▲早餐的晤談。左爲Foster，中爲Ashby，右爲Barton。 ——Peter Lee 攝

▼三位歐洲學者。左爲Barca，中爲Alavi，右爲Foster。 ——Peter Lee 攝

▲研討會進行中。主持人蕭啓慶教授（右二），報告人Barton教授（左二），葉
　小兵教授（右一）及口譯宋家復先生（左一）。──陳志銘攝

▼午餐前的交換意見。由左至右：Chong、宋家復、Alavi及Lee。──Ashby 攝

▲討論時的發言（宋佩芬）。——陳肇萱攝

▼圓滿結束，合影留念。——陳肇萱攝

▲茶敘時間。——陳肇萱攝

▼會後的花蓮參訪。——Peter Lee 攝

學生如何學歷史？

歷史的理解與學習國際學術研討會論文集

張 元
蕭憶梅　主編

臺灣 學生書局 印行

緒言

張　元・蕭憶梅

　　對於大多數人來說，「教學」是一個非常熟悉的詞彙，因為我們都曾進過學校，都曾跟著老師的教導，學習一門又一門的課程。各門科目的教學中，歷史教學似乎是大家最為熟悉的，好像只要上過歷史課，人人都可以對它提出意見，這是在其他科目中很少見到的現象。但是，歷史教學真的只是在課堂上，教師把過去發生的事，擇其重要，加以講述，要學生記得嗎？我們仔細想想，就可以知道，「歷史教學」不是如此簡單，其中盡有十分專業的內容，絕非僅只上過歷史課就能知悉的。

　　所謂「歷史教學」，不外是問幾個問題：歷史是一門怎樣的課程？老師應該怎樣教歷史？學生應該怎樣學歷史？儘管這些不是一個讓人耳目一新的問題，大家會覺得，多少年來，歷史不就是這樣一門課程嗎？老師不就是這麼教，學生不就是這麼學嗎？也許，問題正在這裡，我們太習以為常了。其實，近一、二十年來，世界的變動不可謂不巨大，我們已經不能用一種以不變應萬變的態度來看學校裡的這門稱作「歷史」的課程了。

　　首先，「歷史」是什麼？「歷史」只是發生在過去，而記於教科書中的一些重大事件嗎？如果，老師仍然相信自己教的就是這樣的「知識」，要學生學習的也就是這樣的內容，我們認為這樣的認知是不妥的，至少是太過陳舊了。我們必須強調，「歷史知識」指的不是過去的事情，而是對過去事情的理解，這是一個極其重要的觀念。也就是說，我們必須牢記：「歷史」一詞，應有兩層意思，一是過去發生的事件，二是我們對過去事

件的理解與表述。課堂教學中的「歷史」這門課程，所要傳授的知識，不是前者，而是後者。用另外的話說，我們必須分辨「過去」與「歷史」的不同，我們要清楚了解，「過去」是已經發生的事，「歷史」是依據資料而作出來的表述，是後人「建構」起來的。所以，歷史家如何建構，讓我們認識過去的世界，成了「歷史知識」的主要部分。歷史知識中的客觀，就不再是陳述事件的真相，而是指論證、闡釋過去事件的嚴謹過程。

其次，歷史課堂教學應該怎樣進行？關於課堂教學，雖說應該以學生的學習為主，但教師仍須扮演主導的角色，教師的教學，可以採取許多不同的「方法」，教學的目標卻應該是一致的，那就是引導並幫助學生取得歷史知識，同時培養學生自我學習的能力。教學方法的高下，並不在於新穎與陳舊，而是能否達成教學目標。舉例而言，演講法常被譏諷為「滿堂灌」，似乎過於落伍，應予捨棄。其實不然，如果老師講的內容十分重要，而且口才便給，表述精彩，情意真摯，學生聽得如醉如癡，深受感動，請問：有何不好？相對而言，如果把學生分成若干小組，各自選一題目，收集資料，寫成小論文，再上臺報告，老師講評，教學方式可謂新穎，但學生能夠從這門課中學到多少，不能無疑。所以，老師採取怎樣的教學方法，方能取得良好的成效，確實是一個需要三思的複雜問題。老師怎樣看待教科書？怎樣看待考試？怎樣使用補充教材？如何提出問題？如何與學生進行討論？老師這樣做、那樣做，理據為何？與「歷史知識」的關係如何？都不是簡單的事，都需要仔細考量。

第三、談到學生如何學習的問題，我們似乎應該先問：學生為什麼要學歷史？我們必須為廣大的中、小學生好好想想，歷史這門科目對於他們究竟有著怎樣的意義，為什麼是一門非學不可的課程？如果我們說，這門科目可以培養其他科目不能提供的能力、態度和樂趣，對每一個人的成長過程都會產生正面的影響；像是：訓練他思考人世事物的能力，讓他明白一些基本的道理；培育他待人處世的態度，使他成為今日社會的好公民；

也讓他覺得理解過去，有助於認識今天，展望未來，是十分有趣的事，進而喜歡了「歷史」。那麼，我們怎麼藉課堂教學，達成學生學習歷史的真正目的，就是必須仔細思考的事了。這麼說來，所謂的「應試教學」，就是為了學生準備升學考試而在課堂的所作所為，不應該成為課堂教學的主要活動。我們可以這麼說：如果學生的學習，只是為了升學考試，考過之後，對於辛勤學習的成果大都不復記得，這樣的事實，我們作為老師，應該難以接受的。如果學生的學習只是為了升學考試，我們說歷史是一門有價值的學問，一門有意義的課程，學生同樣也是難以接受的。再說，歷史學界常有一種觀念，認為歷史教學只不過是把學者研究的成果加以普及而已，這種說法，很需要檢討。請問：學生真的需要知道今天歷史學界的研究成果嗎？今天歷史研究的課題，固然有其學術上的意義，但是否切合廣大學生對認識過去世界的需要，仍然令人不能無疑。我們應該從學生的角度好好想想：他們為什麼要學歷史？然後才能接著問：學生應該怎樣學歷史？再者，學生在上歷史課的時候、讀教科書與補充教材的時候、看到考卷中試題的時候，他們心中是怎麼想的，我們似乎所知不多，而這正是我們了解學生如何學習時不可或缺的重要部分，如何取得這方面的信息，也是我們需要仔細思考，並且多下功夫的地方。

　　學生是學習的中心，我們當然贊同，不過，我們也不要忘了，學生的學習需要引導，這就是老師的職責。而老師的教學也需要引導，這就是對於這門課程的正確認知。老師必須清楚認識，歷史是怎樣的一門知識，才能帶領學生走上學習歷史的正確道路。當我們讀到一本名為《學生如何學習歷史》(*How Students Learn History in the Classroom*) 的書，書中對歷史教學的重要概念有十分深刻而又簡要的闡釋，又有教學實例的詳細解說，無疑把英、美歷史教育界的最新研究成果與實際操作，作了一次最為精簡的陳述。我們多位關心歷史教學的朋友，有在大學任教的，但大多是中學歷史老師，看了此書的共同想法是，我們能不能辦一次國際研討會，也請

國外的專家學者前來臺灣，一起探討學生如何學習歷史的問題。通過蕭憶梅博士，我們請她的指導教授——英國倫敦大學的李彼得 (Peter Lee) 教授，推薦參加的國外學者，我們也邀請曾在《清華歷史教學》上刊出大作的 Bettina Alavi、葉小兵和張靜三位教授前來參加。

國立清華大學歷史研究所主辦的「歷史的理解與學習：學生如何學歷史」國際學術研討會，於 2006 年 11 月 17、18 日，在新竹清華大學國際會議廳舉行。這次研討會報告精彩、討論熱烈，可謂成功圓滿。與會的外國學者與在場的朋友，無不滿意。關鍵在於我們非但準備好了中、英文文章的摘要，中文的有英文摘要，英文的有中文節譯或投影片的全譯。而且我們請到了極好的現場口譯，報告人與發言提問者的每一句話，都作了非常清楚的表述。尤其是當時尚為哈佛大學博士候選人，現任臺灣大學歷史系助理教授的宋家復先生，擔任的場次最多，譯述最為清晰、精彩。我們十分感謝宋家復、蕭憶梅、徐兆安的口譯，以及英文節譯與投影片全譯的葉毅均、蔡蔚群、張百廷諸位先生、女士。主持研討會進行，用雙語作各項報告的鐘月岑教授的傑出表現，也讓人留下深刻印象。歷史研究所的老師、祕書、同學，亦多方協助，貢獻良多，在此一併致謝。本次研討會的經費主要由教育部顧問室贊助，不足款項由清華大學撥付，我們謹致謝忱。本論文集的印製經費，由清華大學歷史研究所暑期中學教師進修班結業學員捐贈，我們也要對有的曾經、有的仍然，在課堂教學第一線的歷史教師們致以感謝之忱。

茲將本論文集中的文章，作一簡要的介紹。欲知其詳，仍請閱讀原文。

〈學生應在學校裡接觸那種過去？〉，Peter Lee 撰。主要在討論學生在學校裡應學習哪種歷史，作者認為學科性知識(disciplinary knowledge)較重要，它的影響力能夠超越學生所學的知識範圍，有助學生理解課堂外可能會面對的歷史。作者在文中特別提醒，當我們試圖用歷史來證明某種

價值與信念時，我們就錯失原本歷史可以告訴我們其它東西的可能性，因此最佳對策應是「歷史性地思考過去」。但作者也承認歷史學科知識的「反直覺」特性，與學生日常觀念有很大差異，因此學校中的歷史教育需要著重了解學生對歷史的迷思概念。

〈敘事在歷史教育中的得失〉，Keith C. Barton 撰。學生如何理解歷史敘事，無疑是歷史教育的重點之一。作者舉出學生學習歷史過程中的三項優點與三項缺點，並作了簡要的說明；進而對如何改進缺陷提出三個途徑，也作了精細的分析。最後作者強調歷史敘事在歷史教育中扮演重要角色，我們應該教導學生了解歷史敘事是建構出來的，史家、教科書、教師所注重的內容，都是有其選擇。學生有了這樣的歷史認知，將有助於參與現代的民主社會。

〈課堂上學生提出的「意外問題」〉，葉小兵撰。學生在上課時，往往會臨時起意，提出一些意想不到的問題，並引起其他學生的興趣。這類的問題有時造成教師的困擾，一時之間不知如何回答。作者就這類問題的性質與學生思維的特點，作了深入的分析，也針對教學如何回應，提出具體建議，值得我們參考。

〈藉由歷史教科書提升學科理解：挑戰與機會〉，Stuart Foster 撰。本文闡述過去四十年間英國在教科書編寫與發展的變遷過程，說明歷史教科書如何從傳統民族主義的單一敘述，轉變為強調歷史敘事的建構過程與其多元性。作者不否認這種「新史學」教科書也曾遭受批評並有其限制，但作者認為這種教科書提供學生一個更周延的方法來檢視過去。作者在文章最後更強調個別教師仍可在受限於單一且權威性教科書文本的情況下，使用不同教學法來增進學生對歷史知識的理解。

〈對學生歷史探究學習的研究〉，張靜撰。為了深入研究歷史課程，作者於 2003 年針對北京市三千多名八年級學生進行調查；2004 年，作觀察了二百多節課，訪談了八十多位歷史教師。在這個基礎上，作者對探究

學習在歷史課程上的運用，提出一些基本觀點與具體做法，諸如：學習過程模式、教學設計以及學生技能系統等，可以讓我們對北京市基礎教研中心的工作有所了解。

〈「學科背景重要嗎？」——九年一貫社會領域的研究〉，宋佩芬、楊孟麗撰。兩位作者探究教師專業訓練與教學效果之間的關係，進行實行研究，做法是以歷史科為例，對全臺灣公私立國中社會領域教師進行普查，探究不同專業訓練背景的教師，在歷史知識、歷史觀念和教學內容、教學方法，是否呈現顯著差異。兩位作者得出一些明確的成果，對於課程統整政策的義涵有了進一步的理解，也提出了建議。

〈歷史與倫理學——以女性主義為例〉，許全義撰。該文主張訓練學生讀寫能力的教學模式，關鍵在於設計適合深入討論的問題。即以威尼斯商人與漢茲的難題為例，引導學生思考關懷倫理與正義倫理的優劣。當學生進行歷史倫理學的思辨時，展現出另類的、比較有彈性的倫理觀，既不同於正義倫理，也跟關懷倫理有些許差異。此發現或可對於文化女性主義在闡述關懷倫理時，忽視學生在做倫理抉擇時，文化脈絡所產生的影響，而有所修正。」

〈歷史探究與證據概念：課程目標、教與學的挑戰、學生理解〉，Rosalyn Ashby 撰。本文是以理解學生對歷史的先入之見的前提所展開，她認為學生須掌握「證據」概念後才能區辨那些是論證合理的歷史敘事而那些是神話、傳說或宣傳故事。文中所舉的實徵資料顯示，許多學生不是將史料看成提供過去的「現成」訊息界就是視為證詞(testimony)。所以作者認為教師最具有挑戰性的任務是要如何使學生從只重視史料表面意義的階段提升到將史料理解為「證據」的思維層次。她認為歷史教育目標中須教導學生如何區分過去與歷史，史料與證據。

〈「怎麼會有兩個故事？」——探究兒童如何看待多元敘述〉，林慈淑撰。該文以 54 名十至十四歲兒童如何面對「一段歷史、兩種敘述」為研究

主軸，試圖探索中小學生如何看待多元「歷史記述」(historical account)。文章內採用的分析資料來自 1999 年 8 月至 2001 年 12 月期間，由蔣經國基金會贊助所進行的計畫：「台英兒童歷史認知模式的分析：歷史敘述與歷史理解」(Children's Ideas about Historical Narrative: Understanding Historical Accounts，簡稱 CHIN)。在此計畫中，研究者選取「羅馬人在不列顛」和「秦始皇」為主題，分別設計與此主題相關的不同記述或故事，以了解小學四年級、六年級以及國中二年級兒童，如何解釋：一段歷史卻有兩個不同的敘述，並從中歸納這些不同年齡層的學生有何共同或不同的思考趨向。

〈歷史教育中的客觀性與視野〉，Isabel Barca 撰。今天的歷史教學，不能夠只對史事作單一的敘述，但不同的敘述中，那個可靠又成了問題。作者針對一百多位分別就讀鄉村與城市的七、九、十一年級的學生，以「葡萄牙如何能在十六世紀的印度洋建立海權帝國」為題，要學生對不同的解釋作出抉擇，說明要由。作者歸納學生的回答，作一分析，並加以說明。值得我們參考。

〈「沒有課本怎麼學歷史？」──談中學生對歷史教科書的想法〉，蕭憶梅撰。作者透過書面問卷與訪談來檢測高中生對使用教科書來學習歷史的想法，與他們對歷史學科概念的掌握情形。作者對於教科書如何影響學生學習歷史的討論，與學生對於歷史性質迷思的分析，均可讓我們對於學生的歷史認知與學習情形有所認識。

〈學生如何從「學習者為本」的歷史教學軟體中得益？〉，Bettina Alavi 撰。歷史學習如何使用軟體來進行？作者以 2005 年出版的一套「學習任務」軟體，針對學習策略與方法，進行實證研究。研究以「口述思考進程」方式，對八位十二歲的學生進行測試。作者得出了初步的結果，也作了精要的分析，最後指出學生應用軟體學習的表現並不比課堂學習為佳，學生惟有在專業能力上有所進步，才會對「學習者為本」的軟體更有

興趣。

〈狩獵與採集過去：誰的歷史以及我們怎麼教它？〉Stanley Hallman-Chong 撰。加拿大是一個多民族的社會，多元文化至為顯著，歷史課程中如何講述呢？尤其是相對英裔、法裔而言，屬於弱勢的少數族裔的過去，怎樣才能呈現出它的歷史意義，需要細思。作者提出延續性和主動性的觀念，並作了簡要的分析與闡釋，很值得一讀。

〈學生應該學習怎樣的中國歷史〉，張元撰。撰者以為長期以來學校的中國歷史教學成效不彰，考試因素之外，不論臺灣或大陸，課堂教學均在西方現代史學觀念支配下，刻板簡化，致使學生不喜歡這門科目，成效乏善可陳。撰者進而舉例說明中國傳統史學，可謂層次分明、結構嚴謹、思慮細密、理想高遠，具有既完整又深刻的理論。若能在此一理論指導下，結合現代史學研究成果，或可發展出受到學生喜愛，而且成效佳良的教學模式。

目次

緒言 ································· 張　元・蕭憶梅···I

◆What Kind of Past Should Students Encounter in School? ·········· Peter Lee···1

學生應在學校裡接觸那種過去？ ························ 葉毅均　譯···25

◆Advantages and Disadvantages of Narrative in History
Education ······························· Keith C. Barton···45

敘事在歷史教育中的得失 ··················· 葉毅均　節譯···64

◆歷史課堂上學生提出的「意外問題」 ··············· 葉小兵···71

Unexpected Questions Raised by Students in History Class ··· Ye Xiaobing···86

◆Advancing Disciplinary Understandings with History Textbooks:
Challenges and Opportunities ···················· Stuart Foster···89

藉由歷史教科書提升學科理解：挑戰與機會 ·············· 溫楨文　譯···113

◆對學生歷史探究學習的研究 ··················· 張　靜···127

A Study on Students' Inquiry Learning of History ············· Zhang Jing···171

◆學科背景重要嗎？——九年一貫社會領域的研究 ····· 宋佩芬・楊孟麗···175

Do Teachers' Disciplinary Backgrounds Matter?
－A Study of the Grade1-9 Integrated Field of
Social Studies ··················· Pei-Fen Song & Meng-Li Yang···206

◆How to Help Students Develop Their Problematics?
－A Research on Taiwanese High School Male
Students' Ethics ·························· Cyuan-Yi Syu···207

歷史與倫理學——以女性主義為例 ……………………………… 許全義…227

◆Historical Enquiry Curriculum Goals, Teaching and
　Learning Challenges, and Student Understandings………Rosalyn Ashby…231
　歷史探究與證據概念：課程目標、教與學的挑戰、學生理解
　………………………………………………………… 詹怡娜　譯…261

◆"How Can There Be Two Stories?"
　－An Investigation of Children's Responses to Different Accounts
　………………………………………………… Lin, Tzu-Shu…281
　「怎麼會有兩個故事？」——探究兒童如何看待多元敘述…… 林慈淑…301

◆Objectivity and Perspective in History Education:
　The Ideas of Portuguese Students……………………… Isabel Barca…307
　歷史教育中的客觀性與視野：葡萄牙學生的觀念 ……… 葉毅均　節譯…330

◆「沒有課本怎麼學歷史？」——談中學生對歷史教科書的想法 蕭憶梅…335
　"How Can You Learn History Without Textbooks?"
　—Secondary Students' Perception of History Textbooks…· Yi-Mei Hsiao…353

◆How Can Pupils Profit from Historical Learner-centred Software?
　……………………………………………………… Bettina Alavi…355
　學生如何從「學習者為本」的歷史學習軟體中得益？ ·徐兆安　節譯…376

◆Hunting and Gathering the Past:
　Whose History and How Do We Teach It? ……· Stanley Hallman-Chong…381
　狩獵與採集過去：誰的歷史以及我們怎麼教它？ ………· 葉毅均　譯…388

◆學生應該學習怎樣的中國歷史 ………………………………… 張　元…395
　What Kind of Chinese History Should Student Learn? ……· Chang Yuan…423

What Kind of Past Should Students Encounter in School?

Peter Lee[*]

I want to begin by looking at what there is to be learned in history. Obviously students will need to leave school with knowledge about the past. In what follows I will take that for granted, although there are plenty of problems about what content the students should know.

But this paper is concerned with *what else* is involved in knowing history. If we take research and experience seriously there is more to history than historical content. It is often assumed that history is just common sense, and that there is little problematic about it except for feats of memory. But this may be a serious mistake. Knowing history is more than knowing about the past; it also involves understanding a sophisticated way of looking at the world. What do students need to know if they are to understand history, or even find it an intelligible activity?

Let's begin with a conversation between three 13 year-old girls, trying to decide why the Second World War started, and whether it could have been avoided. At the time of the conversation recorded in this excerpt they have *not* studied World War II in school, but they *have* done some work on World

---

[*] Institute of Education, University of London

War I.

Angela	*I think Hitler was a madman, and I think that's what...*
Susan	*He was... a complete nutter, he should have been put in a... um...*
Angela	*He wanted a super-race of blond, blue-eyed people to rule the world.*
Susan	*Yeah — that followed him...*
Angela	*I mean, but he was a short, fat, dark-haired sort of person.*
Susan	*... little person.*
Katie	*Could it be avoided? I don't think it could have.*
Angela	*No.*
Katie	*If Hitler hadn't started... I mean I can't blame it on him, but if he hadn't started that and provoked... you know... us... if, to say, you know, that's wrong...*
Susan	*It would have been [avoided]...*
Katie	*Yeah, it would have been, but it wasn't.*
Susan	*Yeah, if you think about it, every war could've been avoided.*
Angela	*I reckon if Hitler hadn't come on the scene that would never have happened.*
Katie	*Oh yeah, yes, yes.*
Angela	*There must've been other underlying things, like World War One we found out there was lots of underlying causes, not only...Franz Ferdinand being shot...*
Susan	*Yeah.*
Angela	*... but loads of other stuff as well.*
Katie	*Oh yeah, I don't think he was so far...*

Angela   Yeah, there must've been a few other main currents...

Katie   But, like that Franz Ferdinand, he didn't get, that was the main starting point for it all, that really blew it up...

Angela   But I don't know whether... because we don't know any underlying causes.   If Hitler hadn't been there, I don't know whether it could've been avoided or not.

Susan   Yeah but most wars can be avoided anyway, I mean if you think about it we could've avoided the First World War and any war...

Katie   ... by discussing it.

Susan   Exactly.

Katie   Yeah, you can avoid it, but I don't think...

Angela   Yeah but not everybody's willing to discuss....[1]

Compare the different ways in which Susan and Angela use their knowledge of the First World War. Susan has learned something from thinking about the First World War: she generalizes from the confusions and mistakes that played a part in the slide into war in 1914, and declares that '*Every* war could have been avoided'.   This looks a plausible 'lesson' to draw from the history she has studied, but it is a mistaken one.   Angela is using a different kind of knowledge from Susan.   She is thinking about what counts as a proper explanation, and she knows she may need to look for 'underlying causes'. Angela's search for underlying causes encourages her to be cautious about her explanation, and even to doubt whether it is good enough to do the job properly. She is thinking about her own thinking.

---

[1] Lee, P.J. and Ashby, R., unpublished research, University of London Institute of Education.

So in this conversation the girls display two kinds of knowledge.　On the one hand we have content or substantive knowledge, which is the kind of knowledge historians offer us when they write accounts of the past.　It uses concepts like *emperor*, *constitution*, *profit*, *peasant*, or *Buddhism*.　On the other hand we also find a different kind of knowledge that historians do not generally write *about* as they write history, but nevertheless *use* in order to be able to write anything at all about the past, namely second-order or disciplinary knowledge.　This deals with concepts like *evidence*, *accounts*, *empathy*, *cause* and *change*.[2]　Second-order knowledge is not about the substance of the past, but about how we can know anything or explain anything in the past at all.　In organizing and making sense of the discipline of history, second-order knowledge stands above or behind the ordinary factual knowledge or content of history (which is why it is often called 'second-order' knowledge).

Both kinds of knowledge (substantive and disciplinary or second-order) are required, but disciplinary knowledge has a longer reach, because it goes beyond any prescribed content students are taught, and has a chance of extending to new content beyond school.　It is this kind of knowledge, for example, that allows Angela to go beyond the mistaken lessons of the First World War when she thinks about the Second, whereas Susan's attempt to use

---

[2] Note that the borders between these two kinds of knowledge can be fuzzy, depending on what exactly we have in mind.　For example, we can think of 'the nature of change' as a characterization of patterns of change in a particular passage of the past.　So someone knowing the nature of change will know what changes have occurred in some particular place over some period of time.　This is in large part a substantive understanding. Alternatively, we can think of 'the nature of change' as a characterization of the *kind of thing* students think a 'change' is.　Some students think anything whatsoever that happens counts as a change, and all changes are definitely locatable like small-scale events or actions.

her substantive factual knowledge fails her.

As we can see, this excerpt tells us something *else* about disciplinary knowledge: it gives Angela a strategy for checking on the adequacy of her own explanatory thinking. Hence, she asks, 'But I don't know whether... because we don't know any underlying causes. If Hitler hadn't been there, I don't know whether it could've been avoided or not.' She is asking whether she knows the right information to enable her to give a good explanation, and one question this suggests to her is what would have happened *without Hitler*. She is clearly aware that simply explaining the war by reference to Hitler may not be good enough. She has a better understanding of what counts as a good historical explanation than the other girls in the group, and her disciplinary understanding helps her deal better with a substantive historical problem.

This kind of thinking is what the US National Research Council's *How People Learn* study would call *metacognitive thinking*. The *How People Learn* study set out to find key principles of learning from research over the past three or more decades.[3] These principles are supported by a huge mass of research in many areas of learning (for example mathematics, science and history) but they have to be applied differently in different areas, because different disciplines ask different sorts of questions and have developed their own specific concepts and approaches. One of the three key principles picked out by the *How People Learn* study (actually Principle Three) stressed the

---

3 The principles are listed in M.S. Donovan, J.D. Bransford and J.W. Pellegrino (eds), *How People Learn: Bridging Research and Practice*, Washington DC: National Academy Press, 1999, which summarizes HPL findings and sets out a research agenda. A fuller treatment, with a chapter on American work in history by Sam Wineburg, is in Bransford, J.D., Brown, A. L. and Cocking, R.R. (eds) (1999). *How People Learn: Brain, Mind, Experience and School*. Washington DC: National Academy Press.

importance of metacognitive thinking, in which students think about their own thinking and learning as they try to tackle the problems they encounter. This principle states:

> *A metacognitive approach to instruction can help students learn to take control of their own learning by defining learning goals and monitoring their progress in achieving them.*[4]

In history, second-order or disciplinary understandings provide powerful tools to enable students to think metacognitively, as Angela does in the example we have seen.

If we want to think seriously about the kind of knowledge involved in learning history, we had also better pay attention to the other principles of learning set out by *How People Learn*. Principle Two sets out what it is to have competence in an area of knowledge:

> *To develop competence in an area of inquiry, students must:*
>
> *(a) have a deep foundation of factual knowledge,*
>
> *(b) understand facts and ideas in the context of a conceptual framework, and*
>
> *(c) organize knowledge in ways that facilitate retrieval and application.*[5]

4　M.S. Donovan, J.D. Bransford and J.W. Pellegrino (eds), *How People Learn: Bridging Research and Practice*, Washington DC: National Academy Press, 1999, p.13.

5　M.S. Donovan, J.D. Bransford and J.W. Pellegrino (eds), *How People Learn: Bridging Research and Practice*, Washington DC: National Academy Press, 1999, p.12.

Notice that a deep factual foundation is linked to a *conceptual framework* that organizes knowledge and makes it meaningful. Moreover it is this conceptual framework that allows knowledge not to be *inert* (that is, it allows the retrieval and application of knowledge). Only by 'clumping' or 'grouping' knowledge in meaningful ways can we remember it for use. *How People Learn* recognized that major disciplines – including history – have their own organizing concepts. What is special about history?

The discipline of history as we know it is, of course, the achievement of a particular moment in time, but it *is* nevertheless an achievement, and is the most powerful way of thinking about the past as yet available to us. History has to meet criteria: it attempts to give the best arguments for whatever stories we tell relative to our *questions* and *presuppositions*. In so doing it appeals to the *validity* of the accounts it offers and the *truth* of its singular factual statements. The consequences of these standards are very strong: we may have to tell different stories from the ones we would prefer to tell (even to the extent of having to question our presuppositions). Moreover history also respects the past, treating people in it as we would want to be treated, and emphatically *not* plundering the past for present ends.

Arguably, as the philosopher of history Michael Oakeshott pointed out, the historical past is not the same as the everyday or practical past.[6] The lawyer sees the past as proving rights or obligations, the cleric sees it as proving a moral point and the politician sees it as proving there is no alternative to current policy. These ways of thinking about the past do not

---

6 See Oakeshott, M., 'The Activity of Being an Historian', in M. Oakeshott (ed.), *Rationalism in Politics*, London: Methuen, 1962; Oakeshott, M. *On History, and Other Essays*. Oxford: Basil Blackwell, 1983.

always meet the standards required by history. Organizing the past to prove some present point or favour some current purpose allows the past to be presented as helping or hindering present goals. But if we want to understand the world historically, we have to understand that the past is more complex and interesting than that.

A past organized to prove present points is likely to have a short useful life. As our world changes, a story designed to produce one set of values soon begins to look dated and to cease being useful even for the limited aims it originally had. In the 1950s English students were taught a history organized to explain two outcomes: first, the achievement of a socially stable British parliamentary democracy, and second, British expansion and influence in the world. Because British parliamentary democracy was treated as a culmination to be explained, the past was arranged in terms of what expedited or impeded this achievement. For example, the Glorious Revolution of 1688 confirmed the positive benefits of the Civil War, which was treated as an unfortunately extreme but necessary response to royal interference with the 'natural' course of development, namely, the extension of the power of Parliament. Similarly, events like the Indian Mutiny were treated as significant only as minor setbacks to the growth of British power in India. Such a history closed down questions and left its recipients unable to cope with alternative versions as they arose.

There is a paradox here: *Organizing history to teach lessons about present concerns makes it less useful, not more.* We cannot use history as a kind of shortcut to 'lessons' and 'morals'. We cannot know in advance what questions we will need to ask of the past, so our best bet is to think about it historically. If we try to organize it to suit our present demands, we are in danger of missing out precisely what it *can* tell us. (A partial analogy can be made here with the story of cancer research. Money spent in the 1960s and 1970s on what seemed to be 'promising' cures was wasted. What actually proved useful was research on fundamental scientific questions, which are now beginning to supply the prospect of real cures. Trying to short-cut the science by organizing it to deal with short term goals was an unproductive mistake.) There is more to the past than a narrow little path to the present, and construing and organizing the past so that it leads to today's practical or even moral interests is likely to mean that we will not even properly understand the latter, while missing out on much more.

There is a similar paradox in trying to organize the past to make our students patriotic or even democratic. If we do this we are likely to run into the problems already discussed. It cannot be the central aim of history to create patriots or democrats. This is because if it were the central aim, and we discovered that our students were not becoming patriots or democrats, we would have to fix the history in whatever way was required to produce them. But then it would cease to be history, because if it is to be *history* we must tell whatever stories best meet historical criteria regardless of whether we like the consequences. So we have a kind of Heisenberg or 'uncertainty' principle for history education: we can guarantee history, or we can guarantee patriots or democrats, but not both at once.

History is a *part* of an open society, not a means of sanctifying particular political arrangements. And because we have no reason to believe that even the best story will last, and we cannot protect students against other stories they will meet in the wider world outside school, we must try to ensure that students leave school understanding key ideas about the discipline, the kinds of claims it makes, and how we can test them.[7] History has enormous value for citizenship and democracy, but only if it *is* history. Its value is precisely that it is our most powerful way of thinking about the past. If we attempt to shortcut historical understanding by teaching 'lessons' for citizenship or anything else, we will fail to achieve what we are trying to get to with the shortcut, and — worse — lose exactly what makes a history education worthwhile.

A central part of history education, then, involves students understanding the discipline of history. Hence students by the end of formal school education should understand (among other things) how historical knowledge is possible, which means that they need a concept of evidence. We might expect them to understand that historical explanations may be contingent or conditional, and that explanation of action requires the reconstruction of the agent's beliefs about the situation, together with his or her values and relevant intentions. We would want them to know that historical accounts are not copies of the past, but may nevertheless be evaluated as answers to questions in terms of (at least) the range of evidence they explain, their explanatory power and their congruence with other knowledge.

---

7 For the impact of the stories outside school, see Levstik L.S., 'Articulating the Silences: Teachers' and Adolescents' Conceptions of Historical Significance', in P. Seixas, P. Stearns and S. Wineburg (eds), *Teaching, Learning and Knowing History*, New York: New York University Press, 2000, pp.284-305; Wertsch, J.V. and Rozin, M. 'The Russian Revolution: Official and Unofficial Accounts', in J.F. Voss and M. Carretero (eds.) *International Review of History Education Vol.2: Learning and Reasoning in History*. London: Woburn Press, 1998, pp.39-60; Wineburg, S. 'Making Historical Sense', in P. Seixas, P. Stearns and S. Wineburg (eds), *Teaching, Learning and Knowing History*, New York: New York University Press, 2000, pp.306-25.

Learning the discipline as well as learning the content (acquiring second-order understanding as well as substantive understanding) is all the more important because of what research over the last thirty years or more suggests. It is often said that history has few special concepts of the kind found in science, and it uses ordinary everyday ideas (even if they have to be set in the context of the past). This leads to the idea that history is basically common-sense. But this is almost certainly a mistake. We have increasing research evidence that students' everyday ideas make the discipline of history counter-intuitive.[8] History is NOT just common sense.

How can history be counter intuitive? In science students have to discard common sense ideas to begin to understand natural phenomena, abandoning ideas like *size* and *weight* for *volume* and *mass*. But is there anything like this in history? What could possibly make history like this? The research suggests that many students work with everyday ideas that make them believe historical knowledge is impossible. Some examples will help to show how this can happen. (See Figure 1.)

---

8 See, for example, P.J. Lee and R. Ashby, 'Progression in historical understanding among students ages 7-14', in P. Seixas, P. Stearns and S. Wineburg (eds), Teaching, Learning and Knowing History, New York: New York University Press, 2000, pp.199-222; R. Ashby, 'Students' Approaches to Validating Historical Claims' in Ashby, R., Gordon, P. and Lee, P.J. (eds), *International Review of History Education, Vol.4: Understanding History – Recent Research in History Education*, London: Woburn Press, 2005, pp.21-36; D. Shemilt, 'Adolescent Ideas about Evidence and Methodology in History', in C. Portal (ed.), *The History Curriculum for Teachers*, Lewes: Falmer Press, 1987, pp.39-61. There is also international research: for a brief summary, see P.J Lee, 'Putting principles into practice: understanding history' in M. Suzanne Donovan and John D. Bransford (eds), *How Students Learn: History in the Classroom*, US National Research Council, Washington DC: National Academies Press, 2005, pp. 31-77, especially note 1.

Figure 1.   Everyday ideas that make history counter-intuitive

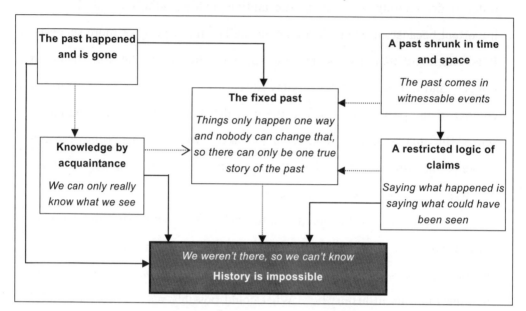

First, common-sense tells us that the past happened and is gone. This is a basic idea about the past for most people in everyday life.   Second, since the past has gone it is fixed and finished.   It happened in just one way — the way it actually did — and nothing we can do can change that.   So there can only be one true story of the past.   Third, we can only *really* know what we directly see.

If knowledge by acquaintance is the model for all knowledge, it follows that the only way we could really know the past would be if we had been there when it happened and had witnessed it.   Betty, an 11 year-old, for example, tells us, 'It is impossible to tell what really happened because we were not there'.[9]   Some students see a way out: 'There could be a book which has

---

9   For many young children the past has a similar status to the present, so questions as to how we know do not even arise.   Kimberley, aged 11, explains that there is only one

someone who wrote about when it happened', or maybe 'If you found an old diary or something it might help.' (Emily and Sally, both aged 11.)   So even if we were not there ourselves, someone who *was* there can report truthfully what happened.   Adolescents, however, soon realize that this does not solve the crucial problem, because we are dependent on people telling us truthfully 'what happened', and they know that even if no one actually lies, people may distort the truth for their own purposes — usually because they take sides. So in the end, they too believe that if we want safe knowledge, only 'being there' will do.   In everyday life this idea makes a good deal of sense, although it does not work for many knowledge claims even there.   And it makes no sense in history at all, because history exists precisely to give us knowledge of what we *cannot* directly see.

Taken together, these ideas mean that for many students history is impossible.   If we were not there to see the past, we cannot say what happened and so we cannot tell the single true story.   This is a serious situation, and means that many younger children and a considerable proportion of adolescents believe that history is simply wrong, or even made up like fiction.   At best they believe that historians and history teachers give their opinions, and opinions are what you give when you don't know the facts, or even just feel free to take a personal view.

These ideas are reinforced by some other, closely linked ideas.   Younger children and many older students think the past is made up entirely of events or actions, not widespread states of affairs or gradual processes.   The past is

---

story of the past 'because it says one way in the book.' Unless otherwise stated examples are taken from data collected by Project CHATA (Concepts of History and Teaching Approaches 7-14).

shrunk in time and space. Moreover, actions and events on this daily-life scale happen because someone *decided* to do them or make them happen. So changes in history are small-scale and occur as a result of deliberate decisions.[10] A past like this, made up of small-scale actions and events, is a past that could have been *seen* (if only we had been there).

A corollary of this is that statements about what happened are statements of *what could have been seen*. (That is, all historical claims, even stories themselves, are like reports of small-scale events.) So our claims about the past are also shrunk, and students imagine that historians' claims are about what could have been directly witnessed. In fact, of course, historians spend much of their time writing about processes, states of affairs and stories that could not have been directly witnessed *even if we had been there*. Shifts in population or economic growth are not directly observable, and nor are many political events and processes, let alone stories.

We should not be surprised to find such ideas, because they work well enough in everyday life. Children typically learn how to 'tell the truth' by appeal to a fixed past. Mum asks her child, 'Did you break the window?', and the child sees the past as a fixed and known touchstone in terms of which the truth is measured. Either he tells the truth (which mirrors the past) or he does not. Because adults and children share conventions on what is relevant to report in these sorts of circumstances, this view of a fixed past against which we can measure our assertions is adequately workable in day-to-day affairs. But it fails utterly in history, where different views may exist about what

---

10 Barton, K.C., 'Narrative simplifications in Elementary Students' Historical Thinking', in J. Brophy (ed.), *Advances in Research on Teaching Vol. 6: Teaching and Learning History*, Greenwich: JAI Press, 1996, pp.51-83.

questions to ask, the conventions of relevance may be contested, and what is asserted may not be something that could have been witnessed by anyone.

The everyday ideas which many students bring to history can therefore actually make the whole enterprise seem unintelligible or pointless. This is all the more important because of what is known about how students learn. Here we need to consider Principle One of the *How People Learn* study. This puts students' preconceptions at the centre of learning:

> *Students come to the classroom with preconceptions about how the world works. If their initial understanding is not engaged, they may fail to grasp the new concepts and information that are taught, or they may learn them for purposes of a test but revert to their preconceptions outside the classroom.*[11]

Unless we know what ideas students are likely to be working with, we cannot effectively address their prior conceptions. Teaching without such knowledge is likely to mean that students will simply assimilate much of what we say to their pre-existing ideas. Knowing what preconceptions we are likely to meet is therefore central to effective teaching.

However, there is something else at stake here too. I said earlier that history was not just a common sense subject, and part of the reason for saying *that* was that everyday common-sense ideas make it difficult for students to see how history is possible at all. But another reason for thinking it is not just common sense is that we can trace a progression of ideas in history. Learning

---

11 M.S. Donovan, J.D. Bransford and J.W. Pellegrino (eds), *How People Learn: Bridging Research and Practice*, Washington DC: National Academy Press, 1999, p.10.

history is not just learning one thing after another.   It is also acquiring new ideas that are more powerful than the ones they replace.

Figure 2.   Increasingly powerful ideas about how history is possible

History is given in books	=	History possible
We were not there so we can't know	=	History impossible
We can rely on testimony (diaries, reports)	=	History possible again
But what if they were lying or biased?	=	History impossible after all
Accounts are constructed from evidence (we can find out things no one was trying to tell us)	=	History possible again

Progression in history can be understood as moving from less powerful everyday 'default' ideas, ones that make history impossible, to more powerful ideas that allow it to take place.   We can see how this works by considering what we know about the development of students' ideas about how we can know the past. The more powerful ideas make history possible as a genuine cognitive activity, while the less powerful ideas close it down.

If students think that history is simply *given*, just somehow out there and copied into books, then authoritative books make history possible.   Younger students cite encyclopaedias and dictionaries, as well as history books, as the authoritative sources of all information about the past.   But, of course, once students realize that books do not always agree, the question arises as to how the authors of the books know what they are claiming.

At this point some students decide that the authors of history books cannot know about the past at all.   How could they, if they were not there to see what happened?   If we were not there, we cannot possibly know.   For these students history is at best a guessing game, and at worst just a pack of lies.   It is clearly impossible.

As students think further about this, or when they listen to their teacher's explanations of how history is 'discovered', they realize that the past left things behind that historians may indeed find.   They typically think in terms of diaries left by people who saw what happened and wrote it down.   Hence reports from the past tell us what happened, and are substitutes for being there to see for ourselves.   History becomes possible once again. Unfortunately, although this solution to the problem of how we can know is a major step forward from the idea that the past is somehow just out there and given in big books, it is inadequate and unstable.

It is unstable because students are well aware that people do not always tell the truth.   So if historians rely on true reports from the past, and people lie, we are back to the need to be there ourselves, and this we cannot do.   History becomes impossible once again.

The big step is the move from working with a concept of *testimony* to working with a concept of *evidence*.   The key idea for students to abandon is the notion of sources as *reports*.   Once they understand that we can ask questions of sources that those sources were not designed to answer, it becomes possible for them to think in evidential terms.   They can see history as inferential, constructing knowledge of the past in ways that go beyond anything reports could have told us.

This sort of progression in ideas is not limited to ideas about evidence. We can also give research based models of progression for students' ideas about other matters, for example about *explanation, change,* and *historical accounts.*[12]

There is not space in this paper to pursue all these, but we can conclude this discussion by turning to an example of progression in students' ideas about historical accounts. Project CHATA (Concepts of History and Teaching Approaches 7-14) asked 320 students in England, aged between 7 and 14, how it was possible for there to be two different stories about the same piece of history. On three separate occasions they were given two competing stories running side by side down a single page. The examples here are from a pair of stories about the end of the Roman Empire. One story was mainly about barbarian invasions, and ended with the fall of the Western Empire in 476. The other focussed more on administrative and economic problems, and ended with the fall of the Eastern Empire with the capture by the Turks of Constantinople in 1453.

From a choice of sentences offering different explanations as to why accounts might differ Louise (aged 14) chose the sentence: *It happened so long ago no-one really knows when it ended*, and said that that is what she actually

---

[12] For examples of a progression model for historical accounts see Lee P.J. and Ashby, R., 'Progression in historical understanding among students ages 7-14', in P. Seixas, P. Stearns and S. Wineburg op.cit., pp.199-222; Lee, P.J. and Shemilt, D., '"I just wish we could go back in the past and find out what really happened": Progression in understanding about historical accounts', *Teaching History, 117 (December 2004, 25-31.* A full progression model for evidence is in Lee, P.J. and Shemilt, D., 'A Scaffold, not a Cage: Progression and progression models', *Teaching History, 113 (December 2003), 13-23.* On empathy, see Lee, P. J. and Ashby, R., 'Empathy, Perspective Taking and Rational Understanding', in O. L. Davis Jr., E. A. Yeager and S. J. Foster (eds) *Historical Empathy and Perspective Taking in the Social Studies,* Lanham: Rowman and Littlefield, 2001, pp. 21-50; Ashby, R. and Lee, P.J., 'Children's Concepts of Empathy and Understanding', in C Portal (ed.), *History in the Curriculum,* Falmer Press,1987; Shemilt, D., 'Beauty and the Philosopher: Empathy in History and Classroom', in A. K. Dickinson, P. J. Lee and P. J. Rogers (eds), *Learning History* London: Heinemann Educational Books 1984, pp.39-84.

thought. When asked how we could decide when the Empire ended, she replied 'By looking it up in a few books and take the time that most of the books say.' She agreed that the Empire might have ended at another time, but thought this 'because no-one really knows when it ended, it could be any time.' Asked if the difference between the stories mattered, she answered, 'Yes, because they are supposed to be the truth. If you looked in one book you would like to know what you were reading is the complete truth'.

Louise thinks that the issue as to when the Roman Empire ended is simply a question of fact, and that differences in historical accounts arise because of lack of knowledge. It was all a long time ago, and our only recourse is to books, but the question of how they acquire the knowledge they recount is left unasked. If they do not tell the truth, there is nothing we can do beyond counting what most books say.

Chris (aged 14) chose the sentence: *It's just a matter of opinion.* He explained this by saying: 'Because different people think in different ways [and] have different opinions etc.' Asked how could we decide when the Empire ended, he replied: 'When a primary source from a strong Roman influence states that the Empire is over (it should be unbiased).' He thought that the Empire could be said to have ended at other possible times, 'because you can have other biased sources etc. stating different dates.' He believed the differences in the stories did not matter 'because in history you need every bit of information to make a fair conclusion, it all counts.'

Chris still thinks the problem about the end of the Roman Empire is a factual one. He stresses historians' opinions, but he thinks of opinions as illegitimate biases. The implication is that they distort a single true account. It is OK to have more versions because we need every bit of information. But in the end it is clear that only an unbiased source from the time can tell us what happened.   Here we can see the power of the idea of true reports as our only access to the past.

Lara, aged 14, chose the sentence: *There was no one single time when the Empire ended*, and said that this was 'because there is no definite way of telling when it ended.   Some think it is when its city was captured or when it was first invaded or some other time.'   When asked how could we decide when it ended, she answered: 'By setting a fixed thing what happened for example when its capitals were taken, or when it was totally annihilated or something and then finding the date.'   She agreed that there were other possible times that we could say the Empire could have ended, 'because it depends on what you think ended it, whether it was the taking of Rome or Constantinople or when it was first invaded or some other time.'   She thought the differences in the stories mattered 'if they are big differences.   Because people will not know the whole story.'

Lara makes a huge step forward.   She can see that the question about the end of the Roman Empire is not just one about reporting events, but is also about criteria.   We have to decide what counts as the end of the Empire, to set a 'fixed thing' as she puts it.   She is implicitly recognizing that historical accounts are not just copies of the past, but have to be constructed to answer questions, and that we have to make such choices if we are to be able to tell a story at all.   But Lara still thinks there can be a 'whole story', and she probably thinks of this as the sum of all the possible stories we can give by setting different criteria.

Finally, Natasha, aged 14, chose the sentence: *There was no one single time when the Empire ended*, and explained: 'Because it all depends on your opinion and whether you are thinking about the Empire physically ending or mentally ending. If people still thought about the Empire and talked about it in 1453 then it hadn't ended until then, mentally.   I think different bits of it ended at different times, i.e. it ended physically before it ended mentally.   The Empire ended physically when it was all no longer governed by the same person, mentally, when it was no longer thought about and spiritually when there was no longer a shadow of it in people's lives, we still use Latin derivatives now so the Empire's influences still haven't ended now.'

Natasha also thinks of the problem as a criterial one, and this kind of thinking enables her not just to explain the differences in the two stories, but to give her own version that shows how they can be reconciled.   She is not helpless in the face of different stories about the past, but has the conceptual tools to relate them to one another in meaningful ways.   She knows that any historical account is an answer to a question (explicit or implicit) and that there are legitimate differences between accounts.

We can see, then, that the first principle of *How People Learn* is critical. If we do not know what students' preconceptions are likely to be, much of our teaching will achieve very different outcomes from what we expect.   Suppose, for example, we wanted to teach Chris and Natasha about how historians write from different standpoints. If we compare their existing preconceptions, we can see that we would have to treat each of them differently. Chris still believes that viewpoints distort a single true story.   We would therefore have to be very careful to ensure that he did not assimilate the idea that historians have different philosophies to lower level preconceptions about opinion as bias and taking sides.

Natasha, however, is thinking at a higher level.   Because she already understands that stories are not copies of the past, she knows that differences between stories are not a matter of distorting a fixed true story. She understands that accounts may differ for legitimate reasons. This would allow us to teach her about historians' standpoints without too much danger of sophisticated ideas being assimilated to simple ideas about personal bias.

The principles identified by the *How People Learn* study together give the notion of progression in ideas about the discipline of history central importance in history education. Principle one reminds us that if we are to teach effectively, we need to know how students' preconceptions are likely to develop. Principle two stresses the importance of conceptual tools, and once we recognize that progression in the understanding of key second-order or disciplinary ideas is possible, we can see how such conceptual tools can be developed. And those same second-order conceptual tools allow students to think about their historical understanding (principle three), as we saw at the beginning with Angela's thinking about the Second World War. Progression means equipping students with more powerful ideas about, for example, how we can know about the past and why historians' accounts differ. Furnished with such ideas they are likely to be able to operate more effectively in handling substantive history. Natasha is able to make better sense of the historical content — the end of the Roman Empire — than Chris, precisely because she has more powerful ideas about the discipline.

In short, as students develop more powerful ideas about history as a discipline, they acquire the intellectual tools they need in order to cope with the multiplicity of competing stories they will encounter outside school. This in turn enables them to think more effectively about their substantive content knowledge. Understanding the discipline and understanding the past go hand in hand.

History education is a serious matter. We should, first and foremost, insist that it is indeed a *history* education, and not an exercise in social bonding, patriotism, or even the production of democrats. History shares some key values with democracy, and respect for other people, for truth and for rational argument are built into both. Historians are committed to freedom of speech, because without it there can be no open search for truth and no testing of argument. In this sense, history is a key part of open societies, and may be a necessary condition of their success, but it does not subscribe to any set of institutional structures or even to any particular current notions of democracy. We should teach history with the aim that students will be better able to think about their world, and that they will be more likely to understand the importance of values and rights that are central to any open society. But they have to be free to think historically and reach their own conclusions about these matters, and that means that guaranteeing democrats cannot be an overriding aim for history education.

History education should give students a sense of where they are located in multiple sets of stories that allow them to orientate themselves in time. It goes without saying that they should know a great deal about the past, although there is much we do not yet understand about how we can give them a historical framework without appearing to sanctify a single 'correct' story.[13]

---

13 See Lee, P.J., '"Walking backwards into tomorrow": Historical consciousness and understanding history', *International Journal of History Learning, Teaching and Research*, 4, 1, January 2004. www.ex.ac.uk/historyresource/journal7/contents.htm and, in a shorter version, 'Historical literacy: theory and research', *International Journal of Historical Learning Teaching and Research, Vol.5 No.1, 2004* www.ex.ac.uk/historyresource/journal9/contents.htm

What is clear, however, is that unless students are equipped with key ideas about how we know and explain the past, and the nature and status of the stories we tell about it, they are likely to regard history as not much better than fiction, and will be helpless in the face of the competing accounts they meet once they leave school.　History education requires that students end their formal schooling understanding how history is possible, despite its uncertainties and notwithstanding people's reasons for wanting to tell stories that suit them.　History obliges us to give accounts of the past we might not always like: if students learn this, we have not failed them.

中文全譯

學生應在學校裡接觸那種過去？

Peter Lee　著
葉毅均[*]譯

　　我想要從檢視我們在歷史中學習到的是些什麼東西開始。很顯然地，學生將會需要帶著關於過去的知識離開校園。在下文中我將視此為理所當然，儘管關於學生應該知道哪些東西有著相當多的爭議。

　　本文關心的是認識歷史還牽涉到其他什麼東西。如果我們認真看待研究成果與相關經驗，將會發現歷史不僅僅是歷史性的內容而已。歷史通常被認為不過是常識罷了，除了記憶裡的豐功偉業之外毫無問題性(problematic)可言。但這也許是個嚴重的錯誤。認識歷史不只是了解過去，還涉及理解一種看待世界的精深方式。假如學生們要理解歷史，或甚而發現歷史是一種知性的活動，那麼他們需要知道些什麼？

　　讓我們從三位十三歲女孩之間的一場對話開始，她們試著理出頭緒為何第二次世界大戰會爆發，以及這場戰爭是否可能避免。此一摘錄中所記載的對話當時她們尚未自學校中學習到二次大戰，但是她們已經針對第一次世界大戰做過一些作業。

　　　　Angela：我覺得希特勒是個瘋子，而且我覺得那就是……

---

[*]　清華大學歷史研究所博士班

Susan：他⋯⋯完全是個瘋子，他早就該被送進⋯⋯呃⋯⋯

Angela：他想讓一個金髮碧眼的民族作為優越人種來統治世界。

Susan：是啊，隨之而來的是⋯⋯

Angela：我的意思是，可他不過是個矮小、肥胖、黑髮的那種人。

Susan：⋯⋯小人。

Katie：這場戰爭可以避免嗎？我不這麼認為。

Angela：的確不行。

Katie：假如希特勒沒有發動⋯⋯我的意思是說我不能全怪在他頭上，但是假如他不曾發動並挑釁⋯⋯你知道⋯⋯我們⋯⋯如果⋯⋯也就是說，你知道，那是錯的⋯⋯

Susan：那麼大戰就可以（避免）⋯⋯

Katie：是啊，那就可以，但實際上沒有發生。

Susan：沒錯，你想想看，每一場戰爭都可以避免。

Angela：我想假如希特勒不曾出現在歷史舞台上，那麼大戰絕不會發生。

Katie：喔是啊，沒錯沒錯。

Angela：勢必還有其他潛在的東西，就像第一次世界大戰我們就發現了許多潛在因素，不只是⋯⋯斐迪南大公(Franz Ferdinand)遇刺⋯⋯

Susan：是啊。

Angela：⋯⋯還有很多其他因素在內。

Katie：喔是啊，我不覺得他到目前為止⋯⋯

Angela：是的，必定還有其他一些主要趨勢⋯⋯

Katie：但是，像斐迪南大公，那是整件事的主要起點，真正的引爆點⋯⋯

Angela：但我不確知是否如此⋯⋯因為我們不知道任何潛在因素。

假如希特勒未曾出現，我不知道大戰能否避免。

Susan：是的，但無論如何大多數的戰爭都可以避免，我的意思是
你想想看，我們可以避免一次大戰和其他任何戰爭……

Katie：……透過討論的方式。

Susan：正是如此。

Katie：是啊，你可以避免它，但我不認為……

Angela：沒錯，但不是每個人都樂意討論……[1]

　　比較 Susan 和 Angela 運用她們對於第一次世界大戰之知識的不同方
式。Susan 已經從思考一次大戰中學到了一些東西：她從引發 1914 年的
戰爭裡占有相當分量的混亂與錯誤中得到概括，並宣稱「每一場戰爭都可
以避免」。從她所學到的歷史來看，這似乎是個合理的「教訓」，但其實這
是個誤解。Angela 運用的則是和 Susan 不同種類的知識。她思考的是什
麼才稱得上是一個適當的解釋，而且她知道她可能必須尋找「潛在因素」
(underlying causes)。Angela 對潛在因素的探索，促使她對自己的解釋小
心謹慎，甚至進一步懷疑這項解釋工作是否得當。她正在進行自我反思。

　　因此在這場對話中，女孩們顯示出兩種知識。一方面我們擁有內容或
實質性知識 (content or substantive knowledge)，也就是當歷史學家記述過
去時所提供給我們的一種知識。這種知識運用的概念是諸如皇帝、憲法、
利益、農民或佛教。另一方面我們也發現另外一種不同的知識，史家撰寫
歷史時通常並未明言，然而為了能夠寫下任何過去卻必須加以利用，也就
是第二序或學科性知識 (second-order or disciplinary knowledge)。這種知識
處理的概念是譬如證據、記載、移情、原因與變遷。[2]第二序知識不是關

1　Lee, P.J. and Ashby, R., 未出版研究, University of London Institute of Education.

2　要注意到這兩類知識之間的界線並不分明，完全視乎我們心中所思而定。舉例而
　　言，我們可以將「變遷性質」(the nature of change) 視為過去某一特定時段中之變遷

於過去的實質內容，而是與我們如何能夠認識或解釋過去任何事情有關。在歷史學門之組建，以及使之獲得意義這方面，第二序知識較諸一般事實性的知識或歷史的內容尤為重要，或者隱身其後（這是為什麼它通常被稱為「第二序」知識）。

兩種知識（實質性知識以及學科性或第二序知識）都是必要的，但學科性知識的範圍所及影響較為廣泛，因為它超越了任何學生受教的指定內容，並且有機會在學校之外擴展到新的領域。舉例來說，正是這種知識使得 Angela 一旦思考到二次大戰，便能夠避免得到有關一次大戰的錯誤教訓，而 Susan 企圖運用自己的實質性／事實性知識則使她見不及此。

正如我們所見，此一摘錄告訴我們有關學科性知識的一些其他東西：它使 Angela 得以藉此檢驗她自身解釋性思維 (explanatory thinking) 的正確性。因此她才會問道，「但我不確知是否如此……因為我們不知道任何潛在因素。假如希特勒未曾出現，我不知道大戰能否避免。」她問的是她自己是否擁有正確的資訊足以得出一個好的解釋，而此一疑問對她來說則表示，若沒有希特勒的話會發生什麼事。她很清楚地理解到，僅僅透過希特勒來解釋這場戰爭可能是不夠的。對於什麼才算是一個好的歷史解釋的理解，她勝過此一團體中的其他女孩，而且她的學科性理解有助於她更好地處理一個實質性的歷史問題。

美國國家研究會 (US National Research Council) 的《人們如何學習》(*How People Learn*) 之研究稱這種思維為後設認知性思維 (*metacognitive thinking*)。此一研究從事自過去三十年或更多年裡的研究成果中找出學習

模式的特徵描述，因此了解此一變遷性質的某人，知道何種變遷經過某段時間在某一特定地點發生。這在大體上說是一種實質性的理解。另一方面，我們也可以將「變遷性質」視為學生們所認為的「變遷」之事物種類的特徵描述。某些學生認為任何已經發生的事都算是一種變遷，而所有的變遷都必定像小規模的事件或行動一樣可以加以定位。

的關鍵性原則。[3]這些原則是由來自許多不同學習領域（如數學、科學與歷史）裡的大量研究成果所支持，但這些原則在不同領域裡必須被區別運用，因為個別學科問的是不同種類的問題，並且也發展出自己特定的概念與研究取徑。《人們如何學習》之研究所選取的三項關鍵性原則之一（事實上是「原則三」）強調後設認知性思維的重要性，也就是當學生試著處理他們所遇到的問題時，同時對他們自身的思考與學習加以反思。這個原則認為：

> 一個後設認知性取徑的教誨能幫助學生透過界定學習目標，並監督達成這些目標的進展，來學著掌握他們自己的學習過程。[4]

在歷史學裡，第二序或學科性理解為學生得以後設認知地去思考提供了強而有力的工具，正如我們在例子中所看到的 Angela 所做的。

如果我們想要對學習歷史所牽涉到的知識類型進行嚴肅的思考，我們最好也顧及到《人們如何學習》所提出的其他學習原則。「原則二」設定何謂在一個知識領域中勝任無虞：

> 要在一個探索領域中發展出能力，學生必須：
> (a) 對於事實性知識有深厚的基礎，
> (b) 在概念架構的脈絡中了解事實與觀念，以及

3　這些原則皆載於 M.S. Donovan, J.D. Bransford and J.W. Pellegrino (eds), *How People Learn: Bridging Research and Practice*, Washington DC: National Academy Press, 1999, 摘述此項研究的發現並著手建立一項研究議程。另一更為完整的論述，是由 Sam Wineburg 以整章篇幅處理美國的歷史研究工作，收錄於 Bransford, J.D., Brown, A. L. and Cocking, R.R. (eds) (1999). *How People Learn: Brain, Mind, Experience and School.* Washington DC: National Academy Press.

4　M.S. Donovan, J.D. Bransford and J.W. Pellegrino (eds), *How People Learn: Bridging Research and Practice*, Washington DC: National Academy Press, 1999, p.13.

(c) 以有利於修正與應用的方式去組織知識。[5]

　　必須注意到深厚的事實性基礎，是與組織知識並使知識產生意義的概念架構 (*conceptual framework*) 有關。更有甚者，正是此一概念架構才能使知識不至於鈍化 (*inert*)，也就是容許修正與應用知識。只有以有意義的方式「聚集」或「組織」知識，我們才能為了運用而記住這些知識。《人們如何學習》認識到主要的學科（包括歷史學）都有自己的組織概念。那麼歷史學在這方面有何特殊之處呢？

　　我們所知道的歷史之學科訓練，當然是在時間之流中某個特定時刻所達到的，但它卻是一項成就，也是到目前為止我們所能擁有的在思考過去上最有效力的方式。歷史必須達到標準 (criteria)：它試圖為我們所說的任何故事（關乎我們的問題〔*questions*〕與預設〔*presuppositions*〕而定）給予最佳論證。而在此一過程中，它訴諸記載的可靠性 (*validity*) 以及單一事實陳述的真實性 (*truth*)。依據這些標準的結果是非常強而有力的：相較於我們所偏好的故事，我們可能必須說出不一樣的版本（甚至於到必須質疑我們自身預設的地步）。更有甚者，歷史也尊重過去，對待過去的人們就像我們希望得到的對待一樣，並且絕不為了當前的目的而侵占過去。

　　可以這麼說，正如歷史哲學家 Michael Oakeshott 所指出的，歷史性的過去和日常的或實際的過去 (everyday or practical past) 並不相同。[6]律師視過去為證明權利或義務的一種途徑，牧師視之為證明一個道德觀點的方法，而政客則將之當成論證除了當前政策之外別無他法的手段。這些思考過去的方式未必經常能達到歷史所要求的標準。組織安排過去以證明當前

5　M.S. Donovan, J.D. Bransford and J.W. Pellegrino (eds), *How People Learn: Bridging Research and Practice*, Washington DC: National Academy Press, 1999, p.12.

6　見於 Oakeshott, M., 'The Activity of Being an Historian', in M. Oakeshott (ed.), *Rationalism in Politics*, London: Methuen, 1962; Oakeshott, M. *On History, and Other Essays.*　Oxford: Basil Blackwell, 1983.

某個論點或偏向某種現實目的，將使過去被呈現為有助於或有礙於眼前的目標。但是假如我們想要歷史地了解過去，我們就必須了解到過去是遠為複雜而有趣的。

　　一個被安排用來證明當前論點的過去，大概只會有短暫有用的生命。當我們的世界改變了，一個設計用來產生一組價值 (values) 的故事很快就會開始顯得過時，並且不再有用。即使就其原先設想的有限目標亦然。在 1950 年代，英國學生所學到的歷史被安排用以解釋兩項成果：其一是英國式議會民主制穩定社會的成就，其二是英國在世界上的擴張及其影響。由於英國式議會民主制被當作需要解釋的某種顛峰，過去便以促進或阻礙此一成就的方式來加以編排。舉例來說，1688 年的光榮革命證實了內戰 (Civil War) 的正面效益。儘管這場內戰被當成不幸的極端事件，卻又是針對皇室干涉議會權力的擴張——此一「自然」發展方向的必要回應。同樣地，像印軍叛變 (Indian Mutiny) 這樣的事件，只有當作為英國勢力在印度的伸展過程中之微小阻礙時，才有其意義。如此這般的歷史不但封閉了問題，也從而使收受者在不同的版本出現時，無法從容應對。

　　這裡有個弔詭之處：為了當前的關切而編排歷史以提供教訓，只會使歷史變得更無用，而非更有用。我們不能將歷史當作通往「教訓」與「道德訓誡」的一條捷徑。我們無法預知我們將會需要對過去提出何種問題，所以我們的最佳對策是歷史性地思考過去。假如我們嘗試著古為今用，我們即將冒著失去過去真正可以告訴我們什麼的危險（這裡可以用癌症研究的故事當作部分類比。1960 與 70 年代的經費花在當時看來似乎「頗有希望」的治療方法，最後是白忙一場。真正證明有用的是對於基礎科學問題所做的研究，現在正開始被用來支持實際治療方法的前景。用走捷徑的方式來進行科學研究，以之應付短程目標的嘗試，是個毫無效益的錯誤）。過去不僅僅是一條通往現在的狹隘小徑，解釋與安排過去使之導向今日的實際利益，甚或是道德利益，大概只意味著我們將無法恰當地了解後者，

同時又錯過了更多東西。

　　類似的弔詭是，嘗試組織過去以促使我們的學生變得愛國，或甚至變得民主。假如我們這麼做，我們很可能便會陷入前述討論的問題。歷史的中心目標不可能是創造愛國者或民主人士。這是因為設若如此，而我們又發覺我們的學生並沒有變成愛國者或民主人士，我們就必須用各種方式來修改歷史，以圖達到上述目標。但如此一來，這就不再是歷史了，因為這要是歷史的話，我們就必須說出最為符合歷史標準的故事，無論我們是否樂意見到其後果。因此，對於歷史教育我們有一種 Heisenberg 或謂「不確定」原則：我們能保有 (guarantee) 歷史，抑或保有愛國者或民主人士，但不能同時保證兩者。

　　歷史是一個開放社會的一部分，而不是認可特定政治安排的一種手段。而且由於我們沒有理由相信甚至可以說是最佳的故事都將會持久留存，我們又無法保護學生免於在學校之外更廣大的世界裡碰到其他故事，那麼我們就必須試著確保學生在離開學校後理解此一學門的關鍵觀念，其內涵主張的類別，以及我們如何對之加以檢驗。[7]歷史對於公民身分 (citizenship) 與民主制度來說有著巨大的價值，但只有在它是歷史的時候才稱得上是如此。歷史的價值正在於，它是我們在思考過去上最有效力的方式。假如我們試圖教導為了公民身分或其他任何事物而來的「教訓」，以求抄捷徑達致歷史理解，我們不但將無法從此一捷徑達成我們想要的目的，而且更糟的是失去真正使得歷史教育有其價值的成分。

---

[7]　對於學校以外的故事所帶來的衝擊，可見 Levstik L.S., 'Articulating the Silences: Teachers' and Adolescents' Conceptions of Historical Significance', in P. Seixas, P. Stearns and S. Wineburg (eds), *Teaching, Learning and Knowing History*, New York: New York University Press, 2000, pp.284-305; Wertsch, J.V. and Rozin, M. 'The Russian Revolution: Official and Unofficial Accounts', in J.F. Voss and M. Carretero (eds.) *International Review of History Education Vol.2: Learning and Reasoning in History*. London: Woburn Press, 1998, pp.39-60; Wineburg, S. 'Making Historical Sense', in P. Seixas, P. Stearns and S. Wineburg (eds), *Teaching, Learning and Knowing History*, New York: New York University Press, 2000, pp.306-25.

　　歷史教育的一個核心成分，涉及學生理解到歷史的學科訓練。因此，學生們在正規的學校教育結束之後，應該了解到歷史知識（以及其他事物）如何可能，這就意味著他們需要證據的概念。我們可以期望他們了解，歷史解釋也許是不必然如此的或有條件性的 (contingent or conditional)，針對行動的解釋需要重建行動者對於其處境的信念，乃至於他或她個人的價值觀及相關意圖。我們將會要求他們知道歷史記載並不是對於過去的複製品，而是可以從它們所解釋的證據範圍、解釋效力，以及與其他知識的一致性等方面來加以評估。

　　過去三十年，或更多年來的研究結果顯示，學習歷史的學科訓練及其內容（獲得第二序和實質性理解）愈加重要。人們時常說，歷史學缺乏像在科學中見到的那種特殊概念，歷史學運用的是一般的日常觀念（即便必須被安置在過去的脈絡中）。這種說法導致人們以為歷史學基本上是一種常識。但這根本就是錯的。愈來愈多的研究證實，學生們的日常觀念使得歷史成為一門反直覺的學科訓練。[8]歷史學並不僅僅是常識而已。

　　歷史學如何是反直覺的呢？學生們在科學中必須拋下常識性的觀念才能開始理解自然現象，丟棄諸如尺寸 (size) 和重量(weight)，改為體積 (volume) 和質量 (mass) 等觀念。但在歷史學裡有什麼類似的例子嗎？有可能使歷史學變成如此這般的是什麼呢？研究顯示，許多帶著日常觀念思

8　舉例來說，可見 P.J. Lee and R. Ashby, 'Progression in historical understanding among students ages 7-14', in P. Seixas, P. Stearns and S. Wineburg (eds), *Teaching, Learning and Knowing History*, New York: New York University Press, 2000, pp.199-222; R. Ashby, 'Students' Approaches to Validating Historical Claims' in Ashby, R., Gordon, P. and Lee, P.J. (eds), *International Review of History Education, Vol.4: Understanding History – Recent Research in History Education*, London: Woburn Press, 2005, pp.21-36; D. Shemilt, 'Adolescent Ideas about Evidence and Methodology in History', in C. Portal (ed.), *The History Curriculum for Teachers*, Lewes: Falmer Press, 1987, pp.39-61. 在這方面也有國際上的研究，一個簡短的摘述可見： P.J Lee, 'Putting principles into practice: understanding history' in M. Suzanne Donovan and John D. Bransford (eds), *How Students Learn: History in the Classroom*, US National Research Council, Washington DC: National Academies Press, 2005, pp. 31-77, 特別是註 1.

考的學生們以為歷史知識是無法成立的。舉出一些例證將有助於顯示這種情況如何產生。（見圖 1）

圖 1　日常觀念使歷史學變得反直覺

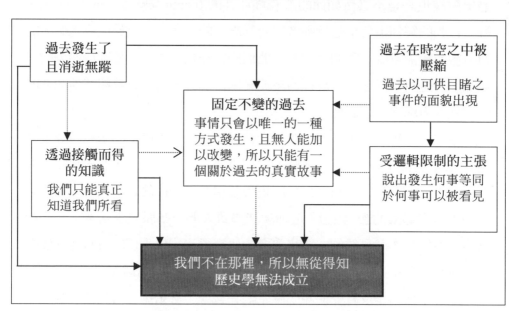

首先，常識告訴我們，過去發生了而且消逝無蹤。這是在大多數人的日常生活裡對於過去的基本觀念。其次，既然過去已然消逝，它就是固定不變而已結束完成的。過去僅以一種方式發生，也就是它實際發生的那種方式，我們沒有任何辦法加以改變。因此，關於過去只能有唯一的一個真實故事可言。再次，我們只可能真正知道我們所直接看到的東西。

假如透過接觸 (acquaintance) 而得的知識是一切知識的模型，那麼我們可以確實知道過去的唯一方式，便是當過去發生的時候，我們就在那兒目擊此事。比如說，一個十一歲的孩子 Betty 告訴我們，「因為我們不在那兒，所以我們不可能知道真正發生了什麼事。」[9]有些學生找到了出

9　對於許多年幼的孩童來說，過去與現在有著相似的地位，因此關於我們如何得知過去的問題甚至不曾被提出。十一歲的 Kimberley 解釋何以關於過去只有唯一的一個

路：「可能有某本書，記載了某個人寫下某件事發生的經過」；或者也許「假如你找到一本舊日記或某物就可以派得上用場」。（同樣皆為十一歲的 Emily 和 Sally）因此，即使我們自己不在那兒，但確實在當場的某人可以據實以告發生了何事。然而，青少年很快就了解到這並沒有解決關鍵性的問題，因為我們仍然得依賴別人據實以告「發生何事」(what happened)。況且他們明白，就算沒有人真的說謊，人們也會為了自身的目的而扭曲真相，因為人們通常會選邊站的緣故。所以到了最後，他們同樣相信我們只有「在那裡」(being there) 才能得到正確可靠的知識。這個觀念在日常生活中非常具有意義，儘管在日常生活中也無法適用於許多種知識的主張。況且這個觀念在歷史學中毫無意義可言，因為歷史的存在正是要給我們不能直接看到的知識。

　　總而言之，這些觀念表示對許多學生來說，歷史是不可能的 (history is impossible)。如果我們不曾在那裡見到過去，我們就不能說發生了何事，同時我們也不能講述一個單一的真實故事。這是一個令人擔憂的情況，亦即許多年幼的兒童以及相當一部分的青少年相信，歷史基本上是錯誤的，或甚至像小說一樣是虛構的。他們至多相信史學家和歷史教師提供了他們的意見，而意見則是當你不知道事實的時候所提出的東西，或甚至是隨意為之的個人觀點。

　　這些觀念由於其他密切相關的觀念而隨之加強。年幼的兒童和許多年齡較長的學生們認為，過去全然是由事件或行動所組成，而非充斥著事態的狀況或逐步的進程 (states of affairs or gradual processes)。過去因而在時空之中被壓縮 (The past is shrunk in time and space)。更有甚者，行動和事件在此一日常生活的範圍中產生，是因為某人決定要這麼做或使之發生。

故事，「因為書中只講到一種方式」。本文所舉案例皆來自 CHATA 計畫（歷史概念與教學取向 7-14）所收集的資料，除非另外指明出處。

因此歷史上的變化都是小規模的，而且都是出於刻意決策的結果。[10]如此這般由小規模的行動和事件所組成之過去，是可以被看見的過去（只要我們能夠到達過去的話）。

如此一來，必然的結果是有關發生何事的陳述，都是可以被看見之事的陳述（也就是說，所有的歷史主張，甚至故事本身，都像是小規模事件的報告）。因此我們關於過去的主張也同樣被壓縮了，而學生們則猜想史家的主張是關於可以被直接目擊之事。事實上，歷史學家當然花費了大多數的時間在於撰寫有關進程、事態的狀況，以及不能被直接目擊的故事，即使我們人在那裡。人口變化或經濟增長是無法直接觀察到的，許多政治事件和過程同樣如此，遑論故事。

我們不應該為發覺上述這些觀念而感到驚訝，因為它們在日常生活中運作良好。兒童通常基於一個固定不變的過去，從而學習如何「說出真相」。當母親問孩子說：「是你打破窗戶的嗎？」這個孩子便將過去視為固定不變而已知的標準，用以檢驗真實。要麼他說出真相（從而反映出過去），要麼則否。由於成人和兒童共享在這種情況下，何者屬於應適切道出實情的常規，此一固定不變之過去相對於我們用來檢驗自身說詞的觀點，在日復一日的事物中是確實可行的。但這在歷史學裡是完全不可行的，當中各種不同的觀點存在於所提出的不同問題，適切性的常規可能會受到挑戰，而且各種說法可能不是可以被任何人所目擊到的事物。

因此，許多學生帶往歷史的日常觀念，確實使得這整個行當變得似乎晦澀難解或者無關宏旨。由於我們已知的學生如何學習之方式，這點變得更加重要。此處我們需要考量《人們如何學習》之研究中的「原則一」。它將學生們的先入之見 (preconceptions) 置於學習的中心：

---

10 Barton, K.C., 'Narrative simplifications in Elementary Students' Historical Thinking', in J. Brophy (ed.), *Advances in Research on Teaching Vol. 6: Teaching and Learning History*, Greenwich: JAI Press, 1996, pp.51-83.

學生來到教室時，對於世界如何運作已經有了先入之見。如果不能契合 (engage) 他們原有的理解，他們也許就無法掌握被教導的新概念和訊息，或者他們會出於考試的目的而學習，但是一旦出了教室就恢復到原來的先入之見。[11]

除非我們知道學生們可能運用的是什麼觀念，否則我們就無法有效地應付他們的先入之見。缺少這種知識的教育，很可能意味著學生們只是將我們所說的大多數東西，吸收消化為他們早已存在的觀念。因此，了解我們可能遭遇的先入之見是有效教學 (effective teaching) 的中心。

然而，這裡還有其他東西岌岌可危。我早先說歷史並不僅僅是常識性的題材而已，這麼說的部分理由在於，平日常識性的觀念使學生們難以理解歷史究竟是如何可能的。但另一個可供思考的理由並不止於常識而已，而是我們可以在歷史裡追溯觀念的演進。學習歷史並非只是學習一件又一件的事物，同時也是獲得較諸替換前之觀念更為有力的新觀念。

圖 2　關乎歷史如何可能 (how history is possible) 逐步有力的觀念

歷史由書籍講述	=	歷史成為可能
我們不在那裡，所以不可能得知	=	歷史變成不可能
我們可以依靠證詞（日記、報告）	=	歷史再次成為可能
但假如它們說謊或帶有偏見的話呢？	=	歷史畢竟不可能
解釋是由證據所構成（我們可以發現無人嘗試告訴我們的事）	=	歷史再次成為可能

歷史的進步可以被理解為從較不有力的平日「隱含」觀念，移轉到較有效力的觀念，從而使歷史的可能性從無到有。透過考慮我們所知道的，

11　M.S. Donovan, J.D. Bransford and J.W. Pellegrino (eds), *How People Learn: Bridging Research and Practice*, Washington DC: National Academy Press, 1999, p.10.

有關學生們對於我們如何得知過去的觀念發展，可以看到這一點如何運作。更有效力的觀念使歷史作為名副其實的認知活動而成為可能，而較不有力的觀念則封閉了歷史。

假如學生們以為，歷史僅僅是給定的，只因不知何故就在那裡，並且被複製於書中，接著具有權威性的專書便使歷史成為可能。更年輕的學生們引用百科全書和字典，以及歷史類書籍，作為所有關於過去的資訊之權威性來源。但是想當然爾，一旦學生們認識到書本並不總是相互一致，問題就出現了，也就是書籍作者們如何得出他們的主張？

到了此時，有些學生就會認為歷史書的作者們根本完全不了解過去。如果他們不在那兒看到發生了何事，他們如何能夠得知過去？如果我們不在現場，我們也不可能知道過去。對這些學生們來說，歷史從好的方面來說只是個猜謎遊戲，從壞的方面來說則是一團謊言。歷史很顯然無法成立。

當學生們對此思考得更加深入，或當他們聆聽其教師解釋歷史是如何被「發現」的，他們便會曉得過去留下了歷史學家確實可能找到的事物。他們通常會想到日記這一類由曾經親眼目睹過去的人所寫下的東西。因此，來自過去的報告能夠告訴我們發生何事，作為替代品取代我們本身在現場的目擊。歷史再次成為可能。不幸的是，儘管此一解決方式回答了我們如何得知過去的問題，較諸僅因過去不知何故就在那裡，且存身於大部頭著作中的觀念來說，已經往前邁進了一大步，這仍然是不準確又不穩定的辦法。

不穩定的原因在於，學生們很清楚的知道人們並不總是道出事實。所以假如史家依靠的是來自過去的真實報告，而報告人卻說謊，那麼我們就回到須得靠自己人在現場，但是這點我們又無法做到。歷史於是再次變成不可能。

邁進的這一大步是從運用證詞 (testimony) 的概念到運用證據 (evidence)

的概念。需要學生們棄絕的關鍵觀念是將史料作為報告 (reports) 的想法。一旦他們了解到，我們可以針對史料所問出的問題，不限於它們原本設計用來回答的答案，他們就有可能以證據的方式來加以思考。他們能夠視歷史為一種關於過去推理性的建構知識，超越報告所能告訴我們的任何東西。

這種觀念上的進展並不限於證據的觀念。我們同樣可以得出以研究為基礎的模型，說明學生們其他觀念的進展，例如解釋、變遷和歷史記載。[12]

本文沒有足夠的篇幅討論上述所有的觀念，但是我們可以看看另一個學生們在觀念上進展的例子：歷史記載，來為這項討論作結。CHATA 計畫（歷史概念與教學取向 7-14）訪問了英國 320 位七到十四歲之間的學生，問到對於同一段歷史如何可能會有兩個不同的故事。在三個不同的場合，分別給他們兩個相互對立的故事並排在同一處。這裡所用的例子是關於羅馬帝國結局的一對故事。其中一個故事主要是有關蠻族入侵，結局是476 年西羅馬帝國的滅亡。另一個故事更關注行政和經濟問題，結束於1453 年東羅馬帝國的君士坦丁堡遭土耳其人攻占而傾覆。

從一系列關於記載何以不同所提供的解釋裡，Louise（14 歲）選擇的

12　關於針對歷史記載的進展模型之例證，可見 Lee P.J. and Ashby, R., 'Progression in historical understanding among students ages 7-14', in P. Seixas, P. Stearns and S. Wineburg op.cit., pp.199-222; Lee, P.J. and Shemilt, D., '"I just wish we could go back in the past and find out what really happened": Progression in understanding about historical accounts', *Teaching History*, 117 (December 2004), 25-31. 針對證據的完整進展模型可見於 Lee, P.J. and Shemilt, D., 'A Scaffold, not a Cage: Progression and progression models', *Teaching History*, 113 (December 2003), 13-23. 關於移情，見 Lee, P. J. and Ashby, R., 'Empathy, Perspective Taking and Rational Understanding', in O. L. Davis Jr., E. A. Yeager and S. J. Foster (eds) *Historical Empathy and Perspective Taking in the Social Studies*, Lanham: Rowman and Littlefield, 2001, pp. 21-50; Ashby, R. and Lee, P.J., 'Children's Concepts of Empathy and Understanding', in C Portal (ed.), *History in the Curriculum*, Falmer Press,1987; Shemilt, D., 'Beauty and the Philosopher: Empathy in History and Classroom', in A. K. Dickinson, P. J. Lee and P. J. Rogers (eds), *Learning History* London: Heinemann Educational Books 1984, pp.39-84.

想法是：這是太久以前所發生的事，沒有人確實知道何時結束，而且她說她真的這麼想。當被問到我們如何可以決定羅馬帝國何時結束時，她回答說：「透過查閱一些書籍，選擇大多數書籍所描寫的時候就是了。」她同意羅馬帝國有可能在另一個不同的時候結束，但認為這是「因為沒有人確實知道何時結束，因此可以是任何時候。」當被問及這些故事之間的差異是否重要時，她回答說，「是的，因為它們應該就是真相。假如你閱讀一本書，你會希望知道你讀到的東西是完全的真相。」

Louise 以為，關於羅馬帝國何時結束這樣的議題，僅僅是一個關乎事實的問題，而歷史記載之間的差異是因為缺乏知識所導致的。這全是很久以前的事，而我們唯一的辦法就是依靠書本，但是這些書本如何得到它們所講述的知識這個問題，卻被忽略不問了。如果它們說的不是真相，除了依靠大多數書本所說的之外，我們也就無能為力了。

Chris（14 歲）選擇的想法是：這只是關乎意見的問題。他就此解釋說：「因為不同的人以不同的方式思考（以及）有不同的意見等等。」當被問到我們如何可以決定羅馬帝國何時結束時，他回答說：「當有一份來自羅馬強烈影響的一手史料陳述帝國已經結束時（這應該沒有偏見）。」他以為羅馬帝國可以出現其他可能不同的結束時間，「因為你可以找到其他受偏見左右的史料，陳述不同的日期。」他相信故事之間的差異並不重要，「因為在歷史中，你需要每一份資訊以達成公正的結論，所有的東西都有其意義。」

Chris 仍然以為羅馬帝國的結局問題是個事實問題。他強調的是史家的意見，但他認為意見是一種不正當的偏見，意思是它們扭曲了單一的真實記載。由於我們需要每一份資訊，因此有更多版本也無妨。但是到了最後很清楚的是，只有一個來自當時、不受偏見左右的史料來源，才可以告訴我們發生了什麼事。此處我們可以看到一種觀念的力量，也就是作為我們接近過去之唯一手段的真實報告 (true reports) 的觀念。

　　Lara（14 歲）選擇的想法是：羅馬帝國結束於何時沒有一個單一的時刻，而且說道這是「因為沒有一個明確的方式說明它何時結束。有的人認為羅馬帝國結束於其城市遭到占領，或首次遭受入侵，抑或其他時候。」當被問到我們如何可以決定它何時結束時，她回答說：「透過設定一個發生何事的固定標的，譬如當其首都被攻下，或當它被徹底殲滅，或者其他何事，然後就可以找到這個日期。」她同意我們可以說羅馬帝國結束於其他可能的不同時候，「因為這取決於你認為的結局是什麼，可以是羅馬或君士坦丁堡的陷落，或它首次遭受侵略，抑或其他時候。」她認為故事之間的差異是重要的，「如果它們是重大差異的話。因為人們並不知道整個故事的來龍去脈。」

　　Lara 向前邁進了一大步。她可以看到關於羅馬帝國結局的問題，不只是一個關於報導事件的問題，同時也關乎標準。我們必須決定何者算作帝國的結局，或者如她所說設立一個「固定標的」。她隱隱約約地認識到，歷史記載並不僅僅是過去的複製品，而是必須被重建來回答問題，以及假若我們要有能力講述一個故事，我們就必須做出如此這般的抉擇。但是 Lara 還是以為可以有「整個故事」，她可能還將它當成透過設定不同的標準所能得出的所有可能存在之故事的總和。

　　最後，Natasha（14 歲）選擇的想法是：羅馬帝國結束於何時沒有一個單一的時刻，而且解釋說：「因為這都取決於你的意見，以及你思考的是羅馬帝國在實體上的結局或心理上的結局。如果人們直到 1453 年仍然會想到或談到羅馬帝國，那麼直到那時，羅馬帝國在心理層面仍尚未結束。我認為羅馬帝國的不同層面結束於不同的時刻，舉例來說，它在實體上的結束早於心理上之結束。羅馬帝國在實體上結束於不再由同樣的人所統治，心理上結束於不再被人想起，精神上結束於不再成為人們生活中的陰影，我們現在仍然在使用拉丁衍生詞，因此羅馬帝國的影響至今尚未結束。」

Natasha 也想到這是一個關於標準的問題，而這種思維則使她得以不僅止於解釋兩個故事之間的差異，還能給出她自己的故事版本，顯示這兩個故事是如何被整合一致的。面對關於過去的不同故事，她並非徬徨無助，而是擁有概念工具，從而以有意義的方式來聯繫彼此不同的諸多故事。她了解任何一項歷史記載都是對於一個（明確的或含糊的）問題之答案，而且記載之間的差異都是正當合理的。

我們由此可見，《人們如何學習》的「原則一」是很要緊的。假如我們不了解學生們的先入之見很可能是些什麼，我們大多數的教學都將得到迥然有異於我們所期望的結果。例如，假定我們要教 Chris 和 Natasha 有關史家如何自不同的立場出發而寫作。如果我們比較他們帶有的先入之見，我們將會發現必須對他們因材施教。Chris 仍然深信觀點會扭曲一個單一真實的故事，因此我們就必須非常謹慎小心地確保他不會將史學家們擁有不同哲學的這種觀念，比擬作為較低層次的先入之見，也就是會變成偏見的意見和選邊站。

Natasha 則不然，她在一個較高的層次上思考。由於她已經理解到故事不是過去的複製品，因此她知道故事之間的差異，並非關乎扭曲一個固定的真實故事之問題。她了解到出於合理的理由，記載是有可能不同的。這就使我們可以教導她關於史家的立場問題，而不至於過分冒著將精深複雜的觀念轉化為簡單之個人偏見的危險。

《人們如何學習》研究所指出的這些原則，共同給予歷史之學科訓練在觀念上的進展此種見解在歷史教育中的中心地位。「原則一」提醒我們，假如我們想要有效地教學，我們便需要知道學生們的先入之見是如何發展出來的。「原則二」強調概念工具的重要性，以及我們一旦認識到，對於關鍵性的第二序或學科性觀念在理解上之進展是有可能的，我們就可以看到這種概念工具如何可能加以發展。而同樣是那些第二序的概念工具，則使學生們能思考他們的歷史理解（「原則三」），就像我們在本文起

始所見到的 Angela 對於二次大戰的思考一樣。進展意味著賦予學生們更強而有力的觀念，比如說我們如何可能得知過去，以及為何史家們的記載會有所不同。帶有這種觀念，他們就更可能有能力在處理實質的歷史時運作得更為有效。Natasha 比起 Chris 來說，更能對於歷史內容（羅馬帝國的結局）提出較好的理解，正是因為她對於這門學科訓練擁有更為有力的觀念。

簡而言之，當學生們對於作為一門學科訓練的歷史，發展出更為強而有力的觀念時，他們就能獲得所需的思想工具，以應付他們在學校之外將會遭遇到的多種不同而彼此競爭的故事。這也會反過來使他們在思考其實質性的內容知識時更加有效。理解歷史這門學科訓練與理解過去，兩者是相伴而來的。

歷史教育是一件莊嚴慎重之事。我們首先必須堅持它確實是一門歷史教育，而非一種社會性的人際結合活動、愛國主義訓練，或甚至是一種民主人士的製造活動。歷史與民主共享某些關鍵性的價值，而且尊重他人，尊重真理，以及建基於此二者之中的理性論證。史學家獻身於言論自由，因為若缺乏言論自由，對於真理的公開追求以及對於論證的檢驗也就無法存在。就此而言，歷史是開放社會的一個關鍵成分，或許也是開放社會得以成功的一個必要前提。然而，歷史並不支持任何一組制度結構，或甚至是任何特定的現存民主觀念。我們應該出於這樣的目標來教授歷史：學生們將更有能力去思考他們身處的世界，他們將更有可能理解對於任何一個開放社會來說最核心的價值與權利的重要性。但是他們必須自由地從事歷史思考，並對於上述事項達成他們自己的結論，這意味著保證成為民主人士絕不能是歷史教育的壓倒性優先目標。

歷史教育應該給予學生們一種在多樣組合的故事之間得以定位他們自身的判斷力，從而使他們能在時間之流中自我導航。不必多說的是，他們應當對過去了解甚多，儘管對於我們如何可能給他們一個歷史性的框架，

同時又不認可一個單一的「正確」故事這方面，我們依然所知甚少。[13]然而清楚的是，除非學生們被賦予了關鍵性的觀念，諸如我們如何了解和解釋過去，以及我們所說的關於過去的故事之性質與地位，他們就很可能認為歷史並不比小說更精當，而且一旦離開學校碰到與面對其他具競爭性的記載時，他們便將會手足無措。歷史教育要求學生們終止他們被灌輸的刻板教育中對於歷史如何可能的理解，儘管歷史存在其不確定性，以及存在人們想要說的是自己中意的故事之動機。歷史迫使我們給出我們可能並不總是喜歡的過往記載：如果學生們學到了這一點，我們也就不負於人。

13　見於 Lee, P.J., '"Walking backwards into tomorrow": Historical consciousness and understanding history', *International Journal of History Learning, Teaching and Research*, 4, 1, January 2004. www.ex.ac.uk/historyresource/journal7/contents.htm 以及較短的版本，'Historical literacy: theory and research', *International Journal of Historical Learning Teaching and Research*, Vol.5 No.1, 2004. www.ex.ac.uk/historyresource/journal9/contents.htm

Advantages and Disadvantages of Narrative in History Education

Keith C. Barton[*]

I'd like to share some of my ideas on how we can help young people learn history. My research has been on how students think about the past—what they know about history, where they've learned it, what they're interested in, and how they make sense of historical information. I've done several studies with students from 6 to 16 years old in the United States and Northern Ireland. Sometimes I've observed in classrooms as children study history, and other times I've talked to them outside the classroom, often having them sequence or organize historical photographs as a way of getting at their ideas about the past. Today I want to share some of what I've learned about students' historical thinking and to suggest some possible implications for history teaching.

As a history educator, I don't like to travel any place without knowing about that country's history, and so I've spent the past few weeks learning about Taiwan's past, and also about some of the controversies here about what kind of history should be taught in school. I think that some of the ideas I've developed in an American and European context may also be useful here, and I think you'll see some connections between these ideas and the issues facing history educators in Taiwan or other countries. Because of my limited

* Indiana University

knowledge of Taiwanese history and Taiwanese education, I don't want to make too many assumptions about what would be effective here, but my observations should help us think about how history can be taught more effectively.

Today I'll focus primarily on one aspect of students' understanding—how they make sense of historical narratives. I want to discuss the advantages of using narrative to teach history, based on research with students, but I also want to point out some of the drawbacks of narrative in history education, again using research on children's thinking.[1] Finally, I'm going to suggest strategies for using narrative while overcoming some of these obstacles.

When I talk about narrative history, I mean an account of a series of events that take place in chronological order and that are causally connected. Not all history is narrative; a description of how people lived long ago—such as life in Ancient Egypt, or the historical culture of the aborigines, or even daily life during World War II—is not narrative, because there is no connected series of events, just a description of social interactions, economic patterns, or cultural practices. But much of the history we teach is narrative, because it involves a plot in which one action causes another. This plot often involves the transformation of some state of affairs, and frequently focuses on an attempt to solve some kind of problem. For example, a narrative may begin with people in a given area under the political or economic dominance of a colonial power; this leads some people to protest against that power; and this resistance may lead to conflict that either results in independence or leads to new levels of

---

[1] This research is discussed in more detail in Keith C. Barton and Linda S. Levstik, *Teaching History for the Common Good* (Mahwah, NJ, and London: Lawrence Erlbaum Associates, 2004).

repression. Many nations tell such stories as part of their history curriculum.

Narratives also have settings and actors. Fifty years ago, a great deal of narrative history focused on nations, and history in schools often took the nation as its most important subject. More recently, other kinds of narrative have become common in history, and these have begun to make their way into schools as well. Some narratives focus on developments much larger than those that take place within a single nation, and over a much longer time period. This has been particularly common in the study of world history, which has focused on large-scale patterns of migration and the development of human societies. Here, the subject of the narrative is not any single nation but a social or economic phenomenon such as "agricultural production" or "transportation." At the other end of the scale, smaller narratives that focus on individuals have become popular—stories not of nations or even the "great men" who lead those nations, but of everyday people whose lives reflect important aspects of the historical setting. These narratives may focus on only one person, and may only deal with a small portion of their lives. For example, students in the United States who are studying the nineteenth century may read a story about a Chinese immigrant who works building a railroad, or of the attempt by an African slave in the South to escape from his master.

The actors in narratives, then, can be individuals, groups of people, nations, or abstract forces such as the environment. The setting can be one neighborhood, a nation, or a region of the world, and the story may extend over centuries or be limited a few days. The chief characteristic of narratives, though, is that they always go beyond simple description or listing to show connections among a series of events.

There are some important advantages of using narrative in teaching history. First, students are already familiar with narrative. They're exposed to narratives from their earliest encounters with bedtime stories and picture books, as well as through cartoons, movies, television, and the everyday stories of peers and relatives. And a number of psychological researchers have shown that people develop expectations for narratives from a young age—they expect a narrative to have a plot with causal connections, they expect it to have characters, and so on—and when they encounter stories that have all these elements, they're more likely to understand and remember them. When people hear a story in which some of the elements of narrative are missing, they have trouble remembering the story accurately, and they often go so far as to fill in the missing parts based on their overall understanding of the story and their own assumptions about how the world works.

One of the ways we can make history more understandable to students, then, is by using their familiarity with narrative. Not only have children heard stories from an early age, but they've also begun to pick up information about the past; in my interviews with children, even those as young as 6 years old have shown that they know about a variety of people, events, and trends from the past, and they've learned about these from a wide range of sources— relatives, cartoons, movies, books, historic sites, artifacts, and so on. But this information doesn't just clutter up their mind in some random way; instead, students mentally structure historical information in ways that make sense to them—and one of the ways that makes most sense is narrative. When students encounter history at school, for example, they try to make sense of it in terms of a narrative. Two colleagues of mine, Bruce VanSledright and Jere Brophy, for example, interviewed students in the U.S. to find out what they knew about common topics in the elementary history curriculum—the colonies, the

American Revolution, the Civil War, and so on. They found that students often confused information about different topics (for example, they would mix together details of two completely different wars) or they combined accurate details with misconceptions or even with fantasies that they had invented. But despite the inaccuracies in their description of historical events, students' accounts made sense when viewed as narratives—that is, they contained all the elements of a story, even when the historical details were wrong. They often explained causal relationships or attributed motivations, for example, based not on any specific knowledge of historical events, but simply on their understanding of human nature. In this study and others, there's strong evidence that students take historical information in whatever form they find it and transform it into narratives that make sense to them.

That can have important advantages for history teachers, because it means that we don't always have to teach students a new way of thinking when we present historical information; it's not like when students have to learn to write an essay or use a formula to find the volume of a cylinder—they don't usually have much experience with those until they study them at school. But they *do* have previous experience with narrative—they can be expected to know something about how narrative works even before they come to school, and by the time they're 10 years old they should have well-developed expectations for setting, agents, causality and so on. Narrative, then, can serve as a kind of scaffolding for history; teachers can expect that students already know what stories are, so they can focus their attention on helping students learn particular stories. Teachers in the United States who are teaching about the Westward Movement of the 1800s, for example, can focus on the motivation of the pioneers, the routes they took, and the challenges they faced without having to worry about students asking, "Why do we need to know *why* they moved? Why do we need to know what *the problems* were?" Students expect a story to have problems, and they expect to learn why people did things. They'd have trouble making sense of if it didn't, so we can use students' familiarity with narrative to focus their attention on the content rather than the form of history.

A second important advantage of historical narratives is that students like them, particularly when they focus on the actions of individuals. Students are captivated by stories that help them explore how people responded to dramatic situations or that give them the chance to imagine taking part in the events of the past. My colleague Linda Levstik, for example, did a study with eleven-year-olds who were taking part in independent reading of historical literature, as preparation for a project. Most students in that study were interested in exploring historical events through the eyes of the individuals involved, as though they themselves were present or could relive the experiences of people in the past. They read about World War II, for example, in order to learn about brave children like Anne Frank or "madmen" like Hitler. They were interested in reading about individuals who were part of historical events rather than about stories of troop deployments or conflict among countries.

Students in that study were particularly interested in the "border areas" of human experience: times when people had to respond to situations of fear, discrimination, or tragedy. Students often reflected on how they would have responded if put in the same situations, with comments such as "I would have run away! Why didn't they run away?" or, after reading about Amelia Earhardt, "I would never have the guts to fly a plane across the Atlantic alone." Students speculated on the nature of bravery and inhumanity, and the motivations for each—exploring what might have led Hitler to undertake such insane actions, or why ordinary people joined the Nazis' cause. The emotional relevance of the stories, and students' personal identification with the characters, were among the most important reasons for their interest in history. Narratives about individuals, then, can build on students' interests by helping them see history from the eyes of the people who were involved. I recognize, though, that this focus on the individual may be the result, at least in part, of the American emphasis on individualism, and so it may not be as important in other nations.

There's a third advantage of narrative that I think is especially important: Narratives promote a search for meaning in history. As I've already mentioned, a narrative isn't a random list of events; narratives aim at causal explanation— they attempt to lay out how one thing caused another, as well as the factors that influenced those links. Narratives are what help us make sense of the past—the whole purpose of a historical narrative, after all, is to identify a meaningful pattern, a plot, out of the massive array of facts that can be established for any given time. When we present history in a narrative fashion to students, then, we encourage them to look for patterns, for logical and chronological sequences, for causes and consequences, for agents and their motivations. Narratives help students make sense of the past, to see it as meaningful. The story of World War II helps students understand that this was a struggle over the future of the modern world, that different countries, and groups of people within those countries, had conflicting stakes in the outcome of that struggle, and that the result of the war had important consequences that remain with us today. It isn't just a series of battles; it's a coherent story that means something to us.

My research with children in the United States suggests that they almost always place historical events into these larger narrative patterns, and that as young as 10 years old, they see coherent patterns in national history—although this may not be the case in other countries where narrative history is less common. This is surely the most important justification for using narrative in teaching about the past—it promotes the search for meaning. And after all, if the past has no meaning, why would we bother with it?

But the very thing that's most important about historical narrative—its shaping of the past into coherent sequences of meaning—is also potentially its greatest drawback. The key word here is "shaping." The past itself doesn't have shape or coherence—the past is just a countless number of people, events, and places. We impose meaning and coherence onto the events of the past when we shape them into narratives. The past doesn't come to us already arranged: We decide how to arrange it, how to group its elements into the causal sequence of a narrative. Historians don't try to describe everything that went on—a history of World War II won't describe every time that a soldier bent over to tie his shoes, or every time a nurse bandaged a patient. That would take forever, no one would read it, and it would be literally meaningless. Rather, when writing narratives, historians select some events as being the most important ones and they arrange those events together as part of a coherent sequence.

This kind of selection requires a great deal of interpretation, and it depends on what the historian is trying to accomplish. If I tell the story of exploration of North America, for example, do I begin with the first migrants over 15,000 years ago? Or with European explorers 600 years ago? What about Chinese explorers of the Americas—are they part of the story, or are they not important enough to be included? And when is the story over—does present-day immigration from South America or Asia count as part of the "exploration" of North America? In making these decisions, historians impose order on the infinite variety of facts from which they could draw, and obviously, others might tell the story differently—with different beginnings or endings, different causal links, or different actors. It's not that historical facts change from one narrative to another, but that their selection and significance changes. Perhaps there are also issues here related to when and where the story of Taiwanese history began, and who should be included.

The first drawback to narratives, then, is that we may confuse them with history itself—that is, we may lose sight of the fact that they're composed not just of what happened in the past, but of our interpretation of the past. Because narratives are so common, so widely used in our attempts to make meaning of the world, it's easy to forget that they've been intentionally constructed—that someone has sifted through the evidence and made decisions about where the story begins and ends, who the agents are, and how the actions are related. Rather than seeing any particular historical narrative as *one way* of making sense of a period in history, it's tempting—for children or adults—to regard that narrative *as history itself.* That is, we may think of the structure found in narratives as being a part of the past, rather than a structure that has been imposed—in our quest for meaning—on a limitless number of discrete happenings. And if children only encounter the products of historical narration—if the process of constructing the narrative isn't transparent—then they may not recognize that the story could be told other ways. Linda Levstik found this in her work, when students who had read historical narratives were confident they knew the truth or as they said, "what really happened." They didn't seek alternative explanations or viewpoints; the narratives they encountered were so powerful that they weren't critical of them. In my own experience, I've found that students tend to cling tightly to the first narrative they hear about a topic. If they hear the story of Betsy Ross sewing the first U.S. flag—a story that's completely fictional—they have great difficulty giving it up later on, even as adults. They already know the story, so why consider alternatives? This is no trivial issue, because if students believe that narratives are *found in the past*, rather than *imposed* by people today *on the past*, then they won't be prepared to look at history from multiple perspectives or to understand why other people may have different interpretations than their own. The strength of narrative makes it very difficult to look at history critically.

A second drawback to narrative also relates to interpretation: Narratives simplify the past, and in doing so they sometimes *oversimplify* it. A narrative necessarily includes some things and leaves out others, and there are gains and losses with each of these inclusions and omissions. For example, historical narratives for many years included mainly elite white males, and they omitted women, minorities, and the poor. This kind of narrative may have had the advantage of helping us understand the actions of those who held political, legal, and economic power in society, but it had the disadvantage of providing little insight into the lives of the majority of the population. Recently, a great deal of historical writing has examined the lives of marginalized groups—moving them from the margins to the center of the narrative—but such works have also been criticized for attributing too much agency to those who lacked formal power and thus for neglecting the larger structural constraints on their lives. No matter where we focus our attention, then, it seems that we will miss out on some other, potentially significant part of the situation. There's no getting away from this—it's just what history is.

But when we look at how children think about the past, we begin to notice some important consequences of leaving things out of historical narratives. In a study I did with 10- and 11-year-olds, I found that they consistently simplified the past into a minimal number of characters and events. When studying the American Revolution, for example, they didn't recognize that there were many thousands of participants, engaged in many different conflicts throughout the colonies. Instead, they thought there were just two bodies of troops who kept meeting each other in battle, and that all the colonists were closely involved with major political figures and events. They also thought of long-term historical processes as having consisted of a small number of happenings, each of which took place at one point in time. That is, they collapse gradual and long-term historical processes into single events to make more effective narratives.

This was especially noticeable when students talked about immigration to North America. Rather than recognizing immigration as a process that took place over centuries and involved millions of people, most students described it as though it happened all at once, with a limited number of ships. In looking at a picture of an immigrant ship from 1906, for example, one student suggested that "this is one of the main ships that brought everybody over to America." Another noted that "it looks like it was when the queen and king went over to sail to get like more people." When asked to put the picture in chronological order, as part of a set of pictures from the past four hundred years, many students thought it must be the oldest in the set because it showed people coming to America—and people had to come here before anything else in the pictures could have happened. For these students, history wasn't about ongoing processes, but about simple events that happened at a given time and then were over with. Students don't just interpret history in terms of narrative, but in terms of very simple narratives.

The clearest example of this kind of simplification came in two different studies I've done with the same pictures, of a city from the early 1800s and a family moving west in the late 1800s. Most students put these pictures in the wrong order. Their explanations point to the more developed, more settled nature of the city—they explain that people first lived in places with grass and fields, and only later built cities. One student explained, "They had plains before they had whole towns like that" and another said, "I *know* it didn't go from brick buildings to wagons and carriages *after* the brick buildings." They thought that any time in history could be characterized by only one image, and that these images stood in a definite chronological order—just like the events in a story.

We have to simplify history in order to teach it, and we can hardly be surprised that students simplify it even further when they learn it—but we need to think carefully about the nature of these simplifications. Does it matter that they think immigration happened at one point in time, rather than extending over centuries, or that everyone at a given time lived the same way? That may be important, because it stands in the way of students' understanding of the variety of experiences faced by people in different periods, including today. And if we think that simplifications such as this should be avoided, then we have to examine whether we're *creating* these simplifications through education. For example, if we only study military conflicts and political leaders, are we encouraging students to think that social developments occur mainly because of the actions of a few important men? If we study about aboriginal people only in the distant past, instead of during later time periods, are we encouraging students to think that they no longer matter, or maybe even that they no longer exist? In the United States, other countries are usually only mentioned in history during time periods when we were at war with them—and I think we all know that Americans have a reputation for not understanding other countries. We have to simplify, but we need to be careful which simplifications we make, because students aren't going to seek out complexity and nuance on their own. As adults, we recognize that there were always other things going on at any given time in history, and that not everyone's experiences were the same, but students won't recognize that unless we make it clear to them.

A final drawback to narrative relates to just one kind of story—the kind students like best, at least in the United States, those that focus on individual experience. In my research with 10- and 11-year-olds, they consistently explained historical events, and even long-term historical changes, as though they were the result of individual motivation and achievement. They almost completely ignored the impact of collective action, as well as the role of societal institutions such as political, legal, and economic systems. When asked to explain why they thought people in the past treated women and minorities differently than they do today, for example, students pointed to individual attitudes: They suggested that men were "bossy" and "wouldn't share," and that whites were "lazy" and thought "black people weren't as good as white people." These explanations may be true, but they are inadequate as explanations for racism or sexism, because they leave out crucial factors such as socially-sanctioned norms and beliefs, the role of the legal system in creating and sustaining systems of oppression, and the economic underpinnings of slavery or patriarchy.

In the same way, when explaining why these practices have changed over time, students pointed to the impact of individuals in changing attitudes and beliefs: They thought famous people, particularly Abraham Lincoln and Martin Luther King, Jr., single-handedly changed the lives of minorities and even women in American society:　As one student put it, Martin Luther King "said a speech, and then everybody started realizing that the black people were the same as them." Almost completely lacking was any sense of the larger structural dimensions of such change, and entirely absent was any focus on collective action. History, for these students, was about a few famous individuals changing the minds of other individuals. Interpreting the past solely in terms of individual motivation and achievement, though, seriously limits students' understanding of many historical events. If students think the lives of African Americans and other minorities in the U.S. changed because a speech by Martin Luther King altered the attitudes of white people, then we could say that they haven't really understood this topic at all. To understand the history of civil rights, students need to understand changes in legislation and political representation, as well as the collective actions that brought about those institutional changes. Focusing on individual beliefs and actions fundamentally misrepresents those events and, perhaps more importantly, leaves students ill-equipped to understand institutional racism and other forms of discrimination today, when individuals are less likely to publicly affirm personal prejudices.

So where does this leave us? Narrative helps students understand history, it leads them to look for meaning in the past, and they find it interesting, especially when it focuses on individuals. Yet narrative may also blind them to the fact that history itself has no particular plot, it may encourage oversimplification of the past, and when it focuses on individuals, it may stand in the way of a fuller understanding of larger societal forces. These conflicting advantages and disadvantages are significant, but I don't think we have to throw our hands up in despair. I think it is possible to use narrative productively, and to do so in a way that makes students aware of the complicated nature of historical narratives, even when they're younger.

First, we need to help students understand that narratives are constructed—that anytime we hear or read a story about the past, we're looking at something that's been put together by someone at a later time. Children already understand that fictional stories are created—they know that an identifiable author sat down and wrote the story, and they also recognize that she or he made choices when writing it—deciding how to describe the setting, what the characters would be like, and how to include action in the story. They know this because they've written stories themselves, and so they've had to make similar decisions, and they often discuss authors' choices and intentions when studying literature at school. I've also found that students are familiar with artwork as a constructed medium—again, because they've had to make choices themselves when drawing or paining, they know that other artists have done the same, and I've found that they can easily discuss why an artist might have composed a piece in a particular way. So students are already comfortable with the idea of interpretation.

What they aren't usually familiar with is the idea of history as an interpretation. They don't perceive a human author behind works of history, and even when reading historical fiction they're often uncritical—they think that such works provide them with "the truth" of what happened, rather than with one interpretation. One way to help them come to a better understanding of the constructed nature of historical narratives is simply to ask the same questions of historical texts that we do of fiction: Who wrote this? Why do you think they wrote it? Why do you think they focused on these particular people or events? How might they have done it differently?

Just as important, we need to give students experience in creating their own historical narratives. Just as writing fictional stories and drawing pictures helps students understand those genres, creating history can help them understand how narratives about the past are constructed. Students at all ages need to work with original historical sources and to shape those sources into narrative accounts. To take just one example: In our book *Doing History*, Linda Levstik and I describe a teacher who had her students interview recent immigrants and tell their stories to the rest of the class.[2] Students had to make choices about what was important enough to include, what could be left out, and how the story could be made interesting to their classmates—and how to fit it into the 15 minutes they had for their presentations. These students were engaging in all the same interpretive acts of professional historians. Other students, in other classrooms, might create historical narratives based on photographs, letters, diaries, statistics, and so on. By creating their own narratives, students should be better able to understand that all historical stories are the outcome of interpretive choices, and not simply reflections of the past.

A second way of overcoming some problems with narrative is to focus students' attention on the diversity of people and events in the past. As adults,

---

[2] Linda S. Levstik and Keith C. Barton, *Doing History: Investigating with Children in Elementary and Middle Schools*, 3rd ed. (Mahwah, NJ, and London: Lawrence Erlbaum Associates, 2006).

we all know that there were lots of things going on at any given time, and that different groups of people were having different experiences. Women's lives may have been different than men's, rural peasants' lives were different than those of urban workers, the lives of different ethnic groups may not have been the same. We know that there was more than one story going on at any point in history—but the research I've talked about suggests that students are not always aware of that, or at least that it's not a very salient aspect of history to them. So we need to draw their attention to it. For each period of time that we study, we need to make students aware of how multiple groups of people were experiencing the events of the day, and how different stories could be told about their experiences. What was going on in the countryside, and in the cities? How did social changes affect men, and how did they affect women? Which people in a country benefited from events, and which ones in the same country suffered? We can always remind students to think, "Whose story is this? What other stories were going on at the time?"

Finally, how do we overcome students' tendency to focus on individuals rather than larger societal forces such as the government or the economy? We don't want to leave out stories of individuals, but we need to show how individuals were caught up in societal institutions: how their behavior was constrained by social forces, how their actions influenced government or the economy, and how they banded together with other people to form groups. In the United States, for example, nearly all students learn the story of Rosa Parks, the African American woman who initiated the Montgomery Bus boycott that was an important element of the Civil Rights Movement. But what they usually learn, or at least what they come away with, was that she was a tired old woman who didn't want to walk to the back of the bus, and who stood up to the prejudice of Whites. What they should learn is that Rosa Parks was part of an organized social movement; that she wasn't tired, but that she was intentionally trying to get arrested, that the social movement wasn't challenging individual prejudice but a system of legal segregation, and that the effectiveness of the boycott was due to its economic impact. Students do need to learn about Rosa Parks' story, and about her courage and determination, but they also need to learn about the societal context in which her courage arose, and about the societal institutions toward which her determination was directed. They already understand what bravery is; they don't understand what an economic boycott is. Of course, that's a U.S. example that may have limited relevance to other nations, but I'm sure most countries have historical incidents where the experience of one individual, or a small group of ordinary people, can help students understand larger social and economic forces, and students will understand history better when they see how individual actions and social forces are linked. However, we have to call their attention to the social aspect, because that's something they may not understand very well.

In summary, I want to emphasize that we need to think very carefully about the role of narrative in history education. We all know that historical narratives can be controversial, because most political debates over the curriculum involve arguments over which narratives we should be telling our young people. Politicians and other public figures are quick to complain whenever they think that schools are not telling children the "correct" stories, especially those relating to the national past. In a sense, their complaints are well-justified, because if all we do is expose students to stories about the past, then we mislead them into thinking that history provides us with the true and correct way of thinking about politics and society—and we all know that what one group considers true and correct may be considered an outright lie by others. The alternative is not to do away with narratives in history, but to teach students how those narratives are constructed, so that they see what choices historians, teachers, textbooks, or politicians have made when they focus on some events rather than others, and when they explain historical changes in one way rather than another. By not only telling stories, but helping students understand how stories come to be told in the first place, we will improve their understanding of history, and we may also better prepare them to take part in modern democratic society.

中文節譯

敘事在歷史教育中的得失

Keith C. Barton　著
葉毅均　節譯

　　學生如何理解歷史敘事？基於我們對兒童思考方式的研究，本文想討論的是在歷史教學中運用敘事的優點與缺失，並建議一些使用敘事的策略，以求克服可能的阻礙。

　　我所謂的敘事式歷史，指的是對一系列在時間順序上相繼發生，並有因果關係之事件的描述。並非所有的歷史都是敘事式的，但是許多我們教授的歷史都是敘事式的，因為涉及了一定的情節。其中，一項行動導致另一項行動的發生。這種情節通常牽涉到某些事態的轉變，並且時常注意到解決某種問題的企圖。舉例來說，一個敘事也許始於某個既定地域裡的人群，他們遭受殖民政權的政治或經濟支配。這會導致某些人開始抗爭，從而引發衝突，最終將造成獨立或更新一層的壓迫。有許多國家在他們的歷史課程中都訴說著這樣的故事。

　　敘事亦有其場景與演出角色。在五十年前，相當大一部分的敘事史皆聚焦於國族 (nation)，學校中的歷史也時常將國族視為最重要的主題。近來，其他種類的敘事開始在歷史中出現，也開始進入學校的課程。有些敘事專注於遠大於單一國族之內的發展，以及更長的時段。這點在世界史的研究中特別常見，關注於大規模的移民模式，以及人類社會的發展。此處敘事的主題不再是單一國族，而是如「農業生產」或「運輸」之類的社會或經濟現象。在另一個極端，專注於個人的更小的敘事開始流行，其故事

不再是關於國族，或甚至是領導國族的「偉人」，而是關乎日常生活中的凡人，其生活反映出歷史背景中的重要面向。這些敘事也許只注意到一個人，甚至只涉及其人生活中的一小部分。舉例來說，學習十九世紀的美國學生可能會讀到一個開築鐵路的中國移民的故事，或者是一個企圖逃離雇主的美國南方非洲裔黑奴的故事。

因此，敘事中的演出角色可以是單一個人、人群、國族，或者如環境這樣的抽象力量。而場景則可以是一個地區、一個國家，或世界裡的某個地域。這樣的故事可能跨越數個世紀，或局限於幾天的日子。然而，敘事的首要特點總是超越單純的描述或列舉，進而凸顯一系列事件之間的聯繫。

在歷史教學中運用敘事有幾項重要的優點。第一，學生們早已熟悉敘事。他們在最初遇到床邊故事和圖畫書的時候，乃至於透過卡通、電影、電視，以及同儕和親戚的日常故事，便已置身於敘事之中。一些心理學家也已說明，人們從幼年時就對敘事發展出期待：期望一個敘事帶有因果連結的情節，包含各種角色等等。當他們讀到含有所有這些要素的故事時，就更能領會並記住這些故事。當人們聽到的故事遺漏了某些敘事要素，他們就很難精確地記住此一故事，並且通常會基於他們對整個故事的了解，以及他們自身對於世界如何運作的假設，來填補這個故事所遺漏的部分。

因此，我們可以用來使學生更容易理解歷史的方法之一，就是利用他們對於敘事的熟悉程度。孩童不僅在年幼時便聽聞故事，他們也已開始汲取關於過去的訊息。在我針對兒童的訪談中，甚至年幼如六歲的孩童都表示知曉一些過去的人物、事件和潮流。他們從相當廣泛的來源獲知這些訊息，如親戚、卡通、電影、書籍、歷史遺跡、史前遺物等等。然而，這些資訊並非只是漫無章法地堆積於他們的腦中。相反地，學生們在心智上以對他們來說有意義的方式組織這些歷史訊息，而其中最有意義的方式之一就是敘事。舉例而言，當學生們在學校中遇到歷史，他們會試著用敘事的

方式來理解歷史。

　　這對歷史教師來說有重要的優點，因為這意味著當我們在呈現歷史資訊時，我們不需要總是得教學生們一種新的思考方式。他們先前確實有過敘事的經驗：甚至在入學之前，可以期待他們對於敘事如何運作已經有所了解。而當他們十歲大的時候，他們應該已經擁有對於場景、角色與因果關係等等完整的領會。因此，敘事可以作為歷史的一種支架。教師可以預期學生們早已了解何謂故事，從而也就可以致力於幫助學生去學習特定的故事。學生們預料一個故事中有其難題 (problem)，並且期望了解人們為何從事某一件事。如果故事中不存在難題，反而會使學生感到困擾。所以我們可以利用學生對於敘事的嫻熟，使他們專注於歷史的內容而非其形式。

　　歷史敘事第二項重要的優點是學生們的喜愛，特別當他們關注的是個人行動之時。學生們著迷於能使他們探索人類如何應對變局的故事，或是能使他們想像自身參與其中的過往事件之類的故事。他們有興趣讀的是關乎歷史事件之中的個人，而非軍隊部署的故事或國家之間的衝突。

　　故事在情感上令人感到與己切身相關，以及學生們對其中角色的個人認同，是他們對歷史感興趣最重要的理由。因此，有關個別人物的敘事可以培養學生們的興趣，使他們得以從相關人物的眼光來看歷史。當然我也了解，對個人的注重（至少有部分）可能是美式個人主義的結果，因而在其他國家可能就不會有同樣的重要性。

　　敘事的第三個優點，我認為特別的重要，就是敘事有助於在歷史中尋求意義。敘事有助於我們理解過去，畢竟一個歷史敘事的整體目標，是從任何一個時代裡無邊無盡的事實中，指出一個有意義的模式、一個情節。因此，當我們將歷史以敘事的方式呈現給學生，我們其實是在鼓勵學生尋找模式、邏輯的或時間的順序、原因與結果，乃至於行為者及其動機。敘事能幫助學生理解過去，使之產生意義。

　　但歷史敘事最為重要之處，也就是形塑過去，使過去成為意義融貫而連續的序列，同樣是其潛在可能最大的缺點。此處的關鍵詞為「形塑」(shaping)。過去本身並沒有形狀或條理可言，只是無數的人物、事件、地點。當我們將過去的事件形塑為敘事之時，我們強加了意義與條理於其上。過去並非以整頓好的面貌出現在我們眼前，是我們在決定如何安排過去，如何分類清理其要素，以完成敘事的因果序列。當寫下敘事時，史家選擇某些事件作為最重要的部分，並將那些事件擺在一起，形成一個融貫而連續的序列。

　　這種選擇性需要的是大量的詮釋，並且將依史家試圖達成的不同目標而定。在作抉擇的時候，史家將次序加諸於他們所能找到的無窮盡的事實，而且很顯然地，若由其他人來講述這個故事將會有所不同。不同的開端或結尾，不同的因果連結，或者是不同的角色。這並不是說，史實在不同的敘事之間有所不同，而是史實的揀選及其意義改變了。也許在台灣史自何時何處開始，以及誰應該被納入的問題上，也同樣存在著爭議。

　　敘事的第一項缺點，是我們可能混淆敘事與歷史本身。也就是說，我們可能會看不見一項事實，那就是敘事不僅僅是由過去所發生過的事所組成，也是由我們對過去的詮釋所構成的。相較於視任何特定的歷史敘事為理解一段歷史的方式之一，對兒童或成人來說，將之視為歷史本身是更為誘人的。也就是說，我們可能會以為敘事裡的結構就是過去中的一部分，而非出於我們對意義的渴求，強加於無數個別不連續的事件的一種結構。假如兒童只遇到歷史敘事的成品，而建構敘事的過程又是不透明的，那麼他們可能就無法了解此一故事可以用其他的方式來說。這不是個無足輕重的小問題。因為如果學生們深信敘事存在於過去之中，而非由今人加諸於過去，那麼他們將不會有本事從多元的視野來看待歷史，或去理解為何其他人可能對歷史有不同於他們本身的解釋。敘事的威力使得批判性地看待歷史變得極為困難。

　　敘事的第二項缺點也與詮釋有關：敘事簡化了過去，有時甚至過分簡化了。一個敘事必然包納某些事物，省略其他事物，這樣的包納與省略自然有其得失。舉例來說，多年來的歷史敘事主要包含的是精英白種男性，從而遺漏了女性、少數族群與窮人。這種敘事的長處可能是能幫助我們了解在社會上擁有政治、法律與經濟權力之人的所作所為，但其短處是對於佔人口大多數的一般人的生活缺乏省察。

　　當我們看一看兒童如何思考過去，我們開始注意到歷史敘事省略了某些事物所帶來的一些重要後果。在我所做的一項關於十歲和十一歲兒童的研究裡，我發現他們時常將過去簡化為最低限度的人物和事件。他們也將長時段的歷史過程想像成由少數的事件所組成，每個事件則在時間之流上的某一點發生。也就是說，他們將漸進而長程的歷史過程拆解為單一的事件，以使敘事更為有力。

　　我們必須為了教歷史而簡化歷史。同時，我們不該訝異於學生們在學習的過程中加倍地簡化歷史。但是我們必須仔細地思考這種簡化的本質。學生們以為移民是在時間上的某一點才發生，而非長達數個世紀的變化，或者又以為一定時期中的每個人都以相同的方式過活，這些足關緊要嗎？這也許是重要的，因為它阻礙了學生理解不同時期的人們所面臨的不同經驗，乃至於今日的人們亦然。如果我們認為應該避免這類的簡化，那麼我們就必須檢討，是否我們本身正在透過教育製造這些簡化。在美國，其他國家通常只有在與我們交戰的時期才會在歷史上被提及。我認為大家都知道，美國人是出了名的不了解其他國家。我們必須簡化，但我們得要對我們所做的簡化謹慎小心，因為學生們將不會自行尋找複雜性和細微的差異之處。

　　敘事的最後一項缺點，只與其中一種故事有關，就是學生們最喜愛的（至少在美國如此）聚焦於個人經驗的故事。在我對十歲和十一歲兒童所做的研究裡，他們經常將歷史事件，甚至長程的歷史變遷，解釋為個人動

機與成就的結果。他們幾乎全然無視於集體行動的影響，以及社會機制諸如政治、法律和經濟體系所扮演的角色。

那麼我們該怎麼辦？上述這些優點和缺失都是有意義的，但我不認為我們只能束手無策。我認為有可能有效地運用敘事，甚至在學生們更小的時候使他們了解到歷史敘事的複雜本質。

首先，我們需要幫助學生們了解到敘事是被建構出來的。無論何時我們聽到或讀到一個關於過去的故事，我們碰到的是由某個人在後來的時候湊在一起的東西。兒童早已熟知小說故事是被創作出來的。他們通常不熟悉的是歷史是一種詮釋的觀念。他們不曾感受到歷史作品背後有個人為的作者，甚至當閱讀歷史小說的時候，他們通常也不會加以批判性的閱讀，以為這樣的作品告訴他們的是過去發生的「真相」，而非僅僅是一種詮釋。有助於他們得到對歷史敘事的建構本質更好的理解的方式之一，就是拿我們詰問小說的同樣問題來詰問歷史文本：這是誰寫的？你認為他們為何書寫？你認為他們為何關注這些特定的人或事？他們有可能寫出如何不同的東西？

同樣重要的是，我們需要給予學生們創造自身歷史敘事的經驗。任何年齡的學生都需要處理原始的歷史材料，並將那些材料形塑為敘事式的說明。只舉一例：在我們的《做歷史》(*Doing History: Investigating with Children in Elementary and Middle Schools*) 一書中，Linda Levstik 和我描述了一位教師讓她的學生們訪問新近的移民，並讓他們在課堂上向其他學生講述所得出的故事。學生們必須選擇哪些是重要的東西得納入，哪些部分可以省略，以及故事要怎樣才會對他們的同學來說變得有趣，乃至於如何將故事濃縮成他們講述的十五分鐘以內。藉由自己創造的敘事，學生們應該可以更好的理解到所有的歷史故事都是詮釋的結果，而不僅僅是過去的反映。

第二個克服敘事所帶來的問題的方法，是將學生們的注意轉移至過去

人物和事件的多樣性上。對於我們所探究的每個時代，我們都須使學生明白有多少各種各樣不同的人類群體在經歷著當日的事件，以及針對這些群體自身的經驗而言，又有多少不同的故事可說。鄉村和城市裡分別發生了什麼事？社會變遷如何影響到男性，又如何影響到女性？一個國家裡的那些人自事件中得益，同一國家裡的那些人反而受害？我們總是可以提醒學生們思考：「這是誰的故事？同時還有那些其他的故事正在發生？」

最後，我們如何才能克服學生們習慣於關注個人，而非更大的社會力量諸如政府或經濟的問題？我們不希望摒棄有關個人的故事，但我們需要呈現出個人如何被捲入社會機制的情況：他們的行為如何受到社會力量的限制？他們的行動如何影響到政府或經濟？以及他們如何與其他人團結起來形成組織？

總而言之，我想要強調的是，我們需要極為仔細地思考敘事在歷史教育中所扮演的角色。我們都知道歷史敘事具有爭議性，因為多數針對課程的政治性辯論都涉及到我們該告訴我們的年輕人那些敘事。我們也都知道，被一個團體認為是真實與正確的事物，可能會被其他團體看作是全然的謊言。解決之道不是在歷史中排除敘事，而是教導學生們了解那些敘事是如何被建構出來的，讓他們知道當史家、教師、教科書或政客關注某些事件而非其他事件，以及用某些方式而非其他方式來解釋歷史變遷之時，這些人究竟做了什麼樣的選擇。藉由不僅僅講述故事，而是首先幫助學生了解故事是怎樣被講述的，我們將能增進他們對歷史的認識，而且更能使他們有心理準備以參與現代的民主社會。

歷史課堂上學生提出的「意外問題」

葉小兵[*]

一、引言

在中學的課堂教學中，教學的內容、進程等一般都是由教師掌控的，教師為此也事先做了準備。在教師準備的教學方案以及組織的教學活動中，幾乎所有的問題都是預設的，也是有標準答案的。因此，在課堂教學時，教學的過程是按照教師的設計而進行的，即使教學的實際情況會有臨場的、隨時的變動，那也多在教師的預料之中，是教師可以解決的。然而，在歷史教學中，有時就會出現教師意想不到的情況，下引兩例就是在實際教學中發生的。

例一

這是在初二歷史《中日甲午戰爭》一課教學時出現的情況：

教師：致遠艦被魚雷擊中後，漸漸沉沒。鄧世昌墜海後，部下用救生圈救他，但他看到艦上的官兵遇難，義不獨生，推開了救生圈。鄧世昌養的一隻叫「太陽犬」的狗，游到他的身邊，叼住他髮辮，

---

* 北京首都師範大學歷史系

欲救其主，但鄧世昌抱著決死之心，毅然用手按狗頭入水，自己也隨之沉入大海的波濤之中。這位愛國將領犧牲時年僅四十歲。

一學生：老師，軍艦上怎麼可以養狗呢？

當時教師講得慷慨激昂，課堂氛圍亦是一片凝重。然而，就是這個學生的疑問，改變了課堂的氣氛，教師沒有想到有學生會提出這樣的問題，一下子愣在了講臺上。

例二

這是在講授初一歷史《秦漢文化》一課時出現的情況：

教師：張衡發明的地動儀，形狀像一個大酒罈，周圍鑲著八條龍，龍頭分別朝著八個方向，每個龍嘴裡含有一個銅球，下面各趴著一隻蛤蟆，對著龍嘴仰首張嘴。如果哪個方向發生了地震，這個方向的龍嘴裡的銅球就會落到蛤蟆嘴裡，人們就知道地震的方位了。這個地動儀當時放在洛陽，有一次甘肅發生地震，洛陽沒有震感，而地動儀朝西龍嘴裡的球掉了下來，證明了地動儀測定地震方位的準確性。

學生甲：老師，我想不明白，地震波的擴散，不會是一條直線的吧？應該是圓形的，向一個方向擴散也應該是弧形的，傳到地震儀，怎麼就震掉了一個球？

學生乙：是啊，地震波來得很快，一下子衝過來，球應該是全被震了下來。

學生丙：那地震儀還有什麼用？

　　此時班上的學生交頭接耳，議論紛紛，教師有些束手無策。

　　案例所示，是當教師傳授歷史知識時，學生突然發問，對教師的講述內容提出了質疑。學生提出的問題，是教師完全沒有想到，又一時不知道該怎麼解答，以致打亂了教師原有的教學計畫，甚至使教師感到難以應對。

　　這裡，我們可將學生提出的這種質疑，稱之為「意外問題」，因為這類問題對於教師和學生來說，都是事先完全沒有想到的。

　　對這些「意外問題」進行分析[1]，可以看出它們有以下特點：1.問題是臨時生成的。提出問題的學生，也沒有事先的考慮和準備，而是在教學的過程中即刻想到了的。2.問題的直覺性和針對性較強。提出的問題，與學生的直接判斷有關，而且直接針對教師講述的內容。3.問題一提出，其他的學生也感興趣。儘管其他學生並沒有想到有同學會提出這樣的問題，但問題提出來後即引起共鳴，都非常想知道答案。4.問題是教師想不到的。雖然教師可能有著一定的教學經驗，在備課時也認真做了準備，但學生在課堂上提出的這類質疑，教師完全沒有想到。5.問題是教師感到困惑的。對於教師來說，這些問題有點古怪、刁鑽，教師不知道如何解答；又由於問題具有突發性，使得教師不知道該怎麼辦，只靠教師的教學經驗和應變能力還不足以應對學生的問題。

　　歷史教學中出現的這種「意外問題」，是一種頗為有趣的現象[2]。本文擬對此進行初步的探討。

1　近兩年來，筆者留意收集這方面的實例，一些中學歷史教師提供了不少實際教學中的情況，目前已彙集了五十多個這方面的教學案例。

2　雖然「意外問題」這種現象不是經常發生，但也有著一定的普遍性。筆者以問卷的形式對北京市的五十位中學歷史教師（初中和高中各半）進行調查，他們的教齡都在五年以上，所在學校都是在城區。結果是有三十八位教師（占被調查教師的 76%）回答說遇到過這類情況，其中初中教師要比高中教師遇到的比例略高，有些教師甚至說他們的學生常會提出這類問題。

二、「意外問題」的種類

從筆者所蒐集到案例看，學生提出的「意外問題」有各種各樣，可以說是五花八門。若對其進行分類，可將其分為兩種類型：史事類的問題和認識類的問題。前者涉及學生所學的具體歷史知識，後者涉及到對歷史的認識和解釋。

（一）史事類的「意外問題」

史事類的問題，是指對所謂「陳述性知識」(declarative knowledge) 本身提出疑問，即學生對歷史教科書和歷史教師的敘述產生質疑，要求了解更多的內容。

在中學歷史教學中，歷史知識的範圍、廣度和深度大都已經過教育者的選擇和編排，是確定了的。從教的角度來說，傳授給學生的史事，本屬於是既成的、明確的，教科書和教師的敘述就是要告訴學生歷史「是什麼」。這好像不會有什麼問題，學生注意接受就是了。然而，就有學生要對史事性的知識作進一步的追尋，希望得到更多的了解。他們所提出的問題，恰恰是針對已經明確了的歷史知識，是從教育者認為「沒有問題」的史事中發現了問題。

在這方面，學生提出的問題可大致概括為幾種：

1.針對知識的細節提出問題。如前引例一，學生對軍艦上養狗的不理解，即是對細節產生了疑問。又如，教師講授山頂洞人時，提到發掘出骨針並展示圖片，學生看到後提出疑問：「骨針頭上的眼那麼小，原始人是怎麼鑽出來的？」這類問題的提出，顯示了學生對既成知識的內容細節有不理解之處。

2.問題涉及到知識的深度。如教師在介紹「春秋五霸」時，學生對他們的稱謂產生疑問：「為什麼齊桓公、宋襄公、晉文公、秦穆公等都是稱『公』，而楚莊王卻稱『王』呢？」再如，教師在講述鄭和下西洋時，介紹鄭和的寶船長四十四丈、寬十八丈，有學生提出問題：「這船的長與寬比例還不到三比一，是不是太寬了？為什麼要把船造得那麼寬？」這類問題，涉及到歷史知識中更深一層的內容，而這更深的內容又好像不必讓學生知道，可學生恰恰就想進一步搞清楚。

3.問題越過了知識的範圍。較為典型的例子是北京大學李零教授在《天不生蔡倫》一文中提到的：「有一天，歷史課，歷史講『四大發明』，我兒子問：『蔡倫發明紙以前，我們用什麼擦屁股？』老師大怒，把他趕出教室。」[3]再如，在學習歐洲文藝復興的歷史時，有學生問道：「文藝復興時期在文學藝術領域出現了那麼多的成就，有詩歌、小說、戲劇、繪畫、雕塑等等，怎麼沒有音樂方面的呢？」以及學生對稱鄭和為「三寶太監」提出疑問的例子等[4]，這些都是將問題的指向擴展到教材範圍之外，突破了中學教學既定知識的「界限」，觸及到原本並不是教學內容的成分。

涉及史事的「意外問題」，儘管會使教師一時不知道如何解答，但其實並不屬於爭議性的問題，因為這些問題還都是有解的。這就是說，這類問題雖然是從既定知識中派生出來的，但還是屬於歷史學科知識本身的內涵，是「客觀」的史事，只不過中學歷史教學沒有要求學生了解，而教師又未關注到或不掌握實情，結果出現了學生提出教師想不到的問題，成為教學中的「意外」。

3　李零：《花間一壺酒》，同心出版社，北京，2005 年版，第 301-302 頁。

4　筆者在聽課隨筆《學生的提問》中引過此例，見《歷史教學》（天津）2005 年第 10 期。另，在《知識的延伸》中引述的帝王自稱「孤家寡人」之例，亦可屬於這種類型，見《歷史教學》2006 年第 6 期。

(二) 認識類的「意外問題」

認識類的問題，則屬於「程序性知識」(procedural knowledge) 的範圍，是學生在認知發展中運用思維能力對所學知識加以評判，對教科書和教師的敘述和闡釋提出質疑。

一般地說，歷史知識雖然是歷史事實的反映與記述，但其中蘊涵了對歷史的解釋。從這一意義上講，歷史知識也是某種歷史認識，教科書和教師對歷史的敘述本身也是對歷史的闡釋。學生是否接受、認同、內化所學的歷史闡釋，是與他們認知的水平、策略等相關。學生在學習歷史知識時，他們的思維水平有不同的程度，對歷史的理解是逐步發展的，也是有反復的[5]。在這一過程中，有些學生會主動地思考「為什麼是這樣」，對教科書和教師的闡釋產生疑問。

學生提出的認識類「意外問題」，主要有兩種情況：

一種是對既定歷史知識的質疑。如前引候風地動儀的例子，就是對地動儀的公認功能產生疑惑。再如，教師在講秦統一的過程時，說到長平之戰秦軍獲勝後坑殺趙卒四十萬人，就有學生提出：「這不大可能吧？要把四十萬人都挖坑活埋了，這要多少人花多少時間才能幹完啊？」這類問題的提出，顯示了學生對歷史記述的不認可，以致懷疑所學歷史知識的真實性。

另一種則是在歷史評價上的疑問。這主要表現在對史事的評論上，學生並不認同教科書中的寫法或教師的說法，會提出自己的見解和觀點，甚至引發爭論。筆者在聽課隨筆《學生的提問》中提到一學生對趙括的評論，認為趙括不是在紙上談兵，而是情勢所迫，即可屬典型的一例，這裡再次引用：

---

[5] 這方面的研究，當推英國學者 P. J. Lee，A. K. Dickinson 和 R. Ashby 主持的 CHATA 計畫。

長平被圍三年了，幾十萬趙軍和城中老百姓的吃喝怎麼解決？外面的援兵又沒有。擺在趙括面前的出路，要不就是活活餓死，要不就是投降秦軍，但他既不是等死也不是投降，而是冒死突圍。他就這麼做了，雖然戰敗而死，但也是為國捐軀，怎麼能說他是紙上談兵呢？

學生在歷史評價上的不同見解，多是在分析歷史人物和歷史事件的性質、歷史地位及其影響時提出的。

這種認識類的「意外問題」，往往是對公認的、權威的、現成的說法提出質疑。問題本身雖然是從知識性的角度上提出來，但明顯帶有一定的探究性，在對歷史的認識和闡釋上與現成說法發生衝突，使提出的問題帶有一定的爭議性。而且，教師即使有對這類問題的正解或別解，也不一定能夠解決學生心裡的疑惑，使他們的看法「歸附」到「正統」的解說上來。這類問題的提出，正是學生對歷史闡釋的積極反應，是他們在了解歷史和認識歷史的過程中表現出來的獨立思考和真實想法。

以上的分類，是為了明晰學生提出的「意外問題」的性質，以便加以研究。要說明的是，在教學實際中出現的情況是多樣而複雜的，筆者所做的分類還只是大致性的，並不能夠完全將學生提出的「意外問題」嚴格區分和歸類[6]。

---

6 例如，學生提出的問題起碼還有兩類也是「意外」的。一類是屬於對歷史的假設。歷史教學中有時會出現這樣的情況：學生並不只是思考「為什麼是這樣」，還琢磨著「如果不是這樣，那會是怎麼樣？」這方面的例子有不少，諸如「如果美國不扔原子彈、蘇聯不出兵東北，中國的抗日戰爭能取得勝利嗎？」「希特勒上臺後，很快恢復了德國的經濟。如果他不發動世界大戰，他就不是一個英雄式的人物嗎？」另一類是類似對歷史的神入，即假想自己是歷史上的人。在聽到歷史人物的事蹟後，有時學生會思考「如果我是這個人物，我肯定不會這麼做，我要怎麼做呢？」這方面的例子也有很多。對於這兩類問題，教師也是很少事先想到的，要進行解答又要費些工夫。由於這兩種情況具有發散性、猜測性，與本文所指的有針對性的「意外問題」還有不同，故在此暫不作討論。

三、學生提出「意外問題」的原因

學生在課堂上提出「意外問題」，雖是意料之外，卻在情理之中。

在一般的情況下，學生對所學的歷史知識（包括歷史的闡釋），多是表現為認同和接受，並不會產生懷疑。但這並不能證明我們所教給他們的知識就是完整無缺、正確無疑的；也不能說教師認為不會有問題的歷史知識，學生就一定也認為沒有問題。的確，在實際上，學生對遙遠的歷史知道的不多，不掌握較多的歷史材料，又不具備研究歷史的專業能力和方法，也不了解對歷史的其他闡釋；而教給他們的知識，又是編排好了的，是現成的，學生若在這種限制了的、既定了的條件下進行歷史的學習與認識，提不出問題來就是一種常態了。然而，就是在這樣的情況下，還是有學生將自己的思索越出了教師和教材圈定好了的範圍，提出了「意外問題」。為什麼會是這樣呢？這的確需要進行分析。

總的說來，造成學生有「意外問題」的原因是多方面的。例如，教學氛圍是學生能夠提出問題的重要條件，教師的民主作風、課堂上的寬鬆氣氛、班集體的活躍風氣等，都可以促使學生積極地學習與思考，使學生主動提出問題來。但這些還都是外在的、表層的因素。筆者認為，其中主要的原因，一是同學生的認知習慣及思維特點有關，二是同中學歷史知識的特點有關。

對於兒童的認知水平、規律及特點，近代以來的心理學各流派都有深入的研究，形成了各種學習理論。其中，建構主義 (constructivism) 學習理論認為，學習是學習者主動建構知識之意義的過程。兒童的學習與理解，不是像在一張白紙上繪畫，即他們在學習時，其思維並不是空白的、停滯的。學生的學習過程，是他們在其現有的知識、自身的經驗和信念的基礎上，對所學的信息進行選擇、加工，從而建構起自己的理解，進而使

原有的認識系統發生改變，使認知水平得以發展。這就是說，學生的學習並不是被動地接受信息的刺激，而是能主動地對知識進行處理與轉換，主動地建構知識的意義。這種學習的建構過程，不僅僅是結構性知識的建構，還有在具體情境中產生的非結構性經驗背景的建構。學生具有著利用現有知識、經驗進行推論的智力潛能，在課堂學習時，他們對知識的接收會以自己的經驗為背景，分辨其合理性。而這種從經驗背景出發所提出的質疑、假設、判斷等，並不是沒有根據的懷疑猜測和不著邊際的胡思亂想。建構主義理論的意義，在於揭示了學生的學習是在自己原有經驗的基礎上的主動學習，學生是可以成為自己知識的建構者的。從這樣的意義上講，學生獲得知識的多少，是取決於他們根據自身經驗來建構有關知識的意義之能力，而不是取決於他們記憶或背誦教師講授內容的能力[7]。如果我們借用建構主義學習理論的原理，對歷史教學中學生提出「意外問題」的原因加以分析，就可以看出學生在學習和認識歷史時的一些思維特點。

首先，「意外問題」的產生，是學生好奇心的表現，這與學生的直覺思維有直接關係。雖然學生對所學歷史知識可能是陌生的，甚至是不感興趣的，但當他們進入歷史學習的過程時，他們原有的經驗、已形成的常識以及此前掌握的知識就會作為他們認知過程的背景和基礎，用以對新知識進行判斷和選擇。「他們在接受正式教育之前，就有了廣泛的先備知識(prior knowledge)、技巧、想法及概念，這些都會很明顯地影響到環境中的什麼訊息會引起他們的注意，還有他們如何組織和解釋這些訊息。」[8]從前引的一些例子中我們可以看出，學生提出疑問是與他們具有的常識有直接的關係，他們是以經驗判斷來辨別所學知識的。例如本文引言中的例

---

7 張建偉、陳琦：《從認知主義到建構主義》，《北京師範大學學報》（社會科學版），1996 年第 4 期。

8 John D. Bransford 等編：《學習原理：心智、經驗與學校》，鄭谷苑、郭俊賢譯，遠流出版公司，臺北，2004 年版，第 33 頁。

一，學生並不清楚北洋艦隊的內部管理狀況、海軍成員的來源以及軍隊風氣等情況，但憑常識認為軍艦上養狗是一件難以理解的事情。再如，學生對長平坑卒的懷疑，雖然是與胡三省注《資治通鑑》所言「四十萬人安肯束手而死邪」[9]有些類似，但這不能說明學生有多少史學素養，因為此時的學生並不是用史家的視野觀察這一事件的，而是在用常理進行判斷，覺得要將四十萬人活埋是不可思議的。學生的經驗判斷，在歷史學習中有著相當的作用，也會導致他們對史事的不理解。同時，學生的經驗、直覺也促使他們產生疑問，尤其是學習內容與學生的經驗發生衝突時，他們就會發現問題。學生的這種經驗判斷的直覺，有時是很活躍又很敏感的，能夠快速地做出反應，甚至是未經深思熟慮就可以直接產生問題。

其次，學生形象思維的活躍是「意外問題」產生的重要條件。認識歷史的基礎是對歷史的感知，形成歷史的表象。學生在接受歷史信息的過程中，他們的形象思維操作有時是比較主動和活躍的，尤其是其聯想和想像的開展，可將抽象的歷史信息活化。但如果有限的信息限制了學生的形象思維運作，他們的頭腦中就會產生出問題來。例如，學生對史事細節的追尋，對既定知識的深層探究，就是由於現有的知識信息尚不足以構成學生頭腦中的歷史表象，使他們想了解更多的具體信息。在學生感知歷史的過程中，他們的聯想力和想像力經常會發生作用。如上引鄭和寶船的例子，就是學生從寶船的長寬比例聯想到他們所熟悉的船隻長寬比例，因而產生疑問，提出的問題觸及到古代海船以風力和海流為動力的造船技術。再如，上引造紙術發明以前人們出恭用品的問題，也是一種典型的聯想，雖然這種聯想是從他們的生活經驗出發的，但直接涉及到紙的功用，儘管既定的教學內容中沒有涉及到。又如，學生對候風地動儀的疑問，是由於以他們對地震的了解和機械構造的知識進行想像，又實在是想像不出來地震

9　《資治通鑑》卷五，中華書局，北京，1956 年版，第 170 頁。

儀是怎麼測定地震波的，問題就出來了。

再次，學生在學習歷史時也要運用邏輯思維進行推理。儘管學生具有的歷史知識和掌握的歷史資料是有限的，但他們仍然會對歷史進行一定的分析、概括、比較、歸納等思維操作，尤其是在歷史評價時，學生會在現有知識的基礎上進行理性的思考，作出自己的判斷。上引學生對趙括的看法，就是學生進行邏輯推理的一種表現[10]。當然，學生的判斷、推理不一定嚴謹和正確，立論的證據支撐也許不充分和確鑿，但仍表明他們在接收某種歷史評判時會對其進行篩選和再加工，並且會將他們認為不合邏輯的因素提出來。這就是說，與學生用已有經驗、常識作為接受新知識的基礎相類似，學生也是以他們所具有的邏輯思維的方式、方法為基礎，對要認同的新認識展開進一步的思考，如果新認識符合他們的思維邏輯，便能夠將其同化到認知結構中；若是有不相符之處，結果就是提出自己的看法，或質疑所要接受的歷史評判。

總之，從學習主體的角度而言，學生在認知、思維上的基礎、方法、特點、習慣等，導致了他們在學習時提出問題。另一方面，從學習客體的角度上看，學生之所以會提出老師想不到的問題，還與他們所學習的內容（即歷史知識）的特點也有一定的關係。

中學歷史知識所具有的體系、結構、層次，所涉及的範圍、廣度、深度，及其內部包含的概念之內涵與外延，是自成一體、相對獨立的，既與專業歷史知識有所不同，又與大眾傳媒中的歷史知識有差別。這種歷史知識雖然來源廣泛，但已是經過教育者的挑選、編排、組織，因而並不是歷史的原本 (context) 的直接反映了。中學歷史知識只是相對的系統，承載有基本的內容，但尚不能完全體現本學科所認識的歷史客體。當學生感覺到歷史的有意義或有趣時（如對歷史評價的思考），當學生想探尋歷史的

---

10 學生推理的結論是否符合歷史事實，則另當別論。對此例提出的問題所涉及到的如何進行歷史理解，可見張元：《歷史的理解》，《歷史教學》（天津），2005 年第 11 期。

真相時（如對細節的查問），當學生想了解更多的情況時（如追問更多、更深的內容），這種相對系統的歷史知識就顯得不能滿足了。這就是說，在學生的認知需求與知識本身之間，會發生不對稱之處，因而會產生「意外問題」。尤其是如果教師採用的是照搬課本既定內容的教學方式，簡單、機械地複述編排好了的教學內容，而不是主動建立知識與知識反映的事實之間的聯繫，那就會有想不到的「意外問題」出現在自己的課堂上。中學歷史知識的「度」與「層面」，很容易造成教學中的各種情況，學生提出「意外問題」也就是見怪不怪的事了。

這種編排好的中學歷史知識，也容易對教師的學科知識結構及內涵產生潛移默化的影響，甚至使教師的學養逐漸固化在圈定的知識體系中。教師為完成教學的任務，往往關注於中學知識體系內的內容，對其他相關或表面不相關的內容則有所忽略，原本學科的素養漸漸轉為教學的固定套路。而一旦學生提出的問題觸及中學知識體系的邊際或外圍，教師就可能想不到，就會感到意外。有些問題本應是教師能夠解答的，但由於教師的知識面被束縛住了，也就不知道如何解決學生的問題。因此，「意外問題」的出現，也與既定知識對教師學養的影響有關。

四、「意外問題」的教學意義

不可否認的是，學生提出「意外問題」，往往是提到了「點」上。這所謂的「點」，也許對教師來說是「盲點」，而且不是教學的「重點」；然而，這確是學生學習時的「疑點」，是他們思維活躍的「燃點」，也是他們認識拓展的「接點」。學生只有真正進入到學習與思考的狀態，才會有這樣的問題提出來。作為教師來說，對學生的「意外問題」可能會感到一時的尷尬，但應該認識到，這一現象的出現，有著一定的教學上的意義，可以使我們得到一些啟示，這裡略談幾點。

（一）歷史學習的對象是過往的史事，要使學生發生對歷史的認識活動，很重要的手段是引導學生盡可能地貼近歷史的實際，了解歷史的實況。這就要努力創設歷史情境，並使學生進入情境，觀察和感受到情景下的歷史。學生頭腦中歷史情境的生成，是要建立在具體的歷史信息的基礎上的。信息越具體、全面，建構出來的歷史情境就越清晰，越有認識上的意義；而過於籠統的、粗略的、零散的信息，不利於學生形成歷史的表象。因此，教師在教學時，應注意史事的過程、脈絡、重點、細節等內容及其相關材料的提供，以有助於學生探尋到歷史的實際，從而加以把握和進行探究。

（二）學生的認識是以原有的經驗為基礎的，而歷史上所發生的情況又是千變萬化的，與學生現有的生活經驗肯定會產生衝突。這種衝突並不是認識的障礙，而應看作是認識發生的條件。從學習與發展的角度上講，教學就是要對學生的經驗判斷加以激活、豐富和提升。因此，教師要盡可能地了解學生的認知水平及特點，找準他們思維發展的連接點，有效地利用學生已具備的常識、經驗和已有的知識，以及思維的方法、習慣等，主動地設計和提出有探究意義的問題，使自己對歷史的敘述具有疑難性[11]，以引導學生積極思考，促進學生在學習時進行正遷移，從而導致他們的認知結構發生新的變化。

（三）中學歷史知識體系是相對成型的，它只是一個搭建起來的學習平臺，供學生在上面進行認識歷史的活動。這就要求教師既要對其重視，又要不被其限制。如果拘泥和局限在現成體系裡，緊盯臺面，畫地為牢，教師的專業素養難以拓展提升，學生的學習需求也難以滿足，甚至會導致

---

11 關於教師歷史敘述的疑難化，可參見：Robert B. Bain (2005). "They Thought the Word Was Flat?": Applying the Principles of How People Lear in Teaching High School History, in M. S. Donovan & J. D. Bransford (Eds.), *How Students Lear: History in the Classroom* (pp.184-188). Washington D.C.: The National Academies Press.

學生的歷史學習成為對臺面知識的機械儲運，而脫離了歷史學習的本意。所以，歷史教師要將學科素養看得與教學理念同樣重要，注重加強自己的史學功底。史學功底厚實了，對學生提出的問題就可以迎刃而解，也就不會感到意外了。

（四）教學是教師與學生雙邊的活動，二者之間的互動、交流和合作是教學活動展開的必要條件。在以書本知識為主的教學中，學生多是處在被動學習的狀態，是被教師和教材所左右的，其學習的動機、興趣、策略等是被束縛著的。而當學生在教學關係中的主體地位被重視起來，他們的主體意識必然增強，他們的思維潛能就會表現出來，一改被動的學習方式，主動地進行思維，積極地參與教學，甚至去促動教師，提出一些有難度的問題。這應該是教師樂於見到的。學生的主動探究，也是需要教師不斷地調整自己的教學策略[12]，更好地與學生共同完成教學的任務。

作為歷史教育工作者，以往我們比較關注歷史課程的編製、歷史教材的編排以及教學方法的技巧和歷史考試的指向等領域，思考的多是怎麼教好，甚至是怎麼教好書。而歷史教學發展到今天，教學的理念已經發生了很大的變化，越來越重視研究學生認識和理解歷史的條件、過程及方式、方法等。過去我們思考的這一切，都要回歸和落實到學生如何進行歷史學習這一核心的問題上。

最後，引述一段英國學者的話[13]，作為本文的結束。

---

12 「意外問題」的處置，也是教師教學策略的運用，有學者提出的對策有：感謝或稱讚提問的學生；鼓勵學生試著回答自己提出的問題；教師回答不了時要承認，並採取以下某一種方法：1.問班裡是否有同學可以解答；2.告訴學生可以利用哪些資源找到答案；3.告訴學生應如何對問題進行思考；4.主動承擔查找答案的任務，然後在下一堂課上告訴學生。參見巴巴拉 G 大衛斯：《教學方法手冊》，嚴慧仙譯，浙江大學出版社，杭州，2006 年版，第 71-74 頁。此書談的是大學的教學方法，但對中學教學亦有參考價值。

13 A. K. Dickinson & P. J. Lee，Making Sense of History, 陳冠華譯，《清華歷史教學》第十四期，第 53 頁，2003 年 9 月。

兒童有進行歷史思考的能力，他們也確實做到了。對學校歷史課產
生限制的常常不是學生歷史思維的品質，而是某些教師無法認知到
其所從事者之複雜性。……我們的教學方法要有足夠的彈性好給予
學生空間來告訴我們他們發覺了什麼疑問，並有足夠的想像力來提
供利用這些疑問的作業，進而使學生有機會能在理解上逐漸進步。

Abstract

Unexpected Questions Raised by Students
in History Class

Ye Xiaobing

In the secondary-school history class, students sometimes ask the teacher unexpected questions on the descriptions in the textbook or the teacher's narrative. These are referred to as unexpected questions because they have similar features as listed below: (1) the questions appear impromptu. The student who asks the question has no consideration and preparation before hand. The question comes into his mind right on the spot. (2) The question that the student asks relates to the student's direct judgment. Also, it directly aims at the knowledge they have learned. (3) Although the questions may come as surprising to other students, they are also interested when such a question is raised. (4) The teacher usually does not expect the question at all. (5) The teacher feels puzzled by the question. And he does not have a ready answer to it. In order to analyze unexpected questions in the history class, we can classify them into two categories: the historical questions and the cognitive questions.

The historical question is one which shows that the student has doubt about the declarative knowledge, that is, the student has doubted about the textbook and the teacher's narrative. He wants to learn about more facts. Mostly, this kind of question can be further divided as follows :(1) The question aims at detailed knowledge. (2) The question refers to the depth of knowledge. (3) The question is beyond the range of knowledge covered by the textbook. It touches information that was not taught prevoiusly.

The cognitive question is in the range of procedural knowledge. It is the student's judgment of the knowledge acquired. It puts forward doubt towards the textbooks as well as the teacher's narrative and description. This generally has two cases: the first one is that the student disapproves of the historical knowledge itself. In other words, the student disapproves of the textbook content or the teacher's translation. The second case is that the student disapproves of the evaluation of the historical knowledge. They raise their understanding and view, even if it arouses argument.

The reasons why students ask unexpected questions in class are in fact multiple. For one thing, it is related to the students' cognitive character and pattern of thinking. For another, it is related to the features of history knowledge at the secondary-school level.

Students' procedure of history study is their understanding. It is based on their own knowledge, experience and faith. Their understanding is established by choosing and improving the acquired information. Firstly, unexpected question displays students' curiosity. It is directly related to the students' intuitive thinking. Also it is related to the students' judgment by their experience. When a contradiction appears between content of learning and students' experience, students will face the problem. Secondly, students' thinking, especially association and imagination is an important condition. An unexpected question emerges right under this condition. If finite information limits the operation of the student's imagery thinking, the question will be formed in their mind. And they want to get more concrete information. Thirdly, when a student learns history, he also reasons by logical thinking to work out his judgment. The emergence of an unexpected question also has some relation with the features of learning content and history knowledge. There is systematicity to history knowledge on the secondary-school level. It is integral and independent. It is selected, arranged and organized by the educator into a system which is structured within a range as determined by the syllabus in terms of both its width and depth. However, if the student possesses a deeper interest in certain historical events or periods (e.g. reflections on historical judgment), or when the student wants to further explore the given facts of history (e.g. asking about details or probing into deeper levels beyond the confines of the syllabus), the relatively systematic history knowledge will not satisfy such needs. Moreover, the structuring of historical knowledge specially set up for the secondary-school level may also affect teacher's knowledge structure and its content in the relevant academic discipline. The effect is unconscious. It can make the teacher's basic level be fixed on the enclosed knowledge system as time goes by. It may even make the teacher ignorant to the knowledge which is relative or not relative on the surface. So once the questions asked by students reach the margin of the knowledge system at the secondary-school level, the teacher will feel surprised.

The phenomenon of students' unexpected questions poses some implications on our teaching. The teaching of history is to lead students into cognitive activities in the realm of history. An important way is for the teacher to take students to historical facts as close as possible by helping them approach authentic historical accounts. In other words, historical imagination in students' mind has to be based on authentic historical information provided by the teacher.

The more specific and comprehensive the information is, the clearer the established historical imagination, and the more significant impact it has on students' cognition. Therefore, when the teacher is teaching, he should focus on providing process, skeleton, key points and details of knowledge, with relevant supportive materials included. This will help students approach historical facts. Clearly, what students learn in history class is more often than not in conflict with students' own life experience. However, such conflict should not be seen as hindrance but a positive condition on which cognition takes place. Viewed from a learning and developmental perspective, teaching is the activation, enrichment and advancement to the students' experience judgment. Therefore, the teacher should be aware of the level and features of students' cognition, and on this basis, design his teaching on a tolerably demanding level of difficulty and complexity so as to lead students think actively. As for the secondary-school history knowledge system, we should treat it as a platform of learning established for students to engage themselves in cognitive activities in history learning. And here comes an important requirement for the teacher to make full use of the system on the one hand but not to be limited by it. The teacher should constantly adjust his teaching strategy in order to accomplish the teaching assignment with students.

Advancing Disciplinary Understandings with History Textbooks: Challenges and Opportunities

Stuart Foster[*]

Introduction and Overview

Despite some important exceptions, school history textbooks in many nations across the world typically are shaped by two characteristics. First, they are overtly nationalistic. Second, they adopt an authoritative, single "best story" narrative style. This paper argues that these textbook developments are problematic because they offer the students no sense of the interpretive, contested, or disciplinary nature of history. Rather, these authoritative textbooks serve as instruments of propaganda often attempting to appease social and political agendas in the present. However, as the experience in England illustrates, textbooks do not have to be written this way. By focusing on changes in history education and textbook development in England during the past 40 years this paper outlines the significant shift from traditional

[*] Institute of Education, University of London

textbooks based on authoritative and nationalistic narratives to "new history" textbooks often produced to advance pupils' understandings of history as a discipline. As will be discussed, this change in practice was (and is) not without its critics and problems. Nevertheless it is argued that "new history" textbooks offer more desirable possibilities for a meaningful history education. The paper concludes by (a) examining some of the obstacles to change faced by history educators operating under traditional systems (b) considering what individual teachers might do to challenge conventional practice.

History Textbooks: Different Systems - Different Practices

History is one of the few curriculum subjects commonly mandated in education systems throughout the world. Furthermore, the use of history textbooks to support student learning is almost universally accepted practice (Foster and Crawford, 2006). However, despite this commonality, the production, selection, and deployment of history textbooks differs considerably in international settings (Hein and Selden 2000; Nicholls, 2006; Pingel 2001; Vickers and Jones 2005). In particular, textbooks have different authority and status in different countries. For example, *What Shall We Tell the Children? International Perspectives in History Education,* graphically illustrates the different approaches to textbook selection and deployment in various nations in East Asia, Europe, the Middle East, Africa, the USA, and South Asia. The chart in Appendix A, further serves to illustrate the key differences in textbook selection and usage in just two countries, Japan and England.

As the chart shows important differences exist. For example, whereas in

Japan the state controlled ministry of education has enormous influence on what textbooks are approved for official use in classroom, in England no such direct influence is apparent.[1]   However, whereas in Japan student ownership of recently published textbooks is guaranteed, in England this is not common practice.   Whilst helpful in identifying key differences between nations, however, simplistic charts disguise some of the complexities and subtleties of textbook usage in classrooms.   In addition they fail to reveal the various functions that textbooks serve in different settings and in different nations across the globe.   Typically textbooks perform multiple functions simultaneously.   For example, they are used to "cover" stipulated historical topics, to respond to curriculum needs, and to address the requirements of standardized tests.   Often they are used as a support mechanism and as a source of information for teachers, students, and parents.   Occasionally they are used critically exemplifying one narrative account among many of a particular historical perspective.

The whole process of textbook selection and use is further complicated when consideration is given to the possibility that what is "in" the textbook may not be taught and, even if it is taught, it may not be understood by students in the way desired by national governments, textbook authors, and teachers.   Therefore to easily accept that textbook content neatly equates to what teachers teach, or, more importantly, to what students learn would be unwise (Apple and Christian-Smith 1991).   The many ways in which students

---

[1] It is undoubtedly true, however, that the textbook market is narrowing considerably in England as publishers respond to the demands of the National Curriculum and national examinations. For a detailed discussion of this development see Crawford and Foster (2006).

and teachers variously understand, negotiate, and transform their personal understandings of textual material is a complex process. Rarely is textbook content simply accepted, absorbed, and then regurgitated by students (see, for example, Apple, 1991; Barthes, 1976; Foster and Crawford, 2006a; Porat 1994).

Generalisations About Textbooks

Despite these cautions and considerations enough research exists to suggest that textbooks remain an important factor in determining how students learn history (Anyon, 1978; Anyon, 1979; Apple & Christian-Smith, 1991; Foster 1999; Marsden, 2001). In the United States, for example, a 2002 survey of elementary and high school teachers indicated that classroom and homework assignments were typically textbook-driven or textbook-centred (Whitman, 2004). Indeed, Gilbert Sewall, director of the American Textbook Council, further argued that textbooks often constituted the *de facto* curriculum and that "to many teachers and almost all students, the textbook is taken to be a well of truthful and expert information" (Sewall, 1987, pp. 61-62). Significantly, because of their importance, the contents of history textbooks often are sites of intense national and international conflict and controversy (Corcuff 2005; Foster, & Davis, 2004; Foster, & Nicholls, 2005; Hein & Selden, 2000; Moreau 2004; Nicholls & Foster 2005; Nozaki, 2005; Vickers & Jones, 2005).

Although it is difficult (and possibly unwise) to make sweeping generalisations about history textbooks, international research in textbook production and use suggests that textbooks in many nations share similar perspectives and characteristics.[2] Furthermore these commonalities appear more pronounced in countries where textbooks are approved centrally. In these settings two features prove salient. First, textbooks often adopt a nationalistic perspective on historical events.[3] Second, textbooks typically present an "official," single narrative.

• Nationalistic and Official Textbooks

In nations throughout the world it is inescapable that textbooks represent a powerful means to render a particular version of the nation's past in the history classroom. Largely influenced by official policies, textbook authors consciously attempt to shape and inform students' understanding of their national history and the relationship between their country and other nations. As Keith Crawford and I have written:

> *In some nation states history teaching is used openly and unashamedly to promote specific ideologies and sets of political ideas. In other countries, under the guise of patriotism, the history of a nation served up for student consumption is what its leaders decide it is to be. In states which consider their existence to be under threat, or in states which are struggling to create an identity, or in those which are reinventing themselves following a period of colonial rule, teaching a*

---

[2] It would be misleading, however, to argue that all nations share these characteristics. For example, in Germany conscious efforts have been made on the part of national and regional government to de-emphasise a nationalistic agenda. Rather, German textbooks are more likely to appeal to a sense of European identity. For an interesting discussion of this development, see Soysal, Bertilotti, and Mannitz (2005).

[3] Not all scholars share this view. For example Schissler and Soyal (2005) argue that in Europe national identities are becoming less important.

*nationalistic and mono-cultural form of history can prove to be the
cement which binds people together. In its worst form the manufacture
and teaching of such an official past can create, sponsor, maintain and
justify xenophobic hatred, racism and the obscenity of ethnic cleansing
(Foster and Crawford 2006a, pp. 6-7).*

Embedded in history textbooks, therefore, are narratives that nation states
choose to tell about themselves and their relationships with other nations.
Often they represent a body of core cultural knowledge which the younger
generation is expected both to assimilate and to support.　As a result
textbooks often are used to convey a story of past as a means to unite people in
the present and to emphasise national unity and pride.　Similarly, textbooks
typically focus on national achievements and triumphs and ignore or downplay
the contributions of other nations. Revealingly, in some nations, textbook
narratives use expressions such as "we," "our" and "us" to differentiate
national citizens from the "them," "their," and "they" assigned to "other"
peoples.

The second characteristic of textbooks used in many nations is the
appearance of a single, authoritative, "official" narrative.[4]　In these textbooks
historical content typically is presented as uncontested and objective.
Accounts are authoritative, detached, and technical and no source material or
alternative evidence is presented. Furthermore, opinions often are stated as
facts and in-text questions for students either do not exist or are based on

---

4　For example, an interesting discussion of the perpetuation of a single "master narrative"
in the United States, is offered by Keith Barton and Linda Levstik (2004).　See,
specifically, chapter 9 "The Story of National Freedom and Progress."

factual recall of given information.

Unfortunately, however, textbooks that present both a narrow nationalistic perspective and an uncontested singular narrative fail to provide students with any respect for the disciplinary nature of history. Often what students are presented with is not history but propaganda and polemic. Rather than presenting young people with an understanding of how history operates, students are too often confronted with narratives that adopt a particular (and often narrow and limited) perspective. Regrettably these "history" textbooks offer no sense of dispute or interpretation, no appreciation of historical evidence or argument, and no understanding of the basis on which historical accounts are constructed. As Peter Lee (1991) has argued this is serious failing because,

> ···*it is absurd* ···*to say that schoolchildren know any history if they have no understanding of how historical knowledge is attained* ···*the ability to recall accounts without any understanding of the problems involved in constructing them or the criteria involved in evaluating them has nothing historical about it (pp.48-49).*

Re-thinking History Textbooks

Changing practice in any educational setting often is difficult and involves overcoming a complex array of challenges and historical legacies. A common obstacle to change is the failure to appreciate the existence of alternatives. Typically it is easier and safer for individuals, institutions, or governments to continue with accepted practice and received wisdoms. The next section, however, offers a window into significant changes in history education and history textbook production that occurred in England during the past 40 years. The account is not comprehensive. Moreover, changes in textbook practice in England are by no means offered as a fully acceptable model of how change should take place. Nevertheless, the dramatic shift in the character and content of history textbooks in England does offer some opportunities for reflection and consideration. Certainly the shift from the widespread use of "traditional textbooks" to "new history" textbooks that occurred during the past four decades offers intriguing insights into the possibilities and appropriateness of change.

• Traditional Textbooks

In the years before the late 1970s most history textbooks used in classrooms in England adopted the characteristics described above. Routinely they offered a nationalistic, single narrative, which focused on Britain's imperial past, the achievements of great men, and the activities of ruling monarchs. Attention to constitutional, military, and political events dominated and insular reference to "we" and "us" proved commonplace amidst ubiquitous patriotic narratives. For example, the following extract from a chapter on World War II in a "traditional textbook" produced in 1948 but in widespread use throughout the 1950s, 1960s, and 1970s exemplifies the tone of many books published in this period:

In Russia the casualties were higher and destruction more widespread; in America more munitions were produced; in China the War had been going on longer; but nowhere was there a more stubborn determination, a more crusading spirit against the Nazi creed than that which

*Churchill led in Britain and the Commonwealth. For a year – to all
the world' s surprise – we fought Hitler alone, and (what is more)
successfully: our prestige was greater than it had ever been···(Carter
and Mears, A History of Britain, p. 1042)*

In most textbooks written in the age of the "great tradition" almost
without exception the authors' opinions were stated as objective fact and
historical accounts typically were presented as uncontested "truths". On the
few occasions when in-text activities or questions were included students were
required to recall stated "facts" or to complete comprehension questions.
Students never were exposed to alternative accounts or source material and
visual representations proved exceptional.   Furthermore, although some
textbooks provided lively and engaging narratives, most were dull and
uninspiring.   Textbook pages were crammed full with detailed information
and densely written text dominated.   Beginning in the late 1970s and early
1980s, however, dramatic and important changes occurred in history education
and history textbook production.   Indeed, by the end of the 1980s
"traditional" textbooks based on conventions established for generations
largely disappeared from the educational landscape.

• Dramatic Changes: "New History" Textbooks

During the late 1970s and early 1980s, important developments took place
in history education in England.   In particular the 1980s proved a fascinating
and dynamic time as the decade witnessed the clash between "traditional
history" teaching and "new history". Essentially the "clash" resulted in a fierce
and ideologically driven debate between, on the one hand, proponents of a
traditional chronological and nationalistic approach to history teaching and

those who, on the other, argued for a "new" history which placed greater emphasis on the structure of the discipline and the interpretive nature of history (Crawford 1996; Dickinson, 2000; Foster 1998; Haydn 2004; Phillips 1998; Sylvester 1994).[5] The reasons why new history increasingly offered a serious challenge to established practices are numerous and complex. Fundamental to this important shift in practice and philosophy however was the increasing concern that history education needed to be revitalized with a more considered and contemporary approach. Undoubtedly the cognitive revolution in the psychology of learning proved influential in challenging existing theories of how children acquired knowledge and understandings. Constructivist approaches to learning also seriously challenged the widespread use of didactic teaching methods common in the era of the "great tradition." Similarly, a number of influential researchers in England (e.g., Booth, Fines, Lee, Shemilt) challenged the domination of Piagetian thinking and suggested that pupils' abilities in history previously had been underestimated. Significantly, an increasing number of researchers and educators pursued the notion that students of all ages could and should acquire a greater appreciation of history as a discipline (not just as a body of knowledge to be learned).[6]

---

[5] Although educational and ideological battles over history surfaced most acutely in arguments over the introduction of the national curriculum for history in the late 1980s, the clash between competing traditions was apparent many years earlier. For example the shift, in 1986, from the traditional and stratified "O" level and CSE examination courses to the more inclusive and arguably more innovative GCSE examination course already ensured that history teachers would have to embrace (or at least accept) many of the key influences and ideas of "new history".

[6] In this respect "new history" followed Bruner's classic assertion that "any subject can be taught effectively in some intellectually honest form to any child at any stage of development" (Bruner, 1960).

In addition to these important developments, it is no coincidence that new history emerged in a period in which socio-cultural shifts in society led to the ubiquitous questioning of tradition and "inherited thinking". An important aspect of the "new history" revolution therefore was also the increased attention given to more social, inclusive and critical history. Finally, the emergence of new history occurred at a time when history education was perceived to be seriously under threat. Unquestionably, a growing anxiety existed among history educators that the subject was in crisis and that traditional history appeared increasingly irrelevant to young people. As Shemilt (1980) wrote in the opening page to the classic SHP "Evaluation Study",

> *The Schools Council Project History 13-16 was established in 1972 as a result of teacher's dissatisfaction with 'traditional history' and their concern at the apparent erosion of its position within the secondary curriculum (p.1).*

At its core new history challenged the notion of history as a "received" subject. Advocates of "new history" wanted students to understand how history was created and become more active in their study of the subject. They recognised that in order to know history pupils must understand the structure of the discipline and be concerned not only with knowing *that* but also with knowing *how*. The most effective embodiment of these changes was the Schools History Project (SHP) which, from the late 1970s onwards, offered teachers and students an innovative, thoughtful, and publicly examined curriculum driven by the philosophy of new history (Dickinson, 2000; Haydn

2004; Phillips 1998; Shemilt, 1980; Sylvester 1994; Wineburg, 2001). It was widely applauded the history profession. According to John Slater (1989) the project remained,

> ···*the most significant and beneficent influence on the learning of history and the raising of its standard to emerge this century. It gives young people not just knowledge, but the tools to reflect on, critically to evaluate, and to apply that knowledge. It proclaims the crucial distinction between knowing the past and thinking historically. It sums up what is often called "the new history" (pp. 2-3).*

New history gradually grew in popularity among teachers and although some reactionary forces harked back to history of the "great tradition," at the time of the implementation of National Curriculum history in 1988, few educators were willing to abandon the achievements made (Lee, 1999; Dickinson, 2000; Haydn, 2004). Accordingly, most textbooks produced during the 1980s undoubtedly bore many of the hallmarks of "new history." Although narrative structures often were preserved, textbooks typically contained an array of source material that both supported and, at times, questioned accepted interpretations. Books invited enquiry and pupil engagement. Activities and questions typically asked students to assess and analyse evidence to reach historical conclusions. Textbooks also began to support the notion that historical narratives were not given and agreed, but were constructed and contested. Certainly all publishers considered more carefully the accessibility and visual appeal of textbooks. The inclusion of significantly more visual sources, many of which appeared in colour, was a common feature of textbooks produced in this period.

Above all "new history" textbooks were more appreciative of history as a discipline. A typical example of a new history textbook is, *Peace and War*, authored by Shephard, Reid and Shephard. It was published in 1993 under the auspices of the SHP and it exemplified a number of features typical of the "new history" genre. In particular four elements stood out. First, the book chapters were organised around a question to be investigated. For example on two double-pages students were asked to consider: "Why did the USA drop the atomic bomb on Japan in August 1945?" In other sections of the book other similarly provocative questions invited student exploration (e.g., Were the Victorian racist?). Second, sources (which included photographs, newspaper extracts, maps, and political cartoons) dominated textbooks pages, while explicit narrative proved very limited. Moreover the central narrative was less authoritative, and the language used appeared more tentative and conditional. For example, the book used phrases like "some historians argue..." or "several reasons have been suggested". Third, historical sources often provided different perspectives on an event or issue (for example, the section on Truman's decision to drop the bombs on Japan included sources from other Americans who argued against the fateful decision). Accordingly historical accounts were often left open to interpretation. Fourth, student questions rarely focused on comprehension or factual recall. Instead, textbook questions appeared more likely to focus on the utility and reliability of sources, the competing claims of evidence, or ask for evidence from sources that refuted or supported statements made.

As a result of important changes in textbook development begun in the 1980s, students studying history today encounter history in a very different way to those who studied history in previous generations. Although the textbooks alone cannot guarantee a shift in students' understanding of the nature of history, young people today are more likely to appreciate that history is a discipline based on the interpretation and construction of historical evidence.

Of course this is not to say that new history textbooks were (or are) without critics. It might be argued for example that the inclusion of a mosaic of competing sources at the expense of a clear and coherent narrative invites confusion among students. Also it is widely recognised that if more attention is given to providing students with alternative historical evidence and interpretations then less time will be devoted to covering a range of "important" historical topics. Furthermore, the inclusion of sources alone cannot guarantee more sophisticated learning. The inclusion of sources ripped out of context, unattributed, and devoid of provenance are unlikely to help students develop their historical understandings. Finally, and perhaps most importantly, it is vital to recognise that textbook content never represents neutral knowledge. Indeed, the selection and inclusion of some source material and the exclusion of others arguably can lead students to certain conclusions and opinions about the past.[7]

---

[7] It is of course important to realise that any textbook is underpinned by a set of values, assumptions and ideologies. This explains why battles over textbooks are so often bitterly contested. It also explains why powerful groups in society often view history textbooks as central in the creation of a collective national memory designed to meet specific cultural, economic and social imperatives. For additional discussion of this issue see, for example, Anyon, 1979; Apple, 1991; Crawford 2000. Beyond these considerations it is also worth exploring the extent to which "new history" textbooks provide students with a coherent framework for orienting themselves in time.

Nevertheless, despite these limitations, textbooks produced in accordance with the philosophy of "new history" undoubtedly offer students a more thoughtful way to examine the past. Textbooks that shun a single, "official" narrative and eschew an overtly nationalistic perspective are more likely to help students acquire a sophisticated appreciation of the complexities and subtleties of history. Furthermore "new history" textbooks are more likely to help students acquire important understandings. These include an appreciation that that history is not the past, but a reconstruction of the past. An awareness that although history provides us with stories and explanations, the past did not happen in stories and explanations any more than it does in the present. And, as a result of these understandings, students should begin to appreciate what sort of knowledge history is and understand the legitimacy of that knowledge.

New History Textbooks: Lessons to Learn?

Although dramatic and often salutary changes in textbook production and development undoubtedly occurred in England during the past 40 years, it would be unwise and inappropriate to suggest that developments in England stand as a model to other nations. What is certain, however, is that significant change in textbook writing and provision requires a massive commitment on the part of any local, regional or national education system. At its core it involves a widespread re-assessment of the aims and purposes of history education. Changes might also include revisions to the history curriculum with less emphasis on coverage and more on promoting disciplinary understandings; the abandonment of examination systems solely based on factual recall and multiple choice testing; changes in teacher education in keeping with shifts in philosophy; and serious changes in the remit given to educational publishers.

Given the political, educational, and philosophical complexities of advancing such changes in any regional or national system of education it is, perhaps, worth considering what individual teachers might do to promote a more informed and enlightened appreciation of historical knowledge among their students. Of course the choices of individual teachers are context-dependent and are often directly related to the amount of pedagogical freedom a teacher perceives he or she possesses. Individual teachers always will make curriculum and pedagogical choices based on a number of considerations including the political context in which they work and the system of examination to which they and their students are held accountable. Accordingly the following are offered as examples of possibilities rather than as a blueprint for action. Nevertheless teachers who often are restricted by the domination of a single, authoritative text might introduce other alternative accounts into the history classroom and further discuss how and why the accounts differ. Importantly teachers may consider with their students how different accounts can be reconciled and evaluated.

Other possibilities also exist. Teachers might, for example, introduce a range of historical evidence into the classroom and ask students to construct a narrative account based on this evidence. This activity could then be broadened to an informed discussion about what legitimately can, and cannot, be said based on this evidence. Another possibility is to ask students to read a given textbook topic. Then require students to research the topic to identity and evaluate information that may have been excluded from the text. An interesting discussion might then take place that requires students to consider why some information is included and why some is not.

Naturally teachers in different contexts will have to consider carefully their pedagogical approach. On the one hand some teachers will enjoy the freedom to be innovative and to challenge textbook conventions in the ways outlined above. On the other hand, many teachers will find themselves more constrained by political, curriculum, assessment, or parental pressures. How individual teachers operate in their given context will therefore be driven to a large extent by a practical assessment of what is possible and desirable. Nevertheless if, as educators, we want to seriously challenge the authority of one dimensional, nationalist textbooks and encourage a broader appreciation of the interpretive nature of history, then new approaches must be explored.

Conclusions

This paper has briefly mapped the changes in textbook writing and development in England over the past 40 years. It has also explained and how and why these changes came about. Most importantly it has explicated the significant shift from textbooks based on the conventions of the "great tradition" of history education to the innovative textbooks produced under the philosophy of "new history". These important and dramatic changes in textbook design and content did not occur without resistance and challenge. Indeed, the battles over school history in England often were bitterly divisive and deeply contested. It is also important to appreciate that although it has been argued in this paper that changes were largely for the better, critics across the political and educational spectrum remain. Moreover it is very important to realise that textbooks alone guarantee nothing. Textbooks can only be effective when they are employed by thoughtful teachers and considered by willing pupils.   In the right hands, however, history textbooks have the potential to shape and deepen understandings.   In this respect good history textbooks offer students the opportunity to appreciate the complexities of uncovering and understanding the past.   They are not driven by nationalistic sentiments or propaganda, nor are they based on a single, authoritative story line.   Rather, good history textbooks allow students to appreciate that history is a constructed discipline worthy of interrogation.   Good textbooks also allow students to be comfortable with the idea that that different versions of the past always will exist.   One of our primary goals as educators is, therefore, not to require students to learn a single official account of the past, but to give students the tools and mental apparatus to help them make sense of different versions of the past.   If we can accomplish this we will have gone a long way to ensuring that students have a worthwhile and meaningful education in history.

References

Anyon, J. (1978), "Elementary Social Studies Textbooks and Legitimate Knowledge." *Theory and Research in Social Education* (6), 40-55.

Anyon, J. (1979), "Ideology and United States History Textbooks." *Harvard Educational Review* (49), 361-386.

Apple, M. W. (1991), "Culture and Commerce of the Textbook" in *The Politics of the Textbook*, eds. M. W. Apple and L. K. Christian-Smith (New York, Routledge).

Apple, M. W. and Christian-Smith, L. K. (1991), "The politics of the textbook," in *The Politics of the Textbook*, eds. M. W. Apple and L. K. Christian-Smith (New York, Routledge).

Barthes, R. (1976), *The Pleasure of Text* (London: Cape).

Barton, K. C. and Levstik, L. S. (2004), *Teaching History for the Common Good* (Mahwah, NJ: Lawrence Earlbaum).

Bruner, J. (1960), *The Process of Education* (Cambridge, MA: Harvard University Press).

Carter, E. H. and Mears, R. A. F. (1948), *A History of Britain*, Oxford: Clarendon Press.

Corcuff, S. (2005), "History Textbooks, Identity Politics, and Ethnic Introspection in Taiwan: the June 1997 *Knowing Taiwan* Textbook Controversy and the Questions It Raised on the Various Approaches to "Han" Identity," in *History Education and National Identity in East Asia,* eds., E. Vickers and A. Jones (London: Routledge).

Crawford, K. A. (2000), "Researching the Ideological and Political Role of the History Textbook: Issues and Methods," *International Journal of Historical Learning Teaching and Research*, (1), 1-11.

Crawford K. A. and Foster, S. J. (2006), "The Political Economy of Textbook Publishing in England," in *School History Textbooks Across Cultures: International Debates and Perspectives,* ed. J. Nicholls (Oxford: Symposium Books).

Dickinson, A. (2000), "What Should History Be?" in *School Subject Teaching: The History and Future of the Curriculum,* ed. A. Kent (London: KoganPage).

Foster, S. J. (1998) "Politics, Parallels, and Perennial Curriculum Questions: The Battle Over School History in England and the United States" *The Curriculum Journal*, (9), 153-164.

Foster, S. J. (1999), "The Struggle for American Identity: Treatment of Ethnic Groups in United States History Textbooks," *History of Education*, (28), 251-279.

Foster, S. J. and Crawford, K. A. (eds.) (2006a), *What Shall We Tell the Children? International Perspectives on School History Textbooks* (Greenwich, CT: Information Age Publishing).

Foster, S. J. and Crawford, K. A. (2006b), "The Critical Importance of History Textbook Research," in *What Shall We Tell the Children? International Perspectives on School History Textbooks,* eds. S. J. Foster and K. A. Crawford (Greenwich, CT: Information Age Publishing).

Foster, S. J. and Davis, O. L., Jr. (2004), "Conservative Battles for Public Education within America's Culture Wars: poignant lessons for today from the red scare of the 1950s." *London Review of Education* (2), 123-

135.

Foster, S. J. and Nicholls, J. (2005), "America's in World War II: An Analysis of History Textbooks from England, Japan, Sweden, and the United States," *The Journal of Curriculum and Supervision* (20), 214-234.

Hein, L. and Selden, M. (eds.) (2000), Censoring History: History, Citizenship and Memory in Japan, Germany and the United States (London: M. E. Sharpe).

Haydn, T. (2004), "History," in *Rethinking the School Curriculum, ed.* J. White (London: RoutledgeFalmer), 87-103.

Lee, P. J. (1991), "Historical Knowledge and the National Curriculum," in *History in the National Curriculum*, ed. R. Aldrich (London: KoganPage).

Lee, P. J. (1999), "Learning the Right Stories or Learning History? Developments in History Education in England." *Newsletter of the Organization of American Historians*, (27), 7-9.

Moreau, J. (2004), School Book Nation: Conflicts over American History Textbooks from the Civil War to the Present (Ann Arbor, MI: University of Michigan Press).

Marsden, W. E. (2001), The School Textbook: Geography, History and Social Studies (London: Routledge).

Nicholls, J. and Foster, S. J. (2005), "'Interpreting the Past, Serving the Present': US and English Textbook Portrayals of the Soviet Union During World War II," in *International Review of History Education, Volume IV,* eds. R. Ashby, P. Gordon, and P. Lee (London: Woburn Press).

Nicholls, J. (2006), School History Textbooks Across Cultures: International Debates and Perspectives (Oxford: Symposium Books).

Nozaki, Y. (2005), "Japanese Politics and the History Textbook Controversy,

1945-2001" in *History Education and National Identity in East Asia,* eds. E. Vickers and A. Jones (London: Routledge).

Phillips, R. (1998) History Teaching, Nationhood, and the State: A Study in Educational Politics (London: Cassell).

Pingel, F. (1999) *UNESCO Guidebook on Textbook Research and Textbook Revision* (Hanover: Hahnsche Buchhandlung, Studien zur Internationalen Schulbuchforschung).

Pingel, F. (2000) The European Home: Representations of 20th Century Europe in History Textbooks (Strasbourg: Council of Europe).

Porat, D. (2004), "'It's Not Written Here, But This Is What Happened': Students' Cultural Comprehension of Textbook Narratives on the Israeli-Arab Conflict," *American Educational Research Journal* (41), 963-996.

Schissler, H. and Soysal, Y. (eds.) (2005), The Nation Europe and the World: Textbooks and Curricula in Transition (Oxford: Beghahn Press).

Sewall, G. T. (1987), *American History Textbooks: An Assessment of Quality* (New York: American Textbook Council).

Sewall G. T. and Cannon, P. (1991), "New world of textbooks: Industry consolidation and its consequences", in *Textbooks in American Society: Politics, Policy, and Pedagogy*, eds. P. G. Altbach, G. P. Kelly, H. G. Petrie. L. Weis (Albany, NY: SUNY Press).

Shemilt, D. (1980), History 13-16, Evaluation Study: Schools Counci; History 13-16 Project (Edinburgh: Holmes McDougall).

Shephard, C., Reid, A. and Shephard, K. (1993), *Peace and War: Discovering the Past, Year 9* (London: John Murray).

Slater, J. (1989), The politics of history teaching: a humanity dehumanized? (London: Institute of Education).

Soysal, Y., Bertilotti, T. and Mannitz, S. (2005), "Projections of Identity in French and German History Textbooks," in *The Nation Europe and the World: Textbooks and Curricula in Transition*, eds. H. Schissler and Y. Soysal (Oxford: Beghahn Press).

Sylvester, D. (1994), "Change and continuity in history teaching, 1900-93," in *Teaching History*, ed. H. Bourdillon (London: Routledge).

Vickers, E. and Jones, A. (eds.) (2005), *History Education and National Identity in East Asia* (London: Routledge).

Whitman, D. (2004), *The Mad, Mad World of Textbook Adoption* (Washington D. C.: Thomas Fordham Institute).

Wineburg, S. (2001), *Historical Thinking and Other Unnatural Acts* (Philadelphia: Temple University Press).

Appendix A

Different Systems: Different Practices

Textbook production and selection in Japan and England:

	Japan	England
Producers	Small number of commercial publishers (and ministry)	A range of commercial publishers
Level of government control	Approved by ministry of education	No government approval process
Textbook selection	Local school boards select from approved lists	Individual teachers and individual history departments decide – no approved lists
Students and textbooks	Students receive textbooks free of charge and they become the students' property	No student is guaranteed a textbook. Individual schools decide. Often books are shared and remain in school.
Duration of textbook	Textbooks revised and approved every 4 years	No fixed period.

中文全譯

藉由歷史教科書提升學科理解：
挑戰與機會

Stuart Foster　著

溫楨文[*]　譯

一、前言

　　儘管存在著重要的例外，但在全世界的許多國家中，歷史教科書通常俱由兩種特徵所形成：第一，具有非常明顯的民族主義。第二，採用一種權威且單一「最佳故事」的敘事風格。本文認為這些教科書的編寫是極有問題的，因為他們向學生提供了不具解釋性及辯駁空間或學科特質意識的歷史。更確切地說，這些權威性的教科書通常是試圖在當時時空背景下，作為安撫社會和政治宣傳的工具。不過英國的經驗卻說明，教科書不必以上述這種方式編寫。藉由關注過去四十年間英國歷史教育及其教科書編寫的歷程變化，本文概述了從奠基於權威性與民族主義敘事形式的傳統教科書，轉變為促使學童認知歷史是作為一門學科而予以編寫的「新史學」教科書的重要變化。正如我們將討論的，這種改變在實行上不無批評者及其問題存在。然而，「新史學」教科書仍為有意義的歷史教育提供了較好的發展可能。本文將含括兩個課題：1.檢討在傳統體制下，歷史教師為了迎

* 政治大學歷史系研究部博士候選人

接變革所面臨的某些阻礙；2.考慮個別教師挑戰傳統慣例的可能作為。

二、歷史教科書：不同的體制——不同的慣例

在全世界的教育體制中，歷史是少數幾門被明令規定在學校課程裡須開設的學科。此外，利用歷史教科書來輔助學生學習幾乎已經成為普遍的慣例。(Foster and Crawford, 2006) 然而，儘管有這種共通性，歷史教科書在生產、選擇和搭配上，各國仍有不同。(Hein and Selden 2000; Nicholls, 2006; Pingel 2001; Vickers and Jones 2005) 特別是教科書在不同的國家有著不同的權威性和地位。例如：《我們應該告訴孩子們什麼？學校歷史教科書的國際視野》(*What Shall We Tell the Children? International Perspectives on School History Textbooks*) 一書，透過圖表來說明在東亞、歐洲、中東、非洲、美國與南亞教科書的選擇與使用方式，在上述各個國家皆有所不同。附錄 (A) 的圖表，將進一步說明日本與英國這兩個國家在教科書的選擇與使用上，基本上有著極度的不同之處。

正如圖表所示，兩者存在著重大的差別。例如，在日本由國家所控制的教育部，所產生的巨大影響便是教科書需經過官方審查才能在教室裡使用。但是在英國並未如此。[1]另一方面，日本學生能夠確保獲得新近出版的教科書，這在英國卻不是通行的慣例。雖然指出不同國家之間的關鍵差異是有益的，但是簡化的圖表掩蓋了在教室中實際使用教科書的一些複雜情形與細微差別。另外，它們也不能呈現出全球所有不同的國家，各自所設定教科書適用於不同目的的各種功能。教科書通常同時執行多項功能。例如，它們習慣「包含」規定的歷史題材、回應課程需求，並且能回饋標準化測驗的要求。這些通常被老師、學生與家長當作支援機制與訊息來源

---

[1] 真實的情況是當英國出版商們回應國定課程及國家考試需求時，教科書市場卻明顯縮小。對此概況的詳細討論參見 Crawford and Foster (2006)。

使用。偶爾它們也被批判性地用來展現基於特定的歷史觀而來的單一敘述。

　　這整個教科書選擇與使用的過程，更由於考慮到教科書「裡面」所存在的內容可能不會被講授而更為複雜。或者即使得到講授，學生也不一定能以政府、教科書作者與老師們所想要的那種方式來加以理解。因此輕易的相信教科書內容等同於老師的講授內容，或者更重要的是等同於學生所學習到的內容，這是相當不明智的。(Apple and Christian-Smith 1991) 學生們與老師們理解、協商乃至於轉化他們自身對文本材料之理解的各種方式，都是一個複雜的過程。很少教科書內容能簡單的被學生接受、吸收，然後產生反饋。（參見 Apple, 1991; Barthes, 1976; Foster and Crawford, 2006a; Porat 1994）

三、關於教科書的通則

　　儘管有這些警告與考量，但仍有足夠的研究顯示，教科書依然是決定學生如何學習歷史的一個重要因素。(Anyon, 1978; Anyon, 1979; Apple & Christian-Smith, 1991; Foster 1999; Marsden, 2001) 例如在 2002 年，美國一項針對小學與中學教師的調查指出，課堂與家庭作業通常受教科書驅策或以教科書為中心。(Whitman, 2004) 美國教科書委員會的主管 Gilbert Sewall 更進一步論證，教科書甚至常等於事實上的課程，「對許多老師與幾乎全數的學生而言，教科書被視為真實的、專業的知識來源。」(Sewall, 1987, pp. 61-62)。值得注意的是，正由於這層重要性，歷史教科書的內容經常是國內和國際衝突與爭論的場所。(Corcuff 2005; Foster, & Davis, 2004; Foster, & Nicholls, 2005; Hein & Selden, 2000; Moreau 2004; Nicholls & Foster 2005; Nozaki, 2005; Vickers & Jones, 2005)

　　雖然對於歷史教科書得出全面性的通則是很困難的（甚至是不智

的），但是關於教科書生產與使用的跨國研究，仍顯示各國教科書有著相似的觀點與特徵。[2]此外，這些共通性在教科書需由中央核可的國家裡顯得更加突出。它們呈現了兩個特點：首先，教科書在歷史事件上通常採納民族主義式的觀點。[3]其次，教科書典型地呈現一種「官方的」單一敘述。

民族主義與官定教科書

在世界各國中，教科書不可避免地代表一種強而有力的工具，它們在歷史課堂上提供一種特定的版本來訴說國家的過去。受到官方政策的強力影響，教科書的作者有意識的企圖去形塑和教導學生對於本國歷史及其與他國之間關係的了解。如同 Keith Crawford 與我曾經寫過：

> 有些民族國家的歷史教育習於公開且無恥地去發揚特定的意識型態與政治理念。其他國家在愛國主義的偽裝之下，提供學生學習的國族歷史是由國家領導者所決定的。在那些認為他們的存在受到威脅的國家，或是正在努力建立認同的國家，或經過一段時間的殖民統治正重新找回自我的國家，講授民族主義與單一文化形式的歷史可以加強人民的團結。最糟糕的情況是，這種官定過去的生產與教學可以創造、支持、維繫、證成排外仇恨、種族主義和令人髮指的種族淨化。(Foster and Crawford 2006a, pp. 6-7)

因此，被寫入歷史教科書中的是一種由民族國家所選擇講述，關於其自身及其與其他國家之間關係的敘事。通常它們代表一種核心的文化知

---

2 主張所有國家共享某些特徵可能會產生誤導。例如，德國中央和地方政府都努力降低對國家主義教條的重視。更確切地說，德國教科書更傾向於訴諸一種歐洲認同感。對此發展的有趣討論參見 Soysal, Bertilotti, and Mannitz (2005)。

3 並非所有的學者都同意這個看法。例如，Schissler and Soyal (2005)即主張在歐洲，國家認同已變得較不重要。

識，年輕的一代被期待加以接納與支持。結果，教科書經常被使用於以傳達過去的故事為手段，團結現在的人群，並強調國家的統一與驕傲。同樣地，正因為這些教科書通常關注己方國家的成就與勝利，因此對於其他國家的貢獻也就顯得較為忽略或輕描淡寫。意味深遠的還在於人以群分的表述。在某些國家裡，教科書的敘述是藉由措辭來表達如「我們」、「我們的」與「是我們」來區分國家公民，有別於「是他們」、「他們的」與「他們」等「其他」的人們。

　　另一個特徵是，教科書在許多國家顯露出它單一、權威性、「官方」的敘述。[4] 在這些教科書中，歷史內容通常被呈現為無須爭論與客觀的存在。其記事是權威性的、超然的、技術性的，而且沒有提出原始資料或其他可供選擇的證據。此外，這些觀點時常被當作一種事實來加以陳述，並且在正文中，提供給學生的問題若非不存在，就是基於其所給予訊息的事實來回想。

　　令人遺憾地是，不論是呈現狹隘的民族主義觀點或者是未經質疑的單一敘述，具備這兩者的教科書均無法帶給學生對於歷史的學科本質有任何尊重。它們通常呈現給學生的不是歷史，而是宣傳與爭執。相較於呈現給年輕人有關歷史如何運作的理解，學生們太常遇到的是採用一個特定（而且常常是狹隘而帶有限制的）觀點的敘事。這些「歷史」教科書不提供辯論與解釋的感度，其中沒有歷史證據與論證的鑑定，也沒有對於歷史敘述是以何為基礎被建構出來的理解。正如同 Peter Lee (1991) 針對這個嚴重的缺失評論道：

　　　……這是荒謬的……如果說學童們懂得歷史，卻不知道歷史知識是

4　例如在 2004 年由 Keith Barton 及 Linda Levstik 所提供的關於美國一個單一「主導敘述」的持久性的有趣討論。詳見該書的第9章 "The Story of National Freedom and Progress"。

如何獲得的……對建構歷史敘述所涉問題，或評估史實所涉準則沒有任何理解，這樣的記憶史事之技能與歷史渺不相關。(pp. 48-49)

四、歷史教科書的再思考

在任何教育體制下，改變慣例通常是困難的，並且需要克服一系列複雜的挑戰和歷史遺留下來的問題。無法找到可以採用的方法是改革常見的障礙。一般來說，對個人、機構或政府而言，較為容易與安全的做法是繼續接受慣例與師法故智。接下來，本文將提供一扇窗口，得窺過去四十年間英國歷史教育與歷史教科書生產的重大改變。這絕非是無所不包的描述。此外，英國的教科書改革也決非是全然可行的典範以指導改變應如何進行。儘管如此，英國歷史教科書在特性與內容上的巨大改變，確實為反省和考慮革新提供了些許契機。當然，過去四十年間由「傳統教科書」過渡到「新史學」教科書的廣泛使用，提供了洞見改革的可能性與妥適性。

傳統教科書

在 1970 年代後期之前，英國課堂所採用的大部分歷史教科書都還繼承了如上所述的特色。它們照例提供一種民族主義式的單一敘述，聚焦於大不列顛帝國的過去、偉大人物的成就與統治君主的活動。憲政、軍事和政治事件方面的關注主導了一切，在無所不在的愛國主義敘事中孤立的使用「we」及「us」成為常見的手法。舉例來說，以下這一段編寫自 1948年，但廣泛地使用於整個 1950 年代到 1970 年代的「傳統教科書」中關於二次世界大戰章節的引文，便能印證許多產生於這個時期之書籍的論調：

俄羅斯的傷亡人數更高、破壞遠甚；美國生產了更多的軍需品；中國的戰事繼續延長；但沒有別的地方比邱吉爾所領導的英國與國協

在對抗納粹信條上展現更頑強的決心、更崇高的奮鬥精神。那一年——令全世界驚奇的是——我們單獨跟希特勒作戰，並（更有甚者）獲得成功：我們的威望更是前所未見……(Carter and Mears, *A History of Britain*, p. 1042)

幾乎毫無例外地，在大部分成書於「大傳統」時代的教科書中，作者的看法均被視為客觀事實，而且歷史記述通常被呈現為無庸置疑的「真實」。在少數時候當課文內的習作或問題出現，學生們被要求回想那些已陳述的「事實」，或去回答無所不包的問題。但學生卻從未有可供自己選擇的陳述或史料，也很少有視覺圖像。再者，儘管某些教科書提供生動、迷人的故事，但絕大部分是枯燥而無趣的。教科書裡充斥著詳細的資訊與支配性的內文。不過在 1970 年代末至 1980 年代初開始，歷史教育和歷史教科書編寫產生了重要且巨大的變化。更確切的說，在 1980 年代末期，基於成立數個世代之久的慣例而來的所謂「傳統」教科書，基本上已在教育版圖中消失。

巨大的變化：「新史學」教科書

在 1970 年代末期至 1980 年代初期，英國的歷史教育有了重要的發展。特別是 1980 年代這十年之間，「傳統歷史」教學與「新史學」教學兩者產生衝擊與火花。基本上這衝擊肇始於一場激烈的意識型態爭論，一方是傳統依照時序編年與民族主義方式從事歷史教學的擁護者，另一方是較強調學科架構與歷史之解釋性本質的「新」史學主張者(Crawford 1996; Dickinson, 2000; Foster 1998; Haydn 2004; Phillips 1998; Sylvester 1994)[5]。

---

5 儘管歷史領域的教育和意識型態鬥爭，在 1980 年代後期採用國定歷史課程的論爭中顯得最為激烈，不同傳統之間的衝突顯然更早了許多年。舉例來說，1986 年從傳統分級「O」和 CSE 英國中等教育證書考試課程，轉變到更具包容性和可以說是更具創新性的 GCSE 普通中等教育證書考試課程，已經確保歷史教師都必須欣然接

新史學為何逐漸對於既有的教學成規形成嚴重的挑戰，其理由極其複雜而多樣。帶來這個重要轉變的原因，不管在實踐還是哲學層次上，都是因為歷史教育藉由更深思熟慮與貼近當代的方式來恢復生機的關切日增。無疑地，學習心理學的認知革命在挑戰兒童如何獲得知識與理解的現存理論方面產生了一定的影響。而建構論者在學習途徑上也嚴厲地質疑「大傳統」時代普遍使用的教誨式教學法。與此相類的是，一些在英國有影響力的研究人員（例如：Booth, Fines, Lee, Shemilt）質疑佔支配地位的皮亞傑式思維，並提出小學生的歷史相關能力長久以來是被低估的。值得注意的是，越來越多的研究人員和教育工作者追求一種理念，認為各個年齡層的學生都可以、也應該對於作為一門學科的歷史擁有更深的體會（而不僅僅是當作一種被學習的知識而已）。[6]

除了這些重要的發展之外，新史學出現於一個因社會文化的轉變而導致對於傳統與「慣性思維」普遍質疑的時期，並非偶然。因此「新史學」革命的一個重要面向是更多社會性的、包容性的和批判性的歷史日益得到關注。最後當歷史教育被認為遭遇嚴重威脅時，新史學便適時出現。毫無疑問地，歷史教育工作者的憂慮日增，因為這門學科正處於危機之中，而且傳統的歷史對年輕人而言是越來越漠不相關。正如 Shemilt (1980) 在對學校歷史計畫 (SHP) 的「歷史 13-16」教學計畫評估研究中開宗明義寫道：

> 學校委員會歷史項目（13-16 歲）建立於 1972 年，作為教師對「傳統歷史」的不滿，以及他們關切歷史在中學課程地位明顯遭到削弱的結果。（頁 1）

受「新史學」的許多關鍵影響和觀念。

[6] 在這方面「新史學」追隨了 Bruner 的經典主張：「任何題材都可依循某種智識上的坦率形式，有效地教給處於任一發展階段的任何兒童」(Bruner 1960)。

　　新史學在其核心挑戰了將歷史視為一門「被授與」科目的觀念。新史學的倡導者希望學生能了解歷史是如何被建立的，也希望學生在這門學科的學習過程中變得較為主動。他們認為，為了了解歷史，小學生必須懂得這門學科的結構，不僅關心了解歷史的內容，還必須知道這些歷史是如何形成的。這些變化最實際的體現是學校歷史計畫 (SHP) 的實行。自 1970 年代末期起，這項計畫提供教師與學生由新史學之哲學思考所帶來的創新、深思，且經公開檢驗的課程。(Dickinson, 2000; Haydn 2004; Phillips 1998; Shemilt, 1980; Sylvester 1994; Wineburg, 2001) 根據 John Slater (1989) 提及此計畫所示：

> ……對學習歷史而言，最重要、最有益的影響及其標準的提升出現於本世紀。它帶給年輕人的不僅是知識本身，還包括進行反思、批判性評估及運用知識的工具。這是在於知道過去與歷史性思考之間的關鍵區別。總而言之，稱之為「新史學」。(頁 2-3)

　　雖然有些保守勢力想恢復「大傳統」的歷史，但新史學逐漸在教師中獲得支持且逐步成長。當 1988 年國定歷史課程實施時，幾乎沒有教育工作者願意放棄既有的成就 (Lee, 1999; Dickinson, 2000; Haydn, 2004)。因此，大多數 1980 年代所編寫的教科書無疑具有許多「新史學」的標誌。儘管敘事架構通常維持原樣，但教科書總是包含了一系列既可對書中解釋提出支持，或有時產生質疑的原始資料。因此教科書引起了學生的探究興趣和參與感。書中所列舉的活動和問題，通常要求學生去評估和分析證據以求得歷史結論。教科書也開始同意歷史敘述並非是既定的，或只能被贊成的；而是被建構出來的、可以質疑的。當然，所有的出版商都更仔細的考慮教科書的獲取管道和視覺吸引力。這個時期產生的教科書其普遍特徵是包含更多有意義的視覺材料，其中還有許多採用了彩色印刷。

最重要的是，「新史學」教科書更為強調將歷史視為一門學科。一個新史學教科書的典型例子是 Reid, Shephard 和 Shephard 所共同編著的《和平與戰爭》一書。該書在 1993 年由 SHP 的主持下發行，示範了許多「新史學」文類的典型特徵。其中尤以四種要素最為突出。首先，書中章節圍繞著即將探討的問題組織而成。例如，學生常被要求細想：「為什麼美國要在 1945 年 8 月對日本投擲原子彈？」此書的其他部分則有類似的爭論問題引發學生探索，例如：維多利亞時代的人是否是種族主義者？其次，原始資料（包括照片、新聞報紙摘錄、地圖與政治漫畫）佔有教科書多數篇章，明顯的敘事則十分有限。此外，中心敘述手法較不以權威性口吻出之，而代之以更具暫時性與條件式的語彙。例如，書中使用的是這類措辭，像：「一些歷史學家爭論說……」或「有幾個理由顯示……」。第三，史料對於同一事件或議題，通常提供不同的見解（例如：在杜魯門總統決定將原子彈投擲在日本的決策這一部分，便包含其他美國人爭論反對這個致命性決策的資料）。據此，歷史記述通常是開放的以供詮釋。第四，為學生準備的問題極少著重在理解或記誦史實上。相反的，教科書問題顯然更加著重在史料來源的效用與可靠性、不同證據之間孰優孰劣，或要求在史料中找到證據以支持或反對既有的陳述。

由於肇始於 1980 年代教科書編寫的重要變化，今日學習歷史的學生比起過去的世代，是以相當不同的方式來學習歷史。雖然僅僅只是教科書單方面的變革，無法就此保證學生對歷史本質的理解產生變化，但今日的年輕人仍然較可能基於對歷史證據的詮釋及建構，而理解到歷史是一門學科。

當然，這不是說新史學教科書就沒有遭受批評。例如可以反駁說，包含相互矛盾史料的資料拼貼，在失去清晰而有條理的敘述的情況下會造成學生的困擾。此外也廣泛的公認，假如在提供學生其他歷史證據和詮釋上付出更多的關注，那麼用於處理一系列「重要」歷史主題的時間將會變

少。而且，僅有原始資料的內容也不能保證更縝密的學習。因為剝離前後脈絡、出處不可考的原始資料，未必有可能幫助學生發展他們的歷史理解。最後，或許是最重要的，認識到教科書的內容從未代表客觀中立的知識是至關緊要的。事實上，某些原始資料的選擇和排除，按理說會引導學生對於過去得到特定結論與看法。[7]

然而，儘管有這些限制，依照「新史學」哲理所編寫的教科書，無疑給學生提供了一個檢視過去更為周全的方式。避開一個單一、官方的敘述，以及避免明顯民族主義觀點的教科書，將較有可能幫助學生獲得一種對於歷史的複雜性與精妙之處的深層理解。此外，「新史學」教科書亦較有可能幫助學生獲得重要的理解。這些理解包括歷史並不就等同於過去，而是對於過去的重建。自覺意識到儘管歷史提供我們以故事和解釋，但過去本身並未以故事和解釋的形式發生，正如現在並未如此發生一樣。從而自這些理解開始，學生應該領會歷史是何種類的知識，並進而了解其知識上的正當性。

五、新史學教科書：可以參考的一課？

雖然在過去四十年間，英國的教科書編寫與發展發生巨大而有益的改變，但認為在英國的發展可以成為其他國家的典範，則是不明智也不適當的。然而，可以肯定的是，教科書編寫與供應上的重大變化，需要任一地方、地區或國家教育體制的大量投入。其核心牽涉到對於歷史教育的目標

7　認識到任何教科書都是奠基於一套價值觀、預設和意識型態當然是重要的。這也解釋了為何關於教科書的戰爭通常是激烈地爭持。這還說明了為何社會上的有力團體，通常視歷史教科書為創造國家集體記憶以滿足特定文化、經濟和社會需求的核心。有關此一議題，更多討論請參見：Anyon, 1979; Apple, 1991; Crawford 2000。除此之外，「新史學」教科書在多大程度上為學生提供一個用以在時間中導引自身之條理清楚的框架，也是值得探討的問題。

與宗旨廣泛的再評估。可能也包含以下諸種改變：減少對歷史課程內容範圍的強調，轉而增進學科訓練的理解；放棄僅以記誦事實與多重選擇測驗為基礎的考試制度；改變師範教育，以求與哲學上的重點轉移協調一致；給予教育出版商之職權範圍以重大改變。

考量到在任何地區性或全國性教育系統推動這樣的變革在政治、教育和哲學上的複雜性，或許值得考慮的是，個別教師如何可能增進學生對歷史知識更具見地與啟迪的了解。當然，個別教師的選擇是視情況而定的，通常直接與教師所感受到他／她所擁有的教學自由之程度有關。個別教師在課程與教學法選擇上總是基於許多考量，包含他們工作時空的政治背景，及其自身與學生所在的考試系統。因此，以下內容是提供作為可能性的例子，而非作為行動的藍圖。無論如何受限於一個單一而具權威性之文本主導，教師仍然可以在其歷史課堂上介紹其他不同的說法，並進一步討論如何與為何這些說法有所不同。重要的是，教師可與學生一起考量不同的說法如何可以互相調和，並加以評估。

另外，教師也可以在課堂上介紹一定程度的歷史證據，並要求學生們依此證據給出一個說法。然後，這個活動可以擴大為基於此項證據，可以或不可以合理地說出什麼。另一個可能性是要求學生閱讀一個指定的教科書主題。然後要求學生針對此一主題加以研究，進而識別、評估可能被排除在教科書正文之外的訊息。接下來可能會出現有趣的討論，要求學生們思考為何某些訊息被納入，某些則否。

教師在不同的情況下自然必須仔細考慮其教學方式。一方面，某些教師喜愛以上述方式自由創新，並挑戰教科書教學的慣例。另一方面，很多教師發現自己將承受來自政治、課程、評量或家長的壓力。因此，個別教師如何在其特定的情況下教學，在很大程度上取決於可能性和可取性的實際評估。不過，身為教育工作者，如果我們要嚴肅挑戰單面向的民族主義式教科書之權威，並促進歷史詮釋性本質更被普遍地接受，便必須探索新

的教學方法。

六、結論

　　本文簡要地敘述過去四十年間英國在教科書編著和發展的變遷，也解釋了這些改變如何發生以及為何發生。最重要的是，本文闡述了從基於「大傳統」歷史教育慣例而來的教科書，到產生於「新史學」哲理下的創新教科書之間的重大轉變。這些在教科書設計和內容上的重要且巨大的變化，並非從未遭遇抵抗和質疑。事實上，英國關於學校歷史教育的爭執通常是尖銳對立且激烈競爭的。同樣重要的是了解到，儘管本文認為英國歷史教科書的變革大多是正面的，但是橫跨政治與教育光譜的批評者仍然存在。此外，非常重要的是認識到，若單靠教科書本身是擔保不了什麼的。換言之，教科書只有在被認真思考的教師所使用，以及透過積極學生的深思時才具有其效用。而且也只有在如斯正確的使用下，歷史教科書才富有塑造和加深理解的潛能。據此而論，好的歷史教科書將提供學生領略認知錯綜複雜的過去的機會。它們既不受民族主義情感及宣傳的驅使，也不固守於單一而權威性的故事發展。相反地，好的歷史教科書會讓學生體會到，歷史是一門值得審問的、建構而成的學科。好的歷史教科書也使學生能自在地理解到一點，那就是關於過去的不同說法始終是存在的。因此，我們作為教育工作者的主要目標之一，不是要求學生們學習一套獨一無二的有關過去的官方說法，而是給予學生們工具和心智配備，以期幫助他們從這些不同說法的過去中汲取意義。如果我們可以做到這一點，我們即將踏上以確保學生有個值得和有意義的歷史教育的漫長道路。

附錄 A

不同的系統：不同的實踐

日本與英國的教科書生產與選用比較表

	日本	英國
生產者	少數的商業出版社（部定）	一系列的商業出版社
政府管制層級	由教育部核准	不需政府審批程序
教科書選擇	地方教育單位從教育部核可的清單中選擇	個別教師和個別歷史部門自行選擇——沒有部訂清單
學生與教科書	學生免費獲得教科書，為學生所有	不保證學生擁有教科書。由個別學校自行決定，教科書通常是共有的並由學校保管。
教科書使用期限	教科書每四年修訂和審核	沒有固定的期限

對學生歷史探究學習的研究

張　靜[*]

一、問題的提出

國家教育部 1997 年對北京 2,107 位學生的調查結果表明：歷史課被學生視為「枯燥、沒意思的課」，在學生心目中的位置如此之低，令人震驚。這一問題由來已久，且原因是多方面的，既有歷史教育本身的，又有社會環境方面的。從歷史教育本身看，既有課程理念忽視以人為本，課程目標狹窄、唯智輕德，課程結構過於強調學科體系，內容繁、難、多、舊等問題；也有教學觀念滯後，教學過程呆板的問題，還有教學評價內容陳舊、片面，評價手段單一等問題。

自 2002 年新一輪課程改革開始實施以來，情況有所變化，但歷史學科狀況不盡如人意。在 2003 年 11 月，我們採取分層整群抽樣問卷法，對北京市 3,228 名八年級中學生進行了問卷調查和測試，了解學生對歷史學習的態度、學生的歷史學習能力、學生的歷史學習方式、歷史學習與學生情感、態度和價值觀方面的變化等。第二，學生歷史學習的影響因素，包括師生關係、教師的教學態度、課堂教學方式等。第三，學生日常的學業評價方式。同時，又對教這些孩子們的 80 位老師進行調查和訪談。自 2004 年以來，筆者對 200 多節歷史課進行了觀察，並和老師共同研究了 90 節歷史課的教學。發現的問題主要有：

---

[*]　北京教科院基礎教研中心歷史教研室

其一，調查資料表明，對歷史學習持有積極態度的學生占 46.9%，有 39.0%的學生對「歷史學習態度」的回答是難以判斷，說不清楚。還有 14.1%的學生對歷史學習持有消極態度。調查資料說明，仍有一半以上的中學生對歷史學習缺少興趣，不能積極主動地學習。

其二，測試結果表明；學生的歷史學習能力水平低，突出表現在歷史的分析與解釋、運用與表達能力上。例如：第一，不能把問題提到一定的歷史範圍內進行分析，張冠李戴。第二，讀不懂材料，不能有效地從材料中提取相關信息，作出相對合理的判斷。第三，限於細節之中，不能在事物的眾多聯繫中把握主要的、本質聯繫。第四，準確表達力較弱。

其三，對課堂的觀察和對學生的調查資料表明：課程教材改革後，學生歷史學習方式發生的一些變化，出現了討論式、辯論式、角色扮演式、材料研習式等新的學習方式，但是這些新教學方式，只是有時使用，還不能經常使用。「老師講學生聽」的傳統教學方式，仍是目前教師主要採取的教學方式，「照本宣科」是這一方式的基本特徵，學生的學習基本處於被動狀態。

其四，在對學生學業評價上，雖然出現了檔案袋評價、表現性評定等具有發展性、多元性色彩的新變化，仍以紙筆測驗測查學生記憶歷史知識為主，而且教、學、評是割裂的。

在研究國內外歷史教育改革趨勢中我們發現：二十世紀 80 年代以來，以探究性學習為基礎重構基礎教育課程，成為世界各國課程改革的突出特點，使得教學方式和學習方式發生重大改變。在理科教育中出現的探究模式也擴展到文科教學中，人們開始關注發展學生對社會生活的本質進行探究和深思的能力，特別是對自己的生活和社會發展方向思考的能力。這種發展體現在中學歷史教學中表現在教科書的編寫、教與學方式、學生學業評價等方面上向探究性學習轉變。我國新一輪歷史課程標準均提出了開展探究學習的要求。《全日制義務教育歷史課程標準（實驗稿）》指出，

要「注重探究式學習，勇於從不同角度提出問題，學習解決歷史問題的一些基本方法；樂於同他人合作，共同探討問題，交流學習心得；積極參加各種社會實踐活動，學習運用歷史的眼光來分析歷史與現實問題，養成對歷史的理解力。」《普通高中歷史課程標準（實驗）》指出，「掌握學習歷史的基本方法。學習歷史唯物主義的基本觀點和方法，努力做到論從史出、史論結合；注重探究學習，善於從不同的角度發現問題，積極探索解決問題的方法；養成獨立思考的學習習慣，能對所學內容進行較為全面的比較、概括和闡釋；學會同他人，尤其是具有不同見解的人合作學習和交流。」不難發現，不管是初中還是高中，「探究式學習」實施的成效都直接影響、制約著其他目標的達成。又如，二十世紀 90 年代以來，隨著歷史課程地位的上升和「國家歷史標準」爭論的展開，在美國中小學的歷史科中，學習的重心從「固定性的觀念」(received ideas) 轉向「批判性的思維」(critical thinking)。相應地，教育模式也從「編年敘事或信息載體」(a chronological narrative or body of information) 走向「歷史探究」(historical inquiry)。[1]

縱觀國內外歷史學科探究學習的研究和發展狀況，有四點是值得反思和借鑑的：

第一，重在發展學生研究能力和樹立人文精神的教學目標。如加拿大安大略省 11-12 年級《加拿大和世界研究》課程的教學目標規定：首先，要獲得這個科目的基本概念的理解，並將其視為進一步探索的基礎。第二，發展實踐的能力，如交流和探究技能。應用在這一科目學習中獲得的知識和技能，幫助其理解人與自然的相互影響；政治、經濟和文化對社會的影響；科學技術和社會的聯繫；促進社會可持續發展的因素。特別強調對經濟、地理、歷史、法律和政治的學習不是記住一系列事實，而是教會

---

[1] 鄭流愛：美國中小學歷史教育中的「探究」，載於《課程·教材·教法》2005 年第9 期。

學生評價事件、思想和價值如何影響及作用於社會。這一科目的學習涉及到學生的研究活動、批判性思維、問題解決和決策，並且有助於學生發展很強的交流能力，包括口頭交流，閱讀和寫作技能，以及運用現代信息技術收集、組織、闡釋和呈現信息的能力。學生應能將他們在這個科目中獲得的技能運用於其他學科，以及未來的學習和生活中。[2]

第二，編製比較系統的探究技能和方法操作系統。這可從美國、加拿大最新編製和使用的教科書中略見一斑。這些能力和技能包括：運用地球儀、地圖等地理工具；學習圖表和表格；原因和結果的聯繫；區別事實和觀點；小組調查；建立卡片；認識第一手材料和第二手材料；解釋政治漫畫；認識和分析偏見；理解歷史觀點；對比與比較；辯論和討論；在合作小組學習；利用統計資料；創造多媒體的展示；角色扮演；進行採訪；分析現實問題；價值探索；寫研究報告等。[3]這些為有效培養學生的人文素養和探究能力提供了條件。

第三，注重主體性、體驗性、差異性、合作性、激勵性、開放性、發展性的新型教學方式。如美國哈佛大學教育學家哈沃德‧加登納 (Howard Gardner) 和大衛‧帕金斯 (David Perkins) 提出的「為理解而教」的教學模式；在美國社會學習和歷史教學中還普遍運用個體和群體調查模式；圍繞一定的教學主題，以學生的活動為主來設計和進行教學的主題活動教學模式；從學生體驗切入，將個人、家庭的變遷與歷史、社會變遷相連的 Personal profile 教學等等。

第四，強調激勵性、開放性、多樣性和發展性功能的學業評價，評價的指標和工具也更為合理。如美國最近出版了包括多種學科的《促進學校

2　The Ontario Curriculum Grades 11 and 12, Canadian and World Studies, 2000.

3　Colin M. Bain, *Making History – the Story of Canada in the Twentieth Century*, (Toronto, 2000); Leland Graham, *Social Studies Fair Projects and Research Activities*, (Nashville, 2001); William J. Mckee, *World History*, (Needham, 2003).

可持續發展的課程標準指南》。在「社會學習評價指南」中明確提出對學生歷史學習的期望、歷史學習的評價標準、歷史和歷史思維的成就指標。美國社會科教師參照多元智慧理論、建構主義學習理論和腦研究理論，提出的 65 項「使社會學習活起來」的課堂探究過程評價的活動和專案，等等。[4]加拿大安大略省社會科課程標準在評價學生的知識和技能方面提出了理解基本概念、探究與研究技能和利用地圖與地球儀的技能、知識交流、概念與技能應用等四個評價指標。每個評價指標分為四個水平，特別是突出對學生表現性的評價。[5]筆者 2001 年為期三月對加拿大安大略省課程改革的考察，深切感受到其教－學－評整體改革的實踐。

　　歷史教學中存在的問題讓我們焦慮，國際歷史教育的發展趨勢開闊了我們的視野。為了改進歷史教學，促進學生對歷史的理解，繼「學生歷史學習心理與教學對策的研究」課題後，五年來，我們集中進行了學生歷史探究學習的研究。

二、研究的思路

　　本課題研究的目的為：通過對歷史學科探究學習的實驗研究，改變傳統的歷史學科教與學的方式和學業評價方式；引導學生學會學習、自主探究，培養學生的探究精神，提升學生的人文素養。

　　本課題研究的假設為：以建構主義學習理論、多元智能理論、腦研究等理論為指導，借鑑國內外探究性學習的研究成果，在大量教學實驗基礎上，對歷史探究教學的本質、結構、共性和特點、教學目標、教學策略、

4　Kretzer. Marilyn, Slobin. Marlene, Williams ．Madell*a*(1998)，"*Making Social Studies 65 Teacher-Tested Ideas for Classroom Use,* "New York.

5　The Ontario Curriculum, 　Social Studies Grades 1 to 6 History and Geography Grades 7 and 8 (1998).

教學評價等問題深入探討，並付諸於教學實踐，將使學生在認知、情感的進步程度高於目前一般的教育教學工作所能達到的水平，使探究教學不再停留在理論範疇，為新課程教與學方式的轉變提供可資借鑑的案例。

　　本課題以歷史學科教學為載體，採取定性研究和定量研究、群體研究與個案研究相結合，以行動研究為主，以實驗研究為輔的方式，深入探討促進中學歷史學科探究教學的多種策略與評價方式，探察學生在探究學習過程中存在的問題。課題組通過分析國內外開展探究學習的情況，根據我國中學歷史學科課堂教學的實際，科學地為課題的實驗方案定位、並注意不斷學習最新的科學教育理論、聽取專家的意見，多次召開了研討會、以保證研究成果的品質。在本課題研究的主要階段教學實驗階段，主要採取：**調查法**：如選取樣本，通過對北京市中學歷史學科教學現狀的調查，歸納當前教學的問題和影響探究教學的因素；**實驗法**：如制定開展探究教學的實驗方案，初中以北京中學新課程實驗若干校的起始年級學生、高中以若干校的高一學生為實驗對象，進行教學實驗；**觀察法**：觀察實驗對象，做實驗記錄；對教學實驗過程進行觀察、記錄。**行動研究的方法**：各實驗校和實驗區的中學人文社會科學學科教師既是研究者又是實踐者，在教學實驗中，邊實驗、邊研究、邊改進。

　　本課題研究經過了調研論證、制定目標，進行實驗，總結、推廣實驗等幾個階段。

三、研究結果及其分析

　　研究的內容主要包括：建構歷史探究學習過程的結構；歷史探究學習的教學設計及其實施；學生歷史探究學習技能和方法的建構及其培養；學生歷史探究的學業評價；探究學習與歷史教師專業化發展。下面主要對其中三項研究進行交流。

(一) 建構歷史探究學習過程的結構

「探究學習」產生於二十世紀 50 年代末 60 年代初。第二次世界大戰結束後，新的科學理論和技術不斷湧現，科學的發展出現了前所未有的新圖景。而這一發展必然對教育產生深刻的影響，傳統的僅以文化知識教育為目的的教育體系已不適應社會的發展。在這一時期，美國著手進行課程改革。著名教育心理學家布魯納在《教育過程》的報告中提出了應重視科學的知識結構，重視發展學生智力、培養能力的新教育觀，其率先宣導的「發現法」受到教育者的重視。與此同時，美國芝加哥大學教授施瓦布提出了與發現法相似，但更具操作性的教學方法——「探究學習」(Enquiry Learning) 方法。「探究學習」說不是強調兒童中心主義的教學活動，而是通過探究的過程，強調科學概念、科學方法、科學態度三者結合和對科學研究過程的理解。由於「探究學習」在解決教什麼、學什麼方面更具體、適用，加之美國教育心理學家加涅從理論上對「探究學習」進行了論證，而受到人們的重視，因此廣泛傳播到世界其他國家，[6]並由理科教學擴展到文科教學中。如美國國家歷史教育協會曾在 1996 年向全國的歷史教育工作者提出從「學校歷史課程的開設」、「歷史課程內容的更新」、「歷史教師的準備和職業發展」、「課堂上有效而又有趣的教學實踐」和「為歷史的教與學確定最好的資訊和材料」等五個方面改革學校的歷史教學，其中特別提到「基礎歷史教育應該包括基礎知識和對知識的可發現性、可證實性方法的理解」，而這種「理解」存在於「歷史探究的過程中」。[7]

目前，國外有關促進學生探究學習的研究取得了一定的成果（見論文第一部分），在我國的課程改革中探究學習已被納入到各科的課程標準

6　鐘啟泉：《現代教學論發展》，教育科學出版社 1992 年版，第 350-351 頁。

7　*Reinvigorating History in U.S.Schools Reform Recommendation for the States.* http://www.history.org/

中。但是，人們對探究學習始終見解不一，有人認為探究主要是指科學探究，在理科中較明顯；還有人將其等同於研究性學習，認為其不存在於常規課中，常規課還是接受學習的「平臺」，等等。在概念上，我們更傾向於鐘啟泉等在《基礎教育課程改革綱要（試行）解讀》中對探究學習的詮釋：「探究學習是從學科領域或現實社會生活中選擇和確立主題，在教學中創設一種類似於學術（或科學）研究的情景，通過學生自主、獨立地發現問題，以及實驗、操作、調查、蒐集與處理信息、表達與交流等探索活動，獲得知識、技能、情感與態度的發展，特別是獲得探索精神和創新能力的發展的學習方式和學習過程。」可以看出，探究既是學習的過程、又是學習的方式，還是學習的目的。

需要說明的是，我們提出的中學歷史學科探究教學吸納了「問題解決」和「探究學習」的特點，但又具有自身的特色：

其一，從學科本身來講，中學歷史學科探究教學並不特指某種形態的綜合課程的開設，也不是從根本上取消學科分類，而是要從以學科為中心分解知識教學，轉到以學科為基礎或支撐進行問題探究教學，必要時還會就涉及多學科領域的一個主題進行多學科視野、多角度的教學，發展學生的思維，增強問題意識和探究精神。

其二，中學歷史學科探究教學中的「問題」主要是在學習中，教師不是給「結論」，告訴問題答案，而是挖掘、引發不同質的疑問和想法，使其互相碰撞，進行探究，加以解決。這種「問題解決」具有很大的相對性、限定性，同杜威等學者所指的「實際生活經驗的情境中形成問題」不同，與人文學科專家發現並解決的問題也不同。

第三，中學歷史學科探究教學是通過對問題探究的過程，強調人文學科知識、思維能力、正確的情感態度價值觀三者的結合。

在分析了歷史學習的特點和學生的歷史學習心理特點的基礎上，我們歸納出了歷史學習過程模式在操作層面的含義，歷史學習過程應是學生在

教師的引導和幫助下，通過體驗和探究為主的主動性學習，增進歷史智慧，提升人文素養的過程。其結構模式如下圖。

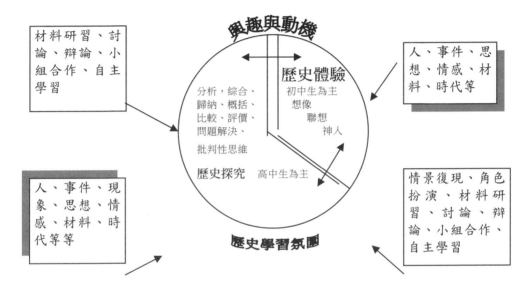

圖 1　歷史探究學習過程結構模式

　　我們認為，歷史學習體驗與探究過程分為內隱與外顯兩個作業系統。其內隱系統如圖所示，如上所述是心智活動，而外顯系統即學生的心智活動通過自主學習和合作學習的方式，將體驗與探究的行為表現出來，如體驗過程可以通過參與角色扮演等活動體驗古人，通過討論將個人的體驗和大家交流、分享。

　　從學生的年齡差異、心理的不同發展水平出發，考慮初中、高中歷史學習任務的不同，我們認為，初中生應以體驗性歷史學習為主，通過對形象直觀的材料的研習和學生喜歡參與的活動，拉近歷史與學生的距離，激發其參與歷史的情感，為進一步學習奠定基礎。高中生應隨著年級的升高，逐步過渡到以探究性學習為主，學會批判，學會多角度、理性的看問題，較合理、客觀地評價社會現象和歷史人物、事件，提出自己的見解。

　　從構成歷史學習過程良性循環的條件看，首先是內在動力，學生在學習上要有可持續發展的興趣和熱情，否則體驗和探究難以進行。再就是良好的學習氛圍，即營造一個和諧、民主、寬鬆、開放的學習氛圍，創設能激發學生對歷史對象感知、想像、聯想、神入、思考的空間和環境。

（二）中學人文科學學科探究的教學設計及其實施

　　教學設計是運用系統方法分析教學問題和確定教學目標，建立解決教學問題的策略方案，試行解決方案，評價試行結果和對方案進行修改的過程。[8] 簡單說，教學設計過程可以歸結為解決三個問題，即「要做什麼」、「怎麼做」和「怎樣判斷已做的事情」。依據教學理論，教學設計過程包括相繼完成的四個環節：(1) 明確並陳述教學目標，解決第一個問題；(2) 分析學習任務；(3) 選擇教學方法與教學媒體，這兩個環節是針對第二個問題的；(4) 評價學習結果，是回答第三個問題的。

　　參照以上教學設計理論，結合文科探究的特點，我們認為，中學人文科學學科探究的教學設計應包括：第一，探究主題或問題的選擇；第二，分析探究任務，確立教學目標；第三，選擇探究方法與教學媒體；第四，探究過程指導；第五，評價學習結果。

1.分析學習內容，選擇探究主題

　　學習內容，是指為實現教學目標，要求學習者系統學習的知識、技能和行為經驗的總和。作為教師，在進行探究教學設計時，對學習內容進行分析，關鍵是探究課題的確定，換句話說就是確定的課題是否具有可探究性，是否有可探究的空間和條件。探究始於問題。由於問題可分為結構良好問題與結構不良問題、或聚合思維問題與發散思維問題、或常規問題與

8　烏美娜：《教學設計》，高等教育出版社 1994 年版，第 11 頁。

非常規問題，因此問題探究的形式也可分為兩類，一種是以學生自主探索為主的探究學習，即由學生自己設計並控制學習的整個過程，包括選題、蒐集信息、處理信息、組織探究、得出結論和展示研究結果等等，教師在其中的作用為參與、指導、幫助。另一種是在教師指導下學生在學習新知識中的探究學習，即主要由教師組織教學過程，師生通過查閱資料、創設情境、研究討論等而進行的學習。儘管這兩種方式在教師的指導程度、學生的參與程度、問題的難易度與複雜度、活動的形式甚至理論基礎等方面有諸多不同，但它們是統一連續體上的兩點，並不相互矛盾，而是相互補充，分別適用於不同的教學內容，而且具有共同特徵，那就是：問題應該具有一定的真實性和複雜性，即不是過於簡單化的習題，而是保留了現實實踐情境的基本特徵的問題，具有較高的思維價值。另外，這種問題應該具有可拓展性、可挖掘性，即問題可以隨著學習者的探究的深入而不斷深化，一個層次上的問題解決了，新的問題出現了。學習者可以不斷確定新一階段上應該聚焦的問題，使得問題的自然延展與知識的生長過程合二為一。

從具體情況看，又可分為兩種，一種是教材中規定的學習內容有一定的難度，也就是說學生現有的認知結構和認知方式無法直接同化吸收這一難度的知識，必須採用探究式學習的教學模式，幫助學生調整、改造自身的認知結構和方式，以便在新知識和自己已有認知結構之間建立內在聯繫，將新知識真正內化到自己的認知結構中去，正確理解知識。適合開展探究式學習的內容是本學科領域的核心內容。運用探究式學習使學生真正掌握了對學科來說具有核心和基礎地位的那些概念和規律性的知識，就等於掌握了該學科知識的主幹，形成了擴充和擴展自己知識結構的能力；適合開展探究式學習的內容是對提高學生的應用能力、學習能力和生活能力具有重要價值的內容；適合開展探究式學習的內容是難度適合於學生的年齡特點和能力水平的內容。

　　另一種信息或者知識雖然在教材中有所體現，但是散落在各章節中，但與現實有著種種聯繫，教師要善於發現這樣的內容，啟迪學生的思維，鼓勵學生質疑，生成探究的問題。例如，清朝前期出現的「康乾盛世」長期以來為史家所稱譽。然而，「康乾盛世」之後僅四十多年，鴉片戰爭的炮火就轟開了中國的大門，中國落入被動挨打的境地。是什麼原因造成了如此戲劇性的大起大落？盛衰榮辱之間何以銜接得這樣緊湊？究竟應怎樣看待「康乾盛世」？「盛世」之下隱藏著什麼危機？課題組設計的《世界歷史上的「康乾盛世」》一課，引導學生把「康乾盛世」放到當時世界大背景下觀察、分析，使他們在科學認識封建「盛世」的基礎上，找到十七、十八世紀中國在世界上落伍的原因。當然更多情形是在常規課中如何進行文科探究，高中二年級《法西斯的擴張和反法西斯鬥爭的開始》一課的教學設計典型地體現了常規課中的問題探究。以往本課的設計是老師講述，如果老師口才好，課堂效果也會很精彩。但是文科探究更注重學生的參與、他們的所思所獲。於是，教師充分發掘相關的課程資源，如影視資料、歷史圖片、重要人物傳記等，使學生對歷史資料的豐富性、多樣性有所了解，嘗試著在學生已有的知識儲備的基礎上，鼓勵學生質疑。課上，同學們就 30 年代法西斯的侵略和反法西斯的鬥爭提出了許多他們感興趣的問題。比如：蘇聯同德國簽訂《蘇德互不侵犯條約》是對英、法等國禍水東引的報復嗎？德意日和英法美各自的戰略意圖是什麼？實力很強的美國為什麼也要推行綏靖政策？法西斯勢力和反法西斯勢力孰強孰弱？為什麼法西斯的陰謀能夠得逞？蘇聯為什麼要簽署《蘇德互不侵犯條約》？如何評價這個條約？西班牙政府的性質是什麼？蘇聯為什麼要援助西班牙？法國長期推行壓制德國的政策，為什麼也要推行綏靖政策？慕尼黑協定和慕尼黑陰謀有何區別？為什麼把慕尼黑協定稱作是綏靖政策的頂峰？等等。當然，一節課不可能把所有的問題都解決，問題也有主有次，不能面面俱到。面臨學生提出的這麼多的問題，老師還要善於引導學生從眾多的

問題歸納出核心問題，如這節課的兩個核心問題「反法西斯局部戰爭為什麼未能遏制第二次世界大戰的爆發」和「二十世紀 30 年代國際風雲的變幻帶給我們那些啟示」就是這樣產生的。

2. 對學習者進行分析，深入了解學生真實的情況

美國認知教育心理學家奧蘇伯爾曾指出：「如果我不得不將教育心理學還原為一條原理的話，我將會說，影響學習的最重要因素是學生已經知道了什麼，我們應當根據學生原有的知識狀況去進行教學。」[9]顯然，奧蘇伯爾是把對學生的了解看成是教學的出發點。在探究教學中，了解學生情況更為重要，其中尤為重要的便是學生的興趣和能力水平。再好的教學設計如不能激發學生的探究興趣，引起學生的積極思維，也不能取得理想效果。

我們認為，對學生的了解主要包括學生的知識基礎和經驗、思維狀況、態度和價值認識等方面。態度是學生學習的一個重要結果，在某種意義上可以說，態度對學生學習效果的影響要比認知大得多，這一點在人文科學學科中尤為突出。在我們選擇某一課題的教學中引導學生採取問題探究學習策略前，在學習態度上首先需要了解學生對所學內容的了解程度和興趣、愛好和需求，並尋因。二是學生對所探究問題的一些初步的價值認識。從發展心理學上講，學生在課堂學習前，並非白板一塊，已經具有富有個性的看法。了解了這些，有助於教師了解學生的自己產生的問題，而不是教材所規定的問題，不是教師主觀的問題，更不是為了提問題而提出的問題」。[10]因此，可以說對學生調研是教師進行探究教學的基本功之基本。

從方法上講，對學生的了解可以採取多種形式。如調查問卷，訪談，

9　轉引自吳文侃主編：《當代國外教學論流派》，p.207。

10　袁振國：《反思科學教育》，《中小學管理》，1999 年第 12 期。

過程觀察，作品分析等，為求調研結果的相對客觀，並具有代表性，幾種方法也可以混合使用。

案例：歷史學科網絡協作探究課「從第二次世界大戰爆發的原因看如何維護世界和平」的學前調查結果。

在開展這項研究前後，我們使用了和張建偉博士共同編制的學習狀況調查問卷。課前問卷內容包括：(1) 網絡學習狀況及感受：包括網絡學習的一般情況、網上協作探究學習行為、對網絡學習的評價及態度等，具體項目詳見結果分析部分。(2) 歷史課上計算機（電腦）使用的情況。(3) 學生對第二次世界大戰的興趣、認識等。

第一，學生每週上網時間、上網學習時間和上網用於歷史學習的時間。調查結果見表 1，僅有 23.9%以上的人每週上網時間在 4 小時以上，學生上網用於學習的時間在 3 小時以下的居多，學生上網進行歷史學習的則更少，由此看來，網絡學習仍有較大的潛力可挖。

表 1　學生每週上網學習（各科學習）和歷史學習的時間

	幾乎沒有	3 小時以下	2-4 小時	4-6 小時	6 小時以上
每週上網時間	7.0%	23.9%	33.8%	23.9%	9.9%
每週上網學習時間	22.52%	45.1%	29.6%	1.4%	0
每週上網歷史學習時間	45.1%	49.3%	4.2%	0	0

第二，目前在歷史課上使用計算機的情況。調查結果見表 2。更多的是教師使用它給學生展示歷史事物的過程，即使用電子展示稿進行展示。另一方面，在師大附中、匯文中學等教學設施較完備的學校學生自主網上學習也在逐步增強。

表 2　歷史課上計算機使用情況

在歷史課上使用計算機情況	是	否
1.多數情況下是教師使用它給我們展示歷史事物的過程	95.8%	2.8%
2.我使用計算機收集、組織和儲存材料	78.9%	19.7%
3.我用它寫報告和論文展示我的研究	71.8%	26.8%
4.我從因特網（網際網路）上收集信息	87.3%	11.3%
5.我使用計算機系統展示我的研究	77.5%	21.1%

　　第三，學生對歷史課採用網上學習的態度。我們讓學生在李克特式四點量表上評定感興趣程度（1.沒興趣 2.較沒興趣 3.較有興趣 4.非常有興趣）。下圖說明了學生的總體反應情況：

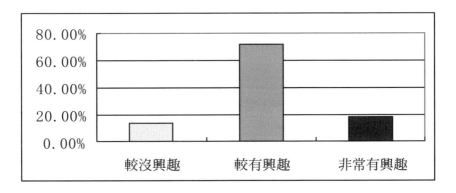

圖2　學生對歷史課採用網上學習的態度

　　首先，沒有學生選擇「沒興趣」。其次，有 14.08%的學生選擇「較沒興趣」，理由分別是：網上資料不典型，涉及面太廣；網絡資源缺乏可靠性；網絡需硬體支援，不太方便；不習慣非語言交流的方式，習慣常規教學方式；不能熟練使用電腦。再次，兩校有71.83%的學生選擇「較有興趣」，理由分別是：網絡探究內容豐富，形式活潑、新穎；有助於鍛鍊分析問題等能力；網絡交流平臺廣闊，不受限制；學生本人喜歡活動和創意；網上歷史探究能夠調

動積極性；網絡探究方便群體合作、交流；希望通過網絡探究提高閱讀、整理資料能力等。最後，有 18.3%的學生選擇「非常有興趣」，理由是：網上探究有吸引力，新穎有趣；增強表達、合作能力；網上學習可以調動積極性；有自由度和開放性，可以獲得更多信息；有時代性，打破了傳統的教學模式等。

第四，對第二次世界大戰的興趣、認識。從表 3 看，學生對二戰的興趣主要集中在以下八項，他們認為二戰戰役「震撼人心」，二戰的原因和影響「與當今關係密切，有借鑑意義」，戰爭內幕，各方態度政策「有意思，很神祕」，新技術在二戰中的運用「趣味性強」，二戰重要人物「是戰爭的重要發動力量、有爭議的人物、很刺激」，還有些學生想探詢戰爭心理和人性的善惡，等等。

表 3　學生對二戰感興趣的內容

對第二次世界大戰的興趣	百分比
1. 二戰的根源、背景	12.7%
2. 二戰經過	9.9%
3. 二戰重要人物	5.6%
4. 二戰戰役	35.2%
5. 二戰的原因和影響	28.2%
6. 戰爭內幕，各方態度政策	15.5%
7. 新技術在二戰中的運用	5.6%
8. 拯救猶太人、二戰中的大屠殺	2.8%

第五，探究第二次世界大戰爆發的原因的意義。從圖 3 看，學生對此的主要想法主要有四個方面，其中持有認為該探究「可以研究如何避免世界大戰再次發生，可以給人警示作用」的學生居多，達到 78.87%，認為「沒有意義」的學生僅有 2.81%。

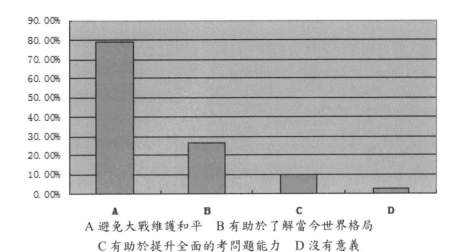

A 避免大戰維護和平　B 有助於了解當今世界格局
C 有助於提升全面的考問題能力　D 沒有意義

圖3　學生對探究二戰原因意義的認識

　　根據調查，對學習者的研究給予我們在教學設計上的參照主要是：在教學設施較完備的學校學生自主網上學習也在逐步增強；多數學生對採取網上探究的學習方式比較感興趣；大多數學生對第二次世界大戰這一歷史事件比較感興趣，對二戰戰役、二戰的原因和影響感興趣的同學相對比例較高；學生對探究二戰爆發原因的價值集中在關注今天如何避免戰爭，維護世界和平上。

3. 教學目標的確定（情感態度價值觀、技能與方法）

　　從學習方式來講，探究學習不同於與農業社會相適應的接受學習，或與工業社會相適應的有意義的接受學習，它是與當今「後工業社會」相適應的學習方式，關注培養思維能力，特別是創造性思維能力的方法和途徑，以及正確的價值觀、人生觀和世界觀的形成，其功能在人文學科學習中表現得尤為突出。人文學習不是靜觀意義認識，而是內在的體驗與直接認同，對其的理解在一定程度上意味著知情意身心的介入。在這樣的學習過程中，學習者是否掌握某個具體知識並不重要，譬如是否清楚地記住秦

始皇統一六國的時間和措施、「光武中興」指的是什麼等等，關鍵是能否會蒐集、整理和運用與學習相關的材料，在正確觀點的指導下，去觀察事物、發現問題、分析問題和解決問題，並在其間，有所悟、有所得，逐漸形成正確的觀念和認識。也就是說，探究學習是利用探究、發現的形式，注重的是在學習過程中促進學生的發展，或者說，其學習的過程本身就是它所追求的結果。

需要說明的是，第一，在確定目標上要注意中學歷史學科探究的教學目標應該是具有整體性、連續性的目標體系。學生中學畢業時要達到的最終目標在課程標準中有明確規定，而其分解可由任務分析按兩個維度進行。例如，高中歷史問題解決的教學目標，橫向可分解為中國近現代史、世界近現代史等各分支的目標，縱向包括各學期、階段、章節、課目標等。教學目標尤其是課目標忌籠而統之，比如「關心祖國和人類的命運，培養愛國主義情感和開放的世界意識。」作為一節課的目標就顯得大而空，應用觀察、測量的語言明確陳述學生學習後應習得解決什麼問題的能力或技能，以及達到什麼水平。

　　案例：初中歷史課《尼雅文明消失探謎》。
　　在本課中我們所強調的並不是讓學生記住在兩漢時期在絲綢之路曾經繁榮一時的綠洲之國──「精絕國」的所在地──尼雅文明的輝煌成果，我們在探究教學目標上是這樣確定的：
　　知識方面：通過大量精美而獨特的考古文物圖片，了解在兩漢時期在絲綢之路曾經繁榮一時的綠洲之國──「精絕國」的所在地──尼雅文明的輝煌成果。通過學生分組討論，初步認識尼雅文明消失的原因。
　　能力方面：利用已經掌握的地理、歷史知識，根據教師提供的相關材料，得出結論的能力。在討論的過程中體驗解決歷史問題的

基本方法和過程，培養合作學習的能力。

態度情感價值觀方面：通過了解尼雅文明輝煌的成果的過程，培養學生對歷史文物考古產生濃厚的興趣。探討尼雅文明消逝的自然和政治、歷史原因。使學生對那些消失的文明感到遺憾的同時，進一步思考和總結其消失的原因，產生一種心靈的震撼。進一步探討尼雅文明消逝給後人留下的啟示。使學生從歷史中看到現實。在討論和探究的過程中，培養學生與他人合作學習和認真傾聽別人的發言的學習態度。

4. 教學方法和教學媒體的選擇

我們認為，不應簡單將探究教學視為一種教學形式，還應該是一種教學思想與原則；不應獨立於常規的教學過程與學習過程之外，等同於活動課、或綜合實踐活動；也不應是教學的「十八般武藝」，即各種「時尚」方法的聚合。我們的思路是：學習的過程應是探究的過程，應圍繞要探究的問題，從以學生發展為本出發，採用適宜的多種教學形式與方法，包括閱讀、必要的講授、討論等。借鑑國外探究的方法[11]，我們對歷史探究作了這樣的分類：從探究涉及的學科來分，中學歷史科學探究可分為單學科探究和文科綜合探究；從探究問題的性質來分，可分為主題探究和問題探究；從信息技術與探究教學的整合程度看，可分為以多媒體課件為展示為主的問題探究和基於網絡環境的網絡探究和網絡協作探究。

(1) 問題探究

在中學歷史探究的教學方法中，最主要、最基本的是問題探討法。這裡的「問題」是指需要通過研究討論加以解決的矛盾、疑難，它是探究的起點和驅動力。材料無言，一則材料可以通過不同的方法提出不同的解

---

11 鄭流愛：《美國中小學歷史教育中的"探究"》，載於《課程。教材。教法》2005 年第 9 期。

釋，關鍵要看我們提出的是什麼樣的問題。從啟發探究的角度，問題可以分為事實性問題、反思性問題和理解性問題三種。事實性問題導向信息積累，反思性問題導向價值判斷，理解性問題導向思維的聚斂或發散。這三類問題都是同樣重要、不可或缺的，因為事實、價值觀和思維都是歷史學科學習的目標所在。問題探究也包括網絡探究，儘管教學條件不盡相同，但探究的本質是相同的。

案例：《中國近代前期鐵路建設延誤原因的探究》（北師大良鄉附中）。

本課的出發點是通過教學方式的轉變，改變學生的學習方法，教會學生學習的方法，培養學生終生學習的能力。鐵路建設是近代化的標誌之一，是西方資本主義國家侵略中國的產物。中國近代鐵路的發展是中國近代化的一個縮影，中國近代前期鐵路建設的艱難曲折印證了中國的近代化是被延誤的近代化。研究近代前期中國鐵路建設延誤的原因，可以從一個側面反映中國近代化被延誤的深層原因。分析近代前期鐵路建設被延誤的原因，深刻領悟與時俱進，順應世界發展潮流的重大意義。本節課在設計上，結合學生認識從感性上升到理性的規律，在錄像、網絡和書籍構成的豐富學習環境下，學生通過各種途徑收集資料、分析資料，取得結論，拓展思維，提升認識，培養學生分析整理資訊、重新構建知識問題的能力，

(2) 主題研究

除了問題探討，較為常見的方法是主題研究，主題研究是問題探究的變式和拓展。歸納起來，主要有以下幾種。

· 調查性探究：如在歷史學科中調查地方文化中各民族的貢獻，調查某一地區在不同時期的歷史變遷，追溯一些歷史遺存曾發生的歷史故事，

採訪社區成員，了解其人生經歷等。

案例：文科綜合主題探究　《新時期中國城鎮化問題探究——以良鄉地區為例》（良鄉附中）

主題選擇思路：城鎮化是一個國家和地區社會經濟發展和生活方式的重大轉變過程。它反映了人類社會歷史的演進，從歷史角度看，是重大歷史現象。從現實角度看，城鎮化也是我國進入現代化建設新時期面臨的一個現實問題。因此，探究城鎮化問題，引導學生思考人與社會發展的關係，具有很強的人文性和社會性。我們住在城鄉結合的地區——北京房山良鄉。良鄉作為北京市衛星城，正在加快城鎮化建設。學生現實生活中遇到許多問題，我們決定讓學生以良鄉地區為例，通過各種社會調查實踐活動，了解良鄉城鎮化及其相關問題，通過各種途徑收集資料、分析資料，取得結論，拓展思維，提升認識。結合我國當前社會發展所遇到的問題和學生生活實際，引導學生探究人與社會發展的關係。

教學設計：在第一階段學習中，教師將城鎮化這一開放性問題通過「腳手架」引導學生經歷體驗專家的思維過程，將項目計畫打碎成三個片段，讓學生能夠繼續鑽研相對單一的任務；通過拼切小組合作方式，讓學生能夠進行充分的交流。引導他們通過研究中相對困難的步驟，從而能夠運用他們的知識。教師從學生個性出發，依據不同學生的實際能力，將全班同學劃分為四個小組。即歷史沿革組、個案研究組、宏觀問題研究組、理論政策研究組。學生在良鄉地區進行社會實地考察，對居民進行問卷調查，對區政府職能部門進行歷史訪談等多樣化的學習活動。學生在活動中收集城鎮化問題的學習資源，在開放式學習情境中感悟、體驗、理解城鎮化。然後，根據城鎮化衡量指標，學生從不同角度提出了良鄉城鎮化的有關問題。課堂上四個小組

的代表利用信息技術展示了各組的初步探究結果。各組彙報完後，師生用《城鎮化問題學生探究活動評價表（一）》對各組的探究結果進行評價。教師引導學生看網頁上的「討論區」，課前全體同學提出的良鄉城鎮化存在的問題。師生共同整合這些信息，歸納出良鄉城鎮化的問題集中在三個點上：即生態環境問題、居民生活質量問題、人口素質問題。

在第二階段學習中，依據同學們對問題的興趣和初步探究，全班同學又重新劃分為四個探究小組。即生態環境問題研究組、人口素質研究組、居民生活質量研究組、綜合研究組。前三個小組分別集中研究三個焦點問題中的一個問題。綜合研究組從整體上思考以上三個問題，要對各組同學的解決方案質疑、補充，還要整合各組同學的結論，形成良鄉城鎮化未來發展的整體方案。

· 設計性探究：如在歷史學科設計國家、州或地方的歷史時間表；以歷史事件為背景創作戲劇活動；用活頁、卡通和社評等形式來強調某一歷史主題，等等。

案例：編輯歷史小報：我眼中的解放戰爭——初二年級歷史課跨學科探究實踐活動（中國人民大學附中）。

這次活動自 04 年 11 月初開始，到 12 月底基本結束，歷時近兩個月。初二年級共十二個班，602 名學生，本次活動是全員參與。每班分為五個小組，各自獨立完成一份報紙的製作，最後全年級共創辦 60 份報紙。

學生們對這次活動是這樣評價的：

「……有一句出自肺腑的話，感謝老師和學校為我們提供了一次這麼好的學習和鍛鍊的機會。」

「……真是其樂融融！我相信，這將是我們難忘的一次經歷！……非常感謝老師能給我們這一次機會！」

「……其實我們從小學一直到現在，這樣的辦報活動也不僅僅只有這一次，但我覺得這次辦歷史小報是規模最大、工程最完善的一次。」

「……我非常喜歡這個活動，提高同學們的合作能力和知識。謝謝老師辦了這次活動！」

通過這次活動，學生不但了解了更多有關解放戰爭的歷史，尤其是關於經濟和文化等課本上介紹較少的知識，而且對歷史課也產生了更加濃厚的興趣。學生們在總結中是這樣寫的：

「……在這次辦報活動中，我們的學習能力以及動手能力都得到了提高。我們通過上網查資料，對我國在解放戰爭時期的經濟和一些當時的內幕，都有了更深入的了解，並且產生了濃厚的興趣。……」

(3) 網絡探究

網絡探究有三種形式，一種是教師和學生共同建立局域網，第二種是webqust 的形式，第三種是強調建立學習共同體、問題跟進的網絡協作探究。幾年來我們除進行了前兩種教學實驗外，還與清華大學張建偉博士合作，進行了網絡協作探究學習的初步嘗試。

網絡協作探究學習主要是受到了建構主義學習理論的推動，注重通過問題解決來學習，基於問題解決來建構知識。為了實現有效的協作探究學習，教師及教學設計者要採取有效的措施創建基於網絡的活躍主動的「學習共同體」(learning community)（或稱為「學習社區」）。所謂學習共同體即由學習者及其助學者（包括教師、專家、輔導者等）共同構成的團體，他們彼此之間經常在學習過程中溝通交流，分享各種學習資源，共同完成一定的學習任務，因而在成員之間形成了相互影響、相互促進的人際聯

繫。設計基於網絡的學習共同體應突出解決好以下問題：[12]第一，主題任務的設計。第二，學習資源設計。第三，交互工具的設計。知識論壇正是這樣一種為支持學習共同體持續的交流協作活動介面友好的溝通工具。知識論壇是一種網上論壇工具，它採用類似 BBS 的形式為學習者建立了一種網上共享知識空間，按照「視窗」(View) 來組織「短文」(Note)，學習者在討論過程中可以通過建立新視窗和新短文來貢獻自己的想法，也可以對其他參與者的短文進行瀏覽和再加工，比如修改、發展、建立鏈結、組織成不同的視窗 (View) 等，為觀點的互動、發展、鏈結、注解、參考引用等提供了強大的條件。

具備了網絡協作探究的理論與平臺，如何在人文社會科學學科運用，以及如何就具體問題進行探究，我們的研究思路是，在信息技術與學科教學不斷整合的今天，我們不否認目前普遍使用的演示型課件在人文社會科學學科教學中的必要作用，但也不應忽視其在教學的開放性、生成性、互動性上的缺憾，特別是受線性思維的限制，難以反映教學中探究問題的延伸與跟進，而採用網絡協作的方式可以引導學生深入研究問題有效地解決存在的問題。

為追求教學的有效性，我們在問題的選擇上出於這樣的考慮：它應是學生感興趣的歷史問題；它應具有豐富的學習資源來支持；它應具有複雜性，體現了歷史事物發生、演變的影響因素的複雜性，而學生在探究時不是一眼看穿問題的真相，而是需要高水平思維的參與；它應與現實有著一定的聯繫，人們對它的探討能閃爍出人文智慧的光芒。

下面以北師大附中和匯文中學兩校高二年級文科班進行的以「從第二次世界大戰爆發的原因看如何維護世界和平」為例，說明我們對網絡協作探究學習教學實踐的嘗試。

12　張建偉：《試論基於網路的學習共同體》[J].《中國遠端教育》2000 專輯。

　　探究問題的選擇：2005 年是第二次世界大戰——世界反法西斯戰爭勝利六十周年。人類在二十世紀打過兩次世界大戰。在新的二十一世紀裡人類還會打世界大戰嗎？當今全球的戰爭與和平前景將是怎樣的呢？在人類進入新世紀的時候，人們紛紛從不同方面和不同角度回首過去，展望未來，探索人類在新世紀的發展趨勢，其中就包含有關戰爭與和平的問題。[13]當今史學界對第二次世界大戰研究的新視角為我們設計本課探究學習提供了新的視野，以及有價值的探究空間。

　　教學設計及實施：在對學習者研究的階段上，我們的教學過程包括以下幾個階段：

　　第一階段為初步查找資料。在 2004 學年寒假期間，每位同學可以利用自己方便的查閱方式（上網、圖書館、書店等）查找有關第二次世界大戰的資料（包括文字、圖片、視頻等），要求盡可能豐富、詳盡，並經過整理。在查閱資料的過程中注意提出問題並做好記錄。

　　第二階段學生通過「知識論壇」（該論壇為加拿大多倫多大學的 Marlene Scardamalia 和 Carl Bereiter 教授及其課題組研製），利用一個月的時間，發布自己的觀點和資料，利用「寫短文」等形式把自己查閱的資料和初步的觀點發布上去，還可以昇華、評價、質疑他人的資料和觀點。在這一過程中要充分關注、利用對方同學的資料和觀點。教師則利用這個平臺提供資源，對學生的探究交流學習過程及時進行監控、調整和評價。

13　邸文：《中國第二次世界大戰史研討會綜述》，〈世界歷史〉2002 年第 2 期；李巨廉：《戰爭與和平歷史運動的轉折——一個中國學者對第二次世界大戰的思考》，《史學理論研究》2005 年第 3 期；劉邦奇、梁瑞紅：《第二次世戰史研究會 2004 年學術研討會綜述》，《世界歷史》2005 年第 4 期。

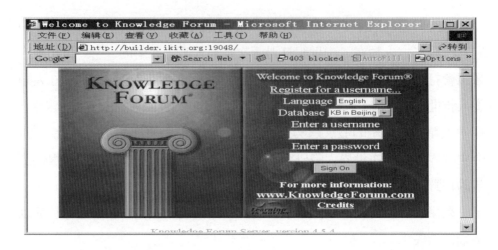

　　但是，僅僅依靠網上的探究是不夠的。為了避免當前在信息技術與教學整合方面存在的「只重技術，忽視人文」、「只見機器，不見師生交流」的偏向，以及實現「問題是學生在學習中自然生成的真問題，而非教師預先設定的」這一問題探究的基本理念，我們注意在教學設計及實施中注意將網上協作探究與「面對面」的探究有機地結合起來，即在第三階段問題生成和分組研究階段，在前兩階段上網的基礎上，利用一課時的時間，師生進行面對面的交流，達成共識，即對二戰爆發原因的探究可以從與其相關的幾個因素或方面，即「法西斯國家」、「英法美等資本主義國家」、「蘇聯」、「其他國家」、「國際組織」五個方面分組進行探究。學生又轉入網上探究，以小組為單位對本組所涉及的方面繼續深入查閱資料，並將資料整理、分類，得出結論，發到「知識論壇」上。

　　第四階段是第二次課堂上「面對面」探究、基本完成探究任務階段。在這個階段，每個小組先發布自己的繼續探究成果，同時可以對其他小組的研究提出質疑；全班討論對如何避免世界大戰再度爆發、維護世界和平形成整體的認識。北師大附中先行一步，先進行了課堂探究，然後師生將其研究成果發到「知識論壇」上。匯文中學在實施這一階段探究的時候，充分利用了師大附中同學的錄像資料作為學習資源，在探究時避免重複北

師大附中的研究結論，而是對探究問題進一步深化。

在學生完成第四階段的探究活動後，我們對學生進行了後測，了解學生對網上協作探究學習的自我評價、對網絡應用效果的評價、對於歷史課採用網上探究的態度與探究表現、網絡使用效果的相關等。

又如地理學科北京工大附中分校的辛欣老師在講授北京市的工業、農業、商業一節內容時，採取了運用網絡啟發式自主學習的策略，為本節課專門策畫、製作了專題網站，網絡教學知識量豐富、可觀性強的特點將能充分滿足學生獲取農業知識的需要，其快捷、生動、互動性好的特點又能極大調動學生上課積極性。本節課通過策劃設立討論題、指導學生上網查閱資料、學生小組的合作交流、學生的探究成果展示等多個環節，立足於改進的傳統填鴨式的教學方式，倡導在教師的引導下進行自主的科學探究，有效實行了地理教學和諧開展，充分顯示了教學以學生為本的教育理念。

(三)對學生探究技能培養的研究

1.課題的提出與研究價值

技能是通過練習形成的按照一定的規則或程式順利完成某種智慧任務的能力。[14]技能被稱為程序性的知識，用於回答「怎麼辦」的問題，屬於學習能力的範疇。

時代的發展和歷史學科的特點提出了培養學生技能的要求。技能培養適應了知識經濟時代素質教育的要求。在基礎教育課程改革的具體目標中，明確提出培養學生處理信息的能力，精選終身學習必備的技能，使學生學會學習。技能的培養成為學習方式、教學內容、教學目標三個層面中的重要內容。技能培養也是歷史學科特點的要求。歷史學科最大的特點就

14　《教育心理學》，上海教育出版社 1997 年版，第 59 頁。

是過去性。客觀的歷史事實本身無法重演，也不可能借助實驗加以再現。人們只能憑藉前人遺留下來的文字、圖像等形態的資料了解歷史。掌握獲取處理歷史信息的技能是學習、認識歷史的基礎。

二十世紀八、九十年代，中學教學改革中，在克服單純傳授知識傾向時，注意到學科能力的培養，一批培養歷史思維能力的論著問世，而有關技能培養尚未引起足夠的重視。自 2000 年高考文科綜合能力測試啟動以來，由於獲取處理綜合信息試題的出現，技能問題受到關注，但僅僅局限於解決特殊題型的應試訓練。脫離了素質教育的應試技能訓練，不僅隱含著把生動的歷史公式化的危險，削弱了歷史對學生正確價值觀形成的作用，而且使技能培養失去了原動力、完整性和發展性。

從理論和教學的層面對技能培養進行深入的研究，把技能的培養作為系統工程，落實在課堂教學中，能有利的推動素質教育。首先，掌握獲取和處理信息的技能，是發現問題，利用已知的條件，發掘未知信息，解決問題的鑰匙，它有利於課堂教學以學生為主體的探究性學習的開展。其次，掌握獲取和處理信息的技能是培養創新能力的重要條件。創造力的培養和發揮，不僅需要思維力、想像力等智力因素，也需要多方面的技能。再次，技能的掌握有利於學生的可持續性發展。我們正處於「知識爆炸」的時代，掌握獲取和處理信息的技能，將為學生的終身學習奠定基礎。

2.研究的思路

歷史探究學習技能包括材料研習與運用、體驗與思考、合作與交流等方面（見附件：歷史學科探究技能和方法）。在實驗中我們集中研究學生探究學習的薄弱點，即歷史信息獲取和處理的學習技能，包括對教科書等歷史書籍的閱讀和理解、歷史知識的梳理和整合、對歷史事物的口頭表達與文字撰述等廣泛的內容。把研究的範圍鎖定於歷史信息獲取和處理的學習技能，包括文字、地圖、圖像、統計數據和網絡信息的利用等五類。引

導學生通過學生感悟、運用、歸納與概括、遷移等過程，學會歷史探究的
方法。研究的思路如下列圖示：

規則研究 ⟶ 技能與教材的整合 ⟶ 教學實施
- 方法滲透
  - 常規課的局部探究
  - 綜合性探究課
- 方法總結（技能方法總結課）
- 方法的遷移

（1）規則的研究

規則是人們在認識世界，發現各種事物內在聯繫的基礎上，得出的處
理某一類事物的一定的公式、法則、原理或定律等[15]。對規則的發現和概
括是培養提高學生技能的前提。在研究中，我們把歷史信息的獲取和處理
的基本的技能分為文字、地圖、圖像、統計數據和網絡信息的利用等五
類。分別對每一類技能的結構和思維操作規則進行了具體研究。

（2）技能與教材的整合

技能與教材的整合是培養提高學生技能的基礎。技能是在對具體歷史
問題的探究過程中逐漸培養形成的。有計畫地進行技能的培養和訓練需要
與各年級課程的具體內容進行整合。為此，我們根據教材對相關技能的培
養進行了整體設計。老師們各自負責本年級的教材，對每一節課用什麼資
料、解決什麼問題、培養什麼技能、如何達到目標等進行具體的設計。

（3）教學實施

教學實施是培養提高學生技能的關鍵。技能從思維規則轉變為支配學
生學習的相對自動化的行為，是複雜的循序漸進的過程。由於規則作為智
慧技能，學習的實質是學生能夠在體現規則的變化的情境中適當的應用規

---

15 《教育心理學》，上海教育出版社 1997 年版，第 103 頁。

則[16]，因此我們在教學實施中採取了發現式學習的方式。

第一階段，通過常規課對某一問題的局部探究或綜合性探究課，使學生對某一種技能或某幾種技能的規則有所發現有所感悟。第二階段，技能方法總結課。主要運用某一種技能探究有關的歷史問題，在專題知識探究與正確價值觀形成的過程中，完成對該種技能規則相對完整的概括。第三階段，在後續性的探究性學習中和階段練習中逐步實現技能的遷移。

3. 研究的成果

(1) 對獲取和處理歷史信息學習技能規則的研究

技能是學生能夠在體現規則的變化的情境中適當的應用規則自動行為。為了有利於學生掌握規則，經過研究，我們把對文字、地圖、圖像、統計數據等技能的規則劃分為不同階段的可操作思維過程，構建了獲取處理歷史信息的探究學習技能體系。

(2) 獲取處理歷史信息技能與教材的整合

技能的形成離不開對具體歷史問題的探究。技能培養和提高的系統工程，需要有計劃地落實在各年級的每一節課中。為了使技能培養與教材內容有機結合，以利於教師從全局出發，選擇每一節課以哪一方面的技能為突破點，考慮某一階段集中培養何種技能，我們對技能與教材進行了整合，根據教材內容對相關技能的培養進行了整體設計。

經過課題組老師的努力，目前已經完成了對高中《中國近代現代史》上下冊、《世界近代現代史》上下冊、《中國古代史》五本教材與技能的整合。對每一節課能培養哪些技能，運用什麼相關資料，如何設問引導學生等進行了整體設計。如《中國近代現代史》上冊第一章《清朝晚期中國開始淪為半殖民地半封建社會》的第一、二節課。

16　《教育心理學》，上海教育出版社 1997 年版，第 103 頁。

(3) 培養提高學生獲取處理歷史信息技能的教學

第一，在探究性學習中對技能的感悟。歷史教材中有大量的文獻資料摘錄、地圖和照片等，這些材料蘊涵著豐富的歷史信息。有意識的選擇其中的資料，補充其他的典型資料，精心設計問題，對教學中的某一問題進行局部的探究性學習，或對一節課的內容進行綜合性的探究學習，不僅有利於學生觸摸歷史，自己做出歷史結論，還可以使學生在獲得知識的同時，感悟和學習技能。

第二，技能方法總結課的創新

技能方法總結課，是選擇具有可探究性、時代性和新穎性的主題，運用某種形式的資料創設新的情境，主要運用某一種技能探究有關的歷史問題。課堂教學除了完成知識、情感態度價值的教學目標外，教師主要對有關技能進行歸納，使學生平時對技能的感悟上升為規則，把單個規則系統化為分階段有步驟的相對完整的規則體系。

案例 1：獲取處理地圖信息方法課的案例。

齊永茂、衛剛老師先後執教的運用地圖的探究性學習《上海：近代中國的縮影》，是一節有關上海近代史的探究課，也是一節歷史地圖學習技能的方法總結課。教師不僅有目的地擇取了有關的地圖資料，而且根據學生的認知水平，精心地設計了由淺入深地獲取處理地圖信息方法的突破點。課堂教學以「列強侵略」、「社會經濟」、「探索抗爭」為主線，學生依託地圖，在探究近代上海變化史實的過程中，經過探討「怎麼發現的？」進一步明確了利用圖例、注記（文字、符號）結合圖題，獲取有效信息，以及將獲取的信息放在特定歷史背景中結合所學知識分析說明信息的規則，並把單個規則系統化為分階段有步驟的相對完整的規則體系。

案例2：獲取處理漫畫信息方法課的案例。

張文燕老師執教的運用漫畫的探究性學習《冷戰面面觀》。是一節關於冷戰爆發原因和影響的探究課，也是一節歷史漫畫學習技能方法的總結課。教師有目的地擇取了不同社會意識形態國家的五幅漫畫，根據學生的認知水平，依據漫畫的特點，精心地設計了獲取處理漫畫信息方法的突破點。在課堂上學生依託漫畫，通過「發現了什麼？」→「怎麼發現的？」→「你是如何認識的？」的探究，從提取漫畫的表面信息，到分析漫畫的寓意，到歷史地辯證地認識漫畫反映的歷史，不僅促進學生多角度的思考冷戰，也進一步明確了從提取信息→分析寓意→闡釋信息的運用漫畫分析認識歷史的方法。

第三，遷移技能的測試

學生技能的形成和發展水平，需要通過階段測試進行評價。編製的試題需要創設新的問題情境，體現相關技能的規則。下面僅以《中國近現代史》上冊的有關試題說明。

例：有關漫畫技能的檢測題

觀察右邊作於 1912 年元月的宣傳畫，結合所學知識回答以下問題：

(1) 圖中「中華民國」，「國」字的寫法是「□」之中有一個「民」字。這是當時民眾創造的一個新字。如此構字要表達的含義是什麼？

(2) 指導辛亥革命的綱領「三民主義」中，最能反映這一創意
內涵的是哪一項？在「新三民主義」中對此有何發展？

有效的培養和提高學生的技能是一個系統工程。對規則的發現和概括
是前提，技能與教材的整合是載體和基礎，教學落實是運用、感悟、提升
技能的關鍵，後續性的探究性學習與階段練習是技能遷移不可缺少的環
節。在這一過程中需要注意：第一，更新教材觀念。技能是在對不同形式
不同情境資料的探究中體現的，因此教師應該重視教材中的地圖、圖片、
統計數據、典籍摘錄等承載的歷史信息，將它們作為以不同形式敘述歷史
的資料，作為探究的物件，而不僅僅是對教材內容的印證。還可以選擇適
合學生心理特徵的其他資料作為教材的補充。第二，更新教學觀念。避免
把知識作為絕對的真理傳授給學生。教學應呈現學科特有的方法，使學生
在探究的過程中獲取知識，發展技能、培養能力，同時受到正確價值觀的
教育，並發展學生的個性。第三，採取即時性探究。為扭轉學生在課餘時
間探究，課業負擔很重的局面，應充分利用課堂教學的主管道，採取即時
性探究。為此，在課前教師需要選擇具有探究性的材料，並精心組織具有
針對性的設問，依託資料，通過「發現了什麼？」→「怎麼發現的？」→
「你是如何認識的？」探究過程，使學生在獲取知識的過程中，感悟或提
高技能。

四、討論與思考

（一）學生的反應

檢驗教學實驗效果的關鍵在於學生的反應、成長與進步。我們通過問
卷、訪談、測試了解學生的反應，其結果可以概括為：

　　學生在知識與技能、過程與方法、情感態度與價值觀等方面都有一定程度的發展。

　　探究學習改變了課程教學過於注重傳授知識的傾向，強調形成積極主動的學習態度，使獲得知識與技能的過程成為學會學習和形成正確價值觀的過程。

　　本課題在探究學習的教學實踐中，將知識與技能、過程與方法、情感態度價值觀的目標三位一體地融合在學生的探究學習活動中，通過真正的「做」科學，學生既學到知識，又體驗到科學探究的一般方法，極大地激發了學生的參與探究學習的興趣，提高了探究能力，同時形成了正確的對待科學問題的態度。通過對學生的測評，結果表明參與教學實驗的學生在對探究方法、思維方式、與人合作、學習毅力與信心等方面顯著高於未參與實驗的學生。

　　(1) 探究學習促進了學生知識和技能的掌握。

　　教學實驗證明探究學習並沒有使學生掌握歷史基礎知識和技能受到影響，相反由於探究學習使絕大多數學生主動參與學習活動，充分調動了學生學習的主動性和積極性，體現了學生在教學過程中的主體地位，探究過程中學生之間的討論、交流，使學生對一些重要的歷史知識有了更加深入的認識和理解，從而達到了突出教學重點、突破教學難點的目的。我們對參加探究學習的學生進行的問卷調查發現 95.1%的學生認為：「探究學習可以擴大知識面，學到很多課本上沒有的知識。」

　　(2) 學生的課堂思維狀態發生了很大的變化，綜合運用知識分析和解決問題的能力、人文素養得到了增強。

　　我們對參與本課題探究學習教學實驗的實驗班和非實驗班學生的課堂思維狀態進行了問卷調查，比較如下：

表 4　實驗班和非實驗班學生的課堂思維狀態比較

在課堂上，你的思維大多數處在	實驗班	非實驗班
跟隨老師的要求積極思考	51.5%	40.1%
多數時間積極思考，偶爾跟不上老師的思路	39.0%	41.9%
對老師的講解不感興趣，常常走神	5.5%	9.3%
因老師講得太快了，雖然努力還是跟不上老師的思路	4.0%	8.7%

　　通過比較我們可以發現：參與探究學習後學生的思維方式發生了很大的變化。這主要體現在實驗班的學生在歷史課堂上，可以跟隨老師的要求積極思考的學生比例要高於非實驗班。

　　這次調查可以看出，課堂教學發生了變化，不僅傳授知識，還加強了能力的培養和訓練。以歷史學科為例，調查結果表明，大多數學生認為歷史學習促進了自己多方面能力的提高（見表 5）。在調查問卷中，「歷史學習是否促進你能力的提高」只有 18 %的學生回答「不明顯」。大多數學生認為，歷史學習有助於提高自己的感知能力、分析闡釋能力和運用表達能力。由此，我們可以看出，歷史教學正在改變只注重知識不重能力的教學傾向。

表 5　學生對歷史學習提高能力的反應 (%)

歷史學習是否明顯促進你能力的提高	不明顯	較明顯	明顯
感知能力	18.0	52.6	29.4
分析、闡釋能力	14.8	45.6	39.6
運用與表達能力	17.7	44.2	38.1

　　我們對學生參與歷史學科探究學習活動後的收穫進行了問卷調查，結果如表 6：問卷的結果顯示：學生參與本課題探究學習後學到了研究的方法，對歷史學習的興趣、合作能力等方面都有較大的提高，觀察社會的能

力也有所提高。由此可見，開展探究學習的教學實踐可以彌補傳統的「注入式」教學在能力培養方面的不足，教師通過創設導致學生認知衝突的問題情境，促使學生調動已有的知識和經驗，提出疑問和各種可能的假設，並實施探究，加以驗證，從而培養學生動腦和動手能力，激發學生的創新意識。在表達與交流過程中，教師有意識地鼓勵學生充分發表自己的意見，通過討論、爭議、歸納得出結論，培養了學生的表達、與人合作、分析解決問題等方面的能力。

表 6　學生參與探究學習後的收穫

參加探究學習活動後，你的收穫有那些	學生人數百分比
A. 學到了研究問題的方法	90.1%
B. 喜歡觀察和思考社會問題了	70%
C. 自己解決了過去解決不了的問題	54%
D. 學習的興趣增強了	65.8%
E. 敢於發表自己的見解，表達能力提高了	55.6%
F. 做事計劃性增強了	43.1%
G. 同學之間的合作加強	60.9%
H. 注意觀察身邊的事情和變化了	23.5%
I. 知道怎樣有創意地展示探究成果了	44.3%

通過本課題的探究學習，學生還了解了文科探究的一般方法。過去很多學生死讀書，遇到需要運用多學科綜合解決問題時茫然無措。現在，通過探究教學的「授之與漁」，他們學會了學習，體驗到了運用文科探究技能和方法解決問題的所帶來的成就感，進一步認識到文科學習的意義。

（3）探究學習使學生學習興趣、毅力、自信心、合作精神等方面發生了變化，促進了學生情感、態度和價值觀方面的變化。

我們對學生情感、態度和價值觀方面的變化進行了調查，調查結果如表 7。可見學生在社會責任感、愛國主義、正確的環境意識、積極進取的

人生態度等方面都有積極的變化。

表 7　探究學習是否促進了你在情感、態度和價值觀方面的變化

項　目	是	否
理解、熱愛中華民族的優秀文化傳統	95.7%	4.3%
祖國的歷史是由各民族共同創造的	96.0%	4.0%
社會責任感	88.9%	11.1%
正確的環境意識	91.0%	9.0%
文物保護意識	95.8%	4.2%
繼承發揚人類創造的優秀文明傳統，面向世界	94.7%	5.3%
求真、求實和創新的科學態度	89.7%	10.3%
進步的歷史意識	90.8%	9.2%
積極進取的人生態度	90.2%	9.8%
健康的審美情趣	86.0%	14.0%

　　我們還通過訪談等了解學生的切身感受。從學生的課後回饋看，對於這樣的學習方式，他們是十分歡迎的。有的學生說：「這是一種截然不同的學習方式，不再限於老師講、同學聽……，通過探究學習，不僅鍛鍊了我查找資料的能力，而且還使我更善於發現問題，並獨立地解決問題，我想，我會把學到的方法運用到平時的學習中去的……。」有的學生平時對歷史學習沒有太大興趣，通過探究學習，對學習有了興趣，她平時不願意在眾人面前講話，在探究活動中卻承擔了代表小組演講的任務，她是這樣談自己的感受的：「這樣的活動，使我的歷史學習產生了跨越式的進步，同時鍛鍊了口才，真是受益匪淺。」探究學習也增強了學生的合作意識。很多同學提到在遇到困難的時候，正是因為想到集體的榮譽，使自己增強了克服困難的勇氣，而且說通過探究學習活動，他們「懂得了什麼叫協作」。許多同學這樣表示：「在這階段的探究學習中，……我們靠我們的能力取得了成功──一次我覺得最值得炫耀的成功。我們還懂得了，我們應

該不斷的挑戰自我，戰勝自我。」

（二）提出探究學習的原則

通過課題研究與實踐，使我們對歷史學科探究教學提高了思想認識，取得了許多理論和實踐成果，特提出探究學習的原則和我們的幾點思考：

原則一：學習目標定向，以保證探究活動不是形式上的「熱鬧」，而是能夠達到實質性的學習效果。

原則二：以問題為基礎，強調問題的真實性和拓展性，即學習始於問題，而非結論。

原則三：以思想成長為中心，即學習過程中最主要的活動是高水平的思維，是思想的持續改進，而不是重複記憶。

實施探究教學最關鍵的在於問題情景的創設和設問的思維力度。探究問題或產生於現實生活中的真實情景之中，或產生於對閱讀材料的反思，或產生於課堂內外的某個衝突，總之探究問題具有一定的真實性，值得探究。探究問題能激發學生的好奇心和探究欲望，需要學生進行解釋並且能夠為學生所解釋，既考慮到學生已有的知識儲備、資源占有度和能力狀況。探究問題要讓學生集中在一個特定的問題上，以小事件、具體問題，以小見大，明確方向，有利於資料收集、問題解決、實現遷移。探究問題展示可採取更為豐富的手段，利用聲光電等技術，把學生帶入更加生動有趣的境界，增強學生的探究欲望。

原則四：創建學習共同體，即由學習者及其幫助其學習者（包括教師、專家、輔導者等）共同構成的團體，他們彼此之間經常在學習過程中溝通交流，分享各種學習資源，共同完成一定的學習任務。

原則五：評價融於過程，教、學、評應當一體化，而且要體現多元與發展的精髓。

提出探究學習的框架

即學習者應當先進入問題情境中，通過對資源的收集和處理，展開探究活動，經過反省性的思維，實現建構性的互動，取得研究成果並交流後，再進入下一個學習流程中。

(三) 思考與啟示

通過研究，我們認為：

第一，文科探究不同於理科探究。理科探究重在探求科學規律；文科探究，特別是歷史學科的探究，重在探求社會現象、歷史現象背後的原因，歷史經驗的總結與反思，重在人文精神的確立與人文素養的養成。因此，文科探究不適合硬搬理科探究的模式與方法。

第二，探究學習，不應簡單視為一種教學形式，更應該是一種教學思想與原則；不應獨立於常規的教學過程與學習過程之外，等同於活動課、或綜合實踐活動；也不應是教學「十八般武藝」，即各種「時尚」方法的聚合。我們的思路是：學習的過程應是探究的過程，應圍繞要探究的問題，從以學生發展為本出發，採用適宜的多種教學形式與方法，包括閱讀、必要的講授、討論等。

第三，探究教學應是教學—學習—評價整體化的過程，其中評價是瓶頸。要改變長期以來將評價割裂於學習過程之外、將評價等同與終結性考試的觀念與行為。發展性評價應融於學習過程之中：診斷性評價應注重了解學生的「前認知」狀態、情感狀態，這是進行探究學習的基礎；過程性評價重在評價學生在探究學習中的表現，如圍繞學習任務的信息蒐集與處理，探究的過程，研究成果的展示，以及學生之間的合作等等；終結性評價要突破現有紙筆測驗中的過於強調「知識覆蓋面」、試題內容偏重記憶、形式呆板僵硬的弊端，在評價內容上要創設情景，不但應當向著知識、能力、情感與價值觀三方面有機結合的方向努力，還應注意學習方法

的考查。

第四，實施探究式學習離不開必備的學習材料、設備以及現代化的學習手段。探究式學習是一種基於資源的學習。在學習過程中，伴隨著情境性問題的產生與假設驗證過程地不斷深入，學生需要了解各種不同的具體信息，這些信息往往不可能預先準備，甚至對學生來說會十分陌生。為解決問題，就需要學生通過各種途徑盡快搜尋與問題解決相關的信息，現代信息技術以其豐富的資源、友好的介面、交互的環境、多樣的展現形式等優勢滿足了探究式學習的需要。為此，教師必須為全體學生提供一定的背景信息，使參與探究的每一位學生都有同一起點的理解水平；教師必須準備數量充足的材料，使每一位學生都有機會使用材料開展探究活動；教師必須能擁有和支配學習資源，使自己不僅能夠選擇出最適合的材料，而且能決定利用資源的時間、地點和方式。

第五，探究教學對教師的角色作了重新定位。突出強調教師的指導作用，在具體的實施過程中教師要處理好「扶」和「放」的關係，要在探究計畫的設計、教學材料的選擇與組織、教學活動的安排、教學過程的指導等方面作深入地思考和實踐。

附件：

歷史學科探究技能和方法

1. 材料研習和運用

(1) 運用地圖等工具

●觀察地圖，知道其特點和功能；

●借助圖例，提取相關信息；

●運用地圖信息，說明歷史問題。

(2) 學習圖表和表格

●知道不同種類的圖表（示意圖、線條圖、條形圖、柱狀圖、餅狀圖等）和表格；

●讀懂圖表和表格所呈現的信息；

●根據學習任務需要創造適用的圖表和表格。

(3) 閱讀理解教科書和課外書

●區分事實和觀點；

●發現和理解主要思想；

●了解歷史事實和文學作品的區別。

(4) 區別和運用第一手材料和第二手材料

●知道材料的種類，第一手材料和第二手材料的區別；

●讀懂材料，了解材料內在的意義；

●運用材料有理有據地論證問題。

(5) 利用統計資料

●讀懂數據；

●知道甄別數據資料的可靠性；

●利用數據資料提出或解決問題。

(6) 解釋圖片和圖畫

　　●描述、解釋圖片和圖畫呈現的主要信息；

　　●能以圖片和圖畫的形式說明解釋問題。

2. 體驗和思考

(1) 角色扮演

　　●收集、閱讀材料，體驗和感受所承擔的角色；

　　●能通過角色扮演加深對所探究問題的認識。

(2) 聯想與想像

　　●認識事物之間具體的聯繫或關係；

　　●依據材料再造或形成新形象。

(3) 分析因果關係

　　●能夠區分不同類型的原因與結果；

　　●理解原因與結果的多樣化和複雜性；

　　●能夠獨立地進行原因與結果聯繫的分析。

(4) 比較與分類

　　●能發現社會現象間的相同點和差異性；

　　●能根據異同將事物區分為不同種類。

(5) 歸納與演繹

　　●知道從個別的事實中歸納出一般的原理；

　　●能從一般原理推理出關於個別對象的結論。

3. 合作與交流

(1) 小組調查

　　●知道調查的種類及其功能；

　　●能夠擬定調查題目和調查計畫；

●會記錄、收集調查資料並進行分析，撰寫調查報告。

(2) 訪談

●能根據調查的目的擬定訪談計畫；

●能依據計畫進行訪談並及時做好記錄，撰寫採訪稿進行交流。

(3) 辯論和討論

●能收集、處理材料，撰寫辯論或討論的提綱；

●能參與辯論，有理有據地論證觀點和進行爭論。

(4) 撰寫研究報告

●會根據確定的題目收集、整理所需的材料；

●能擬定提綱和草稿，修改定稿；

●選擇自己感興趣且適宜的方式呈現報告。

主要參考文獻

皮亞傑:《人文科學認識論》,中央編譯出版社 1999 年版。

李稚勇:《社會科教育展望》,華東師大出版社 2001 年版。

歐陽康:《人文社會科學哲學》,武漢大學出版社 2001 年版。

朱紅文:《人文精神與人文科學——人文科學方法論導論》,中央黨校出版社 1994 年版。

靳玉樂:《探究教學論》,西南師範大學出版社 2001 年版。

烏美娜:《教學設計》,高等教育出版社 1994 年版,第 11 頁。

〔美〕羅伯特·D.坦尼森等:《教學設計的國際觀》第 1 冊,教育科學出版社 2005 年 10 月版。

張建偉等:《建構性學習——學習科學的整合性探索》,上海教育出版社 2005 年 6 月版。

John D. Bransford:《學習原理:心智、經驗與學校》,遠流出版公司 2004 年 11 月版。

〔美〕Ellen Weber:《有效的學生評價》,中國輕工業出版社 2003 年版。

Anthony J. Nitko, *Educational Assessment of Students,* Columbus, Ohio 2004.

Keith C. Barton and Linda S. Levstik, *Teaching History for the Common Good,* London 2004.

Leland Graham and Isabelle McCoy, *Social Studies Fail Project and Research Activities*, Incentive Publications, 2001.

Abstract

A Study on Students' Inquiry Learning of History

Zhang Jing

How is the issue raised

The results of Ministry of Education of China's 1997 survey on 2107 students in Beijing indicated that: the History class has been deemed by students as one of the "tedious and boring classes". This is an astonishing result, for it is now known that the History subject is rated rather low in the minds of students. This issue has been in existence for a long time due to multiple reasons, including not only those relating to the history education work itself but also those relating to our social environment. As far as the history education itself is concerned, the issue is generated not only from the fact that the focus on human being has been neglected in the curriculum, that the course objectives have been narrowly defined, that the faculty members put emphasise on intelligence rather than on morality, that the curriculum structure over-stresses the system of subjects, and that the content of the history classes is complicated, difficult, excessive, and old, etc., but also from the fact that the teaching philosophy is backward, that the teaching process is stiff, that the content of teaching evaluation is outdated and unilateral, and that in fact there is only one evaluation method used.

Since 2002 when the new round of curricula reform was initiated, some changes have been made, but the situation with regard to the history subject is less than satisfactory. In November 2003, we adopted the stratified cluster sampling questionnaire method to carry out the questionnaire-based survey and test on 3228 Grade VIII high school students within the city of Beijing, trying to first of all understand the students' attitude toward studying history, the students' ability to study history, the students' ways of studying history, as well as changes in the relationship between studying history and the students' sentiments, attitudes, and values, etc. Secondly, we tried to understand major factors that affect students' interests in studying history, including the teacher-student relations, teachers' attitude, and classroom teaching techniques, etc. Thirdly, we tried to understand the daily academic assessment methods on students, while at the same time we also conducted surveys and interviews on the 80 teachers who were instructing these students. Since 2004, through observing more than 200 History class sessions and working jointly with teachers to research the teaching activities at 90 History class sessions, the author has found some problems that included:

First of all, it is shown in the survey data that only 46.9% of students have an active attitude toward studying history, 39.0% of students answered "it is hard to judge or hard to say" to the question about "Attitude Toward Studying History", and there were 14.1% of students that showed a passive attitude toward studying history. The survey data indicate that there are still more than half of high school students that lack interest in studying history and cannot pick up learning actively and aggressively.

Secondly, the test results indicate that the students' ability to study history is low, which is primarily reflected in their ability to analyze, interpret, use, and represent their knowledge of history. First of all, for example, some students have a hard time to analyze historic issues or problems by defining them into a certain scope of history, i.e. confusing one thing with another. Some students have a hard time understanding text materials, i.e. are unable to effectively extract relevant information from the text materials to make relatively logical judgments. Other students are often confined focus mainly on details, i.e. are unable to identify correlations out of the substantial number of facts. Also, some students are not good at making precise representations.

Thirdly, it is indicated by classroom observations and in the student survey data that: after the curricula and textbooks were reformed, some changes have arisen in the students' approaches to studying history, i.e. we are now seeing new learning techniques such as discussions, debates, role plays, and literature studying, etc. But these new teaching methods are being used only once in a while, rather than consistently. The traditional "Teacher Talks, Students Listen" teaching method is still, for the time being, the teaching technique that is used by most teachers , the basic characteristic of which is "parroting the textbooks", where students' learning is mainly put to a passive mode.

Fourthly, when it comes to academic assessment of students, although we are now seeing new trends toward enhanced development and colorful diversifications like 'dossier bag assessment', performance appraisals, etc, the paper- and pen-based exams are still the main tool to assess and test students' memory of history knowledge, and teaching, learning, and assessment are isolated from each other.

Since the 1980's, utilizing inquiry learning as the foundation to rebuild basic educational curricula has become one of the major characteristics of curricula reforms in many countries around the world, thus driving both teaching and learning techniques to undergo significant changes. The inquiry model emerging from science education areas is also being extended to liberal arts teaching activities, where people start to pay attention to how to develop students' ability to explore and ponder over the nature of social life, especially the ability to think about their own lives and direction of social development. Looking at the research and development status of inquiry teaching of liberal arts subjects in both China and abroad, there are four aspects that we need to reflect: the teaching objective that focuses on developing students' research capabilities and building the humanistic spirit; the development of very systematic operating system for inquiry skills and methods to provide conditions for effective educating students' humanistic quality and inquiry capabilities; the focus on utilizing experience- and inquiry-based learning techniques; the emphasis on teaching evaluations with motivating, open, diversified, and developing functions, as well as more rational evaluation metrics and tools.

In order to improve History teaching activities and enhance students' understanding of history, we have, following the "A Study on Students' Mentality of Studying History and Instructional Countermeasures" project, conducted a series of studies on inquiry history learning among students, including: building the structure of inquiry history learning processes; teaching design and implementation of inquiry history learning; building and training of students' inquiry history learning skills and methods; academic assessment on students' history inquiries; inquiry learning and development of history teachers. The following is mainly the presentation of three of these studies.

Our Research

Based on the analysis of the characteristics of history learning and psychological characteristics of students in studying history, we have summarized the process model of inquiry history learning. Such model is comprised of two operating systems: the implicit system mainly deals with mental activities, while the explicit system handles students' ability to represent their experiential and inquiry behaviors via mental activities through means of autonomous learning and cooperative learning.

The instructional design of history inquiries should include: first of all, selection of inquiry topic or issue; secondly, analyzing the inquiry task and identifying teaching objectives; thirdly, choosing the inquiry method and teaching media; fourthly, mentoring during the inquiry process; fifthly, evaluating learning results. The realization of the abovementioned process has to be based on our understanding of students. Such understanding of students mainly includes such aspects of students as their knowledge base and experiences, mindset, attitudes, and cognitive values, etc, which can be obtained by using such techniques as survey questionnaires, interviews, process observations, and literature analysis, etc. History inquiries are preliminarily categorized into issue inquiries (e.g. the inquiry on the reasons on delayed construction of railroads during early contemporary era in China), topic inquiries (e.g. an investigation on changes in a region over different historic times —— the Liangxiang area in Beijing, for example, has been the target of A Study on Urbanization Issue in China during the New Age; publishing history tabloids —— The War of Liberation in My Eyes), and online collaborative inquiries. In online collaborative inquiries, in addition to organizing teachers and students to build the LAN, we also adopted knowledge forums to carry out follow-up inquiries on cross-region and cross-school issues such as The Second World War and World Peace, The Evolution of Schools in China during Modern Times, etc.

We have built the History Learning Skills System. Through experiments, we have focused on researching students' vulnerabilities in inquiry learning, i.e. the learning skills in acquiring and processing history information; by focusing on five types of information, i.e. texts, maps, images, statistics data, and online information, we guided the students to learn and master the inquiry history learning method via such processes as their comprehension, utilization, summarization, generalization, and migration, etc.

Conclusions

Inquiries into liberal arts subjects are different from those into science subjects. Science-aimed inquiries are focused on inquiring the laws of sciences; liberal arts-aimed inquiries, especially the inquiry into the history subject, are focused on the causes behind social and historical phenomena as well as the summarization and reflections of historical experiences, thus concentrating on establishment of the humanistic spirit and nurturing of the humanistic quality. The inquiry learning should not be simply deemed as a kind of teaching format, but should be recognized as a type of teaching thought and principle. Our idea therefore is as follows : the learning process should be one of inquiries, which should be centered on the issues we want to inquire into. It should be based on and for the growth of students, and should adopt multiple appropriate teaching forms and methods, including reading, necessary lecturing, and discussions, etc. The inquiry education should be an integrated process of teaching — learning — assessment, where assessment is the bottleneck. The development-focused assessment has to be implemented into the learning process, and enough attention has to be paid to the examination of learning methods. Inquiry learning is a type of resource-based learning, which cannot exist without the necessary learning materials, equipment, and modern learning techniques. Inquiry teaching has redefined the role of teacher by emphasizing the guidance function of instructors.

學科背景重要嗎？
——九年一貫社會領域的研究

宋佩芬* · 楊孟麗**

一、前言

　　九年一貫課程與教學的改革，其中一大政策是推動課程統整 (integrated curriculum)。對於課程統整的政策，學界有認同與反對的聲音。贊成者主要認為知識本身很難以學科劃分，了解知識的全面往往是跨學科的，因此主張以主題式的教學來整合知識 (Beane, 1997; Clark Jr., 1997; Drake, 1998; Forgarty, 1991; Jacobs, 1989)。反對者認為統整的教學往往忽略學科的特性，使知識無法深入 (Gatewood, 1998; Mansilla, Miller, & Gardner, 2000; Mason, 1996; Roth, 1994, 2000)。然而，二者其實都強調學科知識的重要性 (Beane, 1995)。九年一貫課程綱要的能力指標實際上即是學科的能力（宋佩芬，2003），也就是統整的教學必須帶出主題軸中的學科特色，如 Jacobs (1989) 所說，統整應符合學科的效度 (validity within the disciplines)。無論是分科或統整教學，教師都必須了解其學科的本質或特色，始能帶出能力指標中的能力，例如，社會領域「人與時間」軸（歷史）當中的「2-4-5 比較人們因時代、處境、角色的不同，所做的歷史解釋的多元性」；或「人與空間」軸（地理）的「1-4-2 分析自然環境、人文環

---

*　淡江大學課程與教學研究所暨師資培育中心
**　中央研究院人文社會科學研究中心

境及其互動如何影響人類的生活型態」（教育部，2000）。前者指出歷史學
科詮釋的本質，後者指出地理學科系統地理與人文地理的互動特色。

　　長期以來社會領域教師的學科背景對於教學的影響僅止於常識的判
斷，認為專業訓練背景一定影響教學知能。然而，這個假設其實並沒有實
證研究的證實，國內外社會領域亟少有學科訓練背景與教師教學知能的差
異研究。質化研究亟少 (Sung, 1999)，量化研究幾乎沒有，使得統整教學
的支持者容易忽略這個「常識的判斷」，不加以正視，而推動全面的統整
教學。而九年一貫課程改革目前實施的結果是學校並沒有實施統整的教
學，反而皆以「分科」與「合科」的方式進行教學（宋佩芬，2007），統
整教學的實施，事實上造成了不同專業訓練的教師必須負責同一領域內的
所有科目。九年一貫如果繼續朝統整的方向進行，我們就必須釐清是否不
同背景的教師具備教導能力指標所指涉的學科知能。

　　我們以社會領域中的歷史為例（人與時間軸），從教師的學科知識、
對於該學科的觀念，以及教學等三方面來看不同專業背景的教師在此三方
面是否有所不同，以對統整教學的政策提出建議。

　　以下第二部分，首先說明理論根據，接著介紹學科背景對於歷史知
識、史觀及教學之影響的實證研究，並以此建立假設。第三部分，說明使
用的資料及研究方法。第四部分先提供初步的統計結果，再依據假設進行
結果分析。最後我們依據分析結果作討論並提出建議。

二、文獻探討

　　本研究從教師的學科知識、觀念與教學三方面來檢視不同背景教師的
教學知能，原因是我們認為要有好的教學品質，教師不但需要有學科的內
容知識 (substantive knowledge)，也要有結構知識 (syntactical knowledge)
(Schwab, 1964)，以及了解知識本質之後的學科教學知識 (pedagogical

content knowledge) (Shulman, 1987)。

「內容知識」指的是了解該學科的主要概念工具(conceptual devices)，用以定義、規範範疇、分析學科內容的知識。以歷史（人與時間軸）為例，「內容知識」指的是歷史的重要事件以及影響其事件的原因。且知道歷史事件的因果關係，不同觀點下的詮釋。例如，臺灣的歷史老師應該知道中國史與臺灣史在史觀上的差異所造成的知識內容的差別（吳密察，1994）。

「結構知識」指的是知道該學科不同的探究方法，以及如何推論與證實結論，並解釋這些方法如何構成學科架構的知識，此為本文所指稱的學科觀念 (conception)。以歷史為例，具備結構知識的教師能分辨什麼是事實，什麼是詮釋，能夠判斷史料的可信度；結構知識愈清楚，愈能掌握學科的精神，即 Bruner 所倡導的掌握學科結構的教學 (structure of the discipline)，也愈能將學科思考的工具教給學生，不論學生屬於那一個學齡階段 (Bruner, 1960)。

教師要了解結構知識，必須認識學科的本質 (nature of history)，也就是歷史哲學的認識 (historiography)。歷史哲學處理什麼是歷史的問題。新的歷史哲學不再跟過去一樣強調政治、軍事史，而同時重視文化、社會、經濟等社會史與生活史，使得歷史不再只是某些人的歷史記憶傳承。正確的歷史理解是，所有的人、事、物都有過去，都是歷史 (Novick, 1989)，所以動、植物也有歷史，甚至於對於「乳房」也有人寫它的歷史 (Yalom, 1997)。歷史事實不會自己說話，事實本身不是歷史，歷史是需要被詮釋的 (Bailyn, 1994; Carr, 1961)，是一種藉由敘述 (narrative) 所寫出來的詮釋 (Levstik & Barton, 1997)。所有的歷史都是一種建構，所有的故事都僅是部分，總是未完成的，也總是隨著我們的思想行為而改變 (Tuchman, 1981)；因為當我們問不同的問題時，歷史就有可能被重新詮釋，或者新的資料出來增加或改變原來的解釋 (Appleby, Hunt, & Jacob, 1994)。而這

些歷史的證據，即史料，可以包括所有人類留下來的記錄，例如歷史文件、遺物、相片、遺跡、見證人、日記、戶口名簿、地圖等都可以被用來理解過去。

　　歷史的「結構知識」還包括歷史的思維能力。這些思維能力包括了解「事實與詮釋的差別」，強調「時序思考」、「因果關係」、「不同觀點下的不同解釋」以及「歷史同理的想像」(historical empathy) (Davis, Elizabeth Anne Yeager, & Foster, 2001; Wineburg, 2001)。美國 (NCHS, 1994; NCSS, 1994) 與英國（陳冠華，2001）的歷史課程標準十分強調教導歷史思維能力，甚至希望教導學生實作歷史。九年一貫能力指標受到國際課程標準的影響，也強調結構知識，人與時間軸中的「多重因果關係」以及「解釋的多元性」即是（教育部，2000）。

　　「學科教學知識」則是當教師掌握學科精神後，以符合思考工具的方法，將學習內容教給學生。因此，以歷史為例，教師為了使學生明白歷史的解釋有不同的觀點及不同的解釋，因此使用秦始皇的不同歷史評價，並問學生那一個歷史解釋比較正確；或在教學時強調學生能分辨什麼是史實 (facts)，什麼是歷史詮釋 (interpretation)。由此來培養學生「分辨事實與詮釋」，以及「歷史是詮釋的」歷史思維能力，即能力指標中的「歷史解釋的多元性」（教育部，2000）。

　　雖然有關於教師歷史教學與其背景的實證研究有限，仍然有部分研究已經鋪陳出有用的研究方向，這些研究皆指出學科背景的影響。以下我們分三方面探討學科背景對教師表現的影響，包括知識、史觀（即前述的結構知識）與教學。此三方面的研究彼此相關聯，但是仍然可以看到這三面向的不同。最後並根據文獻做成研究假設。

（一）學科背景影響歷史知識

學科背景影響教師的歷史知識的發現，可以從 Wilson & Wineburg

(1988) 的質化研究看到。他們研究四位分別具有考古人類學、國際關係與政治、美國研究，及美國歷史學位的老師。這四位老師從同樣的師資培育機構畢業，取得中等社會科教師資格，在舊金山灣區的不同高中教書。學科背景與訓練成了這些老師教學決定的重要因素。Wilson & Wineburg 發現人類學及政治學背景的老師，在對於歷史事實的理解、詮釋、時間的先後、事件的關係、前因後果皆呈現錯誤的理解，他們容易以考古人類學對事實是科學事實的看法，或政治學對政治與經濟的局部分析來看歷史，缺乏考量歷史整體脈絡情境 (context) 的認知習慣。其歷史知識的理解因此容易是錯誤的。人類學及政治學背景的老師被自己的學科認知框架控制住，知識因此沒有辦法被正確地吸收消化，而學科訓練背景是主要因素。

除了畢業科系影響一個人的學科訓練，所學習的科目也會影響他的歷史內容知識。一個人若僅接受傳統史觀，則其歷史知識便僅限於一般的通史，對於女性史、社會史等新發現的議題則不了解，影響其知識的深廣度 (Sung, 1999; Takaki, 1998)。這也是因為歷史的結構知識，會使教師吸收多元的歷史，因而產生比較多元的內容知識。

(二) 學科背景影響史觀

學科背景影響史觀，上述 Wilson &Wineburg 1988 年的研究，指出教師因不同的學科背景而對歷史有不同的本質性的了解，造成對歷史認知的不同，是此方面最直接的實證研究。

另外，本文第一作者所進行的個案研究發現，教師的歷史觀影響其教學。其個案顯示，受過社會史、女性史、口述歷史訓練或上過其他非主流歷史（如美國歷史與歐洲歷史之外的非洲史及墨西哥史，或亞洲及少數族群史）的老師，在理念上會懂得挑戰正統的歷史詮釋，懂得尋找多元的觀點 (perspectives) 及資料來源。而只受「正統」歷史課程的老師比較堅持美國史有一定的解釋，雖然認知有其他族群的歷史，但是認為正統歷史（主

要是政治與軍事史）仍然是最道地的歷史 ("straight history") (Sung, 1999)。
這個初步研究之後沒有大量的實證研究繼續。但是，Sung (1999) 似乎指出
若教師受過正統歷史以外的非政治軍事菁英的歷史，就可能傾向有歷史多
元的觀點與詮釋，直指歷史的詮釋本質。這個研究發現，同樣是歷史老
師，其歷史的訓練背景不同，史觀也不同。值得探究的是，過去臺灣僅有
中國通史的教學，臺灣史為禁忌的題材（吳密察，1994），教師若受過臺
灣史的訓練，史觀上是否能有學習非傳統歷史後的類似效果，本研究將臺
灣史列為一變項。

再一個實證研究，是在美國緬因州對 160 位歷史老師所做的問卷調查
及訪談 (Evans, 1989)，發現大多數的老師可以被歸類在「說書者」、「歷史
科學者」、「相對者／改革者」、「宇宙哲學觀」與「綜合者」五種類型之
中。「說書者」，強調灌輸知識，與強調歷史的文化知識；影響他們的主要
來源是歷史小說、電影、父母、對故事的著迷，及對祖先的興趣。「宇宙
哲學觀者」，因樣本太少無法綜合出影響因素。「綜合者」，綜合二、三種
不同對歷史的觀點，沒有主要的取向，歷史課學分修得很少，主要歷史觀
念影響來源是家人跟過去的老師。而「歷史科學者」，及「相對者／改革
者」，在史觀上，前者強調歷史的客觀與使用社會學科探究方法，從史料
來發現真相，多角度來看歷史，不強調一種歷史詮釋；後者認為歷史幫助
了解現在的問題，沒有所謂的客觀的歷史，認為歷史有立場，認為歷史應
該要指導現在人的決定。「歷史科學者」及「相對者／改革者」之史觀相
對於其他類型的教師而言，其觀點較接近目前的歷史哲學認知，而這兩種
類型的教師皆受到過去大學教授的思想激發，凸顯學科訓練背景的影響。

背景影響史觀的其他判斷依據是，一般歷史系的學生都必須接受「歷
史方法」的入門課（如史學導論、史學理論、史學方法），進行有關「什
麼是歷史」的探討；歷史學界史觀的轉變 (Appleby et al., 1994; Novick,
1989)，對於有歷史訓練背景的人，也比較容易接觸得到。

（三）學科背景影響教學

　　教師除了具備內容知識與結構知識，仍然需要「學科教學知識」(Shulman, 1986)，即教師選擇合適的方式來連結學生經驗與學科本質。而方法是否合適就是「學科教學知識」的能力表現。許多老師主要考量的是如何讓學生覺得有趣，而非是否在引起學生學習動機的情況下帶出重要的學科性質。例如，歷史老師放歷史電視劇只是為了讓教學多元，甚至只是為了輕鬆，換個學習方式，卻沒有聚焦於歷史問題的探討──事實、觀點、詮釋、情境、因果。同時考量學生的興趣以及學科的基本觀念的「學科教學知識」，是教師專業能力的表現之處。重要的不是方法的「花俏」，而在於方法使用的「合適」上，是否培養具學科精神的思維能力。這方面的例子很多，歷史教育改革者為了使學生能學習歷史思維的能力，會採用第一手資料（「課文內或課外史料」）讓學生直接接觸證據，學習判斷歷史的解釋是否合理 (Kobrin, 1996; Tally & Goldenberg, 2005)；比較「其他二手資料」來評估不同的歷史解釋 (Lee & Ashby, 2000)；用「辯論」的方式使學生能夠進入史料，站在歷史人物的角度思考歷史 (Wilson, Shulman, & Richert, 1987)；說故事（含「講述」與「口頭問答」的方式），將歷史透過精彩的故事軸線鋪陳出來 (Brophy & VanSledright, 1997)。Wilson, Shulman, & Richert (1987) 發現教師只要能掌握學科的本質與目的，沒有一定固定的教學方法，教學方法可以是百變的。

　　除了選擇合適的教法之外，教學理論裡面強調的原則是：教學方法多元 (Good & Brophy, 2003)。一般而言，無論國內外，教師最常採用的就是講述法 (Goodlad, 1984)。多元的教學方法能夠避免無聊，活化教學。臺灣多數人的歷史學習經驗是聆聽教師講授課本內容，背誦整理歷史重點。九年一貫課程改革以後，教科書的編輯多了一些圖片以及思考問題，政策上也鼓勵教師多元教學，因此本研究檢視不同背景的教師是否採用多元歷史

教學相關的方法。

　　歷史學科的訓練背景，有可能使教師的教學不一樣。這個轉變很慢，因為從 1960 年代歷史哲學的改變，到新的史觀在美國大學裡面占有一席之地，穩定開設口述歷史、女性史、社會史等多元課程，已經是 1980 年代以後的事了 (Hu-DeHart, 1993)。等到對臺灣有影響，也必須要等到 1990 年代，如臺灣史研究系所的成立（吳密察，1994；Chang, 2008）。之後，大學的通識課程開設比較多樣的歷史課程，如口述歷史、思想史、經濟史、臺灣史等課；學生撰寫報告，也開始重視過程中學習蒐集資料、觀點內涵的思考，並用多元的方式呈現（喻蓉蓉整理，1999）；歷史學者、教科書撰寫者及教育者，開始討論起什麼是歷史，歷史教育應如何的問題（余玥貞等整理，2000）。東吳大學歷史研究所在 1998 年的方法論國際研討會中已經注意到英國與德國等國家的歷史教學研究，並期望對臺灣有些檢討（張元、周樑楷編，1998）；這種對歷史教育的期望持續在歷史學者間進行中（戴寶村，2000）。

　　這些現象表示，歷史訓練在改變中，大學開始開設包含臺灣史的多元歷史以後，教師的專業訓練開始與過去不同。歷史系背景者比一般人容易接受到新的歷史方法與哲學的探討，也比較容易接受到多元歷史的課程。另外，大學歷史課程的不同也表示，歷史教師若年資越輕，越有可能受教於新思潮，而有對歷史本質有比較正確的理解（如，歷史不是只有一個），其歷史知識可能因而比較正確（因為掌握不止單一的解釋），教學也比較能培養歷史思維。

　　從以上文獻觀察，歷史學科背景對於教師的歷史知識、史觀及教學極可能有深切影響。而此影響必須以實證檢驗。因此，本研究問題是：社會領域教師的背景（畢業科系、上過的課程）是否影響教師的歷史知識、史觀與教學？研究的假設是：

假設一：有歷史專業背景的人，比沒有歷史專業背景的人，前者歷史知識比較高，史觀比較正確，教學比較好（強調歷史思維能力及教學方法多元者被視為教學比較好）。

假設二：受過歷史訓練的人，比沒有受過歷史訓練的人，前者歷史知識比較高，史觀比較正確，教學比較好（歷史訓練包含 1.修過「歷史方法與哲學」的課程或受過「歷史是什麼」的訓練；2.上過女性史、口述歷史、殖民史、庶民史[1]等類「非傳統課程」；3.上過「臺灣史」）。

三、研究方法

(一) 研究對象

本研究於 2005 年 2 月至 6 月間對全國公私立國民中學，私立 10 所，公立 708 所，共 718 所學校之社會領域教師進行普查。正式問卷寄送前，逐一針對全國公私立國民中學進行電訪查詢各校社會領域教師人數，計 5,285 人，共郵寄問卷 5,285 份，寄送正式問卷一個月後，對於未寄回問卷之學校進行電訪及郵寄的問卷催收，再次寄送、催收問卷。有效樣本 2,429 份，回收率 45.96%。

回收的 435 所學校中，430 所為公立學校，5 所為私立學校，大致符合公私立學校母群體比例。依區域分，北部學校占 32%，中部 20%，南部 36%，東部 9%，離島 3%，符合母群體比例（表 1）。專門科目背景上，歷史老師占 40.5%，地理老師 31.9%，公民老師 22.3%，國文老師 4.0%，其他 1.3%。由於教育部沒有分科老師的人數統計資料，樣本代表性僅能從一般學校歷史老師較多，公民老師最少（國文老師配課公民）的經驗法

---

[1] 此四項非傳統歷史僅為舉例。1960、70 年代以後歷史的多元涵蓋了文化、經濟、勞工、環境、心理等各式各樣的歷史 (Appleby et al., 1994; Kessler-Harris, 1990)。

則判斷，應仍然大致符合母群體比例。

表 1　樣本與全國公私立國中學校分布

地區	北部	中部	南部	東部	離島	總和
縣市	臺北縣 桃園縣 新竹縣 苗栗縣 基隆市 新竹市 臺北市	臺中縣 彰化縣 南投縣 臺中市	雲林縣 嘉義縣 臺南縣 高雄縣 屏東縣 嘉義市 臺南市 高雄市	宜蘭縣 臺東縣 花蓮縣	澎湖縣 金門縣 連江縣	
樣本校數	139 (32%)	86 (20%)	156 (36%)	40 (9%)	14 (3%)	435 (100%)
全國校數	255 (35%)	136 (19%)	238 (33%)	67 (9%)	24 (3%)	720 (100%)

（二）研究工具與變項

本研究問卷共分成五部分。第一部分為基本資料。第二部分為歷史觀點（史觀），共五大題。第三部分為歷史知識，共分臺灣史 21 題，中國史 23 題。第四部分為該校九年一貫教學實施現況，共 11 題，並沒有在本論文中使用。第五部分為歷史教學，僅給教過歷史的社會領域教師填答，共六大題。

本問卷建立內容效度的方法是，擬定初稿之後，分別請大學歷史系中國史及臺灣史教授各二位，檢視歷史知識題題目是否正確與是否適合國中教師的程度，而不會過度艱深。由於中國史及臺灣史內容涵蓋為國中歷史通史的範疇，因此一般大學歷史系教授皆可成為審題專家，但是因為題目當中亦包含社會史的部分，因此中國史及臺灣史各兩位專家中皆有一位為社會史（含女性史、生活史、科技史）方面專長，以確保問卷不同的內容面向可以得到好建議。審查結果，其中有 2 題被認為過於深入，不容易令

國中教師判斷，經建議換為比較合適的題目。整份問卷於專家審查後，對
三位歷史、二位地理、二位公民老師做認知訪談，並根據教師建議修改背
景問題 3 題，確定教師對於內容的理解認知與出題者相符。專家及教師建
議都僅一次。

　　以下說明各項出題項目或原則：

1.自變項

　　(1)專門科目背景：分為歷史、地理、公民、與國文等背景（樣本中
有非社會科的教師，是因為他們常被配課教授社會領域的課程）。專門科
目背景包含教師之大學畢業科系、最高學歷畢業科系、具雙主修或輔系學
歷，或具備專門科目教師資格。有以上背景中的任一項，都被視為有該科
的專門科目背景；因此一位教師可能有不只一種專門科目背景，例如某教
師是大學國文系畢業，並具有歷史學碩士，則他同時具有國文及歷史的專
門科目背景。之所以如此粗略的歸類，是因為受歷史訓練的各種經歷不一
而足（例如，有人只是具有歷史的教師專門科目資格，有人只是歷史輔
系，有人是歷史研究所，有人在大學和研究所都是歷史系，等等），如果
一一加以歸類，可能造成複雜、混亂。而且，以如此粗略的分類，如果還
能發現具歷史背景的教師比其他完全沒有歷史背景的教師在知識、史觀和
教學的得分顯著更高，就表示專門科目的背景，整體而言，對於教師的教
學具有相當重要的影響。

　　(2)歷史訓練：以三方面來檢驗教師受訓練的背景因素，分別是 a.歷
史方法與歷史哲學訓練，分為修過課，自行閱讀過，及沒有受過訓練；b.
非傳統歷史，分為修過課，自行閱讀，或沒有受過訓練；c.臺灣史，分為
有上過課或沒有。這三類課程因為和史觀及對歷史本質的理解有關，因此
以其為訓練的指標。將臺灣史分別出來而沒有包括在第二項中，是因為臺
灣特殊的國家認同狀況，臺灣史極可能具備非傳統歷史的特點，即具有挑

戰傳統史觀的效果。

2.依變項

(1) 歷史知識

研究在「學科知識」上以中國史及臺灣史的題目來測試教師的「內容知識」。國中歷史教學包含臺灣史、中國史及世界史，本研究捨棄世界史而僅以前二者為歷史知識的代表，主要是因為題數已經很多（中國史與臺灣史共 44 題），擔心更多的題目會使填答教師失去耐心，影響回收率，且認為臺灣史及中國史為所有歷史教師皆須具備的基本知識，有內容知識的代表性。

問卷出題原則有幾方面：a.以教科書及教師手冊涵蓋的國中內容範疇為主（南一，2003a、2003b、2004a、2004b；康軒，2002a、2002b；翰林，2002）；b.除了政治、軍事史外，涵蓋女性、社會史，如，「太平天國在制度上，提倡男女平等，婦女可以應試、作官、參軍等」；c.題目除有教科書版本的解釋，亦有歷史學界的新詮釋，以測試教師對於歷史是否掌握新的或不同的解釋：如，「鄭成功立志反清復明以臺灣為根據地，再圖發展」，及「鄭成功統治臺灣手段應當歸類為一種『殖民地統治』」；d.題目出現教科書沒有的細節，如「明鄭經濟活動是走私與海上冒險集團的成果」，或傳統的謬誤觀念，如「秦始皇殺了許多讀書人，也就是我們一般所稱的『坑儒』」，以測試教師對於歷史事件了解的深度與廣度；e.以史料為題幹，測試教師對於史料的判斷，如，「從洪秀全說：『妻道在三從，勿違爾夫主，牝雞若司晨，自求家道苦』，是洪秀全主張提升婦女地位的論點。」總共設計臺灣史共 21 題，中國史 23 題。每小題組約 5-6 題，中國史共有秦代與秦始皇、科技史、太平天國、鴉片戰爭等四題組。臺灣史有明鄭與鄭成功、原住民、臺灣社會、日治與現代化等四題組。

各題以「非常同意」、「同意」、「不知道／沒聽過」、「不同意」、「非常

不同意」選擇。由於題目已避免史學界爭議仍大的歷史解釋，各題均有標準答案，分析時視答案為何，答對者，如「非常同意」與「同意」（或「不同意」、「非常不同意」）給 1 分，「不知道／沒聽過」與答錯者給 0 分。加總計分後，分數越高者，歷史知識越高（最高 44 分，最小零分）。內部一致性 Alpha = 0.89 (Crocker & Algina, 1986)。

(2) 史觀

以史觀測試教師是否具備歷史素養的題目分為三大題：a. 什麼是歷史，選項含「動物、植物歷史」、「各國的歷史」、「人物的歷史」、「乳房的歷史」四項，可複選。加總計分，分數越高者，對歷史的認識越正確；b. 什麼是史料，測知教師對於歷史資料的認識，包括「兵馬俑」、「史記」、「日記」、「報紙」、「戶口名簿」、「相片」、「地圖」、「帳簿」八項，可複選。正確答案是全部都是，加總計分後，分數越高者，對歷史的認識越正確；c. 歷史本質的了解，共十題。問填答者是否同意該說法，如，「每一個人都有歷史」，「政治史是最重要的歷史」、「歷史事實自己會說話」，選項為「非常符合」、「還算符合」、「不太符合」、「完全不符合」。每一項依目前歷史哲學的想法 (Appleby et al., 1994; Novick, 1989)，依正確度給 4、3、2、1 分。加總計分，分數越高者對歷史的本質了解越符合目前歷史哲學的發展。此三大題組相關係數約在 .7 及 .75 間，我們將三者加總，作為測量史觀的變項。

(3) 教學

教學部分只針對教過歷史的老師，約占回收問卷 64%（其中歷史老師占 58.9% 人，地理 20.86% 人，公民 14.65%，國文 4.1%，其他 1.4%）。教學方法分為兩部分，第一部分（教學 I）主要測量教師是否強調歷史思維能力的培養，第二部分則詢問教師是否使用多種教學方法（教學 II）。教學 I 強調歷史思維能力的培養主要有兩題：a. 教師教學強調那些歷史思維能力的培養（能分辨事實與詮釋、時間脈絡、不同角色的不同觀點、不

同詮釋、歷史同理的想像），共 5 題，每題依程度（經常、常、不太常、從不），以 3、2、1、0 計分，故量表可能的得分範圍是 15 分到 0 分；b. 老師自己評估學生學到以上這些能力的程度如何。同樣 5 題，每一題依程度（完全學到、還可以、不太熟練、還不會），以 3、2、1、0 計分，故量表可能的得分範圍是 15 分到 0 分。另外又以教師是否使用多元教法（教學 II）來檢視其教學良窳。我們詢問教師，上學期使用了那些教學方法，選項包括「講述」、「口頭問答」、「分組討論」、「角色扮演／歷史戲劇」、「閱讀課本附錄的史料」、「接觸課外史料」、「比較其他二手資料」、「辯論」、「看影片」、「做報告」、「其他」等 11 選項。可以複選。每勾選一項得 1 分。加總後，得分高者，教學方式比較多元。教學固然無法以教學方法多寡來決定教師教學的品質，教學方法多元仍然是好教學的指標之一 (Good & Brophy, 2003)，由於選項皆為歷史相關的教學方法，教師若能採用講述與口頭問答之外的方法，則可被視為一種教學的進步。

3. 控制變項

學歷與年資可能影響教師的教學知能，為本研究的控制變項。學歷作為變項，是因所受智性訓練不同，對知識本質 (epistemology) 比較了解，教師可能藉由找資料與自行閱讀與研究等方式，無論教什麼科目都能使自己具備應有的知識與教學能力。

年資作為變項，是因一般認為年資高者，教學經驗豐富，對於教學內容掌握應該比較多，也應該比較能使用適合的方法教學。然而，年輕的教師可能比較容易接受到新的史觀訓練以及上過非傳統史觀的課程，對於歷史的認識可能比較正確與多元；教學則因為接受新的師資培育，可能比較願意嘗試新的教法。這兩種觀點所指出的方向剛好相反，且都有可能，顯示年資的重要性。

(1) 最高學歷：分大學以及研究所。

(2) 年資：分 3 年以下，3～5 年，5～10 年，10～15 年，15～20 年，20 年以上。5 年以下分為 3 年以下以及 3～5 年，是因為可以藉此比較細分新手教師與有經驗的教師，從實習到剛教書的 2～3 年為教師生涯中的學徒階段 (apprentice phase) (Steffy, Wolfe, Pasch, & Enz, 2000)。

(三) 資料分析方法

本研究使用線性迴歸法分析。依變項有歷史知識、史觀以及教學。歷史知識為中國史及臺灣史的加總。史觀為三大題目之加總。教學則分為教學 I 及教學 II，前者代表教學強調歷史思維能力的訓練，後者代表教學方法多元。

四、分析結果

(一) 變項初步描述

表 2 整理出具有各學科背景者的比例。如前所述，由於一位教師可能受過兩種學科的訓練，表 2 所顯示的人數比實際的樣本數稍多。從表 2 看到，本次的樣本，具有歷史學科背景者所占比例最高，超過 40%。具有地理與公民學科背景的教師，則各占約三分之一。國文教師常常配社會領域的課，所以樣本中有國文老師，約占十分之一。

表 2　學科背景人數表(N=2,429)

科目	歷史	地理	公民	國文
人數 (%)	1,034 (42.6%)	833 (34.3%)	802 (33%)	250 (10.3%)

註：因為部分教師具備一種以上專長背景，所以總數比總樣本數多，且比例和原樣本專業教師比例，稍有不同。

　　歷史知識與史觀的填答者為所有社會領域教師，將這兩依變項的遺漏值扣除後，樣本數為 2,180 人，而教學 I 與教學 II 之填答者為教過歷史之社會領域教師，扣除遺漏值後，樣本數為 1,418 人。表 3 顯示各教師間在歷史知識、史觀、及教學 I 與教學 II 上差異頗大。歷史知識 1 分者幾乎皆為非歷史背景者。教學 II，最小值為 1，這些教師大多使用講述法為其教學方法。

表 3　各依變項的平均數與標準差

	樣本數	最小值	最大值	平均數	標準差
歷史知識	2,180	1.00	40.00	25.1101	7.6198
史觀	2,180	23.00	60.00	41.0179	5.1558
教學 I	1,418	1.00	30.00	16.4076	3.9852
教學 II	1,418	1.00	10.00	3.8808	1.6265

　　表 4 顯示，歷史背景的教師，上過「歷史方法與哲學課」、「非傳統歷史課」及「臺灣史課」的比例，都遠高於非歷史背景的教師。非歷史背景的教師，並非全然沒有接觸過這些課程。自行閱讀「歷史方法與哲學」的歷史背景老師及非歷史背景老師人數相近；自行閱讀「非傳統歷史」的歷史背景者教師為非歷史背景者的 1.7 倍。這部分的樣本數扣除遺漏值後，共有 2,391 人回答。

表 4　歷史背景與是否上過歷史方法、非傳統歷史課、臺灣史的人數 (%)

	歷史方法與哲學課		非傳統歷史課		臺灣史課	
	歷史背景	非歷史背景	歷史背景	非歷史背景	歷史背景	非歷史背景
上過課	820 (80.9)	176 (12.8)	270 (26.7)	90 (6.5)	766 (75.6)	599 (43.5)
自行閱讀	81 (8.0)	87 (6.3)	249 (24.6)	147 (10.7)	NA	NA
沒上過課	112 (11.1)	1,115 (80.9)	494 (48.8)	1,141 (82.8)	247 (24.4)	779 (56.5)
總和	1,013(100.0)	1,378(100.0)	1,013(100.0)	1,378(100.0)	1,013(100.0)	1,378(100.00)

表 5 顯示歷史知識、史觀以及教學 I 與 II 的相關係數。教師本身的學科知識有顯著相關 (.278)；教學 I 與教學 II（教法多元）的相關也類似 (.260)。教學 II 和教師本身的學科知識（無論是內容或結構知識）相關雖較低，也都在 .20 左右；但教師本身的學科知識（知識和史觀）都和他要讓學生學到的思考能力（教學 I）沒有相關 (-.007)，或非常低的相關 (.093)。這些關係，一方面初步顯示內容知識與結構知識的確有關，及知識與教法之間有相關，但另一方面也透露了目前以考試取向為主的升學環境對於歷史教學的內容的影響：由於國中歷史教學仍然以考試為前提，所以老師沒有強調思維能力的培養。雖然如此，教師不同的學科背景仍然對於教學有分別的影響，將於以下分析中呈現。

表 5 四個依變項的皮爾森相關係數

	史觀	教學 I	教學 II
歷史知識	.278** (N=2,180)	.093** (N=1,418)	.203** (N=1,418)
史觀		-.007 (N=1,418)	.199** (N=1,418)
教學 I			.260** (N=1,418)

註：教學部分由教過歷史的老師填寫，其中包括歷史老師占 58.9%人，地理 20.86%人，公民 14.65%，國文 4.1%，其他 1.4%。 *p< .05；**p< .01

（二）迴歸分析結果

1. 測試假設一的迴歸分析

本研究假設一為：有歷史專業背景的人，比沒有歷史專業背景的人，前者歷史知識比較高，史觀比較正確，教學比較好（教學方法多元及強調歷史思維能力）。

迴歸分析結果顯示（表 6），具歷史背景者，其在歷史知識、史觀及教學上都顯著較佳，符合假設一。在歷史知識上，地理、公民、國文背景的係數皆為負，表示非歷史背景的老師，他們在歷史知識上顯著不如具有歷史背景的教師。在史觀以及教學表現上，歷史以外背景的係數仍然多為負或數值小且不顯著。顯示歷史學科背景影響教師的歷史知識、歷史學科觀念與教學。

表 6　測試假設一的迴歸結果

自變項＼依變項	歷史知識	史觀	教學 I	教學 II
常數	24.290 (.508)	42.4857 (.380)	16.088 (.393)	3.471 (.158)
歷史	7.127 (.412)***	1.922 (.308)***	1.210 (.317)***	.715 (.127)***
地理	-.843 (.438)	-.173 (.328)	-.250 (.359)	-.057(.144)
公民	-.833 (383) *	-.288 (.286)	.076 (.277)	-.059 (.111)
國文	-.009(.486)	.121 (.364)	.015 (.366)	-.045 (.147)
學歷—研究所	.461 (.379)	1.328 (.283)***	.297 (.287)	.494 (.115)***
年資	-.571 (.083)***	-.741 (.062)***	-.145 (.063)*	-. 029(.025)
R 平方	.260	.096	.027	.061
使用樣本數	2,180	2,180	1,418	1,418

教學 I 是強調歷史思維的教學；教學 II 是以多元方法教學。*p< .05；**p< .01；***p<.001

控制變項方面，學歷方面，具研究所學歷，對於教師的歷史知識及教學 I（強調歷史思維的教學）上並無顯著影響，但是學歷較高，對史觀及教學 II（多元教學）上則有顯著正面的影響。

年資在歷史知識、史觀及教學三個迴歸分析的係數均顯著為負，顯示年資越高，則歷史知識得分愈低，對史觀的認知愈不完整，教學愈不重視歷史思維，但對教學多元的負面影響則不顯著。支持之前對於年資的預想——年輕教師因為受到新的史學訓練，而知識較佳，以及可能受到新制師

資培育及教育改革的影響，而願意進行比較有挑戰性的教法。

2. 測試假設二的迴歸分析

假設二：受過歷史訓練的人，比沒有受過歷史訓練的人，前者歷史知識比較高，史觀比較正確，教學比較好。

迴歸分析結果顯示（表 7），上過「歷史方法」課，受過歷史哲學訓練的教師，以及上過「非傳統歷史」課程或自行閱讀非傳統歷史課的教師，其歷史知識較高，史觀較正確，教學較重視歷史思維與使用多元方法。上過「臺灣史」的教師，其歷史知識高，教學顯著重視歷史思維訓練。分析結果基本上符合假設二。

「自行閱讀」歷史方法與哲學的教師，其歷史知識與史觀分數雖顯著，從係數上發現，大約是上過歷史方法課的一半；而在教學上，不論是方法的多元或教學注重歷史思維，「自行閱讀」歷史方法或哲學者則都沒有產生加分的作用。方法或哲學的書，大多比較抽象，也許比較需要學有專精的大學教授指導，而史學導論與史學方法等「歷史方法」課是歷史系的必修課，歷史專業背景者比較有機會接觸到，因此修過這門課對於教師的教學有幫助；而「自行閱讀」的理解程度有限，可能因此對於應用於教學方法與課程的精神助益有限。

接觸過「非傳統歷史」者，無論是上過課或自己閱讀，在歷史知識、史觀及教學上都顯著較佳。這表示「非傳統歷史」挑戰了教師對於歷史本質的認識，增加其歷史知識的廣度，也促進其教學上的多元，幫助其教學上強調歷史思維的訓練。這類的歷史透過「自行閱讀」即可產生對歷史不同的理解，其衝擊與效果甚至高於「臺灣史」對於教師的影響。

上過「臺灣史」之教師，其歷史知識較高，教學比較重視歷史思維的訓練，但是在史觀的認識上並不顯著高於沒有上過臺灣史者。可能的解釋是，「臺灣史」不若女性史等「非傳統歷史」挑戰政治與菁英的傳統史

觀。「臺灣史」的教學可能亦若中國史，強調自己的正統，並且大多仍從政治史著手，故教師的史觀並沒有因而更開闊。然而，上過「臺灣史」的教師，在教學上顯著比其他教師著重訓練歷史思維。可能的原因是，歷史思維題目裡涵蓋的重點，例如，「分辨事實與詮釋的差別」、「強調不同角色對事件的看法」、「提供不同於課本的解釋」，由於上過「臺灣史」，教師可能對於這部分有深刻的意識，教師因而會用這些角度提醒學生，臺灣史觀與中國史觀的差異。

研究所學歷仍然在史觀及教學方法多元（教學 II）上有顯著正面影響。年資對在史觀則有顯著的負面影響，對於教學則幾乎沒有影響，也不顯著。與前表相比較，可能因為年輕人（年資較低）比較容易接受到「歷史方法課」與「非傳統歷史課」的影響，使得年資與接觸這些訓練的可能性之間有些重疊（共線性），因此當模型裡明確納入這些訓練時，年資在四個依變項的解釋力就變小了。

表 7　測試假設二的迴歸結果

自變項＼依變項	歷史知識	史觀	教學 I	教學 II
常數	21.192 (.415)	41.308 (.297)	14.998 (.310)	3.055 (.123)
上過歷史方法與哲學課	5.557 (.347) ***	1.614 (.249) ***	.767 (.254)**	.673 (.100)***
自行閱讀歷史方法與哲學	2.874 (.611) ***	.927 (.438)*	.007(.437)	.058 (.173)
上過非傳統歷史課	1.990 (.445) ***	1.888 (.319) ***	.877 (.294)**	.517 (.116)***
自行閱讀非傳統歷史	1.559 (.412) ***	1.261 (.302) ***	.836 (.279)**	.657 (.111)***
上過臺灣史	1.770 (.336) ***	.183 (.241)	.859 (.247)**	.055 (.098)
學歷—研究所	-.489 (.387)	.991 (.278) ***	.098 (.283)	.346 (.112)**
年資	-.066 (.091)	-.563 (.065) ***	.007(.065)	.029 (.026)
R 平方	.218	.119	.049	.107
使用樣本數	2,180	2,180	1,418	1,418

教學 I 是強調歷史思維的教學；教學 II 是以多元方法教學。*p< .05；**p< .01; ***p<.001

3.綜合迴歸分析

我們進一步將假設一與假設二的自變項綜合，進行迴歸分析（表8）。由於自變項彼此有高相關（例如，由表4可知，有歷史背景者較傾向於上過歷史方法課及上過非傳統歷史課，而沒有歷史背景者沒上過這兩種課程的比例較高），一起放入模型之後，共同解釋的部分消失，致使有些自變項變得不顯著。綜合了所有自變項後，歷史訓練背景只有在歷史知識有顯著正面影響，在其他三個依變項無顯著影響。值得注意的是，本文所謂具有歷史訓練背景的教師，分類的方法比較粗略；考量了實際修習的科目後，粗略的背景變項就不再對其他比較需要深度了解歷史本質的依變項有顯著影響力：可見教師實質的背景對學科深度與廣度的認識上之重要性。相對的，歷史哲學與非傳統歷史的學習對於各依變項的影響之顯著模式，則與表7非常近似。

表中倒數第二行是 R 平方項。R 平方項數值愈高，表示模型所含的變項對於依變項的解釋力愈高。其中以對於教學是否注重思維訓練的解釋力最弱。然而，影響實際教學的因素，除了教師本身的知能以外，還受教師本身的人格特質及環境的影響；而臺灣的歷史教育（考試）環境則明顯忽略歷史思維能力的養成。這些都使背景與實際教學之間的關係減弱。然而，儘管有這些外在的影響，本研究仍然發現，教師的不同訓練背景明顯影響他們的教學知能。

表 8　綜合所有背景訓練的迴歸分析

自變項＼依變項	歷史知識	史觀	教學 I	教學 II
常數	22.283 (.566)	41.476 (.424)	15.018 (.438)	3.062 (.174)
歷史	5.218 (.495)***	.585 (.370)	.355 (.375)	.175 (.148)
地理	-.640 (.437)	-.0 (.327)	-.185 (.358)	.013(.142)
公民	-.609 (.382)	-.227 (.286)	.151 (.276)	-.026(.109)

國文	.254 (.484)	.158 (.362)	.125 (.366)	.010 (.145)
上過歷史方法與哲學課	1.793 (.432)***	1.190 (.323)***	.508 (.327)	.561 (.130)***
自行閱讀歷史方法與哲學	.944 (.603)	.710 (.451)	-.157 (.454)	-.007 (.180)
上過非傳統歷史課	.932 (.434)*	1.765 (.325)***	.795 (.300)**	.488 (.119)***
自行閱讀非傳統歷史	1.125 (.404)**	1.206 (.302)***	.812 (.280)**	.646 (.111)***
上過臺灣史	1.444 (.325)***	.128 (.243)	.851 (.249)**	.040 (.099)
學歷—研究所	.118 (.377)	1.091 (.282)***	.10 (.288)	.368 (.114)**
年資	-.350 (.089)***	-.598 (.067)***	-.015 (067)	.019 (.027)
R 平方	.283	.122	.051	.108
使用樣本數	2,180	2,180	1,418	1,418

教學 I 是強調歷史思維的教學；教學 II 是以多元方法教學。*p< .05；**p< .01; ***p<.001

伍、結論與建議

　　教師之專業背景影響其教學，一直是被假設存在的關係，並沒有實證研究。也因為專業是否影響教學的議題被模糊化，因而產生類似社會領域內任一科目背景的教師可以同時教歷史、地理、公民的統整政策。本研究試圖以歷史（人與時間軸）為例，以量化的實證研究，探討學科訓練對於教師的知識、學科觀念及教學是否有影響，以一方面證實學界一直假設的專業背景與教學的關係，另外一方面，回應課程統整政策當中，認為不同專業背景訓練下的教師，有能力將同領域不同學科能力教好的假設。

　　我們發現教師的專業訓練對於其知識、觀念以及教學有顯著影響。亦即，有歷史學科背景的老師，在歷史知識、史觀及歷史教學知能上皆比其他背景的教師佳。歷史背景的教師比較注意引導學生學習歷史思維的相關能力，在教歷史時，教學方法亦比較能使用歷史相關的多元教法。這表示即使是屬於相同的社會領域，不同的學科訓練背景仍然影響教師的專業效

能，證實學者對於教師需要專門知識才能將歷史的思考能力教好的假設 (Ravitch, 2000; VanSledright, 2002)。由此亦可推論，若欲培養學生地理（人與空間軸）或公民（其他社會領域主題軸）的學科能力，教師的專門知識仍然是必要的。

我們發現，即使考量了粗略的專業分類，教師實際修習的課程或自修的內容，仍然對於學科知識與教學有顯著影響。以歷史為例，在歷史訓練上，上過探討歷史是什麼的「歷史方法與哲學」課，或上過女性史、口述歷史、殖民史、庶民史等類「非傳統的歷史課程」者皆顯示比沒有上過此類課程者的教師，在歷史知識、史觀及教學知能上表現佳。這個結果證實了質化研究對於非傳統歷史課程對教師之影響的初步發現，即教師若接觸過非主流的歷史則對於歷史的認知及教學會有所不同 (Sung, 1999)。其中自行閱讀「非傳統歷史」者在歷史知識、史觀及教學上也可以表現突出，在歷史思維教學方面有效果。

上過「臺灣史」對於教師本身的歷史知識，及對於學生歷史思維的訓練，都有顯著正面的影響。但是，令人意外的是，上過臺灣史，對於史觀並沒有額外的正面影響。可能的解釋是，具有臺灣意識的教師，在教學上會強調臺灣史觀與中國史觀的差異，然而此理解未必表示其對於歷史詮釋與多元本質的了解。這個結論仍然有待更多的研究證實。

年資方面，教師年資若越輕，其歷史知識越高，史觀越正確，教學越強調歷史思維。原因是隨著史學的發展，年輕教師比較容易接受到新的史學訓練或上過多元的歷史課，顯示學科訓練背景確實對於教師的學科知識、觀念與教學有重要影響。

而學歷影響方面，則顯示教師若具備研究所學歷，則無論其是否為歷史專業，其史觀分數顯著較大學背景者佳。但是研究所的背景並不會使教師重視歷史思維的教學，仍然是歷史背景的教師，在教學上比較著重歷史思維的訓練，更凸顯學科訓練背景的重要。

　　綜合而論，迴歸分析（表 6、7、8）顯示，雖然歷史訓練的背景在教師的專業知能（知識與教學能力）上有顯著影響，但對於思維的教學影響力明顯偏弱。另外，從相關的分析（表 5）也可看出，在考試與升學取向的大環境下，教師本身的歷史知識或史觀深入與否和歷史思維的教學幾乎沒有關係。也就是，即使歷史知識高或史觀完整的教師，在升學環境不變的情況下，其教學也無法進行學界所倡導的歷史思維訓練。

　　我們從這個研究所得到對於政策的建議是：如果「培養帶得走的能力」（即思維能力）是九年一貫課程統整政策的目標，則應該要解決的是升學的環境。升學環境使教師著重背誦與記憶能力，而忽略理解與歷史思維能力的培養。而九年一貫領域教學的政策排擠了社會領域的總體時數（宋佩芬，2007），讓思維能力的進行更加困難。如果升學大環境沒有解決，則再有理想性的改革也恐怕無法達成培養思維能力的目標。改革可能僅是少數個人的改變，整體的改變仍然非常困難（宋佩芬，2007）。

　　其次，教學品質要改善，其方式並非讓教師在專業知識還沒有預備好的情況下即進行課程統整。統整課程本身並不能使教師知道如何帶出有學科效度（Jacobs, 1989）的思維能力，教師所需的「內容知識」、「結構知識」與「學科教學知識」都需要時間與管道來訓練培養。我們認為分科教學並非不能達成「帶得走的能力」，改革若著重各科教師的「學科教學知識」之培養與落實，反而可能容易達成帶得走的能力。

　　如果領域的教學與統整的政策要繼續進行，則應該加強教師不同學科的教學知能。特別是增加其對於非本科之學科本質的了解（結構知識），以及如何帶領出學科能力的教學知能（學科教學知識）。以歷史而言，這些知識的增加，可以用開設課程的方式來教授（特別是史學導論、史學方法等「歷史方法與哲學」課需要有人指導），或教師自行閱讀多類歷史，或以讀書會的形式對學科教學有更多了解。各校的領域教學研究會更應該妥善朝理解與實踐「結構知識」及「學科教學知識」的目標設計。

　　本研究以歷史（人與時間軸）為例發現教師的知識、觀念與教學能力和教師的學科訓練背景密切相關。而我們認為不僅是歷史、地理與公民學科之間有差異，其他領域的統整也可能面對同樣的學科訓練不同的挑戰，因此認為統整的政策必須審慎評估。

　　本研究是社會科與歷史教學研究領域內，首先嘗試的量化研究。我們採 Jacobs (1989) 的看法主張成功的統整教學應符合學科的效度標準 (Jacobs, 1989)，並以分科的方式來進行研究，這可能是本研究的限制，未來的研究可以朝統整的知識形式來進行。而本研究的結果對於目前「合科」（分科）的教學現象，則有直接的證據可以支持學科背景的影響。

參考文獻

于玥貞等整理 (2000)，〈歷史教科書與歷史教學座談會記錄稿摘要〉，《新史學》，11 (4)，139-194 頁。

宋佩芬 (2007)，〈漸進改革？：九年一貫社會領域教學之調查研究〉，《教育研究學報》，42 (2)，1-17。

宋佩芬 (2004)，〈九年一貫課程改革的變與不變：國中階段社會學習領域的個案研究〉，《淡江人文社會學刊》，18，101-127。

宋佩芬、周鳳美 (2003)，〈教師應付九年一貫課程改革的態度與原因：試辦階段的觀察〉，《課程與教學季刊》，6 (1)，95-112。

宋佩芬 (2003)，〈培養「帶得走的能力」：再思統整與學科知識〉，《教育研究月刊》，115，123-136。

吳翎君 (2002)，〈學童歷史思維的教學方法初探〉，《花蓮師院學報》，15，158-110。

吳翎君 (2003)，〈「神入」歷史與觀點陳述──引導學童歷史思維的教學方法初探〉，《花蓮師院學報》，17，133-152。

吳密察 (1994)，〈臺灣史的成立及其課題〉，《當代》，100，78-97。

林慈淑 (2003)，〈年齡、知識或觀念──試探兒童對多元歷史記述的反應〉，《東吳歷史學報》，10，307-346。

南一 (2003a)，《國民中學社會第三冊》。臺南：南一書局。

南一 (2003a)，《國民中學社會第三冊教師手冊》。臺南：南一書局。

南一 (2004a)，《國民中學社會第四冊》。臺南：南一書局。

南一 (2004a)，《國民中學社會第四冊教師手冊》。臺南：南一書局。

康軒 (2002a)，《國民中學社會課本第一冊》。臺北：康軒出版社。

康軒 (2002b)，《國民中學社會課本教師手冊第一冊》。臺北：康軒出版

社。

翰林 (2002)，《國民中學社會備課用書第一冊》。臺南：翰林出版社。

教育部 (2000)，《國民中小學九年一貫課程暫行綱要》。臺北：教育部。

張元 (1996)，〈十一歲兒童認知能力初探〉，《清華歷史教學》，5 期，4-30 頁。

張元、周樑楷編 (1998)，《方法論：歷史意識與教科書的分析編寫國際學術研討會論文集》。新竹：清華大學歷史研究所。

黃乃琦 (2002)，〈「影視史學」的教學分析〉，《歷史月刊》，3 月號，頁 111-115。

喻蓉蓉整理 (1999)，〈探索歷史教學的新方向〉，《歷史月刊》，140 期，頁 26-32。

陳冠華 (2001)，《追尋更有意義的歷史課：英國中學歷史教育改革》。臺北：龍騰文化。

戴寶村 (2000)，〈概念學習與歷史教學〉，《史匯》，4 期，173-179 頁。

Appleby, J., Hunt, L., & Jacob, M. (1994). *Telling the truth about history.*New York: W. W. Norton & Company.

Bailyn, B. (1994). *On the teaching and writing of history.*Hanover, New Hampshire: University Press of New England.

Beane, J. A. (1995). Curriculum integration and the disciplines of knowledge. *Phi Delta Kappan, 76*(8), 616-622.

Beane, J. A. (1997). *Curriculum integration: Designing the core of democratic education.*New York: Teachers College Press.

Brophy, J., & VanSledright, B. (1997). *Teaching and learning history in elementary schools.*New York: Teachers College Press.

Bruner, J. (1960). *The process of education.*Cambridge, MA: Harvard

University Press.

Carr, E. H. (1961). *What is history?*New York: Penguin Books.

Chang, L.-C. (2008). Re-imagining community from different shores: Nationalism, post-colonialism and colonial modernity in Taiwanese historiogrpahy. In S. Richter (Ed.), *Contested views of a common past* (pp. 139-155). Frankfurt/New York: Campus Verlag.

Clark Jr., E. T. (1997). *Integrated curriculum: A student-centered approach.* Brandon, VT: Holistic Education Press.

Crocker, L., & Algina, J. (1986). *Introduction to classical & modern test theory.*Orlando: Holt, Rinechart and Winston.

Davis, O. L., Elizabeth Anne Yeager, & Foster, S. J. (2001). *Historical empathy and perspective taking in social studies.*New York & Oxford: Rowman & Littlefield.

Drake, S. M. (1998). *Creating integrated curriculum: Proven ways to increase student learning.*Thousand Oaks, CA: Corwin Press.

Evans, R. W. (1989). Teacher conceptions of history. *Theory and Research in Social Education, XVII*(3), 210-240.

Forgarty, R. (1991). Ten ways to integrate curriculum. *Educational Leadership*(49), 61-65.

Gatewood, T. (1998). How valid is integrated curriculum in today's middle schools? *Middle School Journal*(March), 38-41.

Good, T. L., & Brophy, J. E. (2003). *Looking in classrooms* (9th ed.). Boston: Allyn and Bacon.

Goodlad, J. (1984). *A place called school: Prospects for the future.*New York: McGraw Hill.

Hu-DeHart, E. (1993). Rethinking america: The practice and politics of multiculturalism in higher education. In B. W. Thompson & S. Tyagi (Eds.), *Beyond a dream deferred* (pp. 3-17). Minneapolis: University of Minnesota Press.

Jacobs, H. H. (1989). *Interdisciplinary curriculum: Design and implementation.* Alexandria, VA: Association for Supervision and Curriculum Development.

Kessler-Harris, A. (1990). Social history. In E. Foner (Ed.), *The new american history* (pp. 163-183). Philadelphia: Temple University Press.

Kobrin, D. (1996). *Beyond the textbook: Teaching history using documents and primary sources.*Portsmouth, NH: Heinemann.

Lee, P., & Ashby, R. (2000). Progression in historical understanding among students ages 7-14. In P. N. Stearns, P. Seixas & S. Wineburg (Eds.), *Knowing, teaching, and learning history: National and international perspectives* (pp. 199-222). New York & London: New York University Press.

Levstik, L. S., & Barton, K. C. (1997). *Doing history: Investigating with children in elementary and middle schools.*Mahwah, New Jersey: Lawrence Erlbaum.

Mansilla, V. B., Miller, W. C., & Gardner, H. (2000). On disciplinary lenses and interdisciplinary work. In S. Wineburg & P. Grossman (Eds.), *Interdisciplinary curriculum: Challenges to implementation* (pp. 17-38). New York: Teachers College Press.

Mason, T. C. (1996). Integrated curricula: Potential and problems. *Journal of Teacher Education, 47*(4), 263-270.

NCHS. (1994). *National standards for united states history: Grade 5-12.*Los Angeles: National Center for History in the Schools, University of California, Los Angeles.

NCSS. (1994). *Curriculum standards for social studies*.Washington, DC: National Council for the Social Studies.

Novick, P. (1989). *That noble dream*.New York: Cambridge University Press.

Ravitch, D. (2000). The educational backgrounds of history teachers. In P. N. Stearns, P. Seixas & S. Wineburg (Eds.), *Knowing, teaching, and learning history: National and international perspectives* (pp. 143-155). New York & London: New York University Press.

Roth, K. J. (1994). Second thoughts about interdisciplinary studies. *American Educator, 18*(1), 44-48.

Roth, K. J. (2000). The photosynthesis of columbus: Exploring interdisciplinary curriculum from the students' perspectives. In S. Wineburg & P. Grossman (Eds.), *Interdisciplinary curriculum: Challenges to implementation* (pp. 112-133). New York: Teachers College Press.

Schwab, J. J. (1964). The structure of disciplines: Meanings and significance. In G. W. F. L. Pugno (Ed.), *The structure of knowledge and the curriculum*.Chicago: Rand McNally.

Shulman, L. S. (1986). Those who understand: Knowledge growth in teaching. *Educational Researcher, 15*(2), 4-14.

Shulman, L. S. (1987). Knowledge and teaching: Foundations of the new reform. *Harvard Educational Review, 57*(1), 1-22.

Steffy, B. E., Wolfe, M. P., Pasch, S. H., & Enz, B. J. (Eds.). (2000). *Life cycle of the career teacher*.Thousand Oaks, CA: Corwin Press.

Sung, P. F. (1999). *Multicultural history teaching: Views from the field*. Unpublished dissertation, Michigan State University, E. Lansing, Michigan.

Takaki, R. (1998). *A larger memory: A history of our diversity, with voices*.Boston: Little, Brown and Company.

Tally, B., & Goldenberg, L. B. (2005). Fostering historical thinking with digitized primary sources. *Journal of Research on Technology in Education, 38*(1), 1-21.

Tuchman, B. W. (1981). *Practicing history*.New York: Ballantine.

VanSledright, B. (2002). *In search of america's past: Learning to read history in elementary school*.New York & London: Teachers College, Columbia University.

Wilson, S. M., Shulman, L. S., & Richert, A. E. (1987). "150 different ways" of knowing: Representations of knowledge in teaching. In J. Calderhead (Ed.), *Exploring teachers' thinking* (pp. 104-124). London: Cassell.

Wineburg, S. (2001). *Historical thinking and other unnatural acts*.Philadelphia: Temple University Press.

Yalom, M. (1997). *A history of the breast*.New York: Alfred A. Knopf: Distributed by Random House, Inc.

Abstract

Do Teachers' Disciplinary Backgrounds Matter?
－A Study of the Grade1-9 Integrated Field of Social Studies

Pei-Fen Song & Meng-Li Yang

The relationship between teachers' disciplinary backgrounds and their teaching practices in social studies has been assumed, rather than empirically examined. One assumption that seems to underlie the Grade1-9 Integrated Curriculum policy is the notion that teachers of different disciplinary backgrounds bear no significant difference when teaching subjects in the same field. In a culture that teaches to entrance examinations based on textbooks, teachers' knowledge backgrounds can easily be deemed as insignificant. This study uses history as an example and surveys all public and private junior-high school social studies teachers in Taiwan with an intention to clarify if disciplinary backgrounds significantly affect teachers' knowledge, conceptions about the discipline, and teaching practices. Regression analysis shows strong and significant difference in teachers' disciplinary backgrounds in their knowledge, conceptions about the discipline, and teaching practices. Implications and suggestions for the integrated curriculum policy are provided.

How to Help Students Develop Their Problematics?
－ A Research on Taiwanese High School Male Students' Ethics

Cyuan-Yi Syu[*]

Introduction

This paper focuses mainly on a series of high school history classes, of which the objective is to help students develop their problematics—by introducing feminism, especially cultural feminism and radical feminism, and using stories as hypothetical scenarios to help students think further the views of the two schools of feminism.

It should be noted beforehand that cultural feminism is closely related to discourses on ethics, and that lecturing on ethics in a history class may arouse some criticism.[1] However, ethics is one of the important keys to utilizing what one knows about the past to interpret the present; if we simply leave it out, we may unconsciously succumb to the temptation of putting history to the service of particular moral, social, or political values.[2]

---

[*] National Taichung First Senior High School
[1] James Axtell, "Ethnohistory : An Historian's Viewpoint, " *Ethnohistory* 26 (1), pp.1-13.
[2] Bruno Latour, *We Have Never Been Modern* (2005).

An Overview of Feminism

Feminist views are generally based on the political, economic, and social equality of sexes. Through various approaches, feminists have discerned and pointed out gendered components and implications of seemingly neutral laws and practices that inherently entertain men's interests and values. Feminists' beliefs include: that history is written from men's point of view and does not accurately and justly represent women's role in making history and structuring society; that male-written history has cultivated a rooted bias in the concepts of human nature, gender potential, and social arrangements; that the language, logic, and structure of the equality law are created by male and thus inherently reinforce men's values; that by presenting male's character as a "norm" and female's as deviation from the "norm", the prevailing conceptions of law reinforce and perpetuate patriarchal power. Feminists challenge the notion that the biological composition of men and women is so different to the extent that certain differences in behavior can be attributed to sex. Gender, according to feminists, is created socially not biologically; sex determines such matters as physical appearance and reproductive capacity, but not psychological, moral, or social traits.

Although feminists have common commitments to the pursuit of sex equality, they are not uniform in their approaches. Three major schools with varied opinions can be identified among the feminists: traditional or liberal feminism, cultural feminism, and radical or dominant feminism.

Traditional or liberal feminists assert that women are as rational as men and therefore should have equal opportunities to make decisions on their own.

They challenge the presumption of male authority and seek to erase gender-based distinctions, thus enabling women to compete in the marketplace.

Cultural feminists, on the other hand, focus on the differences between men and women and elaborate on those differences. Following the research of psychologist Carol Gilligan, this group of thinkers asserts that women value the importance of relationships, contexts, and reconciliation of conflicting interpersonal positions, whereas men think according to abstract principles of rights and logic. The goal of this school is to give equal recognition to women's moral voice of caring and communal values.

Radical feminists, or dominant feminists, being somewhat similar to the liberal feminists, focus on sex inequality. They assert that men, as a class, have reigned over the entire society, and thus have dominated women as a lower class; for radical feminists, gender is associated with power distribution. Radical feminists urge us to abandon the traditional approaches that set men's values as their reference coordinates; they argue that the construction of sex equality must be based on the realization and recognition of women's difference from men instead of a mere accommodation of that difference.

In the series of history classes, I focused mainly on the views of cultural feminists and radical feminists.

Teaching Procedure

The course basically followed and repeated this teaching procedure in each session:

(1) The teacher provided the background or context by narration, or told a story as a hypothetical scenario.

(2) Students were asked to read some sources about radical feminism or cultural feminism.

(3) The teacher encouraged students to develop their own problematics by freewriting and getting involved in group discussions.

(4) Students were asked to work on their learning sheets（學習單）.

The prototype of this structure was formulated by Professor Chang Yuan when he taught Chinese Classics in Tsinghua University. Under this structure, he taught students history very effectively and also received good feedback from his students. What I had designed in addition to the Professor Chang's original structure was to ask students to work in groups and develop their own problematic, i.e. to expand their questions systematically and try to answer these questions as adequately as possible.

In the third step of the procedure, students were first given 15 minutes to free-write on the questions listed on the learning sheet. (Notice that the learning sheets are handed to the students at the beginning of each session, i.e. before Step 1.) Afterwards, 25 minutes were given for group discussion, of which instructions were as following:

- Read to one another your free writings on the questions listed on the learning sheet.

- Discuss the differences between your responses to the questions and arrive at a consensus position on the questions.

- Construct a "position statement" that reflects the group consensus on the questions.

- Design another question and try to answer your own question through team work and discussion.

- Have one representative from your group to make oral presentation on your position statement and supporting points to the entire class. (All group members shall take turns being the representative.)

Teaching Materials

Appropriate selection of stories (i.e. hypothetical scenarios) is very important; the stories have to be mesmerizing and revealing so as to arouse students' interests, to stimulate discussion, and to further demonstrate the characteristics of the two different schools of feminists.[3]

Radical Feminism

I chose the "American Booksellers v. William H. Hudnut" court case to illuminate radical feminists' opinions and push students to think about the question: **Given that freedom of speech is guaranteed, does the pornography deserve to be protected?**

"American Booksellers v. William H. Hudnut" Court Case

Deep Throat (1972) was the pornographic film which challenged the American obscenity laws and became the first of its kind to be shown in mainstream cinemas. Linda Boreman, who starred as Linda Lovelance in the movie, later wrote a book, *Ordeal* (1981). It revealed that her career had been a catalogue of violent physical and sexual abuse and that interview and public appearance had been scripted by the sadistic Traynor, the production manager of that film as well as Boreman's husband at that time. She claimed that he had forced her at gunpoint into a life of prostitution and pornography. "When you see the movie *Deep Throat*," she told an interviewer that "you are watching me being raped. It is a crime that movie is still showing; there was a gun to my head the entire time."

She allied herself with radical feminism and petitioned the court for a ban on

---

[3] Grant Bage, *Narrative Matters: Teaching and Learning History through Story* (1999).

'*Deep Throat*' and other pornographic products circulating in the market. She toured the US giving lectures on abuses within the pornographic industry. She also testified before several commissions on the effects of pornography on women and children. However, after almost all possible efforts of her, *Deep Throat* is still protected under free speech and *Ordeal* is banned for libel

Cultural Feminism

For cultural feminism, on the other hand, I chose the Heinz dilemma and the story of the Venetian merchant to illustrate their points of view.

Heinz dilemma

A woman is close to death. There is one kind of drug that might save her life but it costs 4000 dollars per dosage, which is extremely expensive. The husband of the sick woman has tried all legal means to get more money but he only has about 2000 dollars. He asked the doctor scientist who discovered and owns the drug for a discount or installment payment, but the doctor scientist refused.

My questions targeted towards the dilemma were：

1. **Should Heinz break into the laboratory to steal the drug？Why or why not?**

2. **If he hates his wife, should Heinz break into the laboratory to steal the drug for his wife？Why or why not?**

3. **If the person who was near death from cancer was a stranger for Heinz, should he break into the laboratory to steal the drug for the stranger？Why or why not?**

The Heinz dilemma was first constructed by Lawrence Kohlberg (1927-1987). He asked questions to probe their reasons for recommending a specific course of action. From his research, he identified six stages of reasoning at three levels:[4]

Kohlberg's Theory of Moral Development

Level One:	Stage1：Punishment-Obedience Orientation
Pre-conventional Morality	Stage2：Instrumental Relativist Orientation
Level Two:	Stage3: Good Boy-Nice Girl Orientation
Conventional Morality	Stage4：Law and Order Orientation
Level Three:	Stage5：Social Contract Orientation
Post-Conventional Morality	Stage6：Universal Ethical Principle Orientation

However, cultural feminists disagree with Kohlberg's theory on how people make decisions when faced with a moral dilemma. Gilligan finds that men and women use fundamentally different approaches in moral reasoning, and since men have dominated the discourses of moral theory, women's perspective is often not taken seriously and is considered to be less developed and sophisticated.[5] As Gilligan states, the male approach is that individuals have certain basic rights, and that you have to respect the rights of others; therefore, morality imposes restrictions on what you can do. The female

---

4 Chang Yung, 'A New Teaching Formula in the History Classroom: Story-telling, Reading and Writing', *Historical Inquiry 37* (2006), pp. 319-349.
5 Carol Gilligan, *In a Different Voice: Psychological Theory and Women's Development* (1993).

approach, on the other hand, is that people have responsibilities towards others, so morality is an imperative to care for others. As Gilligan summarizes, men's moral reasoning is based on the "ethics of justice" and women's on the "ethics of care".

Will Kymlicka further elaborates Gilligan's theory. She explains the differences between the approach of "ethics of care" and that of "ethics of justice".

	ethics of justice	ethics of care
focus	rights, universal principle of morality	relationships, responsibilities
moral capacities	Abstract reason (What are the best principles?)	Sympathy, tolerance (How will individuals best be equipped to act morally?)
procedures	universal principle, logical thinking	thinking in the context
emphasis	respect for distinct individuality	respect for common humanity
conflicting dilemma	conflicting rights	disconnection/abandonment/indifference; oppression/inequality
decision criterion	principle deontological theory (experiences do not matter)	relationships experiences

In order to assess whether students could distinguish between ethics of care and ethics of justice, I brought in another story, the Merchant of Venice, and then asked students: **which character could be the representative of the ethics of justice? Who might represent the voice of the ethics of care? Why?**

The Story of the Merchant of Venice

Antonio, a Venetian Merchant, has a friend named Bassanio, who is desperately in need of money to court Portia, a wealthy heiress. Antonio would like to help Bassanio, but he is unable to make the loan himself because his own money is all invested in a number of trade ships that are still at sea. Antonio and Bassanio finally approach Shylock, a Jewish moneylender, for a loan. Shylock acts agreeably and offers to lend Bassanio three thousand ducats with no interest. Shylock adds that should the loan go unpaid, Shylock will be entitled to a pound of Antonio's own flesh. Antonio agrees.

Portia and Bassanio are joined and celebrate their wedding. However, the celebration is cut short by the news that Antonio has lost his ships, and that he has forfeited his bond to Shylock. Bassanio immediately travel to Venice to try to save Antonio's life. After he leave, Portia also go to Venice disguised as man.

Shylock ignores the many pleas to spare Antonio's life, and a trial is called to decide the matter. The duke of Venice, who presides over the trial, announces that he has sent for a legal expert, who turns out to be Portia disguised as a young man of law. Portia asks Shylock to show mercy, but he remains inflexible and insists on collecting the bond as it is written. Portia examines the contract and, finding it legally binding, declares that Shylock is entitled to the merchant's flesh. Shylock praises her wisdom, but as he in on the verge of collecting his due, Portia reminds him that he must do so without causing Antonio to bleed, as the contract does not entitle him to any blood. Trapped by this logic, Shylock hastily agrees to take Bassanio's money instead, but Portia insists that Shylock take his bond as it is written or nothing at all; she further informs Shylock that he is guilty of conspiring against the life of a Venetian citizen, which means he must turn over half of his property to the state and the other half to Antonio.

At last, the duke spares Shylock's life and Antonio also forgoes his half share of Shylock's wealth. They allow him to live, but only as a Christian, forcing him to give up his faith and identity. They condition their mercy on Shylock's promise to leave his property to his Christian son-in-law.

Almost all students could easily identify Shylock as the representative of the ethics of justice. While facing Portia, they at first identified her as the representative of the ethic of care. However, after group discussions, they reached the point that Portia is a complex character. Then my question emerged：**Which is better to solve conflicts and bring peace to our society, ethics of justice or ethics of care? Why?**

Discussion

Radical Feminism

(1) Given that freedom of speech is guaranteed, does the pornography deserve to be protected? (table 1)

Position	Vague	No	Yes
decided	3	17	4
confused	0	5	4
total	3	22	8

Most of students (22/33, high school freshmen aging from 16-17 years old)[6] did not agree that the pornography deserves protection under freedom of speech. However, some of them (5/22) could not stand firm on their position when pushed to think about another question—"Do you agree with the Indianapolis' banning pornography?" or "Do you agree with the judgment of

---

6 They are almost the best students in Central Taiwan. Students of National Taichung First Senior High School come out of the top 3% range in the Joint High School Entrance Exam.

the U. S. supreme court which stated that it is unconstitutional to ban pornography?"—they are confused. They held that Indianapolis' definition of pornography is too broad to agree with, and they also conceded that the supreme court's decision is right according to the law. Meanwhile, however, they thought that pornography does not deserve protection.

The same confusion occurred to some students (4/8) who agreed that pornography deserves protection—when pushed to think about another question: "What does pornography do as in the *Deep Throat*? It affects the real world, or only the mind?" They thought it affects the real world. They also agreed that pornography does real harm to women. Perhaps they blurred the distinction between "obscenity" and "pornography".

However, after group work, their "position statement" became either more subtle or more concrete in comparison with individual's writing.

For example, group 1, represented by Yang Hangbo, stated that： "A publication, deserving no protection, must, *as a whole*, contain offensive descriptions of sexual conduct, and on the whole have no literary, artistic, political, or scientific value." "Offensiveness could be *assessed* under the *standards of the community*." It seemed that they were able to narrow down their thoughts about freedom of speech to more specific definitions.

Group 2, represented by Hsu Chiawei, insisted on their vague position about banning pornography or not, for there are still many controversies. They listed the reasons for pro or against pornography which they could imagine and find. Thus, it depends on the situation.

Group 3, represented by O Reiyu, strongly recommended banning porn. Here are their reasons：

Beliefs are also facts. People often act in accordance with the images and patterns they find around them. People raised in a religion tend to accept the tenets of that religion, often without independent and thorough examination. People taught from birth that black people are fit only for slavery rarely rebelled against that creed. Words and images act at the level of the subconscious before they persuade at the level of the conscious. Depictions of subordination tend to perpetuate subordination. This subordinate status of women in turn leads to lower pay at work, insult at home, rape on the streets.[7] All of these unhappy effects depend on mental intermediation. Pornography affects how people see the world, their fellows, and social relations.

Their statement had fully comprehended that facts could be biased by our beliefs and that mental intermediation does matter. They could think through the sources and beyond sources.

(2) Should Heinz break into the laboratory to steal the drug? Why or why not? (table 2)

position	yes	no	uncertain	total
ethics of justice	12	1	0	13
mixed ethics	14	1	0	15
ethics of care	0	4	2	6
total	26	6	2	34

If the students viewed the above three moral questions totally in terms of principle, duty and rights, his approach would be classified as "ethics of

---

[7] He also referred to the famous case happened in Taiwan's campus where a young elementary school teacher was raped and killed by two teenagers, one fifth grade and the other seventh grade, who had just watched the AV video and then imitated the offensive descriptions of sexual conduct in the movie.

justice" in this table. If the students made moral decisions based on whether their actions help or harm the people involved, his approach would be classified as being based on "ethics of care". If both approaches toward the dilemmas could be observed, then the student would be classified as using "mixed ethics."

From the table 2, more male students made their decisions according to ethics of justice than ethics of care, which seemed consistent with Gilligan's observation. However, the total number of mixed ethics is even larger than that of ethics of justice. Those students classified as using mixed ethics have the capacity to look at moral dilemmas from the two perspectives and even chose not to stand on either. For example, Ho Hsiaogan wrote, "Yes, she is your wife, that's why you must do everything possible to save her life, including stealing. Besides, 'life's value weighs as much as God's will（人命關天）.' Therefore, the first priority is to save life." They could navigate in the spectrum of relationships and universal principles, connectedness and separation; their image of self could be both that of a male and that of a female.

There are some anomalies. Tang Wenhung thought that the provided information was insufficient to make a decision. "I am really not sure; it depends on the situation." Chang Tinrei said, "It depends, if we have children, I would not go to steal. I cannot risk. If I did not success in stealing, my wife was then dead, and I also had to be imprisoned, so nobody could take care of the children. However, if we have no child, I would go to steal definitely. Even if I failed, I had done my best to save my wife's life." Both of them were uncomfortable responding to hypothetical moral dilemmas. They asked for more information about the characters, their history, their children and their relationships. They were the only two hesitating in making a decision.

Tsai Lida was the only one who refused to steal among those whose decision-makings were based on the ethics of justice. Tsai seemed very faithful to the Ten Commandments, including "never stealing." He thought the true way to love is through wisdom, not through rudeness. He referred to Socrates who would rather die than break the law of Athens. Tsai was also the only one who said direct "no"s to the different variations of the question—his answers were always based on the single principle: never stealing.

Cultural Feminism

(1) If he hates his wife, should Heinz break into the laboratory to steal the drug for his wife? Why or why not? (table 3)

position	yes	no	uncertain	total
ethics of justice	7	2	1	10
mixed ethics	0	0	1	1
ethics of care	9	12	2	23
total	16	14	4	34

In comparison with table 2, the total number of saying "yes, steal the drug" declined dramatically—from 26 down to 16. The number of students using mixed ethics also dropped. About 19 students who said "yes" in table 2 (26-7=19) now had to focus on relationships rather than on universal principles.

(2) If the person who was near death from cancer was a stranger to Heinz, should he break into the laboratory to steal the drug for the stranger？ Why or why not? (table 4)

position	yes	no	uncertain	total
ethics of justice	13	2	1	16
mixed ethics	0	0	0	0
ethics of care	1	16	1	18
total	14	18	2	34

Those who decided to steal the medicine always grounded their choice on the ethics of justice rather than on the ethic of care. Only O Reiyu's action was based on the ethics of care: He always took into consideration the possibilities of being caught while trying to steal the medicine. He said no to the previous two questions, for if he were caught, it would hurt his beloved ones, e.g. nobody taking care of his wife; he said yes to the third question, for if he was caught, it would not be of much impact to that stranger. All that he would do for that stranger could be only good.

In comparison with table 2, the total number of saying "no" arises sharply from 6 to 18. As Chang Chinghang explained, "it goes beyond his imagination to sacrifice so much, being jailed, for a stranger" and "all I could do is to lend him some money or to raise funds for him; after all, he is a stranger." "It seems endless to go help strangers, so we cannot keep stealing on and on. Stealing for strangers is not the right way. We are not thieves." He seemed influenced by the Confucious' thought on "position（位）"—"Gentlemen act purely according to his relevant position. No position, no over action.（君子素其位而行，不在其位，不謀其政）"

We may expect that anyone who makes his choice based on the ethics of justice that life is the first priority, would say "yes" to the third question firmly as to the first and second. However, Hsu Jintang changes his mind from yes to uncertain. He would send the stranger to hospital and raise funds for him because saving one life is much better than any charity（救人一命，勝造七級浮屠）. He insisted in that he could exhaust every means to save the stranger's life, but he was uncertain whether stealing would be an option for him or not. His standpoint on the first priority of life was shaken. He ignored the hidden conflicts between his belief of life and his reserved attitude to help strangers.

(3) There is a Chinese proverb that inferrs the strategic program to solve dilemmas, considering the context first（情）, the principle（理）, and then the law（法）last. Do you agree with this proverb? Why or why not? (table 5)

	agree	disagree	uncertain
total	11	18	6

11 students were very sensitive of the diversity in moral reasoning. They thought it was impossible to converge into one principle, or one law; therefore, we should consider the context first to avoid unnecessary conflicts. Chinese ancient proverb（情理法）did not go wrong. After all, law is too rigid and too uniform to bring about real peace. We should also look at the context.

However, most of the students (18) thought otherwise. Tang Wenhang, for instance, wrote, "If we follow this Chinese proverb, no law could ever bring about real equality. Deprivation of equality results in less trust. If we do not trust our law, it's chaos!"

Only 6 students thought the relationship between the context and the law is flexible and always changing in different times. "If we put too much emphasis on the rigorous laws in the past, we should take more contexts into consideration now. If we used to practice our laws loosely, we must now put laws on the first priority," as Ho Hsiaogan wrote, "That is the way of being— always on the becoming. We should maintain our flexibility."

Some students were very smart. They pointed out that the "law" in the Chinese proverb is equivalent to the ethics of justice, and the "context" to the ethics of care. They could figure out the problematics behind the series of moral dilemma questions. On top of that, they even challenged this problematics for not considering carefully the difference between the transcendent quality of ethics of justice and the instrumental character of traditional Chinese laws—we are not supposed to regard the two as equivalent.

(11,18,6) of table 5 could not correspond to (24, 7, 4) of table 6. On the whole, Table 5 is perhaps more reliable than table 6—many students might have been influenced by the previous leading questions, and talking a great deal about feminism might as well have been regarded as being favorable of feminists' views, i.e. giving recognition to ethics of care. Students could also have interpreted further from the introduction of Linda's miserable life and the indifference of law that could obviously be noticed.

(4) Which is better to solve conflicts and bring peace to our society, ethics of justice or ethics of care? Why? (table 6)

	ethics of care	ethics of justice	mixed ethic
total	24	7	4

24 students thought that our society consists of different voices; it is a multicultural society. For example, Chen Changhong related that the Christians' focus is always far away from the Muslims' orientation; it is

definitely impossible to establish common moral standards for all people in the future. We should, in turn, learn to have respect for one another. In this case, ethics of care is a better option for solving conflicts and bringing peace to our society.

7 students thought ethics of justice to be a better choice. As Hua Yishang said, "Conflicts come from uncertainty. Disputes often arise from interpretation of the principle or the law, not the law itself. If law is clear enough, intricate enough, it's not difficult to settle down conflicts effectively. In other words, objective law brings peace with equality. If we usually bend the law to any specific context, there would be no law. No law, no peace. Everyone hurts."

Some students adopted the mixed ethics. Ho Hsiaogan, for instance, explained as follows: On the large scale, such as international conflicts, we could not establish the consensus of justice and are thus prone to fight for ideology rather than for real justice (while pretending to be insisting on "justice"). In this case, we should focus on the responsibility to discern and alleviate the real and recognizable trouble of the world, rather than on rights. On the small scale, it is easier to settle down the rule of game, or a moral standard that applies to all; therefore, we could put emphasis more on justice and equality rather than on care and responsibility.

This table could not be used to overturn Gilligan's observation on gender differences in moral reasoning. As I have said in the discussion of table 5, students were very likely influenced by my leading questions. In spite of the fact that many of these male students claimed to be in favor of ethics of care in this table, larger number of them still followed Shylock's way in other questions. However, it is also true that not all male students' moral reasoning is based on ethics of justice; some of them speak "in a different voice."

Conclusions

One thing that must be noted first is: story-telling may result in the problem of "leading questions". After hearing the story of the Venetian merchant, for instance students easily identified Shylock as the representative of ethics of justice. However, he was so mean in my narrative that many students gradually altered their choices from the ethics of justice（法）to ethics of care.

Returning to the issue of students' reception of cultural feminism— from the series of high school history classes, it can be concluded that the voices Gilligan recorded are not the final words.

Gilligan conducted extensive interviews with 24 of the women who varied in age, education, marital status, and socioeconomic backgrounds. All were in the first trimester of their pregnancy and planning or considering an abortion, but only four chose to give birth. Their voices are not recorded as examples of care. Her case study approach is not only charged for being non-representative, just as Kohlberg's—but also open to the criticisms of ignoring the influences of cultural contexts.

In Taiwan, male students' morality showed more flexibility than Gilligan and Kohlberg's recordings. Some of the students did not necessarily stand on either ethics of care or ethics of justice. They could keep the balance by standing on both points or navigating between the two according to the occasions.

They were not only suspicious of abstract concepts like justice—Kohlberg stated unequivocally that the universal principle of justice is the highest claim of morality—but also doubted the validity and necessity of ethics of care on smaller scales. On the whole, they are rather good at mixing the two extremes flexibly in comparison with Gilligan and Kohlberg's samples.

中文摘要

歷史與倫理學
——以女性主義為例

許全義

本文旨於在歷史課堂上，透過介紹激進女性主義和文化女性主義，設計學習單，協助學生思索人我，群己關係。

本課程一方面以激進女性主義來鬆動自由主義者的權利論述，讓它不是那麼不證自明，那麼放諸四海皆準；另一方面以文化女性主義提供另一可能性。不過這種設計有誘導之嫌 (leading questions)，讓聰敏的學生感受到，推崇關懷倫理才是老師想要的答案。

本研究發現大部分男同學遇到漢茲難題時，都採取類似正義倫理的取向：確立考慮的優先順序、再比大小來解題。如「自己妻子的一條命要比自己幾年的自由重要得多」、「人命是再多的錢也買不到的」、「違背道德、倫理，破壞法律，產生的結果對漢茲和他的妻子而言會更不利。」徘徊在強烈的二分法，偷與不偷之間，擇一而處。如很少男同學會跳脫出題目的框架，將倫理創造力釋放開來，而像愛彌兒那麼堅定自信的說，漢茲不用偷藥，她太太也不會死。

不過大部分臺中一中的學生並非理論性一貫的堅持用正義倫理來解題。有一小部分認為生命價更高，所以漢茲應該偷藥的同學，當題幹情況轉變成漢茲不愛自己的妻子時，就轉變成不要去偷藥，「而應該花費心力來照顧她……以彌補他對她的歉意」。當然，其中大部分還是認為漢茲應

該偷藥給自己不愛的妻子。可是，他們所持的理由跟漢茲一貫的正義倫理有所不同。而偏向就具體脈絡來審酌，如「當然要，畢竟還是自己的妻子」、「要，不然的話，對不起自己的良心，還會被親戚朋友看不起」、「一個不愛自己妻子的人，要他去偷，那是不可能的，而他卻該偷，因為那人是自己的妻子」等等。換言之，當問題愈來愈具體，細節愈清楚時，臺中一中的男同學偏向採關懷倫理來解題的也就愈多。

當題幹情況轉變成病危的陌生人時，採關懷倫理來解題，貼近現實脈絡的人就更多。如「病危的人對他來說雖然只是陌生人，但是基於人性，遇到需要幫忙的人，我們應該盡力幫助他，但不能用偷的方式，我們想散發愛心要有真實的智慧而不是魯莽的行動」、「以我中國人而言，他不該偷藥。但他可向藥商來商量，請求協助」、「不該偷，他自己還有自己的家人，不能去坐牢」、「不該，否則偷到沒完沒了」、「不該，但可以借他一點錢或發動募捐，但如果每個人有病就去偷藥，那要偷到那時候？」、「看情況，可以去募捐，或者送到醫院，請社會有錢的人或一些基金會來處理，因為命是比什麼都來得重要」。這或許是受到傳統儒家教養「仁」、「有差別的愛」的影響。

在此我們可以看到心理學有關道德發展理論的限制，甚至文化女性主義亦然，他們在理論建構時，並沒有顧慮到不同文化背景的衝擊與影響。亦即，在正義倫理與關懷倫理之外，還有其他的可能性。如孔子的倫理觀，「極高明而道中庸」，一方面試圖確立優先順序，淘汰出必不得已而去之的選項，一方面貼近現實脈絡，為聖之時者，兼具正義倫理與關懷倫理的特色。

但另一方面，我們也要注意，在兼顧情理法，兼具正義倫理與關懷倫理的解題趨勢，在臺灣邁向公民社會時，可能會遭遇的困難。在邱小妹事件中，她之所以會被轉走，醫師們之所以將其未交健保費、又顯無資力付醫療費用，又會拖很久納入考量，未確立生命價值最高，而將其轉診，這

又與臺中一中學生認為「不該，否則偷到沒完沒了」、「不該，如果每個人有病就去偷藥，那要偷到哪時候？」在解決倫理難題的取徑上，並沒有太大的差異。有些學生一方面認為情理法，排序上法要排在最前面才公平，合法合理下才能考量人情，但另一方面又寧願選擇關懷倫理，這似乎是「霹靂手段，菩薩心腸」的倫理取徑的翻版。問題是，關懷倫理強調的是就現實脈絡上倫理上的創意，而非客觀穩定的法理。在關懷倫理下，如何有穩定的法理秩序；在菩薩心腸下，如何能採取霹靂手段呢？這並非不證自明、可輕鬆解決的問題。亦即，就算當大家都是孔子、孟子時，社會不見得便有穩定的法理秩序。個人道德與社會秩序有時還是會有衝突的。

Historical Enquiry Curriculum Goals, Teaching and Learning Challenges, and Student Understandings

Rosalyn Ashby[*]

Introduction

The initial intention of this chapter is to highlight the importance of a history education that includes goals associated with the development of students' understanding of the nature of historical enquiry, and more specifically their concept of historical evidence. However, setting goals of this kind is one thing, asking teachers and students to respond to these goals is quite another. It will therefore be necessary for this chapter to go beyond a justification for these goals and also offer some commentary on the nature of the enterprise, and on the kinds of challenges students are likely to face. These challenges will be discussed in the context of specific research knowledge about students' understanding of the status and nature of historical claims, their approaches to historical sources: their propensity to treat source

---

[*] Institute of Education, University of London

material at face value, and their assumptions that eyewitness accounts offer direct access to the past.

Why Is an Understanding of Historical Evidence an Important Part of a History Education?

In the UK history teachers work with the assumption that, in an open, modern, democratic, and multicultural society, a history education has to go beyond the learning and the regurgitation of a single-track account of the past designed to encourage a particular kind of patriotic identity.

The argument, that children should learn something of the *nature* and *status* of historical knowledge, has been accepted in the UK since the 1970s, mainly as a consequence of the initiative of a group of teachers who founded the Schools Council History Project (SCHP) in 1972, and designed a course of study that attached these goals to a public examination option for 14 – 16 year olds. During the past three decades this 'new' approach to school history has been increasingly embodied in the curriculum: firstly, through the introduction of a new General Certificate of Secondary Education (GCSE) examination in 1986 which extended the principles embodied in this project across all 14 – 16 public examination courses, and secondly, through the introduction in 1992 of a national curriculum for history, for 5-14 year olds. Revisions to this national curriculum in 1995 and 2000 have maintained this *disciplinary* or *form of knowledge* approach to the acquisition of historical knowledge.

In this tradition there is an acceptance that school students historical knowledge ought to rest on an open tradition of enquiry, where students are taught to recognize that the claims made about the past are derived from (and need to be consistent with) the evidence. Teachers strive to develop in their students an understanding that this evidence is gleaned from an interrogation of the material the past has left behind, and from the range of questions and hypotheses this material is able to generate.

In the 1970s the SCHP recognized that 'although children can be taught to believe various things, they cannot be said *to know* anything until they have grasped something of the nature of historical enquiry itself.' (Shemilt, 1980, p.4) The project stressed the importance of understanding history as a *form of knowledge* claiming that 'history has developed characteristic ways of exploring and making sense of human experience' and arguing that 'whilst children can be more or less *well informed* about the conclusions of expert enquiries into the past, they are only *educated* to the extent that they possess understanding of the methods, logic and perspectives proper to these enquiries.' (Shemilt, 1980, p.26) The project identified *evidence* as one of the concepts crucial to the historical enterprise, with recognition also being given to the attendant skills of 'enquiry, hypothesis formation, analysis, inference, judgement and synthesis.' (Shemilt, 1980, p.7)

Writing in support of the Schools Council History Project in 1980, Peter Rogers made his belief in the importance of the project's *disciplinary* goals clear. In a Historical Association Pamphlet entitled 'New History', he argued that school students' historical knowledge should be 'grounded in reason', explaining that although a child:

> *may be sure of what he has learned, he has not the <u>right</u> to be sure, even if what he has learned is in fact correct, for he cannot assess the grounds upon which the 'knowledge' rests.... There can be no*

knowledge, which does not at least partially include 'know how' and 'know how' is largely specific to a particular discipline. In the present context it is the historian's 'know how', and it follows that mere communication of the fruit of scholarship in the absence of any acquaintance with its procedures is quite inadequate.... Clearly the procedures are what make History a discipline ... and study which neglects them can hardly count as History at all. (Rogers, 1980, p.19)

Writing, at the Queen's University, Belfast, Northern Ireland, in 1984 Rogers presented further argument consistent with this previous statement. He expressed concern about the picture of the past children acquired from the everyday world in which they were growing up making the point that 'we cannot have a perception of the present that is not strongly influenced by a version of the past – some sort of version – which we have internalized in the course of growing up, and articulated in our adult lives'. He makes this point to justify the place of history in the curriculum claiming that without the study of history 'there will be nothing to monitor the development of the framework within which [we] will come (largely) to see the world, and the problem of adult misconception will be perpetuated.' (Rogers, 1984, p.21)

But, what kind of a history education should this be? Rogers was clearly concerned that historical controversy should not be avoided convinced that 'to eschew historical content that has implications for present controversial issues achieves nothing except the removal of any possibility of their rational scrutiny'. (Rogers, 1984, p.21) He was insistent that history in school should deal with the nature of historical knowledge and the consequent issues of contested accounts of the past, making the point that because 'history deals largely with matters that are essentially contested' to 'look for unanimity between historical accounts is simply to misunderstand the nature of historical knowledge'. (Rogers, 1980, p.21)   For Rogers this was not to licence the view that any old account of the past will do, or that students should be able to choose whatever version they fancied.   He made it clear that 'to repudiate "one right version" as a feasible objective gives no sanction whatever to polemical and uninformed accounts of the past'. (Rogers, 1984, p.22) He wished instead that school students be educated in ways that enable them to distinguish a 'judicious and well informed opinion as opposed to a silly, ignorant and prejudiced one.' (Rogers, 1984, p.22)

What is at stake here for Rogers is the importance of *evidence,* highlighting an understanding for 'the sort of *ground* for a valid knowledge claim', and stressing that 'history provides much more reliable grounds for such claims about the past because it embodies and employs the techniques and procedures for identifying and handling evidence that have been refined over time into the best available.'   (Rogers, 1984, p.22)   Without an understanding of these 'techniques and procedures' it would surely be difficult to distinguish history stories in school to those acquired from an often unscrupulous multi-media world to which our children are currently exposed. Rogers was not alone in his thinking.   In 1984 Peter Lee, writing from the Institute of Education in London, also stressed that history supplies the only rational means of investigating the past, making the point that this 'claim is founded in part on history's developing concept of (and techniques for handling) evidence.' (Lee, 1984, p.4)

During the national debate on the future of the history curriculum in the 1990s history teachers in England fought fiercely to defend this position.

During some difficult challenges, David Sylvester (Director of SCHP between 1972 and 1975), challenged history teachers to 'keep faith with the professional knowledge which they have developed in the last quarter of a century', asking 'whether enough of them would 'continue to affirm that an historical education is as much about the development of minds as the furnishing of them with facts' and reaffirming his belief that a history education is as much 'about knowing how new knowledge is discovered' as 'remembering the old?' (Sylvester, 1994, p.22)   In the context of this debate about the nature of the history national curriculum Shemilt and Lee also restated their position on the importance of this approach to history education.

Shemilt's voice was clear:

> *Concern with the evidential basis of claims to knowledge, with the developmental logic of historical accounts, and with the modal logic of causal explanation is not [mere] pedantry; on the contrary, it is a moral concern fundamental to the maintenance of an open tradition, and, thereby, of an* 'open society'*. (Shemilt, 1992, p.7)*

In defending the integrity of history as a school subject, from those concerned to exploit it for goals of 'citizenship' and 'patriotism', Lee presented the case that 'history is not just a matter of picking up a new set of beliefs, or even new substantive knowledge.'   He argued that it is also about 'taking on a set of second-order understandings, together with the *rational passions* (eg. for truth and respect for evidence)' suggesting that it is this which gives historical understanding 'a universality that patriotism does not have.' (Lee, 1992)

An important aspect of this position is that it encourages, in students, a sense of responsibility towards people in the past: recognition is given to their experience and their endeavour, offering us, in the present, an important human connection with people beyond our time. As Paddy Walsh highlighted in the context of the above debate, there 'is such a thing as a brotherly and sisterly love directed to the human beings and the human worlds that are dead and gone' and although 'we cannot shape and influence [the past] nor, therefore, take responsibility for it' we are 'not *entirely* helpless' in regard to that past. 'One thing we can do for it is set the record straight posthumously'. (Paddy Walsh: 1992, pp.36-37) An understanding of historical evidence is clearly essential to maintaining some vigilance over the historical record and the validity of the claims that are made about the past.

What does the UK National Curriculum for History Require Students to Understand About Historical Enquiry and the Concept of Evidence?

The national curriculum for history in the UK has indeed kept faith with this open approach to the study of history in school, and as a consequence concepts of evidence and interpretation have maintained a central position in curriculum regulation. The new national curriculum document (to be taught in schools from September 2008) sets out similar goals to the previous versions including those goals that relate directly to the principles of historical enquiry. The Importance Statement on page 3 of this document includes the following statement:

As they develop their understanding of the nature of historical study, pupils ask and answer important questions, evaluate evidence, identify and analyse different interpretations of the past and learn to substantiate any arguments and judgements they make.

In fact these new proposals restate and strengthen objectives that require students' to be taught concepts and skills relating to historical enquiry.

Historical Enquiry:

Pupils should be able to:

- *Identify and investigate, individually and as part of a team, specific historical questions or issues, making and testing hypotheses*
- *Reflect critically on historical questions or issues*

Using Evidence:

Pupils should be able to:

- *Identify, select and use a range of historical sources, including textual, visual and oral sources, artefacts and the historic environment.*
- *Evaluate the sources used in order to reach reasoned conclusions.*

Explanatory Notes are provided that expand on these requirements:

Historical Enquiry: *This includes structured enquiries into different kinds of historical questions and issues. Pupils should begin to devise and refine their own questions to structure an investigation, developing their own hypotheses and selecting and deploying evidence to reach and justify their own conclusions. Pupils can either use their acquired knowledge and understandings to suggest hypotheses, or can suggest hypotheses at the start of the topic based on their own assumptions and values, which they then test against the evidence.*

Using evidence: *Knowledge of the past is based on evidence derived from sources and depends on the questions asked and the sources available rather than making prior assumptions about the validity and reliability of the historical sources used. This includes evaluating the value and reliability of evidence by studying the provenance, purposes and language of sources. (Extracts are from **The National Curriculum 2007**, Qualifications and Curriculum Authority, 2007.)*

These are serious demands for both teachers and their pupils and it is important that, as history teachers in the UK, we understand the nature of this challenge. Research can help and there is an increasingly rich body of research knowledge that has implications for the classroom.

What Does Research Tell Us About the Nature of the Challenge Teachers and Their Students Face in Pursuing These Educational Goals for History?

It is clear from the research available that a classroom culture that identifies students' preconceptions and challenges their misconceptions is necessary for effective learning:

> *Students come to the classroom with preconceptions about how the world works. If their initial understanding is not engaged they may fail to grasp the new concepts and information that they are taught, or they may learn them for purposes of a test but revert to their preconceptions outside the classroom. (M.Suzanne Donovan and John D. Bransford, 2005: p.1)*

But, what kinds of pre-conceptions and misconceptions are we likely to meet in history classrooms and what problems do these pose for teachers who want to work with historical sources and develop their students' concept of historical evidence? There are several difficulties.

The most challenging of these has been how to persuade students whose propensity is to treat historical sources as 'face value' information, to use them instead *as evidence*. In encouraging students to make distinctions between the past and history students are introduced to historical sources. However, this is no straightforward matter, as these sources 'bear neither their meaning nor their authenticity on their face.' (Walsh, 1963; p.20) It is understanding the *nature* of this material that is an essential first move if students are to get beyond the 'face value' treatment of sources and to begin to recognize that the 'meaning and authenticity' of a source will determine how it may, or may not be, used *as evidence*. Understanding the society and the context in which a source came into being is therefore one important facet of being able to understand the weight that can be placed on a source as evidence, and understanding what can *count* as evidence for any given claim, or enquiry, about the past is another.

To challenge students' propensity to treat historical sources at face value (as direct access to information) students are asked by their teachers to interrogate historical sources through questions about who produced them, when were they produced, and for what purpose. While this approach to teaching may shift a students' thinking away from accepting, without question, the information contained within a source, this approach can, in itself, produce further problems and misconceptions: that testimony can be biased, and therefore unreliable, and as a consequence be useless to the historian. At this point a further move, towards a higher level of understanding, is necessary: a move that will support an understanding that a witness report can be examined for what it can yield beyond what it had intended to reveal. This is crucial in encouraging students to consider historical sources as evidence.

We now have a substantial body of research about children's understanding of historical evidence. In the late 1970s and early 1980s small-scale research by Peter Lee, Alaric Dickinson and Rosalyn Ashby, and Denis Shemilt's *Evaluation Study* of the SCHP (Shemilt, 1980) provided a framework of knowledge and understanding about progression (a progression from less to more powerful ideas) in students' understanding about historical evidence.

This research is useful to teachers in indicating their students' likely preconceptions, and misconceptions. In looking at these ideas as less to more powerful, it is possible to describe them as ranging from the treatment of historical sources as offering direct access to 'ready-made' *information* about the past, to the treatment of sources as *testimony*, and beyond this to the more powerful idea that sources need to be understood as *evidence* (as a product of a specific society, and that if understood as such they can be probed and questioned to yield evidence of that society in relation to a specific enquiry).

Throughout the 1990s and beyond, this knowledge base was refined and extended through the ESRC funded *Chata* Project (Concepts of History and Teaching Approaches). A key aspect of the *Chata* project was to explore students' treatment of historical sources, their understanding of evidence and their approaches to testing and validating historical claims. The tendency, even amongst many older students, to treat sources as face value information, to reject sources (seeing them as useless) on the basis of a reliability test that remained detached from the question being asked or the claim being made was apparent in this research context.

Some exemplification is presented here in order to highlight the ideas that children were working with in responding to the research tasks presented to them during the data collection for this project. Appendix A (Lee, Ashby, Dickinson, 1995, pp.65-67) provides an example of one set of material used in this research, and supports an understanding of the example responses used in the discussion that follows. The material consists of three historical claims and six historical sources. Students were asked to consider the *validity* of these three stories (accounts) in the context of the source material, and background information given to them. This background material was an illustrated timeline of events about the Saxon invasions of Britain and the centuries that followed these, during which time stories were told about these invasions and the resistance to them by the Britons.

The only valid story is story B. Story B is able to account for all six sources if these sources are treated as evidence. Story B is also able to account for the existence of the competing stories A and C, specifically the aspect of Story B that claims 'He became a hero'. Story A and C are based on the legend of King Arthur, the hero, told as stories in a much later age. Students were likely to be familiar with these kinds of stories, from television, film and story books. For young students, who do not distinguish history stories from any other kind of story, or who think a test of truth lies in the detail and expanse of a story, there is clearly a difficulty in recognizing the validity of Story B. Students are also, in many lessons, encouraged by their teachers, to write at length and in detail, and as a consequence are likely to place a high value on longer, more detailed and explanatory accounts as opposed to generalized more contracted statements that are short on detail, with no immediate appeal. For young students in particular Story B fails to interest them, it is not at all exciting and is thin on detail. For many students, *detail* is equivalent to facts, and therefore this detail speaks for itself, offering a clear sense of validation. In a teaching context, where history stories come to students as ready packaged stories or accounts, it will be difficult for students to distinguish history from legend, myth or propaganda, and very worrying that they might also equate the existence of detail with the existence of truth.

If we consider one or two of the students' responses, we gain some insight into the problems their teachers are likely to face.   For example, Rachel, aged 10, rejected Story B and chose Story C 'because it 'says more about everything'. Gareth, aged 12, also chose Story C 'because it tells you more about the battle, like who fought and where and also what happens'. Story B stood little chance with students who thought in this way.   Ruth, also aged 12, claimed Story A was best because it 'gives you the time, it dates back the king, etc. It has all the details'. Some students were explicit in labelling this kind of detail as fact. Daniel, aged 12, chose Story A 'because it was very factual. It gave the year, who was involved, where it happened and what happened'. Some of the older students also took this approach.   Stuart, aged 14, chose Story A, 'because it has names and numbers'. The validity of the detail was assured by its very existence.

Some students however, did have a much more sophisticated sense of a test in considering the possible status of information within stories of this kind. For example, Graham, aged 12, decided on Story B because he 'saw that it did not have figures like the other story making it more reliable', and David, aged 14, chose Story B because it was 'more inconclusive. There doesn't always have to be dates, numbers and names'. Layla, only 10 years old, expressed this idea more clearly, recognizing the likely survival qualities of Story B under test conditions, pointing out that 'it did not give many definite dates or anything. This meant not much of it could be wrong'.   These more sophisticated responses help to identify some key teaching points that could be introduced into history classrooms.   If some young students can think like this then it is important that we build on these ideas and incorporate them into our teaching of older students.

The above examples are taken from students who, in coming to a decision about the validity of a story, focused, at least initially, on the stories themselves, not justifying their choice with reference to the source material. Other students took one of four different approaches, and these in the main were age related, but not exclusively so.

One approach was a *matching* one. As a means of validating a story, these students picked out key words in the sources and matched them to the wording in the stories. *Matching* of this kind can be seen clearly in Christine's response, aged 12. She chose story A, because she 'saw that in clue 2 the name and the number of Saxons he killed were exactly the same' as her story. She told us that clue 2 was helpful because 'it said about how many Saxons he killed which was the same and about him having the same name'. There is some persuasive evidence that students taking this approach chose the story first and then scrutinised the clues to find specific information to support that choice. This *post hoc* justification was apparent in both the way students subsequently explained their choice of helpful clues and in the reasons given for rejecting others. Gary, another 12 year old, explained that clue 2 helped him because 'it was the only one that corresponds with Story A' and Martin, aged 10, rejected clue 6, 'because it has nothing about King Arthur in it'. Although these students used a testing strategy, it seems to have begun with them finding a point of reference in a story as a secure point from which to explore the material – a reasonable strategy for coping with the quantity of material available. However, because the point of reference, or starting point for the task, was the story the students had 'come across' from the myths and legends so often portrayed in popular fiction and film, it resulted in students reaching invalid conclusions. For many of these students conflict in the material was ignored, and repetition of detail was seen as redundant information.

Some students were adept at handling the range of material they were presented with. Although they treated the sources as information, they collected information across the range of sources. These students tended to choose Story C, the story that is more extensive in its coverage of the information available. However, although this, *collecting* approach, indicates an ability to handle a wider range of information and a higher number of variables, than those students who took a *matching* approach, and sometimes an ability to arbitrate between the stories, it was clear that these students still treated that information at face value. There was no real *conceptual* shift in their thinking, and they showed no concern about the nature of the sources (who produced them, when, and for what purpose), nor did they treat them in any way as *evidence*. The focus for these students was the information *in* the sources, with nothing to indicate that any information *about* the sources had been considered. Sophie, aged 14, justified her choice of Story C, by rejecting Story B because it 'did not say how many people he killed at Badon Hill, or anything about his armour'. Clue 1 was valued 'because it said that both sides won some of the battles and clue 3, because it tells about the armour'. She tells us that Clue 5 had limitations because although it 'tells me that the battle took place' it did not tell me 'who won or lost'. Clue 6 was given the same treatment: 'it tells me what a soldier might have looked like but not what Arthur was wearing'. Sophie's ability, like some of the students who took this approach, was to arbitrate between all the stories and take account of all the clues. This was impressive, but all these moves still treated the information as a given. However, her selection of information was not just arbitrary; some sense of relevance was at work. This approach was not so much a test of the validity of Story C but an explanation of where the information in this story could be found across the sources.

In responding to this task some students had some sense of what might count as a test in attempting to validate the story of their choice. They considered the sources an important part of this, but still found it difficult to go beyond treating the sources merely as information. The approach they took to a test of validity was *counting* the sources that said the same things, presumably as a means of corroborating what was being claimed by them. If more than one source said the same thing or something similar then this information was given credibility. However, in these cases no consideration was given to whether one source held information that might be derived from the information contained in another, and no attempt was made to consider the time context or the author purpose behind these sources. The fact that 'two clues said the same thing' or that 'all the clues agreed' was sufficient for Phillip, year 11, who chose Story C simply 'because clue 2 and 3 both say the leader was called Arthur' and although Adam, aged 14, used the word 'agree' in his response, the idea was the same. He claimed 'clue 2 and 3 were helpful, because they agreed about the name of the king, approximately how many people he killed and where the fight was at Mount Badon'. Although responses here picked out specific information in the way that responses in the *matching* category did, the validation came from the match across the sources in relation to the story, rather than a direct match between a single source and a story.

Many of the students worked with ideas about the quantity and the corroboration of information in tandem, so decoupling such ideas was not always easy. For example, Stephanie, aged 14, chose Story C, and claimed that 'clue 2, 3 and 5 are particularly helpful because they all agree with each other, and tell you the most information'. Clue 6, was then rejected because 'it only shows a soldier and not much else'.

The *collecting* and *counting* responses, and in some cases the *matching* responses, also showed students willing to ignore conflicts between the sources. For example, Robert, aged 11, claimed 'there are two clues, clue 2 and clue 3 saying that Arthur killed 960 men'.

However, a number of students did go beyond the face value acceptance of the sources as providing direct information about the past, and recognized that the circumstances of their production should be taken into account in their deliberations about how well they could support any of the stories. They asked questions of the sources that enabled some interrogation to take place, *questioning* the authors' position to know what was being claimed by the sources.

There were important distinctions however in this approach, in the way in which the sources were called into question, and in the validity of students' conclusions. In treating the sources as testimony some students questioned the author's intentions, the tone of their claims or their position to know. James, aged 11, was keen to place value on clue 1 'because this is a man of God who wouldn't lie and his parents would have told him on his birthday'. Emily, aged 14, checked the credibility of clue 1 for both its tone and the circumstances of its production, showing how the author of this source would have been made aware of the battle at Mount Badon as a child. She chose Story B because 'it doesn't say anywhere that he won all of his battles, and the monk who was born around that time (clue 1) said that both sides won battles'. She argued that 'the monk was born at the time, and although it would have been a few years before he could understand what happened he would still be around when the original story was being told'. George, aged 10, also chose Story B on the basis of clue 1, but unlike Emily, his response provided no mechanism for knowing, beyond being 'around when it happened'. His rejection of clue 2 and the paintings because they were 'done a long time after' was consistent with this thinking: the author was not in a position to know. Katherine, aged 11, recognized that the problem with the paintings was not just a question of them being 'drawn a long time afterwards' but also that they were 'pictures in the imagination'.

Some students, in *questioning* the status of the clues, made complex disconfirmatory moves, giving weight to the evidence available from the archaeological find in clue 6 to challenge the 'heavy armour' claim in Story C and in sources 3, 4 and 5. In his initial response Craig, aged 14, gave status to clue 1 on the basis of the author's proximity to the event, in claiming that Story B 'fits best with clue 1, the story that was written by someone who lived in the era', and added 'because of this it is more likely to be correct'. He explained that clue 6 was particular helpful as it enabled him 'to eliminate clue 3 and so also Story C because this mentions him wearing heavy armour which was not used at the time'. Laurence, also 14, declared that 'the clues I have seen best fit Story B as being the most accurate of the three stories' justifying this by explaining that 'clue 1 is the more primary source of the three accounts and because clue 6 discounts Story C by having no picture of Mary on the armour and the armour being not too heavy and based on primary finds'. Clues 4 and 5, were not helpful to Laurence, because 'they are not primary sources and do not contain any primary evidence, so they are probably not very reliable'.

In these examples the students' reasoning in support of a clue was consistent with their reasons for rejecting clues. These students are not yet working with a concept of evidence despite their treatment of the sources as testimony. The clues were either reliable or unreliable authorities on the events picked out. A few students however, did take things further, but this required them to recognize that story B was not just a claim about the battle but also the significance of this to later generations. These students pointed out that it was not necessary to reject clues 2 and 3, or 4 and 5, as they actually provided evidence for the last part of Story B's claim, that 'He became a hero'. William, aged 14, rejected Story A and C because 'both of them seem exaggerated' and explained that clue 1 'was written by a British monk who lived at the time this happened', claiming 'he is obviously not biased in any way as he is not putting down either the Britons or the Saxons'. He acknowledged the evidence value of later clues, explaining that 'all the other clues were still useful, even if they were biased, because they show that he was a hero, as they all show him killing or winning fights or tell the tale of how great he was'. Tony, also 14, reported, in a similar vein, that clue 2 'seconds the fact that he became a hero, by telling us that he won all his battles'.

There is an important conceptual difference here between those students who, when interrogating the circumstances surrounding the production of a source, conclude that it has no value, and those students who, working with a concept of evidence *in relation to the claim being made*, recognize that this context does not prevent its use as evidence, only what it may count as evidence *for*. This kind of understanding may well be difficult for many students to apply in the context of the task. The skill level needed to handle three stories in relation to six clues may explain the propensity for students in this and other categories to isolate singular statements in both the story and the clues, rather than consider a story as a whole and the clues as a set. Concept development is likely to be hindered by information overload and has to be a consideration in supporting students' progress, in the context of classroom teaching.

This research knowledge is further exemplified in material presented for the *How Students Learn: History in the Classroom*, 2005 publication by the National Research Council in Washington DC.

It is worth looking at an example of a relatively straightforward way in which teachers can gain access to their students' ideas about sources.

In the context of an enquiry about the arrival and significance of the pilgrims in the Mayflower at Plymouth Harbour, a group of 11 years olds were given two photocopies of paintings with the following captions. (Ashby, Lee, Shemilt, 2001)

'The Mayflower on Her Arrival in Plymouth Harbor' by William Formsby Halsall.   Painted in Massachusetts in 1882.

'The Landing of the Pilgrims' by Michael Felice Corne. Painted in Salem, Massachusetts, between 1903 and 1806.

The students were asked to examine these as part of a set of sources and to jot down any questions that occurred to them while they were looking at them.

The four example responses set out below demonstrate how students' questions reveal some of the ideas they are working with:

How did the painter know what the Mayflower looked like?

How does he know what the Mayflower looked like, and how bad or good the weather was?

How did the artist know what the Mayflower looked like because he drew it at least 200 years after?

How could they know what the ship looked like 200 years after it had sunk in Cape Cod Bay?

How did William Formsby Halsall know the view of when the Mayflower arrived at Plymouth harbour, because the ship would not have stayed in the same position for hours?

These 11 year olds are rightly concerned about the position of these painters in providing accurate testimony of this event, but they are also clearly making assumptions about the intentions of these artists in portraying this event.

However, the teacher was able to use the conflict of information provided by the two paintings, to challenge the thinking of these pupils. In asking them to write down any ideas they had that might solve this conflict one of the pupils had responded with 'I think the Indians are in the picture to show they were there first.' The teacher put this idea to the whole class and asking them what they thought about this. The following dialogue then took place.

Matthew, an 11 year old responded:

Art isn't always total fact it's usually symbolism because you couldn't put tiny men on there, showing they are far away, it could very well symbolize, year, that these Native Americans are here first and it's not really the Pilgrims land at all.

Teacher: *What would we need to know to interpret the painting?*

Adam: *You would need to know about the painter who actually painted it. You need some background information.*

Peter: *Then we could find out the truth about what it's saying.*

Teacher: *Would the information you need just be information about the painter?   What else would you need to know?*

Matthew: *What period of time it was painted and whereabouts it was painted. They could be changed with society, like giving into society [meaning agreeing with predominant ideas?] because like, most people in Salem, Massachusetts, which is where this was painted, were white, so he wanted to portray the white people as the great greats ... or however you want to interpret it.*

In this very straightforward task the teacher has firstly, revealed student thinking – the majority of students were working with an understanding of sources as testimony, and in doing so found it wanting, and secondly used one of the pupil responses to a question that revealed the dilemma about these paintings as testimony to generate a teaching and learning dialogue that moved students from a testimony level to a situation in which she could encourage her pupils away from treating the information in the painting as *information about* the arrival of the Mayflower and the landing of the Pilgrims towards an understanding of the painting *as evidence of* the significance of this event to later generations.

What Does All This Mean?

If it is accepted that school students should understand the nature and status of the historical knowledge they are expected to acquire during their course of study then it is important that the teaching agenda addresses some key goals. Students will need to be taught to distinguish the past from history, and sources from evidence. While the past may be everything that ever happened within the framework of human existence, history is what we claim about that past. It should be clear that we have no direct access to that past, it is gone and our only access to it is through what it might have left behind in the form of artefacts, habits, customs, memories etc. However, these cannot tell us of the societies that produced them in any direct sense, and it is only through asking questions of them that we can get them to yield what might be used as evidence for our enquiries. School students need opportunities to pursue the kind of work that will help them to develop an understanding of these complex relationships, and that might challenge some of the misconceptions they have about these.

However, for them to be precise in their understanding of evidence, students will also need to understand what might count as evidence in any specific case. Enquiries into what happened in the past, what actions took place, and the reasons behind those actions relate to the evidence in different ways. Working with the nature of the questions and asking students what might count as evidence will both develop their understanding of the concept of evidence, and the distinctions between the past, sources, evidence and history. It will also help them to see that different kinds of questions, in relating to the evidence in different ways, are likely to generate claims that differ in their status. For younger students simple distinctions might be made: that demonstrate that actions may relate to the testimony of witnesses in a straightforward manner, whilst reasons for those actions are not so readily available to the historian in this way. For older students more complex ideas can be explored: demonstrating that while factual statements may be established on the basis of source material, historians also use these as evidence for some of the higher level claims they may wish to make, and that in doing so they put these factual statements into relationships with each other, producing complex accounts of past actions, events, processes and changes.

Students can work with source material to generate hypotheses that might be tested against further sources or factual statements. They would need to develop their understanding that a test does not just involve a search for evidence that might support their theories but to consider what evidence might provide disconfirmation of any given claim, and to learn something of the provisional nature of some of our knowledge of the past.

What has become clear to us in the UK is the importance of school students working with source material in the context of historical enquiry; the relationship between sources and the question being asked should be able to demonstrate to school students that the important issue is not the reliability of any given source, but the weight that might be placed on a source *as evidence in the context of the specific claim* it is attempting to substantiate or refute.

Research provides us with knowledge of the challenges we face in developing these understandings in school students. It suggests the importance of teaching that allows these misconceptions and problems to be exposed to the teacher, and that enables the teacher in turn to demonstrate how these less powerful ways of thinking cannot solve the problems that more powerful ideas can.

References

Denis Shemilt, (1980) *History 13-16 Evaluation Study*, Holmes McDougall, Edinburgh.

P.J. Rogers (1980) *The New History: theory into Practice*, Historical Association, Teaching History Series No. 44, London.

Rogers, P.J. (1984) 'Why Teach History?' in *Learning History*, eds. A.K. Dickinson, P.J. Lee, P.J. Rogers, Heinemann, London.

Lee, P.J. (1984) 'Why Learn History?' in *Learning History*, eds. A.K. Dickinson, P.J. Lee, P.J. Rogers, Heinemann, London.

Sylvester, David (1994) 'Change and continuity in history teaching 1900-93' in *Teaching History*, ed. Hilary Bourdillon, Routledge in association with Open University, London and New York.

Shemilt, Denis, (1992) 'Preface' in *The Aims of School History: The National Curriculum and Beyond*, eds. Peter Lee, John Slater, Paddy Walsh, and John White, The London File, Tufnell Press, London.

Lee, Peter, (1992) 'History in School: Aims, Purposes, and Approaches. A Reply to John White' in *The Aims of School History: The National Curriculum and Beyond*, eds. Peter Lee, John Slater, Paddy Walsh, and John White, The London File, Tufnell Press, London.

Walsh, Paddy, (1992) 'History and Love of the Past' in *The Aims of School History: The National Curriculum and Beyond*, eds. Peter Lee, John Slater, Paddy Walsh, and John White, The London File, Tufnell Press, London.

The National Curriculum for History, (2007) Qualifications and Curriculum Authority.

Donovan, M. Suzanne, and Bransford, John D., Chapter 1: 'Introduction', in M. Suzanne Donovan and John D. Bransford, eds. *How Students Learn: History in the Classroom*, National Research Council, National Academies Press. Washington DC. 2005.

W.H. Walsh, (1963) An introduction to the Philosophy of History, Hutchinson, London.

Ashby R. Lee, P.J, Shemilt, D. (2001) 'Putting Principles into Practice: Teaching and Planning' in M. Suzanne Donovan and John D. Bransford, eds. *How Students Learn: History in the Classroom*, National Research Council, National Academies Press. Washington DC. 2005.

Lee, P., Ashby, R. and Dickinson, A.K. (1995) 'Progression in Children's Ideas about History' in M. Hughes (Ed), *Progression in Learning.* Pp. 50-81. (Series editor D. McIntyre) Clevedon, England. Bristol, PA, USA. Adelaide, Australia,. Multilingual Matters, BERA Dialogues 11.

Appendix A

People who are interested in the past sometimes argue about whether something is true or not. Below are three stories from three different books.

READ THE STORIES CAREFULLY

> **Story A:**
> About the year 500 there lived a very brave king of the Britons called Arthur. He fought the Saxons and won all his battles. In his twelfth battle at Mount Badon he killed 960 Saxons himself.

> **Story B:**
> About the year 500 a leader of the Britons fought the Saxon invaders and defeated them several times. One of his battles was at Badon Hill. He became a hero.

> **Story C:**
> About the year 500 there lived a King called Arthur. Arthur and his knights fought a big battle at Mount Badon. Arthur wore heavy armour with a picture of Mary mother of Jesus on it. This helped to make him very brave when he rode into battle. At the battle he killed many Saxons.

Sometimes we have CLUES to help us to decide how true a story is. We have some clues about this story.

STUDY THE CLUES CAREFULLY

> **Clue 1:** Written in 540 by a British Monk called Gildas
>
> Some Britons were murdered by the Saxons, some were made slaves. Some fought back under a leader called Ambrosius. Sometimes the Britons won the battles and sometimes the Saxons won. There was a big battle at Badon Hill. I know about this because I was born in the year it happened.

> **Clue 2:** Written in 800 by a Welsh Monk called Nennius
>
> The war leader was called Arthur. His twelfth battle was on Mount Badon. At the battle Arthur killed 960 Saxons all on his own. He won all the battles he fought.

> **Clue 3:** Written in 1125 by a Monk called William
>
> At the battle of Mount Badon, Arthur killed 900 Saxons all on his own. He had a picture of Mary, mother of Jesus on his armour.

Clue 4: A painting done in 1400 showing King Arthur killing Mordred.

Clue 5: A picture of King Arthur and his knights fighting the Saxons, drawn about 1400.

Clue 6: A drawing of a soldier of the 400s and 500s (based on finds dug up by archaeologists).

中文全譯

歷史探究與證據概念：
課程目標、教與學的挑戰、學生理解

Rosalyn Ashby 　著

詹怡娜* 　譯

一、前言

　　本文的最初意旨在於強調以下歷史教育目標的重要性：歷史教育應包含發展學生對歷史探究 (historical enquiry) 之性質的理解，以及更具體地培養他們有關史料證據的概念。然而，設定此類目標是一回事，要求教師和學生符合這些目標截然是另一回事。因此，本文有必要超越對這些目標的解說，也針對這整套機制的性質以及學生可能面臨的挑戰類型提供一些評論。這些挑戰將被置於學生對歷史論述的定位與本質的理解以及處理史料的方法之特定研究知識背景下討論：學生傾向以表面的意義處理史料，與他們假設目擊者證詞提供關於過去的直接資料。

*中國文化大學史學所博士候選人

二、何以對於歷史證據的理解是
歷史教育的重要部分？

在英國，歷史教師的教學工作前提是：在一個開放、現代、民主、多元文化的社會裡，歷史教育必須擺脫學習與死記硬背旨在鼓勵某種特定種類愛國認同的單軌歷史記事。自 1970 年代起，英國已接受學童須學習歷史知識的性質與定位的看法，這主要是由於一群教師在 1972 年倡議建立學校委員會歷史科計畫 (SCHP)，並計畫將這些目標附屬於十四至十六歲學生升學考試之教學課程的結果。這種歷史教學的新方法在過去三十年間已在學校課程中逐漸體現：首先，透過 1986 年新通過的普通中等教育證書 (GCSE) 考試，延伸這些原理將其具體化到所有十四至十六歲學生公開考試課程中；其次，於 1992 年引進針對五至十四歲學生設計的全國教育歷史課程。1995 年與 2000 年全國教育課程修訂也維持此種獲取歷史知識的學科訓練／知識形式方法。

此一傳統認為學生的歷史知識應奠基於開放的調查，在學校中學生被教導要確認對過去所做出的陳述源自於（且符合）證據。教師努力培養學生理解證據是收集自對過去所遺留資料的檢驗，以及來自這些資料可能產生的一系列問題與假設。

在 1970 年代，學校委員會歷史科計畫 (SCHP) 認識到，「儘管兒童可以學習到各種事物，但是直到他們掌握歷史探究的性質前，他們不能說是了解任何事情」(Shemilt, 1980, p.4) 這個計畫強調將歷史理解為知識形式的重要性，主張「歷史已在探究和了解人類經驗上發展出典型的方法」，並認為「當兒童能或多或少通曉以專業方法調查過去所得到的結論時，他們才被訓練到掌握這些探究的方法、邏輯和觀點本身的程度。」(Shemilt, 1980, p.26) 這個計畫將證據視為歷史事業具關鍵性的觀念之一，也同樣認

可伴隨而來的技巧：「探究、形成假設、分析、推論、判斷與綜合。」
(Shemilt, 1980, p.7)

於 1980 年為支持學校委員會歷史科計畫所寫的著作中，Peter Rogers
在這個計畫的學科訓練目標重要性方面清晰地闡述了他的理念。在歷史協
會手冊《新史學》中，他主張在學學生的歷史知識應該「奠基於理性」，
說明儘管一個孩子：

> 也許相信他已學到的東西，但他無<u>權</u>肯定它們（即使事實上他所學
> 到的東西是正確的），因為他無法評估此一「知識」的根據何
> 在。……沒有完全不包含任何「專門技術」(know how) 的知識，
> 「專門技術」很大程度為個別學科所特有。本文所指的正是歷史學
> 家的「專門技術」，由此可見<u>僅</u>傳播學術研究的成果而缺乏對研究
> 程序的了解是十分不恰當的。……顯然地，研究程序使「歷史」得
> 以成為一門學科……缺乏它們（程序）的研究根本很難算做是「歷
> 史」。(Rogers, 1980, p.19)

1984 年，任教於於北愛爾蘭的貝爾法斯特女皇大學 (Queen's
University) 的 Rogers，在其著作中對前述說法提出了進一步的論證。他關
注孩童自他們成長的日常生活世界中所獲得之有關過去的想像，指出「我
們對於現在的觀念不可能不深受某個版本的過去影響，某個我們在成長過
程中吸收並在長大後的生活中表達出來的版本。」他提出這個論點作為學
校課程設置歷史科的正當理由，因為若不研究歷史，「將無法掌控讓我們
在其中可更大限度看到世界的框架的發展，且已長成的謬論將永遠存
在。」(Rogers, 1984, p.21)

但歷史教育應該是怎樣的呢？Rogers 顯然關注的是，主張歷史爭論辯論不應迴避主張肯定：「避免涉及當前爭議性問題的歷史內容，除了排除理性周密調查的可能性，無法達到任何成果。」(Rogers, 1984, p.21) 他堅持學校歷史教育應涉及歷史知識的性質，以及因過去爭議性記述而來的爭議，因為「歷史大部分處理的事項，基本上都是有爭議的」，「尋找歷史敘述之間的一致性，只是對於歷史知識性質的誤解」。(Rogers, 1980, p.21) 對 Rogers 而言，這並非贊成任何對於過去的記載，也不是認為學生們應可選擇他們喜好的任何描述。他明確表示，「否定『一個正確的版本』是合理可行的目標，但並非因而認可任何具爭議性、毫無根據的關於過去之記述」。(Rogers, 1984, p.22) 相反地，他希望學校裡的學生所受到的教育能使他們區分出「審慎而有根據的看法，與相反的愚蠢、無知和偏見偏頗之見解。」(Rogers, 1984, p.22)

在此對 Rogers 而言證據的重要性攸關成敗。強調對於「有根據的知識主張之基礎方法」的理解，以及「歷史為關於過去的主張提供了更加可靠的根據，因為它體現並運用了通過時間錘鍊而達到最佳效果之用以識別與處理證據的技術和程序」。(Rogers, 1984, p.22) 如果不了解這些「技術和程序」，必定很難把學校教育的歷史故事，與那些兒童學自他們目前所置身之肆無忌憚的多媒體世界的歷史故事區隔開來。Rogers 的想法並非孤明先發。1984 年，任教於英國倫敦大學教育學院的 Peter Lee 在其著作也同樣強調歷史提供了考察過去唯一的理性手段，指出「這個主張在某種程度上建立於歷史逐漸發展中的證據概念，以及處理證據的技術。」(Lee, 1984, p.4)

在 1990 年代，英國歷史教師在歷史課程前景問題的全國論辯中，強烈捍衛此一立場。在某些艱鉅的挑戰中，David Sylvester（於 1972 至 1975 年間領導 SCHP）要求歷史教師「對他們在過去四分之一個世紀以來所發展的專業知識保持信心」，不論他們之中是否有足夠的人將「繼續同

樣肯定歷史教育對心智發展的作用，以及提供事實這方面的作用」，並再度重申歷史教育對於「知道新知識如何被發現」與「記憶過往」這兩方面同樣重要的信念。(Sylvester, 1994, p.22) 在這場關於全國歷史課程性質的論辯中，Shemilt 及 Lee 也在這個歷史教育方法之重要性上重申了他們的立場。

Shemilt 的意見是清楚明瞭的：

> 關注知識主張的證據基礎、歷史記載的發展邏輯，以及因果解釋的模態邏輯並不僅僅只是賣弄學問；恰好相反，它是維持開放傳統的道德觀念基礎，從而也是維持開放社會的道德觀念基礎。(Shemilt, 1992, p.7)

為了捍衛歷史作為學校教育科目的完整性，遠離那些企圖利用它達到「公民資格」與「愛國主義」等目標，Lee 提出「歷史不僅止是學會一套新信念，甚或是新的實質性知識的問題」的論點。他認為歷史也「具有一套第二序理解以及理性熱情（例如對於真理，與對證據的尊重）」，故能給予歷史理解「帶有愛國主義所不具備的普世性」。(Lee, 1992)

這個立場的一個重要面向，是激勵出學生們對過去人們的一種責任感，承認他們的經驗與努力，並提供現今的我們與在我們時代之外的人類一項重要的聯繫。如同 Paddy Walsh 在上述論辯的脈絡下所強調的，這是「對於已死去與消逝的人類和人類世界的手足之愛」。儘管「我們不能形塑與影響〔過去〕，因而也無法為它負責」，但對於過去我們「並非完全是無可奈何的」。「我們對於過去所能做的一件事，就是使其在消逝之後的記錄可靠正確。」(Paddy Walsh: 1992, pp.36-37) 對於歷史證據的理解，在針對歷史記錄與針對過去所提主張的正確性保持警覺方面顯然是必要的。

三、英國國民歷史教育課程要求學生們在歷史探究與證據概念方面理解什麼？

英國國民歷史教育課程確實對此一開放式的學校歷史教學方式保持信念，因而關於證據與解釋的概念在課程規章中持續佔有中心地位。新的國家課程規畫（自 2008 年 9 月開始在學校中使用）在與歷史探究的原則直接相關的目標上，與之前的版本有類似規畫。這份文件第 3 頁的重要聲明包含以下陳述：

> 當中小學生發展他們對歷史學習性質的認知時，他們提問並回答重要的問題、評估證據、辨別與分析對過去不同的解釋，並學習充實他們所做的任何論點與判斷。

事實上，這些新的提案重申並加強要求學生們被教導與歷史探究相關的觀念與技巧之目標。

(一) 歷史探究

學生們應該能夠：

1. 各自獨立或作為團隊的一份子以識別和調查具體的歷史問題或議題，提出假設並加以檢驗。
2. 對歷史問題或議題進行批判性的思考。

(二) 使用證據

學生們應該能夠：

1. 識別、選擇及使用一定範圍內的史料，包含文字、視覺和口述史

料、人工製品及歷史遺跡。

2. 評估用以推理結論所使用的史料。

提供注釋詳述這些要求：

歷史探究：包含針對不同類型的歷史問題與議題進行有組織的探究。學生們應該開始策畫並琢磨他們自己的問題，以便組織一場有組織的考究，發展他們自己的假設，並挑選和安排證據以達到及證明他們的結論。學生們既可以使用他們所獲得的知識與理解提出假說，也可以基於他們自己的預設與價值觀在破題之始提出假說，而後再依證據加以檢驗。

使用證據：對於過去的知識是基於來自史料的證據，並取決於所提問的問題及可以得到的史料，而非基於事先設想所用史料的確實性與可靠程度。這包含透過研究史料的出處、用途和語言來評估證據的價值及可靠性。（摘錄來自於：*The National Curriculum 2007*, Qualifications and Curriculum Authority, 2007.）

這些對於教師及其學生們而言都是嚴格的要求，重要的是作為英國歷史教師，我們理解這項挑戰的性質。學術研究對此有所助益，而且與課堂教學相關的研究知識成果也越來越豐富。

四、關於教師與其學生們在追求這些歷史教學目標所面臨的挑戰之性質上，學術研究告訴我們什麼？

從現有的研究成果可以明瞭，在課堂文化裡，辨別學生們的先入之見

以及挑戰他們的誤解，對於有效的學習是必須的。

> 學生們來到教室時，對於世界如何運作已經有了先入之見。如果不能契合（engage）他們原有的理解，他們也許就無法掌握被教導的新概念和訊息。或者他們會出於考試的目的而學習，但是一旦出了教室就恢復到原來的先入之見。(M.Suzanne Donovan and John D. Bransford, 2005: p.1)

但是什麼類型的先入之見及誤解是我們可能在歷史課堂上面臨的？以及希望運用史料從事教學，並培養學生們有關歷史證據概念的教師在此會遇到什麼問題？此處有幾個難題。

最具挑戰性的難題，來自於如何說服傾向以「字面意義」看待史料的學生們，反之將史料作為證據而使用。為了鼓勵學生們區別過去與歷史之間的差別，史料被引介給學生們。然而，這不是一件簡單的事，因為這些史料「並未在其表面就帶有它們的意義與真偽」。(Walsh, 1963; p.20) 如果學生們要超越以「字面意義」處理史料的程度，並開始認清史料的「意義與真偽」將決定它能或不能作為證據使用，那麼了解一份資料的性質將是基本的第一步驟。了解史料出現的社會背景及其來龍去脈，因此是理解史料能作為證據之份量的重要層面，而了解什麼可以算得上任何對過去的主張及探究的證據，則是另一個重要層面。

為了挑戰學生們以字面意義（作為直接可得的訊息）看待史料的習性，老師要求學生們對史料加以檢驗，透過關於誰產生史料、何時產生，以及產生目的等問題的思考。這個教學方法可能改變學生們的思維方式，不再毫無疑問地接受史料所包含的訊息。然而此一方法本身卻可能造成更進一步的問題與誤解：認為證詞可能存有偏見因而不可靠，結果對史家而言毫無用處。在此時，朝向更高理解層次的進一步措施是必要的：此一措

施將能有助於理解到，對一份目擊者的報告進行檢驗，可使它產生超出其所意欲揭示的訊息。這對於鼓勵學生們將史料考慮作為證據而言極為關鍵。

關於兒童對歷史證據的認知，現今我們有一批可靠的研究成果。在1970 年代晚期和 1980 年代早期，Peter Lee、Alaric Dickinson、Rosalyn Ashby 所進行的小規模研究，以及 Denis Shemilt 的 *Evaluation Study* 對 SCHP 的研究 (Shemilt, 1980)，提供了知識框架，以及關於學生們對歷史證據之認知進程（此一進程為由弱漸強的主導觀念）的理解。

上述這些研究在指出學生們可能擁有的先入之見與誤解上，對教師而言是有用的。一一檢視這些由弱漸強的主導觀念，我們便有可能描繪出其變化範圍：從將史料視為提供了關於過去直接可得的「現成」訊息 (information)，到將史料視為證詞 (testimony)，乃至於超越證詞到了更為強而有力的觀念，亦即必得將史料理解為證據（evidence，作為特定社會之產物。如果能理解至此，作為證據的史料就能夠加以探討與質疑，以便視乎特定的探究而產生有關該社會之證據）。

在整個 1990 年代及其後，透過 ESRC（經濟與社會科學研究協會）所贊助的 CHATA（歷史概念與教學取向）計畫，此一知識庫變得更加完善與擴張。CHATA 計畫的主要方向是研究學生們對史料的態度、他們對證據的理解，以及他們檢驗與證實歷史主張的方法。此項研究成果很明確地顯示，即使是許多年紀較長的學生也有一種傾向，亦即只重視史料的表面價值，或以與所問問題或所作解釋無關的可靠性檢驗為基礎，將史料視為無用而予以貶斥。

此處提出一些例證，以便強調在這個計畫的數據收集期間，孩子藉以回應此項研究任務時所具有的一些觀念。附錄 A (Lee, Ashby, Dickinson, 1995, pp.65-67) 提供一組這個研究中所使用的資料作為例證，並可支持在接下來的討論中所舉出的問答實例。這個資料包含了三個歷史敘述與六項

史料。學生們被要求根據史料的脈絡，以及提供給他們的背景資料來考慮這三個故事（敘述）的確實性。此一背景資料是有關撒克遜人侵略英國及其後幾個世紀的事件時間表，這些入侵與反抗的故事則是由英國人在這個時期中所講述。

唯一有根據的故事是故事 B。如果把這些史料當作證據的話，故事 B 則囊括說明了全部六項史料。故事 B 也能說明為何會有故事 A 與故事 C 的存在，特別是當故事 B 的內容中主張「他成為一位英雄」。故事 A 和故事 C 都是基於亞瑟王的傳說而成，在時間晚得多的時代裡作為英雄故事而流傳。學生們對於這一類的故事由於接觸電視、電影和故事書而相當熟悉。對於那些無法辨別歷史故事與其他類型的故事，或者認為判斷真實可以依靠故事本身的詳盡程度與涵蓋範圍的學生們而言，要想認識故事 B 的確實性顯然相當困難。在許多課程中，學生們亦由於受到老師的鼓勵而寫作長篇大論，結果學生們很可能給予較為冗長、詳細及解說性的敘述較高的評價，反而對於缺乏細節、屬於通論性、較為濃縮的陳述缺乏直接的興趣。故事 B 一點也不刺激且情節單薄，尤其無法引起年輕學生的興趣。對許多學生而言，細節等同於事實，因此細節即可為自己發聲，提供一種明晰的確實感。在教學的情境裡，當歷史故事在學生們眼前以現成包裝過後的故事或記載而出現時，要求學生們從傳說、神話或宣傳中辨別出歷史將是非常困難的。而且令人擔憂的是，他們可能會認為細節的存在就等同於真實的存在。

如果我們仔細思考一項或兩項學生們的回應，我們就能較為深入地了解他們的老師所可能面臨到的問題。例如， 十歲的 Rachel，排除故事 B 而選擇了故事 C，「因為它對每一件事講了更多。」十二歲的 Gareth 也選擇故事 C，「因為它告訴你更多關於這場戰役的情節，像是誰在作戰、在何處作戰，以及發生了什麼事？」以此方式思考的學生們選擇故事 B 的機率很低。同樣是十二歲的 Ruth，主張故事 A 是最佳選擇，因為它「給

了你年代，可以往前追溯到國王等等。它具備所有的細節。」有些學生直率地把這種細節歸類成證據。十二歲的 Daniel 選擇故事 A，「因為它非常真實。它提供了年份、相關人物、事件發生地點及發生了何事。」一些年紀稍長的學生也採取了這種判斷方法。十四歲的 Stuart 選擇故事 A，「因為它有名字與數字。」細節的存在本身是其確實性的保證。

然而，有些學生在考慮這類故事中所含訊息的潛在地位上，展現更為深思熟慮的判斷力。例如，十二歲的 Graham 選擇故事 B，因為他「看到它沒有像其他故事中的數據，使它看起來較為可靠」；而十四歲的 David 選擇故事 B，因為它「更不確定。並不非得要有日期、數字與名字不可。」只有十歲大的 Layla 更清楚地表達了這種觀念。她看出經檢驗過後故事 B 可能擁有的存活價值，並指出「它沒有提供很多明確的日期或任何事。這意味著它可以犯錯的地方不多。」這些較為深思熟慮的回應，有助於發現可以引進歷史課堂中的某些關鍵教學要領。如果一些年幼的學生可以如此這般地思考，那麼重要的是我們以這些觀念為基礎，將之結合到我們對年長的學生之教學中。

以上的例子取自學生們對於一個故事之真實性的判斷，至少在最初焦點是集中於故事本身，而非以史料作為基準來證明他們的選擇。其他學生則採用四種不同方法的其中一種，這在基本上與年齡有關，但是仍有例外。

一種方法是比對法。作為證實一個故事的手段，這些學生會在材料裡選出關鍵字，並在故事中找出匹配的用語。這種比對法可以清楚地見於十二歲的 Christine 的回答中。她選擇故事 A，因為她「看到線索 2 他（亞瑟王）所殺戮的撒克遜人的名字與數量正好符合」她所選的故事。她告訴我們線索 2 是有幫助的，因為「關於他（亞瑟王）殺戮的撒克遜人數量是一致的，而且他有相同的名字。」這是具有某種說服力的證據，使用這種方法的學生首先選擇故事，然後詳細閱讀這些線索，以發現特定的訊息來

支持其選擇。這種帶有前後因果關係的證明法，顯然運用於兩方面：學生們接下來對他們選擇的有用線索之解釋，以及排除其他線索的原因。另一名十二歲的 Gary 解釋道線索 2 對他有幫助，因為「它是唯一一個符合故事 A 的」。而十歲的 Martin 排除線索 6，「因為它完全沒有提到亞瑟王」。儘管這些學生使用了一種檢驗策略，但他們似乎是以在故事中尋找參照點，作為考察資料的安全切入點為始，這是一個處理面對現成資料之數量的合理策略。然而，因為這個參照點或作業的出發點，是學生們從通俗小說與電影裡時常描繪的神話與傳說中曾經「遇見」的故事，導致學生們作出無效的結論。對於許多這類的學生來說，資料中的牴牾會遭受忽略，而重複的細節則會被視為是多餘的訊息。

　　一些學生擅於處理呈現在他們眼前的資料。儘管他們將史料當作訊息，他們卻透過一連串不同的史料來蒐集訊息。這些學生傾向於選擇故事 C，因為這個故事涵蓋更廣泛的可得訊息於其中。不過，雖然蒐集法相較於那些採取比對法的學生們而言，顯示了一種能處理更廣泛訊息與更高程度變量的能力，甚至時有一種能在不同故事之間加以判斷的能力，但很清楚的是，這些學生仍然是將所得訊息加以字面意義的解讀。在他們的思考中沒有真正概念上的轉變，而且他們顯露出既不關心史料的性質（誰製造它們、何時製造、為了什麼目的而製造），也未曾將史料以任何方式視為證據來處理。這些學生注目的是從史料之中得來的訊息，未嘗顯示出有關史料本身的訊息曾經被他們考慮過。十四歲的 Sophie 選擇故事 C 而排除故事 B，因為它「沒有述說他（亞瑟王）在巴頓山殺過多少人，或者說到任何有關他（亞瑟王）部隊的事情。」線索 1 是重要的，「因為它提及雙方都贏了某些戰役。而線索 3 之所以重要，則是因為談到了部隊。」她告訴我們線索 5 有其局限，因為儘管它「告訴我發生了這場戰役」，卻沒有告訴我「誰贏誰輸」。同樣地，線索 6 也是一樣：「它告訴我一位士兵是何模樣，卻沒說亞瑟王穿些什麼。」Sophie 的能力就如同採取這種方法的

某些學生一樣，在於能夠在所有的故事之間做出裁斷，並考慮到所有的線索。這是令人印象深刻的，但是所有這些舉動仍然將訊息作為已知的事實來處理。然而，她的選擇並非只是隨心所欲之舉，某種關連性的判斷力也在起作用。這種方法不太算得上是對於故事 C 之真實性的檢驗，反而是對於如何在不同史料裡找到此一故事的相關訊息之解說。

在回答這項作業時，一些學生企圖去驗證他們所選擇的故事，從而意識到怎樣才可以算得上是一種檢驗。他們認為史料是其中重要的一部分，但也發現要超越將史料僅僅視為訊息是極其困難的。他們採取用來檢驗確實性的計數法，是認為講述了相同事物的史料是較為真實的，這種方法大概是作為確證這些史料說了些什麼的手段。如果不只一份史料講述了同一件事或相似之事，那麼這個訊息就被認為較具可信度。然而，在這些案例中，沒有考慮過一份史料所包含的訊息，有可能是從另一份史料中轉手而來的，而且未曾嘗試去考慮在這些史料背後的時間脈絡或作者目的。事實上，「兩個線索在說相同的事」或者「所有的線索都相同一致」，對於十一歲的 Phillip 來說已經足夠，他因此選擇了故事 C，僅僅「因為線索 2 和線索 3 均說明領導者名叫『亞瑟』」。而十四歲的 Adam 雖然在他的回答中使用了「同意」的字眼，他的觀念也是一樣的。他聲稱「線索 2 與線索 3 是有幫助的，因為它們都同意國王的名字為同一個，以及他（亞瑟王）在巴頓山大約殺了多少人。」儘管此處的回答是揀選出特定的訊息，與比對法中的回答所為如出一轍，但是其確實性來自於比對與故事相關的不同史料，而非在單一史料與單一故事之間尋求直接的對應。

許多學生以有關數量的觀念來進行思考，並習於比較訊息是否前後呼應，因此要消除這樣的觀念並非易事。例如，十四歲的 Stephanie 選擇故事 C，並且宣稱「線索 2、3、5 特別有幫助，因為它們彼此之間相互一致，又告訴你最多訊息」。線索 6 遭到排除，因為「它只秀出一名士兵，別無其他。」

　　蒐集法和計數法的回答，以及在某些案例中的比對法，也顯示學生們會自動忽略史料之間的衝突。例如，十一歲的 Robert 宣稱，「有兩個線索，線索 2 和線索 3 都說亞瑟殺死了 960 個人」。

　　然而，有些學生的確超越了以字面意義解讀史料的方式，不再將史料作為提供關於過去的直接訊息，他們認識到當思索史料在多大程度上能夠支持任何一個故事時，史料產生的背景應該被列入考慮。他們對於史料提出可進行查詢的疑問，質問作者的立場以了解這些史料的主張。

　　但是這個方法在對於史料提出質疑的方式，以及學生們結論的確實性上有著重要的特點。在將史料看作證詞的過程中，一些學生質疑作者的意圖、他們主張的論調，或其何以得知訊息的立場。十一歲的 James 熱切地看重線索 1，「因為這是一位從屬於上帝的人，他不會說謊，而且他的父母應該在他生日時告訴過他此事（巴頓山戰役與他的生日同年）」。十四歲的 Emily 由兩個方面確認線索 1 的可靠性：它的論調及其產生的背景，由此顯示這份史料的作者如何在兒時即已被告知這場在巴頓山的戰役。她選擇故事 B 是因為「它並沒有說他（亞瑟王）贏得所有的戰役之處，而且大約出生於那時的教士（線索 1）說雙方都有取勝的戰役」。她認為「這位教士在那時出生，儘管此事在他真正懂事之前已經過了數年，但是當原來的故事被傳頌時他仍可得知。」十歲的 George 也是根據線索 1 選擇故事 B，但是與 Emily 不同，他的回答並未提供認知的途徑，除了「大約在此事發生時」。他拒絕線索 2 及那些繪畫，因為他們是「完成於很久之後」。這和如此這般的想法是一致的：作者無從得知。十一歲的 Katherine 認為這些繪畫的問題不僅僅在於它們「繪製於很久之後」，還包括了他們是「透過想像而來的畫作」。

　　一些學生當質疑這些線索的地位時，做出複雜的否證意見，他們看重線索 6 由考古發現所得的證據，藉以挑戰故事 C 及線索 3、4、5 中所做之「沉重盔甲」的主張。在十四歲的 Craig 最初的回答中，基於作者與此

一事件（在時間上）的接近而給予線索 1 相當的地位，主張故事 B「最能符合線索 1，此一故事為生活在當時的某人所寫的」，並補充「因為這一點，這看起來較可能是正確的」。他解釋說線索 6 特別有幫助，因為它使他能夠「淘汰線索3 及故事 C，因為它們提到他（亞瑟王）所穿著的沉重盔甲，其實並未使用於這個時期。十四歲的 Laurence 宣布「我看到的線索最符合故事 B，使它成為三個故事中最為準確的」，他透過以下解釋來加以證明：「線索 1 是這三個敘述更為原始的來源；透過線索 6 將故事 C 排除，因為盔甲上沒有瑪莉的圖像、盔甲看起來並不太重，況且線索 6 是基於原始發現。線索 4、5 對 Laurence 來說沒有幫助，因為「它們不是原始資料，也不包含任何主要證據，所以它們可能不是非常可靠」。

　　在這些例子中，學生們支持某個線索的推理，與他們排除其他線索的推理是一致的。這些學生尚未形成證據的概念，儘管他們已將史料作為證詞來處理。這些線索對於揀選出來的事件而言，要麼可靠要麼不可靠。不過，少數的學生的確已更進了一步，但這需要他們認識到故事 B 不僅只是有關此一戰役的說明，還具有對於後世的重要意義。這些學生指出，不見得非得要排除線索 2、3 或 4、5，因為它們確實為故事 B 的最後一部分敘述提供了證據，亦即「他（亞瑟王）成為一位英雄」。十四歲的 William 排除了故事 A 和 C，因為「這兩者似乎皆言過其實」，並解釋線索 1「是由活在事件發生當時的英國教士所寫下」，主張「他顯然不帶有任何偏見，因為他將英國人與撒克遜人一視同仁，不加貶損。」他承認時代較晚的線索也具有證據價值，解釋說「所有其他的線索仍然有用，即使它們帶有偏見。因為它們顯示出他（亞瑟王）是一位英雄，表現出他的殺戮或贏取勝仗，或者述說他是如何的偉大。」同樣是十四歲的 Tony 以相仿的口吻回答，線索 2「支持了他（亞瑟王）成為一位英雄的事實，因為它告訴我們他贏得了所有他所參與的戰爭。」

　　此處有一個概念上的重要差異，當質疑史料來源產生的環境時，一類

學生的結論是該史料毫無價值；而另一類學生則因抱持與所做主張相關聯的證據概念，從而認識到這樣的背景並不妨礙該史料可以作為證據來使用，只是要考慮它能作為什麼的證據。對於許多學生而言，將這種理解運用在這個作業之中是相當困難的。這個技巧的層次需要處理與六個線索相關的三個故事，也許可以解釋學生們在此一範疇和其他範疇中，孤立故事與線索中之個別陳述的傾向，而非傾向於將一個故事作為整體、將線索視為全盤來考慮。概念的發展很可能被負載過多的訊息所阻礙，並且需要在課堂教學的脈絡下，為了支持學生們的進展而加以考慮。

這項研究在 2005 年所出版的《學生們如何學習：在教室中的歷史課》（*How Students Learn: History in the Classroom*，由華盛頓特區國家研究委員會所出版）裡所呈現的材料，得到更進一步的例證。

這是值得一看的例子，教師利用相對而言簡單明瞭的方式，以得知其學生們關於史料的觀念。

關於一項探究搭乘五月花號的清教徒抵達普利茅斯港之意義，一群十一歲的學生們被給予兩份寫著以下說明的畫作影本。(Ashby, Lee, Shemilt, 2001)

> 《來到普利茅斯港的五月花號》，畫家為 William Formsby Halsall，繪於 1882 年的麻薩諸塞州。

> 《清教徒的登陸》，畫家為 Michael Felice Corne，繪於 1806-1903 年間麻薩諸塞州的 Salem 市。

學生們被要求將這兩幅畫作為整組史料中的一部分來加以檢驗，並隨即寫下當他們看到這些材料時出現在他們心裡的任何問題。

以下四個回答的例子，展現了學生們的問題如何顯示出他們自身運作

的觀念：

> 畫家如何得知五月花號的外觀為何？
>
> 他怎麼知道五月花號的樣子？或者當時的天氣是好是壞？
>
> 這至少是在兩百年之後才畫的，這位藝術家如何知道五月花號長啥樣？
>
> 在五月花號沉沒於鱈魚角灣的兩百年後，他們怎麼知道這艘船是何模樣？
>
> 由於五月花號並不會一直停在相同的位置不動，那麼 William Formsby Halsall 如何得知這艘船在抵達普利茅斯港時的景色為何？

　　這些十一歲大的學生們都正確地關注到這些畫家們的立場，並以之為此一事件中之證詞準確與否的條件。但他們也相當明顯地對於這些藝術家們在描繪此一事件時的意圖作了預設。

　　然而，老師可以藉由提供這兩張圖來利用其中相互衝突的訊息，進而挑戰這些小學生們的思維。當要求他們寫下他們覺得可以解決這個衝突的任何想法時，其中一位小學生如此回答：「我想畫中的印地安人是為了顯示他們是早就到了那裡的人。」老師在課堂上公布這個想法，並且詢問他們對此有何看法。以下便是當時出現的談話內容。

　　十一歲的 Matthew 回答：

> 藝術絕非全部的事實。它通常是一種象徵形式。因為你無法在一張圖裡放入渺小的人物以顯示他們人在遙遠的地方。但這極好地象徵

了這些美洲原住民是第一個到達這裡的人，而非清教徒的登陸。

老師：要解釋這幅圖的話，我們需要知道些什麼？

Adam：你需要了解這位真正在作畫的畫家。你需要一些背景資料。

Peter：然後我們就可以找出這幅圖到底在說些什麼的真相。

老師：你需要的資料只是關於這位畫家而已嗎？其他還有什麼是你需要知道的呢？

Matthew：這是在那一段時間裡所畫的，以及在那裡畫的？它們可能會隨著社會而改變，比如像是對社會讓步〔意指同意主流的觀念〕？因為像大部分在麻薩諸塞州 Salem 市（這幅圖創作的地方）的都是白人，所以畫家就想要將白人描繪成是最偉大的偉人……或者你想要怎樣解釋就怎樣解釋。

在這個相當簡單明瞭的作業中，教師首先揭露出學生們的思維方式——大多數的學生們是靠著將史料當作證詞的理解來下判斷，這麼做的時候發現這樣是有所不足的。其次，利用學生們對於某個問題的一項回答，其中顯示了關於將這些畫作視為證詞所導致的困境，從而激發了一場教學對話，使教師得以鼓勵其學生們從先前將畫中的訊息當作有關五月花號抵達與清教徒登陸的訊息，轉而理解到這些畫作乃是此一事件對於後世意義的證據，最後使學生們脫離了證詞的層次。

這一切意味著什麼？

　　如果大家都接受，學校裡的學生們應該了解到他們在課堂學習中所獲得的歷史知識之性質與地位，那麼在教學日程裡提出一些關鍵目標是相當重要的。學生們將需要被教導區分過去與歷史，史料與證據。過去也許是在人類生存框架中曾經發生過的一切事物，歷史則是我們對於過去所做的主張。應該很清楚的是，我們無法直接進入過去，因為逝者如斯。我們僅能憑藉著過去可能遺留下來的物品、習慣、風俗、記憶等等形式來加以了解。然而，這些事物卻無法直接告訴我們，製造了它們的各個社會究竟是怎樣的。況且，也只有透過對之提出問題，我們才能使它們產生對我們的探究而言可能有用的證據。學校裡的學生需要有機會去從事這種工作，以幫助他們發展對於這些複雜關係的理解，如此一來便有可能挑戰他們擁有的某些誤解。

　　不過，為了使他們更準確地了解證據，學生們也需要了解在任何特定事件中，什麼可以算得上是證據。探究過去發生了什麼事，出現了何種活動，以及這些活動背後產生的原因，都是以不同的方式牽涉到證據。以問題的性質來加以思考，並詢問學生們可以將何者視為證據，這兩者將可發展他們對於證據的概念的理解，以及懂得區分過去、史料來源、證據和歷史。這也將有助於他們看到，各種不同的問題聯繫到各種不同的證據，可能會產生不同於它們自身狀況的主張。對於較年輕的學生們可以作一些簡單的區別：展示出一項活動，也許可以用目擊者的證詞這種簡單明瞭的方法，但是若要說明這項活動出現的原因，對於歷史學家而言就並非如此唾手可得了。對於較年長的學生們而言，可以探索更為複雜的觀念：展示出事實性的陳述可以是建立在史料的基礎上，但史家也使用它們作為證據，以達到史家希望做出的某些更高層次的主張。如此一來，史家將這些事實

性的陳述組合成相互關係，從而做出對於過去的活動、事件、過程和變化遠為複雜的解釋。

學生們可以依據史料來做出假設，也可以依據更深入的史料或事實性的陳述來檢驗其假設。他們將需要進一步了解，所謂檢驗並不僅僅是尋找可以支持他們理論的證據，而是考慮到何種證據可能對於既有的主張造成損害，從而學到我們關於過去的知識有著某種過渡的性質。

對於人在英國的我們來說，已經很清楚的是，學校裡的學生們在歷史探究的脈絡下接觸史料有其重要性。史料之間的關係以及所問的問題，都應該能展現給學校裡的學生了解到，重要的議題不在於任何既定史料的可靠性，而在於將某一史料置於特定主張的脈絡下作為證據使用時所具備的份量，以便試圖用以證實或反駁此項特定主張。

這些研究提供給我們當要發展學校裡的學生們這些理解力時，所面臨到的挑戰的相關知識。這顯示了讓這些誤解與問題呈現在教師眼前的教學方式之重要性，使得教師可以接著展示這些較為無力的思維方式，無法解決更有力量的觀念所能解決的問題。

"How Can There Be Two Stories?" — An Investigation of Children's Responses to Different Accounts

Lin, Tzu-Shu[*]

The inquiry into children's cognition and thinking has become one of the dominant interests in the recent studies of historical education. Historical scholars in particular have devoted long years of research and achieved considerable accomplishments.

Since the 1990s, the study of children's historical cognition and thinking has evolved both in width and depth. In the course of which development, one of these trends figured prominently.   There is an apparent shift in the point of emphasis. While the conventional perspective set forth to illuminate general schemes such as "what historical concepts should they absorb" or related to topics that concerns intellectual capacity like "how fully could they grasp certain abstract concepts", the new outlook raises questions about how they "process" historical discourses and try to understanding how they think. Thus, at the core of this latter standpoint laid this basic assumption: the children's mind can not be regarded as a sheet of white paper, void of characters and free of bias, they already contain certain ideas derived from various sources that

* Institute of History, Soochow University

some of them might govern the way they look upon history or even prevent them from acknowledging new concepts. How then, could we strive to expose these hidden notions that are presumably unconscious even to the children themselves and improve the effect of historical education through proper guidance and correction? It is this mere vision of improvement that provides the impetus for those who are deeply dedicated to this cause.

The Designing of "One Historical Event, Two Historical Stories"

Reading is a process that triggers complex psychological activities and requires thinking skills that are genuinely difficult; some readers would take a text at face value while others may exercise a much deeper vision and attempt interpretations。 The unveiling of determining factors in the divergence of the two patterns of reading became an interesting subject for text processing which has gained prominence in recent years. It may easily be assumed that reading historical accounts might prove even more difficult. Historical accounts deal with the remote past, and certain contents uncover themes that go far beyond children's daily experience. Therefore, how do we adapt historical texts to children's understanding is among the driving forces behind the upsurge of Textbook Analysis.

While it is hard enough for children to understand historical account, it would doubtlessly pose a bigger challenge for them to face two different versions of stories concerning one historical incident. However, perhaps the greatest challenge lies not merely in the multiple discourses about "history (namely the past)". Presently our children reside in an age where information overflows, a place where varying opinions and co-existing contrary accounts have already become a "reality" of their life. As a result, the urge for "respect for multiple viewpoints", "plural education", and "learning value-pluralism" are frequently proposed and commonly heard during discussions over projections for current and future education. Such demands were also presented in the newly released *Grade 1-9 Curriculums* in Taiwan. For instance, according to the Competence Indicators under the category "man and time" in the *Curriculum*, grade 7-9 students (junior high level) should learn to understand "the diversity of historical interpretation owning to different ages, situations, and roles". In a similar vein, the second clause of the Competence Indicator under the category "meaning and value" stated that "when dealing with disputed points" students of the same grade level should "be able to carry on rational discussions with others from a multi-angle point of view while offering good reasons to support their own judgments"

And truly, amid the bombardment of information, how do we discern the interrelationships between each and every other individual discourse, and how do we separate the valid from the invalid. The rational thinking and specific standing required by such undertaking are indeed not easy and could only be achieved through long-term endeavor. Unfortunately, in this newly conceived blueprint of educational reform in Taiwan, hollow avocations seem to exceed practical guidelines and strategies for the learning and teaching of such skills. More importantly, the groundwork for building guidelines as such lies in understanding, but do we really understand how our younger generation look upon multi-dimensional or even contradictory discourses and values? Are we truly certain about the underpinning factors of their judgments? Do multiplicity and diversity increase their wisdom simply by providing more alternatives or do they provoke a greater sense of uncertainty? If we could not answer the aforementioned beforehand, the so called "guidelines" might just end up to be nothing but empty theories.

From this, it all bears a strong sense of reality that by examining children's approach toward multiple historical accounts we can inspect the features as well as restraints of their way of thought, and that would in turn equip us with the knowledge as to what to teach in class that might make proper guidance for children when they encounter differing narratives. This particular issue was accommodated into the research design of the CHATA Project (Concepts of History and Teaching Approaches: 7 to 14) which ran from 1992 to 1996 and was led by Professor Peter Lee, Alarick Dickinson, and Rosalyn Ashby of the University of London. In the project, 320 students were given three pairs (six in all) of stories each revealing one particular aspect of British history, with an aim to grasp the unique characteristics of children's historical thinking. Efforts were made to distinguish different patterns in their reactions and to learn how age difference or other variations affect their understanding. The CHIN Project (Children's Ideas about Historical Narrative: Understanding Historical Accounts) in Taiwan has sought inspiration from CHATA, principally in its "One historical event, two historical stories" testing framework, but has otherwise shown contrast in terms of method and objectives.

The CHIN project applied two historical subjects for testing, one is the "Romans and Saxons" which has been used in CHATA but its contents unknown to most Taiwanese students, the other is "The First Emperor (Qin Shi Huang)"which by comparison has been largely studied or widely acquainted. Each subject entails two stories differing in three key respects that will help us determine children's reactions. Below is a list of example of the distinctions between the two stories on "Romans and Saxons": (See Appendix)

Differences/ stories	Story 1	Story 2
Tone	Mildly positive toward Roman rule	Mildly negative toward Roman rule
Theme	With an emphasis on the substantial constructions built by the Romans	Slightly inclined toward the Roman suppression on British primitive culture
Time-scale	Shorter (only asserted in the end that cities resulted in ruins after the Romans left)	Longer (further claiming that intellectual legacies continued to pass down)

Similarly, story 1 of "The First Emperor" took a more critical stance while story 2 focused on the constructive facets of his rule. The former revolved around his "tyrannical" conducts, and the latter addressed his great diligence as a ruler and other admirable ways. At the end, story 1 wrapped up by stressing that the Qin Dynasty had a short reign of merely fifteen years while story 2 concluded that his institutions were inherited by generations to come.

The testing process is consisted of both written tasks and oral interviews. Students were asked to complete a written task which was proceeded by a semi-structured interview within the following two days. In order to keep track of their thoughts, data collected from the written tasks were provided to form the basis for the ensuing interview. The children were asked to expound for their chosen answers, to confirm their responses were genuine. The testing of the other pair of stories was carried out in the fallowing week.

The CHIN Project had accumulated data of written surveys and interviews accomplished by 54 children in total. These 54 children include students from three separate grade levels: primary 4 (age ten), primary 6 (age twelve), and. secondary 2 (age fourteen). Given the consideration that students begin to study history (social studies) from the primary 4, it would make a suitable starting point to observe changes and developments in their modes of thought through the example of these grade levels with an interval of precisely two years.

Judging by the number of students involved, the CHIN Project appeared to be a rather small-scaled positivistic survey. Aside from limited funds, feasibility, desirability for fundamental study, and the poverty of previous works on the positivistic investigation of children's historical thinking, are the primary concerns responsible for confining the scope of this enterprise. On account of the inadequate research background, researchers have so far just come through its primitive stages to exploring the qualitative traits in the historical thinking of Taiwanese students. The experimental objectives behind the CHIN Project were therefore chiefly set to understand and familiarize with children's basic reactions, and if so, a brief but thorough experiment design like the present, might better serve our purpose. The idea of an additional in-depth interview to be directed toward each individual student apart from the written task was also born on the very same cause.

Analysis and Discussion

In the process of analyzing records of Project CHIN, it's not easy for us to code children's ideas neatly or divide them into some obvious categories very specifically like Project CHATA. That's because we only designed two pairs of stories to investigate students' way of thinking. It might not be enough to rely on just two pencil-and- paper task sets to understand how these children really thought. Working through the more detailed interviews perhaps is a better way to alleviate this possible defect. So besides finishing two sets of written tasks, the children also have been interviewed twice to confirm their answers. We asked interviewers to probe student's opinions as deeply as possible while they conversing with the interviewees. Indeed, our interviewers were all undergraduates and not well-trained in interviewing. They sometimes gave strong hints to students. It means we needed to be cautious in differentiating what were children's ideas and what were responses effected by interviewer's will. Nevertheless, we collected a lot of interview data which is very helpful toward our research. We have discovered many children changed their opinions automatically trying to make sense of two stories about a bit of history. Still other students suggested more than one cause for justification. Consequently, it would be hard to follow the basic rule of "one student, one response" during our coding. Rough categories of children's responses have been constructed, but not in a very tidy way. Estimation in quantity could not be achieved yet, at least, in this stage of research.

However, this paper tries to unlock some traits and tendencies of children's ideas from their thinking about two different accounts.

There Can't Be Two Stories

The immediate reactions of many children to two historical accounts of an event are stunningly similar. Lots of them could not accept two stories coexisting for the same bit of history at the beginning. Some students fell into confusion and perplexity by this fact. Li, primary 4, murmured during the interview:' So strange…How can there be two stories?'. Pong, primary 4, also expressed his feelings on the written set: 'Too many stories would be too confusing'. Later at interview, Pong questioned again: ' …(If there's only one story), you just need to read one. How can you do when there are two?'.

Younger children expressed their confusions very straightforward, but that doesn't mean similar doubts didn't appear in other age groups. Chen, primary 6, told the interviewer: ' …because there is only one not two answer about history , if there are two stories, it will raise the doubt that this one is true or that one is true'. Fu, secondary 2, had the same response: '(it matters,) because which one is true? ', 'That is, there are two stories, which one is just the fact? '. Children seemed to be disturbed by those two stories just because of their assumption that there can be only one accurate story about a bit of history. In fact, this presumption of only one accurate story was popularly present in many students' thoughts on two sets of stories. More common was their dichotomous thinking habit, no matter what was revealed or hidden. Children tended to distinguish the true and the false. If any factor is responsible for it, it might be the pervasive influence of the dominant type of multiple-choice text. The most important thing for students in Taiwan is to pursue right answers to pass historical examinations. As Chen, a child of primary 6, mentioned: 'there is only one not two answers about history,' he has disclosed the possible context of children's preconception.

It's Difficult to Ascertain What Really Happened

Among the children who rejected the legitimacy of two different accounts, some even strongly doubted the probability that one could ascertain what really happened before. Students expressing this kind of pessimistic attitude came from every grade we investigated, but more of the elder children shared this feeling while only one primary 4 students mentioned it. Chou, primary 6, wrote on the written task of the first emperor like this : 'a long time has passed, and no-one has lived from that time until now , to prove it to us .' Hu, primary 6, also wrote with nearly the same words: 'No-one lived from that time until now, thus nobody can prove that these two stories ever happened.'

In these children's minds, testimonies of eyewitness were the most authentic evidence. It was a terrible thing for them that people now have lost the direct and valid connections with the far past. In a sense, students seemed to be helpless and passive in the face of the ruthless force of time. They should have opportunities to learn some powerful methods of history discipline which can bridge the gap between the past and the present. This would be a useful way to make sure children do not get involved themselves in a condition of despair or carelessness. But looking from the positive side, it might also reveal that some students of primary 6 and secondary 2 had been aware there was no direct path to go back to an earlier period of history and we need auxiliary sources to lead us to understand it. Comparatively, younger students of primary 4 appeared to have no consciousness about this point yet.

But children didn't stop their thinking here. As Peter Lee has concluded from other investigations, children won't always stay at the stage of incredulity and confusion, although few of them really did.   Other students reconsidered two different accounts, and tried to make sense of the given information. Were the children challenged and changed their minds while confronted by new sources?   Or did they adjust new sources to their previous frame of mind?

The Stories Were Things About Different Times, Places and People

Some children turned to find out reasons for the two stories of Romans in Britain and the First Emperor.   They believed that these stories told different events that happened at different times, places and people.   Chang, secondary 2, explained: 'Because of the two stories,···one knows that there were two places, just two villages on an island···Romans ruled them in different ways,···'   Another child Chen ,studying in primary 4, said : ' ···the Romans have been divided into the south and the north, ···one part of them went to occupy Britain first , then··· .'   In both students' opinions, two stories were different , describing things of different places, times, and people, therefore they could exist at the same time.   They tried to derive the possible reason from a seemingly indubitable result.   Interestingly, Chang and Chen all agreed with this sentence:' there can only be one proper story about the Romans in Britain.'   In other words, what they inferred did not go against the basic principle of only one correct story.   Children supposed a reasonable way to solve the difficulty they faced in two different accounts and to reconcile them with their previous belief.

Some students further mentioned, two stories are indeed parts of a grand story, and putting them together could finish the whole correct story. For example, Yuan, primary 4, wrote down her idea on two stories of the First Emperor: "I think he might have made mistakes, and then he regretted and corrected himself.' Dung, primary 4, said: ' ···because it can describe the good side and the bad side, ···It's just fine to combine these two stories.' Huang, primary 6, expressed the same idea: 'These two stories are two parts separated from a grand story of the First Emperor.'

Certainly, students who held this view were mostly distributed in primary 4 among 3 grades tested, though there's still a high rate of old students showing this kind of thinking. A large number of 10 years old children thought accounts differed because they were related to different pasts. It is more likely that younger students are accustomed to see the problem from the perspective of quantity. They imaged the stories could be taken apart and added together mechanically. Seeing in a quantitative way also appeared in other responses of categories that will be discussed later.

There's another interesting finding here. According to the analysis of Peter Lee and Rosalyn Ashby, only a small part of children in CHATA made this point. On those reasons for difference in accounts, children in the UK who mentioned the factor of "real differences" were fewest (about 5% to 9%) compared with others ascribing to factors of source and author. By contrast, a large number of students in CHIN made this response. 10 year old children of CHIN who thought accounts differing by different pasts were in the majority. This was presumably their most convenient explanation in handling two different accounts. It may be a simple way for students to rationalize the fact. However, the distinction between results of CHATA and CHIN might indicate the influence of culture on children's historical learning and thinking. It lends to the significance for further explorations in the future.

When children attempted to give rational explanations for the existence of two different accounts, one aspect they would think about was 'different pasts,' and another aspect was 'different sources.'

The Stories Were Based on Different Sources

Some students of primary 6 and secondary 2 focused their attentions on the sources of accounts. These children regarded that writers of different stories collected different sources, and they only recorded what they knew. Thus one needed not to be surprised to have two different stories or even more stories about a bit of history. Huang, primary 6, said to the interviewer: 'Maybe⋯the first historian went to ask some people, they told him story one. The second historian asked some other people, they told him story two. This is why there were differences.' Liang, secondary 2, also said: 'It's impossible there's only one story about Romans in Britain, because two scholars discovered different things.'

It seemed that there was a logical development of thinking from 'different pasts 'to 'different sources.' Primary 4 students who accepted the two different accounts generally considered from the view of different pasts. They seldom construed from the view of source problem. On the contrary, more students of secondary 2 supported this idea. Some older students even mentioned simultaneously both of these two points. Furthermore, we observed that some children showed the opinion of integrating story one and story two again so as to get a full story.

While being confronted with two different accounts, students who couldn't accept this fact always tended to assume that there must be truth and fallacy in the contents of two stories. Actually, some students were hesitant to decide what the most possible cause was, and moved around between "different pasts" and "truth and fallacy."

There Must Be Truth and Fallacy in These Two Stories

Conceiving dichotomous thinking, children easily concluded there must be truth and fallacy in two stories. They supposed perhaps one story is true and the other false, or both of the contents of stories having parts of truth and fallacy. When students were asked how this could be done, some thought the main problem was the stories losing their accuracy through the process of transmission. Few students directly appealed to the writer's problem which affected the qualities of the stories in the three age groups.

• Transmission's mistakes

When children thought about the reliability of accounts, some of them, especially primary 6, noticed the errors in transmitting. Jou, primary 6, expressed his idea here. "When they (stories or history) were transmitted, probably from the British, right? They were correct at the beginning. Later while being passed down through the generations, transmitting here and there, the mistakes then occurred. Another student of primary 6 Tsou, also said: "Perhaps the story was true originally, but through the disseminating of people, it went wrong." Interestingly, Jou suggested: "Then just combine these stories, you would find out the more correct story." Other children also believed that through careful contrast of two stories one could gain the final truth.

Children meant that stories passed on by oral tradition were very easily diluted. But they didn't signify obviously that the accuracy of the stories was spoiled by people purposely or unintentionally. Nevertheless, their attitude toward people's opinions seemed to be negative.

It's significant that while very few students in CHATA related two different accounts to the transmission errors, nearly 25% of primary 6 students in CHIN responded in this way. This discrepancy between the results of two projects might represent the effects of the different historical teaching and the different educational milieu. It would be worth further investigation.

However, students were more concerned with the errors of the stories. They seemed to treat the stories as things that happened, not the stories being established by sources. In their statements, these students didn't talk about the problem of the sources. Only one student actually mentioned the defects of sources. Wang, secondary 2, noted that: "Because we couldn't have all the records, some of them got lost. Thus, the historians separately inferred different ends. That's why there were different stories." These sentences probably indicated that this student had some complex ideas. He was aware of the difficulties historians always met in dealing with sources. He understood that the role of historians was important on the making of stories, even though his image of historian's ideas which appeared in the data of interviews was harmful to the truth of history.

• The writer's forgery and bias

Among the three grades, only one to two students of primary 4 and 6 alluded to the writers' responsibilities for the different accounts, but they often meant the bad influences. Huang, primary 6, agreed that there's only one story for every historical event and it's processing. And she continued to write: "If there are others, they were forged."

The explanations from the transmission's error to the writers' forgery and bias were almost made by the students of primary school. It seemed to be a sign that younger children tended to suppose something went wrong to affect the purity of the stories. They easily doubted the history and historians. Whatever causes may be attributed to this kind of historical thinking, how to help children to release them from their distrust should be an important target for this stage of history teaching.

Different Stories Were Resulted from the Writers' Perspective Viewpoints

Most of the children who attended our project were uneasy about two different accounts, and they tried in their own ways to come to terms with it. There were still a small proportion of primary 6 and secondary 2 students who held a normal view to the accounts differing. They looked to the writers' aims, selections and perspectives of observations. Chou, secondary 2, expressed her ideas quite clearly: 'Everyone's point of view is different. Maybe somebody said The First Emperor's rule was dictatorial, the contents of the stories he wrote would include the Emperor's wrongdoings. If others thought the Emperor's rule was merciful, the contents of the stories wouldn't be the same.' Another secondary 2 student, Tzeng also supported this view: 'It matters, because in history, we need a lot of evidences to approach the truth. Viewing From different perspectives, events would have been represented by different ways.'

Conclusions

The responses of students analyzed above can be concluded as follow:

1. Students couldn't accept two different accounts

(1.A) Popular reactions at the beginning

    a. There can't be two stories

    b. It's difficult to ascertain what really happened

(1.B) Further inferring

    a. Reasons for two different stories

        a.1 The stories were things about different times, places and people

        a.2 The stories were based on different sources

    b. There must be truth and fallacy in these two stories

        b.1 Transmission's mistakes

        b.2 The Writer's forgery and bias

2. Students could accept two different accounts

(2.A) Different stories were the results of the writers' viewpoints

Some Feedbacks of students from the three grades are listed as below

1. The most popular response among primary 4 students is that: a.1— the stories were about different "pasts". To them, these "stories" represented "what happened in the past".

2. Other from the a.1 statements, the more prevailing opinions among primary 6 students were b.1— the mistakes were made in the course of transmission and b.2— the writer's forgery and bias, and both answers were scarcely seen in the other two grades. Primary 6 students spoke more negatively about the element of "people" and assumed that individual thoughts would discredit the authenticity of the stories. They considered history and historians as distrustful.

3. The two general observations made by secondary 2 students were that: a.2— the stories were based on different sources and 2.A— the different stories were the results of the writers' viewpoints. Secondary 2 students were capable of looking at the distinctive discourses from the perspective of sources and writers and had recognized their role as the medium connecting the "past" and the "present".

Appendix One

Here are two history stories about the Romans in Britain. Read them both carefully.

STORY 1

Before the Romans came the Britons lived in wooden huts. They had no towns.　Almost no-one could read. The Britons often fought each other. The Romans went to Britain and took most of it over. They made Britain peaceful.

The Romans built towns and cities. Some houses had central heating. Many Britons lived more comfortably. Some Britons learned to read.

Much later, invaders attacked the Romans. The Roman armies went off to protect their other lands. The Anglo-Saxons took over England.

Towns and cities fell into ruins. It was as if the Romans had never been in Britain. It was ages before people in Britain lived　as comfortably as they did when the Romans were there.

STORY 2

Before the Romans came the Britons had their own way of life. They were good at making jewelry and tools. Almost no-one could read.

The Romans took Britain over. They beat the Britons who tried to stop them.

The Romans made Britain like other countries they lived in. Britons copied the Roman way of life. Some learned to read.

Much later, invaders attacked the Romans. The Roman armies went off to protect their other-lands. The Anglo-Saxons took over England.

Once the Romans left, Britain gradually became one country, with a mixture of Britons and Anglo- Saxons. After a time people remembered Roman ideas. Some Roman ideas are still used now.

Appendix Two

Here are two historical stories about the First Emperor (Qin Shi Huang), please read them carefully.

STORY 1

Qin Shi Huang was the first emperor in the history of China.

He was a king of the state of Qin.

At the time, China was divided into seven warring feudal states; each of them had their own writing, language, and life style.

Among them, Qin was the most powerful state. Eventually, Qin conquered the other six states and established the Qin Dynasty, and Qin Shi Huang became the only ruler of all China.

After the Qin Dynasty was founded, Qin Shi Huang ordered the country to adopt the same form of Chinese script and standardized the units of measurements. He banned the possession of private weapons, and burned all previously-existing books owned by civilians. His commands were to be obeyed with immediate obedience, and dissenters were sentenced to death. For his personal glorification, people were mobilized from all over the country for the construction of extravagant palaces.

Qin Shi Huang died at the age of fifty. After his death, people of the former annexed states quickly revolted. The Qin Dynasty had a short reign of merely fifteen years, and Qin Shi Huang was remembered as the most horrifying tyrant throughout Chinese history.

STORY 2

Qin Shi Huang was the first emperor in the history of China.

He was a King of the state of Qin.

At the time, China was divided into seven warring feudal states; they did not share any common language or writing, and were often engaged in warfare. The *Wang* of every state was equally ambitious in taking over others.

Ultimately, Qin Shi Huang defeated the other six states and became emperor.

Once assumed power, Qin Shi Huang introduced a single form of writing and unified the systems of measurements, he also developed a nationwide network of roads. His orders were delivered throughout the country and were all fully implemented. Additionally, the emperor himself was a very diligent man, he made a daily habit of reading 30 kilos of official letters written on bamboo tablets before he would rest for the night.

Qin Shi Huang died at the age of fifty, and the Qin Dynasty ended shortly after. However, some of his institutions remained, and people all over China communicated with the same written language ever since.

中文摘要

「怎麼會有兩個故事？」
——探究兒童如何看待多元敘述

林慈淑

　　本文試圖從十至十四歲兒童面對「一段歷史、兩種敘述」時的反應，探索兒童如何看待多元「歷史記述」(historical account)，藉以了解兒童思考歷史的特質和方式。本文採用的分析資料皆來自 1999 年 8 月至 2001 年 12 月期間，由蔣經國基金會贊助所進行的「臺英兒童歷史認知模式的分析：歷史敘述與歷史理解」(Children's Ideas about Historical Narrative: Understanding Historical Accounts，簡稱 CHIN）計畫。[1]這個計畫的主要目的在探測十到十四歲兒童對歷史記述 (account) 的理解。計畫之初，原擬透過臺灣與英國倫敦大學 Peter Lee、Rosalyn Ashby 等教授的合作，比較臺灣、英國兩地兒童的歷史思考，探測兒童思維與文化背景的關係。然因經費所限，後改為臺灣實驗、英國諮詢的研究案。

一、CHIN 計畫的研究背景

　　近年來歷史教育的研究重心之一，是探討兒童的認知和思考。自 1990 年代以降，關於兒童歷史認知和思考這個領域的研究，主要有兩股

1　本計畫另外兩位主持人是清華大學歷史研究所張元教授、東吳大學歷史系劉靜貞教授。

可見的**趨勢**。其一，過去的研究多專注於兒童應該獲得那些歷史學科概念，或者兒童對某些抽象概念的認知深淺等問題，最近則進而轉求探索兒童理解歷史的「過程」，以及探測兒童進行思考時，盤旋在他們心中的是那些念頭和想法。此一研究趨向隱含的前提是：兒童面對歷史並非如同空白的紙張，他們腦中存有各種從其他管道獲得的某些概念，其中一些似是而非的念頭往往左右了兒童理解歷史的方式，甚至妨礙他們對新的歷史觀念的吸收和接受。如何讓這些連兒童都不自覺的念頭曝光，透過引導疏正，以提高歷史教育的實效，是許多有心歷史教研工作的英國和歐洲學者努力的動力之一。

其二，兒童歷史認知研究的另一個趨勢是探究兒童閱讀歷史教科書的問題。或許因應後現代主義的風潮，文本解讀中的主客體互動問題，激發了知識各界的興趣，也引起美國許多歷史教育學者，關心兒童究竟如何閱讀與他們最是關係密切的教科書。這方面的分析又逐漸形成兩個研究取向：一則檢視歷史教科書的編排與兒童背景知識的關係，一則考察歷史教科書中，文句的安排和表達是否利於讀者的親近，對於兒童的理解是提供了幫助，或者反倒構成阻礙。

相對於國外的進展，臺灣在這個領域的開發顯得較為緩進。目前歷史教育學者思考的焦點多半未能及於兒童的思考能力，這與國外的研究導向，顯然還有一段距離。CHIN 計畫以歷史記述為題，考察兒童面對一段歷史、兩個故事的看法，擬藉此和兒童歷史思考的研究領域，有所對話和交流。

二、「一段歷史兩個故事」的設計源起

閱讀是一件涉及複雜心理和高難度思考的過程，而讀者對於文義的理解是止於字面上的了解和記憶，或是能夠達到更深入的透視，並提出詮

釋，這其中層次的分別，正是近年來流行的文本分析 (text processing) 所興趣的課題。可以想見，閱讀歷史記述所面臨的難度更高。歷史記述談到的都是發生在時空遙遠的過去，尤其有些內容主題根本超乎兒童日常經驗。

兒童理解歷史記述誠然不易，面對一段歷史卻出現兩個故事，對於我們年輕的學子來說，恐怕更是一項挑戰。尤其環顧當今，兒童所身處的已是個資訊充斥的時代，各種論述並陳、甚至互相衝突的現象，早已成為他們生活中的「現實」。因此，「尊重多元觀點」、「多元化教育」、「學習多元的價值觀」的呼聲，總在各種談論當前與未來教育理想的場合中，多所聽聞。

然而引導的基礎在於了解，而我們是否了解年輕世代如何看待多元甚至衝突的論述、價值觀？我們是否清楚主導他們判別的因素是什麼？多元和多樣對他們而言，是帶來更多的選擇、智慧的增進，或者更多的不確定感？如果我們無法預先掌握上述問題，所謂引導和培養，很可能只會流於高論而已。

英國倫敦大學的 Peter Lee、Alarick Dickinson、Rosalyn Ashby 在 1992 年至 1996 年所主持的 CHATA 計畫（Concepts of History and Teaching Approaches: 7-14，「七到十四歲兒童的歷史概念與教學取向」）中，即將此問題納入他們的研究中。CHATA 以三個英國史的主題設計出三對、六個故事，讓 320 名學童閱讀推論，目的是從中歸納出兒童的各種反應類型，觀察年齡或其他因素對於認知的影響，藉此掌握兒童思考歷史的特質。在臺灣我們所進行的 CHIN 計畫，從 CHATA 獲得了啟發，同樣採用一段歷史兩個故事為測試主題，但是在研究方式和旨趣上仍然有所區別。

三、CHIN 計畫的實驗設計與考量

CHIN 計畫用以測試的兩個歷史主題，一個是採用臺灣學生多數陌生、CHATA 也曾經用過的「羅馬人在不列顛」歷史，一個是選取多數學生學過或聽過的「秦始皇」的歷史。每個主題下各自包含兩個故事，兩個故事並呈現出三方面的區隔，以利於試探出兒童的反應。試以「羅馬人在不列顛」的兩個故事為例，表列如下（並請參考附件）：

風格差別＼兩個故事	羅馬人故事一	羅馬人故事二
敘 述 語 氣	對羅馬人的統治偏向正面敘述	對羅馬人的統治偏向負面敘述
內 容 取 向	側重羅馬人為不列顛帶來的物質建設	側重羅馬人對不列顛原始文化的壓制
涵 蓋 時 段	較短——只談及羅馬人離開後物質建設荒廢	較長——談及羅馬人的觀念流傳久遠

同樣的，「秦始皇」故事一批評的意態較為明顯，故事二則認為秦始皇的統治有其正面作用。「秦始皇」故事一著眼他「暴虐」事蹟，故事二則述及始皇理政之勤和可取之處。最後「秦始皇」故事一以秦朝十五年即亡作為結束，故事二總結秦始皇立下的制度仍為後世承襲沿用。

國外研究多已顯示，兒童的思考迂迴間接，不易掌握。針對此因，本計畫的筆測和口訪問題以兩種問題的交叉探詢為原則。一類問題是直接聯繫至兩個故事本身，另一類問題則抽離提問某些觀念或思考前提，藉此環環相扣的設計，探詢學生的反應。同時，為幫助學生更容易掌握故事重點，兩組故事並都配上圖畫。（參見附錄）

在測試方法上，分從筆試和口訪兩方面進行。CHIN 計畫總共收集 54 名兒童的筆試和訪談資料。這 54 名兒童分屬三個年級：國二（十四歲）、

國小六（十二歲）、國小四（十歲）。由於國小四年級學生開始學習歷史（社會科），因此以這個年齡層為起點，觀察每間隔兩年的這三個年齡層，思維的發展和變化。由於諸多考慮，54 名學生分別取自臺北市、縣以及新竹市、苗栗縣等地區的八所中小學：

以訪測學生的人數而言，CHIN 計畫算是個小規模的實證研究。除了經費的限制外，主要的考量在於過去臺灣相關的研究不多，兒童歷史思維的實證探查所累積經驗有限，小規模的實驗較易於掌握，並適合基礎的研究。CHIN 計畫的實驗目的因而側重的是熟悉、了解兒童的基本反應，這也是本計畫除了筆測之外，還針對每一位受試學童進行詳細深入口訪的原因。

四、研究分析

以下為兒童如何思考「一段歷史兩個故事」的分析。本分析重在兒童思考的發展過程以及各年級間的思考趨向。

（一）兒童思考的發展歷程

1. 不能接受「一段歷史兩個故事」

(1) 初始的普遍反應：

　　(a) 兩個故事不能並存，

　　(b) 無法確知過去發生什麼事。

(2) 進一步推論方向：

　　(a) 故事可以並存的理由

　　　　a-1 不同的故事敘述的是不同的「過去」。

　　　　a-2 故事是根據不同的資料而來的。

    (b) 兩個故事中必有真、假

        b-1 流傳中的錯誤。

        b-2 作者的編造和偏見。

2. 可以接受「一段歷史兩個故事」

    2.1 故事是來自作者的選擇和觀點。

(二) 各年級學生思考的某些趨向

1. 小四學生最多數的反應是：a-1 不同的故事敘述的是不同的「過去」。小四學生認為「故事」等於「過去發生的事情」。

2. 小六學生除了 a-1 的反應外，較普遍的看法是：b-1 流傳中的錯誤，以及 b-2 作者的編造和偏見，而這兩種看法在小四學生和國二學生中少見。小六學生從較負面的角度談「人」的影響，認為人們的想法會破壞故事的真確性。對於歷史和歷史家持以不信任的態度。

3. 國二學生較為普遍的兩種反應是：a-2 故事是根據不同的資料而來的，以及 2.1 故事是來自作者的選擇和觀點。國二學生已經能夠從資料和作者的角度去思考兩個不同敘述的問題，可以意識到「現在」與「過去」之間，必須透過資料和作者的中介，才能連結溝通。

Objectivity and Perspective in History Education: The Ideas of Portuguese Students

Isabel Barca[*]

The information society opens to history education a fascinating possibility to expand its scope and further explore diverse points of view, learning about converging and diverging ideas and interchanging them. Such an attitude does not fear the multiplicity of perspectives; it acknowledges variety as a basis for a deeper understanding of the past and present society. As Walsh claimed in 1967, if all points of view were taken away, nothing intelligible would be left in history. Therefore, historically-educated youngsters of nowadays must have the opportunity to gain insight of the actual diversity. History education can have a role in the progression of their views of the world.

Objectivity and Point of View in History

The meaning of historical objectivity as equated to the author's absolute neutrality about a given past might look a naïve idea nowadays as it is no longer supported by leading historians, philosophers and social scientists. Assumptions such as 'documents speak for themselves' or a dichotomic belief

[*] University of Minho, Portugal

on 'the very true theory' versus the false ones, abandoned a long time ago in the debates on the nature of historical knowledge, appear to be challenged in wider, nonacademic circles nowadays.

The early debates about the truth of historical conclusions led to different schools of thought, some of them presupposing the need to controlling the subjects' interference on the object to be known, some others stressing the particular nature of history as a specific form of knowledge. Within the former posture some authors focussed on establishing *the* scientific explanation of social change against the biased ones (although several, competing theories about social change were produced) while some others denied the possibility of scientifically explain the past, emphasising the value of just describing 'what happened' from reliable sources. Among those who viewed history as an autonomous mode of thought some authors welcomed its interpretive element, affirming it as genuine in history provided some methodological criteria were observed. All those views and the debate among them, it must be said, contributed in some way to better clarify the status of historical knowledge, its core concepts and methods.

The positive recognition of subjectivity as inherent to historical production seemed to be confirmed among scholars as the theoretical debates evolved. Parallel to a new paradigm of scientific objectivity accepting the existence of different, competing theories in the field of natural sciences, the notion of existing different perspectives in history appears to be accepted now by the academic community – bringing with it fresh controversies.

Walsh (1967) discussed objectivity by recognising two factors in historical conclusions: point of view (a subjective element) and the evidence (a link to the real past). He analysed the notion of point of view in its components, making a distinction between prejudice and personal principles. Some personal assumptions can be considered as genuine and accepted as such in an objective explanation while some others, linked to practical concerns of an economic, political, or religious kind, can lead to a biased conclusion. In order to get a valid history it is crucial to distinguish general presuppositions from propaganda: when the author relies upon personal emotions and interests she/he will tend to deliberately omit or distort that evidence working against her/his particular purposes. In such a position, only a disposition to search for evidence confirming what is previously expected will be found.

Walsh listed four types of presuppositions leading to disagreement among historians: personal bias, group prejudice, and conflicting theories of historical interpretation and philosophical conflicts. While personal bias, likes and dislikes, are a matter of prejudice and can be overcome by the historian at work, the other assumptions are matters of principle and more difficult to detect. Assumptions shared by identity groups like nation, race, class or religion must be justified on rational grounds; disagreements about the relative importance of causes can rely on conflicting philosophical principles provided they are empirically well-confirmed, not due to mere partisanship. And as the historian reads the past by necessarily using general judgements according to moral conceptions it would be useful that they become aware of their own moral preconceptions so that they could not be used naively.

Dray (1980, 1991) discussed the notion of perspective, a necessary feature of historical inquiry, in terms of value judgement. As history aims to reconstruct a reality which is itself value-ladden, it applies a value-judgement in order to better understand the rationale of the past. He recognised the existence of several points of view with the possibility of mutually understanding each other.

With the recognition of a subjective element in science, the debate on historical objectivity has moved to another central question: if the interpretive element entangled in historical accounts is socially contextualised, how can historical productions be assessed? Martin (1989) focussed his discussion on a systematic examination of criteria used by historians for justifying actual historical explanations. He raised two questions about the logic of explanatory controversy: "How do historians attempt to show that one weighted explanation is better than competing weighted explanations?" and "How should they attempt to show this?" (p. 54). Accordingly, Martin analysed the kinds of arguments adduced as explanatory justifications and the manner in which historians assign relative importance to causes for or against a particular explanation. Concerning the arguments adduced as justification, Martin found three kinds of arguments directed to (a) the truth of the facts entailed in the explanations; (b) the explanatory relevance; or (c) the sufficiency of the explanations. Each of these three kinds of arguments can have a positive and negative pole - positive arguments to increase the likelihood, and negative arguments to decrease the likelihood of a given explanation. Martin found that both positive and negative arguments related to the truth of the *explanans* are often used to justify a favoured explanation by means of exhibiting some data to support it and some data against the other competing ones. Arguments of this kind are thus summed up to show that the favoured explanation is either more consistent with data available than others, or more plausible than others when grounded on some specific set of evidence. Martin clearly emphasised evidential consistency (i.e., confirmation and non-refutation) and plausibility (as referred to a higher degree of probability of the occurrence happening) as criteria for justifying and assessing explanatory adequacy. Affirmative arguments focussing the logic of a given partial explanation are not frequent and negative ones are almost non-existent; they only explicitly appear when the *explanans* is not of a familiar type or when controversy about a given set of factors exists. Concerning arguments on the sufficiency of the *explanans*, Martin found some negative and none positive, which means that historians do not attempt to produce sufficient explanations. Negative arguments of this kind, when they exist, plays a role against the sufficiency of a non-favoured explanation, in order to give room to a more relevant *explanans*. Such negative arguments can be presented in terms of showing the implausibility of a given *explanans* as being sufficient to the *explanandum* or as contradicting evidence.

Concerning the manner in which historians assign relative importance to causes of particular occurrences, Martin discussed whether causal weighting is based on objective or subjective criteria. He criticised the Dray's core criterion of value-judgement for selecting the relevant factors of an explanation. Martin argued for an objective, factual criterion of distinguishing causes from conditions, by means of a comparison-situation. The relevant cause is often constituted by a conjunction of factors, not a single factor, and even at that level it is possible to rank the relevant factors in terms of their relative importance to the occurrence. He stressed that it is always possible to distinguish causes from conditions on factual grounds by formulating an appropriate explanatory question. If an explanatory question is selected according to a specific value-laden framework, that is characteristic of all inquiries, not of historical inquiry only. Thus, Martin stressed that historians mainly justify competing explanations on evidential grounds even when they argue in terms of plausibility and logic of the situation.

But as in this debate about objectivity, 'deconstruction' and fiction approaches have gained some support among different groups of professionals, Fulbrook (2002) entered the objectivity debate having in mind those postmodernist discourses, and came back to the question:

If historians agree on the facts - dates, events, 'what happened' - but do not agree on the broader framework of interpretation or explanation, should we simply accept that all accounts are merely 'perspectives', in principle equally valid (or equally fictitious)? (p. 9)

Discussing ways of adjudicating among *a number of separate, competing, coexisting, mutually incompatible paradigms*, Fullbrook (2002) considers two layers of historical divergence in order to clarify the possibilities or impossibilities of historical convergence: at the macro level of historiographic paradigms, there can exist different, conflicting theories due to *a priori* general assumptions such as those on the nature of relationships between human being and society, culture and material conditions, or on the level at which we look for explanations - at the surface or at the long term. At such a generic level, paradigms may not be open to refutation, like Popper stated in 1961, and a variety of metanarratives may stand. But when we move from a wide framework to specific, competing narratives on a particular past, it is possible then to answer to the question: 'which account is more valid?' In both stances it is possible to find a number of methodological criteria shared by historians - such as being open to revision of particular interpretations in the light of evidence.

Objectivity and Point of View in History Education

Accounts on history curricula suggest that probably in most of the countries history has been taught as a given version of the past, although master narratives have changed according to political moves (cf. Biao, 2001; Roberts, 2004; Barca & Magalhães, 2004). The topic of the subject matter and the time assigned to historical contents across the years of schooling may vary but a single account tends to be transmitted with few concerns about questioning it by cross analysis of different, competing versions conveying different points of view. Countries like UK, where educational laws explicitly point to the need to consider different perspectives in school, are the exceptions to this overall picture. The work carried out in that country has been influential in instilling fresh approaches in history curricula elsewhere. In Portugal, the *Curriculum Essential Competencies* paper issued by the Department of Basic Education-DEB (addressed to 1-9-school grades) gives room to exploring different interpretations of the past and textbooks begin to assume the same concern. A number of empirical studies on how Portuguese students make sense of history - at substantive and second order levels - in the context of postgraduate work and funded projects might have contributed to this yet slight but new movement in history education.

Exploring different perspectives in history is not a single-track task. As Lee (2005) warns us history is counterintuitive. It is not enough to give several sources on a given bit of the past to students interpret; students need to know that historical claims are based on evidence to be interpreted, not merely copied, that explanations of the past are not the same as factual statements, and that existing different versions does not mean that history is simply a matter of opinion.

Students need to be addressed with questions to gradually reason on what grounds are historical descriptions and explanations constructed, and why some explanations can eventually be more valid than others can. To achieve this goal it is required to know which tacit understandings students are working with. Recent work in the field has assumed the rich multiplicity of perspectives in history and investigated students' ideas about this historical feature in accounts, evidence or significance (Ashby & Lee, 2000; Cercadillo, 2001; Ashby, 2005; Gago, 2005; Hsiao, 2005) and in textbooks (Foster, 2005). In spite of particular substantive views, it is amazing to find out how children, youngsters and adults from different countries and cultures share some kinds of arguments when discussing different versions of history.

A Study with Portuguese Adolescents

An empirical study was carried out aiming to highlight students ideas about the provisional nature of historical explanation. This idea was understood in the sense of existing competing explanations at any given time about the same past.

The (national) master narrative implicitly taught in Portugal in the last decades has quickly moved during the 1970s from a nationalistic tale about 'a great people who discovered the world to expand their faith and empire' toward a recognition of some of the complexities of that period of Discoveries and Expansion – exploration, adventure and power but also war, famine and slavery. The old heroic master narrative appears replaced with a central idea of recent conquest of freedom in Portugal and in its former colonies over dictatorship (Barca & Magalhães, 2005). In spite of this move from a linear story biased by the political context toward a more scientific, balanced version, history teaching continued to focus on a given version of the past, now supported by a number of corroborating sources. In this educational context controversy was thought too confusing for adolescents, this revealing little awareness of a changing society where children and youngsters deal with that controversy around them and at the media - everywhere.

A set of tasks based on four versions about a specific, usually discussed historical question was given to 119 students attending grades 7, 9 and 11 from a rural and an urban school. The historical question 'how could the Portuguese establish a maritime empire in the Indian Ocean in the sixteenth-century?' was followed by four adapted versions, three of them being explanations:

Version A

Openly defying the Moslem domain and combating the Moslem faith, the Portuguese had to meet as their main enemies in Asia the Egyptians and the Turks. It helped the Portuguese considerably that none of these major Moslem countries based its power upon the sea."

O. Marques (Portuguese historian), *H. de Portugal*, 1980

Version B

The Islamic naval challenge to the Portuguese, when it came, was ineffective ...

Had the Chinese still been present in the Indian Ocean when the Portuguese

---

arrived, one can only speculate what might have happened. The decision to withdraw the Chinese fleet 60 years before was a momentous one, leaving the "door left open" (to the Europeans) into the Indian Ocean.

A. Pacey   (English researcher), *Technology in World Civilization*, 1990

Version C

This large domain quickly conquered with a few human and financial resources can only be explained by the moral correctness of the Portuguese great leaders, by the sacrifices for the country made by all the people.

A. Matoso (textbook author), *Compêndio de História Universal*, 1946

Version A emphasizing a *Moslem factor* and version B emphasizing a *Chinese factor* may be seen as competing historical explanations; version C emphasizing a *nationalistic factor* may be considered a biased version; the fourth version (D) assumed a descriptive mode conveying information on how Portuguese and Chinese maritime explorations evolved (see Appendix). This last version was given to students so that they could choose between a description or an explanation when answering an explanatory question. The historical materials also included a set of sources to justify mainly versions A and B.

The tasks were designed to provide indicators of students' ideas on several aspects of provisionality and objectivity in history. Among the questions posed, task 3 asked for specific choices on the given substantive versions and arguments for or against them, implying a second order reasoning on criteria for assessing historical explanatory claims:

1. Rank the four versions given in order of importance as an historical explanation.

2. In what respects do you consider the first better than the second in explaining why the Portuguese managed to control the Indian Ocean?

3. Do you consider the first version better justified by the sources? Why?

4. Justify your last two choices.

The inductive analysis of data suggested a network of students' conceptual patterns with less or more elaborate contours in terms of use of information and evidence-explanation relationships. Ana (13 years old, grade 7) appeared to be centred on a descriptive mode when arguing for version D because it 'explains more how discoveries were made', and against version A when she just quoted that the Portuguese 'combated the Moslems'. Teresa (17 years old, grade 11) argued for version D on explanatory grounds, alluding to antecedents, motives and military conditions of the historical situation (' D explains better as it shows the steps [...] and what the Portuguese really went to take due to economic needs at the time. It shows well the various factors in which the Portuguese were superior to the Moslems'). When referring the "various factors" to justify version D consistency it seems that Teresa established an implicit relationship between factors and sources to justify them. Factors conveyed by versions B and C were undervalued by her to give room to her favoured account ('I don't think that morality and leaders' correctness were important, and in relation to version B, I think that the question about the Chinese being or not being in the Ocean is not very important'). Although the explanatory relevance of a negative sign was presented in terms of everyday plausibility, it reminds Martin analysis (1989) about arguments adduced by historians.

Mario (13 years old, grade 7) also valued a set of factors conveyed by version D but in factual terms ('the different steps taken by the Portuguese for the domination of Africa and the Indian Ocean') over a counterfactual speculation given by version B ('while version B only speaks about what would have happened if...'); he gave a low value to explanations A and C using an implicit criterion of multifactoriality ('A and C only speak of one fact about the Portuguese domination in the Indian Ocean'), which also seems to underlie his first choice. In other tasks he reasoned on explanatory rounds, for example when he discussed the explanatory limits of the versions given: 'why did the Chinese or other European people not try to conquer the spice trade when they realized that it was so profitable?'. But his notion of evidential consistency seems still vague, with no explicit concern about evidence as a basis for explanations.

Lurdes (18 years old, grade 11) clearly decided among two historical explanations, chosing version A over version B as the former conveyed a factor which "really happened", while the latter presented a mere hypothesis: [A] 'does not speculate, it only refers to why we defeated the Moslems; the second [B] refers to an aspect which might be very important but, in spite of everything, did not really happen'. Thus, an explanation based on a counterfactual possibility was considered important by Lurdes, but not so much as one based on something that "really" happened. When arguing for evidential justification of version A, she might be confirming this version by evidence conveyed by the sources given. Her arguments against version C, which did not give 'tangible reasons, the Portuguese might be very determined but the enemies could defeat us with their material resources', indicate the use of criteria of consistency with evidence and plausibility. Also she was aware of the descriptive status of version D, which 'only describes the events by order and not why and how they happened'. These responses (in conjunction with others related to the idea of explanations open to refutation) seem to take into account elaborate criteria of explanatory power, on grounds of evidential and logical consistency.

According to the ideas shown above, students argued and seek to explain their thoughts from quoting random fragments of the material given to coherently employing information - some students using just previous, familiar knowledge, others relating it to the fresh information given. As to evidential consistency, some students focused exclusively on facts (a descriptive mode of thought) and others employed the notion of factor; in the latter group some implicitly linked notions of fact and factor with explanatory consistency, discussing the validity of specific factors on grounds of evidential and logical verification, or corroboration/refutation.

The frequency distribution of responses to the different questions revealed a distinctive overall pattern between substantive choices and second order ideas about evidential consistency. Item 1, which asked the pupils to rank the four historical versions given, was considered a relevant question since it propelled the arguments about reasons in terms of explanatory consistency for concrete decisions. However, the ranking attributed by students to the four versions did not reveal the variation in ideas suggested in the arguments for their choices (table 1).

Table 1. How students ranked historical versions

	First rank	Second rank	Third rank	Fourth rank
Version A	8	28	51	32
Version B	7	46	24	41
Version C	9	33	36	40
Version D	94	11	7	5

Kendall's Coefficient of Concordance W=0.345, n.s.

The descriptive version D was clearly the most popular among students (79% of pupils ranked it first), whilst all the other three versions obtained small acceptance as a first choice. Moreover, version D was placed last by five pupils only. This version conveys a descriptive, not overtly explanatory account of the question about the Portuguese maritime power; however, it might be stressed that most students used its information as raw material for their own explanations.

The four versions may be aggregated in two categories: the most popular (chosen as first and second choice) and the least popular accounts (the two ranked last). Next to version D, the most popular second choice was version B - but much less enthusiastically accepted than version D. It might be seen as a counterfactual hypothesis (as far as the speculation about the Chinese is concerned) and critical about the Portuguese naval supremacy. The third rank, which might mean one of the least popular versions, was most frequently given to version A. It was hypothesized that this version would convey information about the Moslem factor not completely new to the students, but stated in a fresh approach (stressing Moslem land power against its naval inefficiency). Although versions C and B, together, exceeded it in the third rank, it consistently took the third place for the first, second and fourth choice. That suggests an attribution of a mild negative sign to it. The last rank, representing the least popular version among pupils, was attributed to version C, conveying a nationalistic view about the Portuguese empire, and to version B which might be seen as an innovative, but also critical approach about Portuguese naval supremacy. These two opposed views seemed to be those against which pupils reacted most.

The ranking of the four historical versions was analysed by grade. Table 2 shows the distribution of the most popular versions (first rank), by grade.

Table 2. The most popular version by grade

Version	Grade			
	7	9	11	Total
A	3	3	2	8 (6.7%)
B	4	1	2	7 (5.9)
C	1	5	3	9 (7.6)
D	41	32	21	94 (79.0)
NR.	1	-	-	1 (0.8)
	50	41	28	119 (100)

Chi-square = 6.23, df = 6, n.s.

The chi-square test revealed that no significant differences among grades were found. Version D clearly appeared the most popular version across grades, the other versions being quite distant from the former. This version was massively chosen first: 82% of the 7th-graders, 78% of the 9th-graders and 75% of the 11th-graders selected it.

The last choice across grades is shown in table 3 and, in a similar way to the choices made for the most favoured explanations, raises a paradox:

Table 3.   The least popular version by grade

Version	Grade			
	7	9	11	Total
A	12	10	10	32 (26.9)
B	14	17	10	41 (34.5)
C	22	11	7	40 (33.6)
D	1	3	1	5 (4.2)
NR.	1	-	-	1 (0.8)
	50	41	28	119 (100)

The frequency mode across grades shows some variation concerning the least favoured version. It corresponds to version C at the 7th grade, version B at the 9th grade, and versions A and B, *ex aequo,* at the 11th grade. Clustering the most valid versions with respect to historical grounds (versions A and B) against the less valid (versions C and D), the frequency distribution shows that 50% of the 7th-graders, 66% of the 9th-graders and 71% of the 11th-graders reacted against the most valid explanations. A negative correlation between a historically-valid substantive choice and grade seems apparent. How to explain such a paradox?

A Brief Discusssion of Results and Some Implications

Portuguese students argue for and against competing explanations on more or less elaborate grounds in spite of a history curriculum centred on substantive historical content. Some of their arguments were proximate in kind of those adduced by historians when assessing differente versions, according to Martin analysis. But at what levels of sophistication do adolescents decide when choosing among different options concerning a given social or historical issue?

The substantive choices revealed a relative homogeneity across the three grades. Students are not much used to applying critical criteria to their practical choices, even when they can thoroughly reason about them. Choices made by students at higher grades and levels of a second order reasoning seemed to follow simple standards, such as clarity of information, description of antecedent steps, quantity of factors, or in terms of personal assumptions such as the positive image of the Portuguese, rather than criteria of explanatory consistency underlying their 'theoretical' arguments. Perhaps there is a huge work to be done in history education around this specific issue which is part of a much bigger challenge: making explicit relationships between what we think and what we do.

It must be stressed that different reasons and *more* or *less* sophisticated arguments of a second order nature may justify similar practical choices. Identifying those underlying motives is crucial to our understanding of the tension between thinking and acting. Students may take concrete decisions which appear to indicate a less elaborate reasoning than that suggested by their arguments. In this study, the descriptive version was the most popular 'explanation' even among students who suggested elaborate conceptual patterns - its information was frequently selected in terms of factors, namely, technological advance (naval equipment and knowledge), economic motivation (the trade spice), organized explorations (systematic trips through the African coast). Moreover, a preference for the nationalistic version based on an emotional choice was in some cases consciously justified in terms of practical concerns, thus overtly distinct from historical criteria; in other cases its *morality* factor was interpreted in terms of current values (*morale* factor) being the nationalistic context rarely grasped.

The attribution of meanings according to everyday values appears to be a common strategy for students coping with historical information, such as Lee (2005) points out. A gradual expansion of more consistent criteria related to objectivity - such as evidential confirmation/refutation and considering the context of the situation - is a task for teachers, teacher educators and researchers. Some similar patterns across countries begin to be encountered (cf. Lee & Ashby, 2000; Hsiao, 2005; Barca, 2005; Gago, 2005). Analysing and reflecting on those similarities and differences might be valuable to history education in these times where different perspectives are publicly discussed and the young people need to be equipped to critically handle them.

References

Ashby, R. (2005). Students' approaches to validating historical claims. In Ashby, R., Gordon, P. & Lee, P. (eds.), *Understanding History: Research in History Education.* International Review of History Education, vol 4 (pp. 21-36). London: Routledge Falmer.

Ashby, R. & Lee, P. (2000). Progression in Historical Understanding among students ages 7-14. In Stearns, P.; Seixas, P. & Wineburg, S. (Eds.). *Knowing, Teaching and Learning History* (pp. 199-222). New York: New York University Press.

Barca, I. (2005). ´Till new facts are discovered´: Students ideas about objectivity in history. In Ashby, R., Gordon, P. & Lee, P. (eds.), *Understanding History: Research in History Education.* International Review of History Education, vol 4 (pp. 68-82). London: Routledge Falmer.

Barca, I & Magalhães (2004). Syllabus change: A view from Portugal. In Roberts, M. (ed.), *After the Wall. History teaching in Europe since 1989* (pp. 109-114). Hamburg: Körber-Stiftung.

Barca, I. & Magalhães, O. (2005). *A bridge between the past and the present§? The perspectives of Portuguese young people.* Paper presented at the International Perspectives on History Teaching Symposium, 2005 AERA Annual Meeting, Montreal, Canadá.

Biao, Y. (2005). The development of history teaching curricula in China. In Dickinson, A., Gordon, P. & Lee, P. (eds), *Raising standards in history education*, International Review of History Education, vol 3 (pp. 168-180).

London: Wolburn Press.

Cercadillo, l. (2001). Significance in history: students' ideas in England and Spain. In Dickinson, A., Gordon, P. & Lee, P. (eds), *Raising standards in history education*, International Review of History Education, vol 3 (pp. 116-145). London: Wolburn Press.

Dray, W. (1980). *Perspectives on history*. London: Routledge and Kegan Paul.

Dray, W. (1991). Comment. In Van der Dussen, W. J. & Rubinoff, L. (Eds.), *Objectivity, method and point of view*: *Essays in the philosophy of history*, (pp. 170-190). Leiden: E. J. Brill.

Foster, S. (2005). Interpreting the past, serving the present: Us and English textbook portrayals of the Soviet Union during the Second World War. In Ashby, R., Gordon, P. & Lee, P. (eds.), *Understanding History: Research in History Education*. International Review of History Education, vol 4 (pp. 173-187). London: Routledge Falmer.

Fulbrook, M. (2002). *Historical Theory*. London: Routledge.

Gago, M. (2005). Children's understanding of historical narratives in Portugal. In Ashby, R., Gordon, P. & Lee, P. (eds.), *Understanding History: Research in History Education*. International Review of History Education, vol 4 (pp. 83-97). London: Routledge Falmer.

Hsiao, H. (2005). Taiwanese students' understanding of differences in history textbooks. In Ashby, R., Gordon, P. & Lee, P. (eds.), *Understanding History: Research in History Education*. International Review of History Education, vol 4 (pp. 54-67). London: Routledge Falmer.

Lee, P. (2005). Putting principles into practice: understanding history. In Donovan, S. and Bransford, J. (eds), *How Stydents Learn* (pp. 31-78). Washington, DC: The National Academy Press.

Lee, P. & Ashby, R. (2001). Empathy, Perspective Taking and Rational Understanding. In Davies Jr, O., Yeager, E. A. & Foster, S. J. (Eds), *Historical Empathy and Perspective Taking in the Social Studies* (pp. 21-50). New York: Rowman and Littlefield.

Martin, R. (1989). *The past within us*. Princeton: Princeton University Press.

Popper, K. (1961). *The poverty of historicism*. London: Routledge.

Roberts, M. (ed.) (2004). *After the Wall. History teaching in Europe since 1989*. Hamburg: Körber-Stiftung.

Walsh, W. (1967). *A Introduction to philosophy of history*. London: Hutchinson.

Appendix

Version D

The sailors of Prince Henry were those who took the first and most difficult steps into the unknown lands for the Europeans ... The western African coast was progressively explored. The Portuguese caravels brought back gold, spices, furs, ivory and slaves from those regions.

Meanwhile, between 1405 and 1433, the emperors of China sent seven expeditions to explore the Indian Ocean, commanded by Cheng Ho, bringing back to China spices and unusual animals, including lions and giraffes.

Upon Bartolomeu Dias having rounded the Cape of Good Hope, a new expedition, commanded by Vasco da Gama, arrived in India, in 1498. After that, the Portuguese quickly took control of the lucrative spice trade, for almost a century by forbidding other people to trade in the Indian Ocean and seizing the main ports through which the spice route passed.

Based on *Explorers*, 1991 and *Exploration & Empire*, 1990

中文節譯

歷史教育中的客觀性與視野：
葡萄牙學生的觀念

Isabel Barca　著

葉毅均　　節譯

　　資訊社會為歷史教育提供了開拓其範圍以及探索多元觀點的絕佳機會，並可學習交替使用各種既融匯又分化的觀念。這樣的態度毫不畏懼多元的視野，反而承認此種多元性乃是深度理解過去和當前社會的基礎所在。因此，今日受歷史教育的年輕人必須把握機會洞察現實的多樣性。歷史教育從而可以在他們世界觀的進展中佔有一席之地。

一、歷史中的客觀性與觀點

　　將歷史客觀性的意涵等同於作者之於過去的絕對中立，在今日看來是個過分天真的想法，也不再受到一流的史家、哲學家和社會科學家們的支持。諸如「文獻自己會說話」的假設，或抱持「真假理論」相對的二分法信念，在有關歷史知識本質的論辯中早已被拋棄，卻似乎在今日更為寬廣的、非學術的圈子裡受到挑戰。

　　一旦認識到科學中的主觀因素，針對歷史客觀性的論辯便轉移到另一個核心問題：如果和歷史敘述糾結在一起的詮釋成分有其社會脈絡，那麼該如何才能評估歷史作品？

在此一針對客觀性的論辯中，「解構」和小說的研究取徑在不同的專業團體中獲得某些支持，Fulbrook (2002) 腦中帶著那些後現代主義者的論述加入辯論，並回到這個問題：

> 如果史家們在事實（日期、事件、「發生了什麼事」）方面得到共識，卻在更寬廣的詮釋或解釋架構上產生歧異，我們是否應該直接認為，所有的敘述都只不過是「觀點」，在原則上一樣可靠（或同屬虛構）？

當探討如何裁決一系列個別、競爭、共存的，乃至於互不相容的典範時，Fulbrook 考量歧異產生的兩個層次，以求澄清調和的可能或不可能：在歷史學典範的宏觀層次，由於先驗的預設諸如有關人與社會之間的關係、文化與物質狀態、或我們尋求解釋的層級（是求表面性抑或長時段的），可以存在各種不同而又相互衝突的理論。在這樣通論性的層次，這些典範也許不夠開放以供人反駁，一些不同的後設敘事也許都能成立。但是當我們從一個廣泛的架構轉移到對於特定過去的各種敘事時，那麼就有可能回答此一問題：「那個敘述更加可靠？」在這兩方之中，有可能找出一系列史家共享的方法論標準，譬如是否可以在證據的考量下，開放特定詮釋以供修正。

二、歷史教育中的客觀性與觀點

針對歷史課程的研究顯示，大多數國家一直到本世紀仍然在教一套固定版本的過去，儘管主要的敘事會依照政治策略的不同而改變。在橫跨多年的學校教育中，歷史課程的內容主題與授課時數也許會改變，但不變的是單一的敘述方式，從而未曾關注透過交叉分析來加以質疑，並檢視不同

說法所帶來的不同觀點。像大英國協 (UK) 這樣的國家是此一整體情勢中的例外，其教育法規明確地指出需要在學校中考量各種不同的觀點。大英國協所實現的成果深具影響力，為其他地方的歷史課程取徑注入了新的活力。在葡萄牙，由基本教育部 (DEB) 所頒發的基本課程權限文件（針對一到九年級）已開放探索對於過去的不同詮釋，教科書也開始承擔起同樣的關注。

在歷史中探索不同的觀點並不是一種單線的任務。正如 Lee (2005) 警告我們的，歷史是反直覺的。提供一小部分關於過去的幾件史料來讓學生詮釋是不夠的。學生需要知道的是，歷史是建築在亟待詮釋而非照抄的證據之上。對於過去的解釋不同於事實性的說明。乃至於現存的各種不同的說法，並不代表歷史僅僅是一種意見而已。

學生需要被提示問題，進而逐漸去思索歷史描述與解釋是建立在什麼樣的基礎上的，以及為何某些解釋最後能夠勝過其他的解釋。要達到此一目標，需要了解學生們是以何種未曾明言的理解 (tacit understanding) 在從事操作的。

三、針對葡萄牙青少年的一項研究

本項經驗性研究旨在強調學生們對於歷史解釋之暫時性 (provisionality) 的觀念。此一暫時性的觀念指的是對於同樣的過去，無論何時都存有不同的解釋。

針對 119 個分別是七、九和十一年級的學生，來自一所鄉間學校和一所城市學校，我們提出一組基於四個版本的常見而特定的歷史問題來請他們作答。這個歷史問題是「葡萄牙如何能在十六世紀的印度洋建立起一個海權帝國？」緊接著是四個改寫的說法，其中三個是一種解釋。（版本 A、B、C 以及附錄中的版本 D）

　　版本 A 強調的是伊斯蘭教徒的因素，版本 B 強調的是中國人的因素，兩者可以視為競爭性的歷史解釋。版本 C 強調的是民族主義的因素，也許可以視為具有偏見的版本。第四個版本 D 是一種描述性的模式，說明了葡萄牙與中國的海權探險是如何演進的。最後一種版本是用來給予學生當回答解釋性問題的時候，可以在一種描述或一種解釋之間作出抉擇。同時，亦包含史料以證明版本 A 和版本 B。

　　需要作答的問題是設計用來顯示學生們對歷史中的暫時性與客觀性等幾個方面所擁有的觀念。在這幾個問題裡，問題三要求學生針對既有的實質說法做出贊成或反對的論證，隱含了第二序的推論標準，用以評估歷史解釋的效力：

　　一、依據一個歷史解釋的重要性，評價排序這四個說法的高低。

　　二、當解釋為何葡萄牙成功地控制了印度洋，你認為在那些方面第一個說法優於第二個說法？

　　三、你是否認為第一個說法較能為史料所證實？為什麼？

　　四、為你排序的最後兩個選擇辯護。

　　結果顯示，相較於完整地引述訊息，學生們隨意引用片段的材料來從事論證，並藉以尋求解釋他們的想法。一些學生僅僅是利用先前所熟悉的知識，其他學生則是將之與新獲得的資訊串連在一起。至於證據的一致性，一些學生將焦點只放在事實 (fact) 之上（一種描述性模式的思想），而其他學生則運用了因素 (factor) 的觀念。在最後這一種群體中，某些學生隱然將事實與因素等觀念連結為解釋的一貫性 (explanatory consistency)，基於對證據和邏輯的確認、證實或否定，來討論特定因素的有效性。

四、結論

　　儘管歷史課程集中於實質性的內容，葡萄牙學生仍然會或多或少基於

某些根據，而去論證支持或反對不同的歷史解釋。其中，他們的某些論證近似於史家評估不同說法時所採用的論證。但是針對一個既有的社會或歷史議題，青少年會在那種程度的世故之中，而對不同的選項做出抉擇呢？

實際的抉擇顯示了跨越這三個年級的一種相對同質性。學生們不太習慣在他們的實際選擇上運用批判性的標準，即使他們完全能夠加以推論。學生們在高年級以及第二序的推論層次所做出的選擇，似乎按照的是簡單的準則以作為他們的「理論」依據，諸如訊息是否清楚明白、對於先前步驟的描述、決定因素的數量多寡，或者乾脆依個人假設而定，例如葡萄牙人的正面形象，而非基於解釋一貫性的標準。或許在歷史教育中圍繞此一議題尚有更多的工作有待完成，因為這是更大的挑戰的一部分：澄清我們的所思所想與我們的所作所為之間的關係。

必須強調的是，不同的理據與在第二序上或多或少老練的論證，也可能得出相似的實際選擇。指認出藏身其下的動機，對我們理解思考與行動之間的張力來說將是關鍵性的一點。學生們可能會採取具體的決定，反映出較未深思熟慮的推論，而非他們在論證中所顯現的那般精巧。在本研究中，描述性的版本 D 甚至在表現出精心結構的概念模式的學生那裡，都是最受到歡迎的「解釋」。更有甚者，基於情感選擇而對民族主義版本 C 的偏好，在某些案例中是被有意識地藉由實際考量而證成的，從而全然與依照歷史性的準則下判斷不同。

依據日常價值來賦予意義，似乎是學生們處理歷史資訊的共同策略，如 Lee (2005) 所指出的。將之逐步擴展至關乎客觀性的更為一致的標準，諸如證據的證實／否定，以及考量特定狀況的脈絡，則是教師、師資培育者以及研究人員的任務。一些相似的模式已經在不同國家中出現。當此時代，不同的視野能夠被公開討論，而年輕人也須具備能力以批判性地處理這些觀點時，分析與反省這些模式的異同對歷史教育來說，可能是有價值的。

「沒有課本怎麼學歷史?」
——談中學生對歷史教科書的想法

蕭憶梅[*]

一、前言

　　在談歷史教育時,我們不能忽略一個基本的核心問題,那就是學習的
主體:「學生」,他們到底在想什麼?因為學生並不是被動的接收我們想要
教給他們的「歷史知識」,而是有自己的邏輯與理解方式在看待歷史,並
且這些對歷史的既有概念深深的影響到他們學習歷史的情形。所以,要使
歷史教學真正達到效果(無論那是為了什麼:民族認同、民主意識,或是
歷史思維),我們必須對學生的認知有初步的認識[1]。而臺灣近年來,對於
學生學習歷史的認知研究已開始發展,主要集中在探測學生對歷史記述的
想法與歷史理解[2]。也有許多教師在探索學生思維與創新歷史教學的可能
性(如清華大學至今已舉辦六屆的「歷史教學新嘗試」研討會),這些研

* 國家教育研究院課程及教學研究中心

1 Bransford, J. D., Brown, A. L. and Cocking, R. R. (1999) *How People Learn: Brain, Mind, Experience and School* (eds), Washington D.C.: National Academy Press.

2 詳見林慈淑,〈史家?偵探?或記錄?— 10-14 歲兒童對歷史記述的一些想法〉,發表於東吳大學歷史系主辦之「第三屆史學與文獻學」學術研討會,收入《史學與文獻(三)》(臺北:東吳大學,2000),頁 171-206;林慈淑,〈年齡、知識或觀念——試探兒童對多元歷史記述的反應〉,東吳歷史學報,第十期,2003,頁 307-346;劉靜貞,〈10～16 歲學生對歷史記述的認知初探——三人組討論方式的嘗試〉,發表於東吳大學歷史系主辦之「第三屆史學與文獻學」學術研討會,收入《史學與文獻(三)》(臺北:東吳大學,2000),頁 119-169。

究都增進我們對臺灣學生歷史認知學習的了解。然而，不可否認的是在目前臺灣的實際教學環境下，除了少數老師使用自己編寫或設計的教材之外，教科書在大部分的歷史課堂裡，仍然扮演著舉足輕重的角色。所以當我們談論學生如何學習歷史時，我們無法忽視在教學環境中很重要的一環：教科書在歷史教學中所扮演的角色及其影響力（至少我們不能在沒有實證研究下就宣稱我們可以對教科書置之不理）。

然而目前在有關歷史教科書的學術研究中，均大量集中在課本內容的編排方式以及其隱含的政治意識。這些問題當然都有它的重要性及意義，但是我們卻不清楚教科書和歷史學習之間的關係。學生對於歷史教科書內容的理解程度是如何[3]？學生對於教科書的論述又有什麼樣的想法？當我們花了許多心思在編寫課本及選擇課本，或是為了課程綱要的政治意涵大動干戈時[4]，我們是不是應該先停下來想一想，到底學生是如何的學習與理解歷史，是如何解讀呈現在他們眼前的教科書？

基於以上理由，筆者在碩士論文研究期間曾嘗試探測國中生對教科書記述的想法，結果顯示大部分學生對於教科書有權威的印象[5]，當他們看到「南京大屠殺」此事件在臺灣、中國大陸、新加坡的教科書中有不同的描寫及解釋時，超過半數的國中生無法接受這樣的情況。有些學生覺得很憤怒，認為這三者之中一定只有一篇是真實，其他則是謊言，而那篇真實的記述一定是臺灣的版本，因為「我們的政府怎麼會欺騙我們？它怎麼會要我們去背誦不正確的歷史，然後還要不斷的考試？」。少部分學生則認

---

3 這方面的研究很少，除了在美國有 Beck 和 McKeown 以及 Wineburg 部分的研究，在臺灣更是缺乏。

4 如 1997 認識臺灣歷史篇及 2006 高中歷史暫行課綱問題所引發的論戰。

5 見 Hsiao, Y. (2002). *Exploring Students' Ideas about Historical Accounts in Textbooks*. Unpublished Masters dissertation, University of London, Institute of Education; Hsiao, Y. (2005). Taiwanese Students' Understanding of Differences in History Textbook Accounts in Ashby, R., Lee, P. and Gordon, P. (Eds), *International Review of History Education Vol. 4: Understanding History: Recent Research in History Education* (pp.54-67), London: RoutledgeFalmer.

為有不同的歷史記述是正常的，因為每個人都會加油添醋，站在自己的立場為自己辯護。從學生的這些回答中可以看出學生對於教科書有某種既定印象，而且對於歷史記述並沒有很成熟的概念。但是因為這份研究施測時，是在國中仍只採行標準版教科書的時候，加上僅此一次的小型施測不足以對中學生的想法有概括的解釋，所以筆者接下來的研究便繼續針對此一主體做進一步的探測。但是研究對象轉往使用開放版本已有數年之久的高中生，研究資料也將教科書和其他坊間的歷史書籍合併使用，期能更精確的了解學生可能對於歷史記述及教科書的想法。

本文的內容是筆者博士論文研究的前測部分，所以樣本數及研究方式都有限制，其目的不是對臺灣高中生的歷史認知做概化推論，而是試著初步探測高中生可能的想法及測試題目方向的效度，所以在研究方法上難免有不盡完善之處。只希望藉此機會，讓大家認識到學生在學習歷史時可能會出現的看法，以及他們對歷史教科書的既有概念。期望在了解學生對教科書的看法後，教科書能成為教師教學的幫助而非絆腳石，讓學生可以真正的理解歷史的意義，而不是一味背誦教科書裡的「歷史事實」或是視歷史為無用之物。

二、問卷的實施與設計

本研究的施測時間為 2004 年 12 月到 2005 年 1 月間，對象是臺北縣兩所高中的兩所班級，學生為高一及高二的學生，研究方法主要是以開放式書面問卷為主，再根據問卷的回答中抽三位同學做非正式的對話訪談，本文中所使用的資料來自於這兩個班的一半數量，總共樣本數為 42 份[6]。

這份書面問卷包含兩個部分，第一部分的問題是開放式題目，讓學生

6　兩個班級的總數為 84 人，但一半的同學作 A 問卷，另一半作 B 問卷，本文只討論 A 問卷的資料部分，故樣本數為兩班總人數的一半。

在沒有太多的限制下去闡述他們對於歷史記述的想法。教科書的議題並沒有直接出現在題目裡，但是在學生拿到的資料中則有放進歷史教科書這個背景因素。學生拿到的資料中，附有兩個有關鴉片戰爭的歷史記述，記述一出自龍騰版高中歷史課本，記述二則出自於史景遷 (Jonathan Spence) 的《追尋現代中國》（請見附錄一）。這兩篇文章都是直接從原書節錄，文章的出處都有刊出，讓學生清楚知道記述一是來自於高中課本，而記述二不是，龍騰版的記述一主要是在陳述鴉片戰爭發生背景及原因，在表現林則徐禁煙的決心時，以史料對話方式呈現出當時的情境。而史景遷之文主要在批判中國及林則徐的政策問題和英國的貿易決心。學生在閱讀這兩篇文章後要回答以下兩個問題：(1) 你覺得為什麼會有兩個「鴉片戰爭」的故事？(2) 你能不能選出你比較相信的？如果可以，請說明是那一則和你的理由？如果不可以，也請說明你的原因。學生們需要在三十分鐘內回答完這兩個題目。

問卷的第二部分則是針對學生對教科書的想法，在十五到二十分鐘的時間內回答以下兩個問題：(1) 你覺得我們使用歷史教科書的目的是什麼？(2) 有人曾說「如果只有用標準版教科書，學生對過去就會有相同的詮釋」，你同不同意這種說法？為什麼？

三、結果分析與討論

（一）比較可信的記述

學生對於是否可以選出比較令人信服的記述此問題時，有各式各樣的回答，他們對於可信歷史記述的選擇情形如下：

表 1　學生對於不同歷史記述的選擇

	A 學校	B 學校	總數
無法決定	7	13	20
第一則（歷史課本）	11	5	16
第二則（非歷史課本）	3	3	6
總數	21	21	42

　　初看這項數據會有一種錯覺，似乎學生比較信賴歷史課本的記述，但這是因為歷史課本呈現「官方核准版本」的形象所造成的關係嗎？我們無法確定，所以必須繼續檢測他們做選擇的思維過程，才能對學生對於歷史記述及歷史教科書的看法有所了解。根據學生所提供的理由，可將其判斷多元記述的想法大略整理成以下幾種反應：

- 無法決定，因為不具備判斷的依據
- 無法決定，因為沒有必要去判斷歷史解釋
- 第一則（歷史課本），因為比較熟悉
- 第一則（歷史課本），因為民族情感
- 第二則（史景遷之文），因為比較客觀

圖 1　學生對判斷多元記述的反應

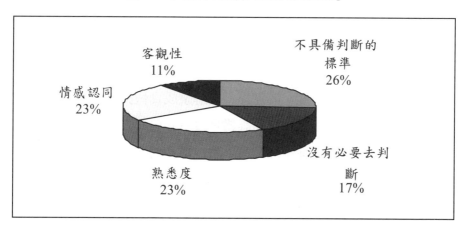

以下針對每一種反應做概略說明，並舉出相關的例子，但這裡的討論重心不在於他們到底能不能作決定，或是他們到底作了什麼決定，而在於探討影響他們是否可以作決定的因素是什麼？[7]

1.不具備判斷的標準

有的學生無法做出決定，主要是因為他們不知道要怎麼判斷。有的學生認為他們不能確定那一個比較可信，因為事情發生的時候他們不在那裡，所以沒有機會去確認事情是不是真如問卷提供的記述內容一般。有些學生則覺得他們沒有足夠的歷史知識去判斷，因為他「歷史不好」。這些學生似乎認為判斷多元記述的標準是在於有沒有親身經歷，或是豐富的歷史知識背景。既然這些條件都不可得，所以他們不能作出可信度的判斷。

2.沒有必要去判斷歷史解釋

有的學生則認為這兩則記述的差別只在於解釋的觀點，而世上沒有一個客觀的判斷標準可以來評價歷史解釋的可信度，所以我們沒有必要去判斷。高二李同學的回答就是一個很清楚的例子：

> 「第一則是屬於從小教科書上給我們的知識，而第二則卻較為精細，對於英國的一切作法有較詳細的介紹，兩者都各有道理，其實兩則只是對於相同史實做不同的歷史解釋，所以沒有誰對誰錯。」

李同學似乎把「可信度」的意思直接解讀成真假對錯，所以對他來說要在不同的歷史記述中去選擇誰對誰錯是沒有必要的。而高二的施同學則認為這兩種說法只不過是從不同角度來看，從他們各自的立場來說，當然

---

[7] 學生的回答中有時包含了不只一種傾向，可能他們選擇記述一是因為這個故事比較常看到，或是情感上比較能認同，在此情況下，學生的這兩種反應都會同時納入。

他們都是對的，所以去作判斷時沒有意義也沒有必要的。

3. 第一則（歷史課本），因為比較熟悉

有將近四分之一的學生認為記述一（歷史課本）是比較可信的，因為他們比較熟悉這個故事。如同高二的王同學所言：「第一則，因為那是在大部分的書裡都會提到的說詞，從小的課本裡也大概是這麼說的。」有三位同學更直接言明他們早已習慣記述一對於鴉片戰爭的這種說法，所以很難接受其他種歷史解釋。

4. 第一則（歷史課本），因為民族情感

也有四分之一左右的學生覺得他們比較相信第一則的說法，是因為情感認同的關係。他們認為與第二則相較之下，第一則歷史課本的敘述是比較站在中國人的立場，讀起來比較舒服。高一陳同學的回答就相當理直氣壯：

> 「我是中國人，當然我支持中國人。英國人在中國非法販賣鴉片，他們還以為發動戰爭是理所當然的。第二則故事竟然還批評中國政府和官員（林則徐）！我不能接受這種說法。」

5. 第二則（史景遷之文），因為比較客觀

有少數同學選擇相信第二則的說法，因為它有顧及到中國和英國雙方的立場，讀起來比較客觀。他們認為第一則的課本敘述中充滿著偏見，而且有為中國辯護的意味。相對之下，第二則敘述的解釋比較公允。

從學生對於判斷不同歷史記述的思維過程中，我們可以看到很多學生對於歷史性質隱而不宣的概念，這些都值得在根據每一個因素再深入分析，但由於本文的討論焦點在於學生對歷史教科書的想法，所以有關學生對於歷史性質的概念會再專文另作探討，這裡只將結果提供作為理解學生

如何看待歷史課本的一個參照背景。

(二) 使用歷史教科書的目的

當學生進一步被直接問到使用歷史課本的目的時，他們的反應可以概括如下：

1. 了解歷史的入門書

有些學生覺得歷史課本涵蓋了基本的歷史知識，所以使用課本很好也很方便，它已經幫我們整理好歷史過去的大事要點。所以我們只要念完歷史課本就可以對過去有基本的認識，可以知道不同的人在不同的時間及地點做了那些不同的事，而對歷史特別有興趣的同學可以再根據自己的需求去找課外書來閱讀。

2. 鑑往知來

有超過一半的學生認為使用歷史課本的目的是讓我們從過去中學到教訓，甚至直接以「鑑往知來」四字作答，沒有再作其他解釋。高一王同學的回答就是其中一個例子如下：「學習歷史的目的就是了解過去的人做了那些事情，然後我們就可以從中學到教訓。」他的回答似乎把使用教科書的原因和學習歷史的目的畫上了等號。

3. 考試的依據

大約三分之一的學生認為歷史教科書是作為考試的依據。這些學生聲稱他們需要一個標準的書面教材，才能夠準備考試。就像林同學所說：「沒有課本我們還考什麼？我們要有課本才能夠回家複習那些歷史年代，才能得到比較好的成績。」

4.控制思想

有少數學生提到歷史教科書可以用來控制思想。而學生對於「思想的控制」有不同的解讀，有的學生認為這是加強民族認同的一種方法，有的人則認為課本被拿來用作洗腦的工具。林同學的回答就闡述他對思想控制的想法：

> 「國家透過歷史課本來控制思想，讓人不會有造反的思想；或是國家有對自我民族的自傲自大概念，不願承認自己過去的失敗。其實我也不確定有沒有效，可能吧。因為要準備考試，所以常反覆看課本的內容，久了大概就習慣這種說法了。」

從學生的回答中可以看到他們認為歷史課本有方法學及理念上的存在因素。在方法學上，他們認為歷史課本可以是個學習歷史很重要的工具，因為它已經把重要的歷史知識整理好，並且按照時間次序逐項解釋，所以讀完這套教科書後就可以掌握「基本的歷史概念」。除此之外，歷史課本對於準備考試有很重要的幫助，因為有一個書面的教材，他們才能夠複習其中的內容。有的學生還表達了他們對於目前高中教科書有數種版本的不滿，因為這讓他們很難準備考試。從這些學生的想法可以看出他們似乎把歷史知識看成一連串的事實資訊，所以需要教科書提供重點大綱和考試的準備素材。然而，我們不能只把學生這樣的想法看作可笑或幼稚後便置之不理。我們應該思考的是：學生的歷史思維有沒有可能其實是受到這些傳統教科書和當前考試制度的限制？如果教科書的內容就是列出重要事件，或直接敘述歷史事件的原因，而沒有解釋作者是依據什麼樣的理由作出這樣的推論時，我們又如何責難學生認為歷史是固定不變的呢？如果考試的內容只是測試歷史知識的熟悉度，那麼學生認為應該只有一種標準教科書讓他們方便準備考試，這樣的想法不也是理所當然嗎？

　　另一方面，超過一半的學生在回答使用歷史教科書的目的時都提到「學習歷史可以鑑往知來」，這樣的反應似乎在回答學習歷史的目的（姑且不論學習歷史是不是真能鑑往知來），甚至有很多學生直接以學習歷史的目的是——作為回答的開頭。學生這樣的反應讓筆者懷疑是不是題意不清，所以學生沒有理解題目想要問的東西。為了確認學生的想法，在閱讀完施測結果後找了有類似回答的三位學生再次詢問，結果學生仍然作了類似的回答。當再進一步詢問他們覺得「使用歷史教科書的目的」和「學習歷史的目的」這兩個題目是否相同時，學生竟然回答說：「一樣啊！我們不是都用課本在學歷史嗎？不用課本的話我們要怎麼上歷史課？」當然這幾位同學的想法不能代表所有高中生的想法，但這樣的回答出在幾位學生的學習過程裡，顯然是習慣教師把歷史課本當成教學的唯一工具，讓他們想不出來還有什麼其他的歷史教學方式，以至於學生的歷史學習便仰賴在課堂上的那本課本，要靠它來讓我們「鑑往知來」。

　　而關於歷史教科書的理念部分，有少數學生也意識到政府的政治立場與意識型態。他們認為政府想透過歷史教科書來達到思想控制與加強民族認同。事實上，歷史教科書之所以在臺灣或是世界引起眾多注意及爭議，就是因為這個因素。然而歷史教科書的論述角度或政治意識會影響到學生的想法，這是大部分人士的假設，但實際上學生又是如何看待歷史教科書對他們想法的形塑呢？在現在眾多歷史資訊充斥的環境下，歷史教科書是不是仍然扮演著學生吸收歷史概念的重要角色呢？學生如果意識到歷史教科書被當作是一種政治工具，他們會極力抗拒還是認為這是理所當然，因為這是加強民族凝聚力的必要手段呢？這些問題都需要日後的研究才能夠加以釐清。

四、結語

從學生的回答中，我們可以初步探測出學生對於歷史的概念，以及他們對歷史教科書的想法，以下分成兩個層面來探討：

（一）教科書的歷史論述對學生有相當程度的影響，但並非來自於它本身的權威性，有可能與學生本身的歷史理解有關，也有可能和教育環境與制度有關。

儘管有很多的學生認為記述一（歷史課本）比較可信，但其中的原因並非是「歷史課本的內容應該比較正確」，或是「這是政府確認正確無誤的歷史知識」等等對教科書的權威印象。大部分的學生明白教科書只是歷史論述的其中一種（當然有少數同學可能還沒有意識到），它不一定是最好的歷史解釋，但卻是他們比較熟悉的說法，因為在別的書籍中有看到類似的說法。或是因為歷史記述本身符合他們情感上的認同與同情。

極端一點的例子就是如同在訪談中出現的某同學之言，「沒有課本怎麼學歷史？」這些學生已經習慣只透過歷史教科書去學習歷史，而考試制度又強化了歷史課本的重要性，如果再加上教師對課本的照本宣科（當然教科書在課堂上的使用情形我們並不是完全清楚），無怪乎歷史教科書好像成為歷史的代言人一樣，提供學生最方便的一套歷史知識與看法，使其鑑往知來。這樣的情形無疑是一個警訊，提醒我們對於歷史教科書在教學中所扮演的角色作深層的省思。

（二）學生對於歷史性質的迷思

從學生的回答中，可以間接看出學生對於歷史的性質並沒有很深刻的掌握。有些學生把歷史看作是固定的歷史資訊，所以教科書便提供了最方

便與最基本的整理。而如果歷史教科書的內容和其他歷史論述不同時，他們也不知道如何抉擇，因為他們沒有親眼目擊，所以無法判斷事情的真相。

有些學生雖然已經可以接受歷史多元記述的存在，但是明白了這一點卻不足以幫助他們去面對歷史的多元記述。有的學生不是以直覺式的方法作判斷（最熟悉的說法，或是最有情感認同的），就是直接歸咎於每個人都有他的看法，所以不需要去也無法去對多元解釋作探討。後者的想法正是 Peter Lee 提醒我們教師要注意的現象：

> 教師應該要努力革除學生「個人意見」和「刻意扭曲」這類的想法，代之以更複雜及成熟的理解方式。如果教科書提供了多元解釋卻沒有去建立這樣的理解，那麼就有可能陷入一個危機，只是將學生從服膺官方過去的信條，轉為面對多元歷史的徬徨無助[8]。

當我們希望學生真正理解歷史時，我們就必須培養他們對歷史的性質及歷史建構過程的理解。教科書只是教學的一種工具，教科書的歷史論述也只是眾多論述中的一種。我們要設法讓學生認識到，不應只是用真假對錯的概念來解讀多元歷史記述的差異，或是全盤接收所有「個人的想法」，而是要去思考這些歷史論述是針對什麼樣的問題在回答？是不是有足夠的史料證據在支持？是不是有考慮到當時的歷史脈絡？如果我們沒有去詳細探討歷史的性質，去幫助學生如何以歷史思維來面對多元記述，那麼我們只是將學生從「固定的歷史真相」的這一端，轉移到接受「各種多元的歷史解釋」的另一端，而他們仍然不能真正的理解歷史。

8　Lee, P. (1998) Children's Ideas about the Nature and Status of Historical Accounts 收入《方法論：歷史意識與歷史教科書的分析編寫國際學術研討會論文集》（新竹：清華大學，1998），頁 219。

附錄

請閱讀以下兩篇有關鴉片戰爭的歷史記述，並回答第一部分的兩個問題。

（一）

因為鴉片引起這麼多嚴重的問題，大臣之間各謀對策，而漸漸形成兩種不同的意見。一派人主張對販賣和吸食者處以重刑；大多數人則認為嚴刑峻罰不能禁止，與其讓白銀長期外流，倒不如就地合法，課以重稅，以解決財政困難。道光皇帝原來在這兩種主張之間搖擺不定，後來看到林則徐的奏摺，大為感動，乃決定禁煙。林則徐在奏摺中提醒皇帝，如果現在不正視鴉片問題，幾十年後，中國將沒有可禦敵的軍隊，也沒有可以發餉的銀兩。他並指出鴉片難禁的原因，是因為衙門中十個人有八、九個吸食。這些執法者一方面自己吸食，一方面又包庇走私，從中獲利，應該從嚴懲處。

林則徐在湖廣總督任內，曾經屬行禁煙，著有成效，所以他的各項見解，格外得到皇帝的信任。道光在七天內連著八次召見他，共商禁煙大計。為了表示對他的寵信，道光先是特准他在紫禁城內騎馬，接著又告訴他：「你不慣騎馬，可坐椅子轎」。蒙受君恩的林則徐，隨即被任命為欽差大臣到廣州禁煙，道光十九年(1839)中，他將繳獲的二百多萬斤鴉片在虎門海灘當眾銷毀。另一方面，他又增添大砲，操練水師，積極備戰。他告訴當地的百姓說：「英吉利夷人本來就很狡詐，又用鴉片殘害中國人性命。只要他們的兵船敢開進內河，人人都可以持刀痛殺」。

在英國國內，各地的商會都主張採取強硬手段對付中國。英國首相認為對付中國唯一的辦法，「就是先揍它一頓，然後再作解釋」，並決定派一支東方遠征軍到中國。英國國會為此展開激辯，反對者認為再也沒有比為鴉片而戰更不正義的戰爭了，他將使英國永遠蒙羞；贊成者則巧妙的操縱輿論，把焦點變成如何擔保未來貿易的平安與英國公民的安全。最後主戰派險勝，一支包括四十艘船隻的艦隊，在道光二十年(1840)中抵達中國，憑著優勢的堅船利砲，英軍在中國沿海一帶取得一連串的勝利。

李孝悌，《高中歷史課本（下）》，龍騰出版社，2001，頁 53-54。

　　（二）

　　欽差大臣林則徐與道光皇帝均是克盡職守、勤奮工作的人，儒家那一套上下尊卑與統治手段都已經深入兩人的心中。他們似乎真心相信，廣州臣民與外國商人的個性皆單純如童稚，會遵奉道德戒條而不悖。可惜實情沒那麼單純，當時很多人也看出這一點。即使鴉片還沒銷毀的時候，就有官員直陳，林則徐此舉並不能真正解決鴉片問題。一個英國鴉片商回想遭清廷封鎖的經驗，只是淡淡告訴一位友人說道：封鎖商館「幸可作為我們提出賠償的理由」。（註一）

　　中、英兩國以兵戎相見似乎已是一觸即發。前面已經提到一些大的原因：清朝已出現社會失序的現象、染上鴉片癮的人日益增加、中國人對洋人越來越不滿、洋人拒不接受清律的規範、國際貿易的丕變、西方文人不再傾慕中國文化。其他的因素則關係到林則徐談判的背景，也有林則徐所不了解的細節。外國商人觀察朝廷於 1836、1838 年就鴉片問題的辯論，趨於相信中國會合法化鴉片買賣，於是屯積了大量鴉片，並頻頻向印度的鴉片農增加訂貨量。然而隨著 1838 年禁革鴉片的強硬路線抬頭，鴉片市場亦跟著萎縮不振，鴉片商警覺到庫存的問題。

　　其次，新上任的英國駐華商務總監督改由英女王選派，而不是東印度公司聘任。倘若中國為難這位商務總監督，這無疑形同侮辱英國，而不是一家普通的商業公司，但中國並未察覺這中間的差別。反過來，商務總監督亦缺乏明確權限約束在華的英國或歐美各國的商人。然而，當他面臨重大問題時，卻能向英國軍隊和皇家海軍直接求援。

　　英國方面也密切注意中國境內鴉片事件的發展。1839 年初夏，義

律就曾發文向倫敦求援，英國外相巴麥尊 (John Henry Temple Palmerston) 爵士起初對於不遵守大清律例的英國商人並不表同情，現在已經轉而支持英國商人了。巴麥尊在「致中國欽命宰相書」中表示，中國官吏竟以「暴力傷害廣州的英國臣民，而這些英國臣民卻是平和地住在廣州城內，信賴中國政府的善意。雖然女皇陛下不會寬赦販賣鴉片的行為，但她絕不容許海外的英國臣民遭到暴力相向，受到侮辱與不公平的待遇。」(註二)，令他「極其詫異」。

註一：韋利 (Arthur Waley)，《中國人眼中的鴉片戰爭》(The Opium War through Chinese Eyes: London, 1958)，頁 47。

註二：馬士，《中華帝國的對外關係，卷一》，頁 622。

史景遷 (Jonathan D. Spence)，《追尋現代中國》，2001，時報出版社，頁 188-189。

第一部分

填寫日期：＿＿＿＿＿＿

學校：＿＿＿＿＿＿　　班級：＿＿＿＿＿　　座號：＿＿＿＿＿　　性別：＿＿＿＿

一、你覺得為什麼會有兩個「鴉片戰爭」的故事？

＿＿＿＿＿＿＿＿＿＿＿＿＿＿＿＿＿＿＿＿＿＿＿＿＿＿＿＿＿＿＿＿＿＿＿

＿＿＿＿＿＿＿＿＿＿＿＿＿＿＿＿＿＿＿＿＿＿＿＿＿＿＿＿＿＿＿＿＿＿＿

＿＿＿＿＿＿＿＿＿＿＿＿＿＿＿＿＿＿＿＿＿＿＿＿＿＿＿＿＿＿＿＿＿＿＿

＿＿＿＿＿＿＿＿＿＿＿＿＿＿＿＿＿＿＿＿＿＿＿＿＿＿＿＿＿＿＿＿＿＿＿

＿＿＿＿＿＿＿＿＿＿＿＿＿＿＿＿＿＿＿＿＿＿＿＿＿＿＿＿＿＿＿＿＿＿＿

＿＿＿＿＿＿＿＿＿＿＿＿＿＿＿＿＿＿＿＿＿＿＿＿＿＿＿＿＿＿＿＿＿＿＿

＿＿＿＿＿＿＿＿＿＿＿＿＿＿＿＿＿＿＿＿＿＿＿＿＿＿＿＿＿＿＿＿＿＿＿

＿＿＿＿＿＿＿＿＿＿＿＿＿＿＿＿＿＿＿＿＿＿＿＿＿＿＿＿＿＿＿＿＿＿＿

二、你能不能選出你比較相信的？如果可以，請說明是那一則和你的理
　　由？如果不可以，也請說明你的原因。

＿＿＿＿＿＿＿＿＿＿＿＿＿＿＿＿＿＿＿＿＿＿＿＿＿＿＿＿＿＿＿＿＿＿＿

＿＿＿＿＿＿＿＿＿＿＿＿＿＿＿＿＿＿＿＿＿＿＿＿＿＿＿＿＿＿＿＿＿＿＿

＿＿＿＿＿＿＿＿＿＿＿＿＿＿＿＿＿＿＿＿＿＿＿＿＿＿＿＿＿＿＿＿＿＿＿

＿＿＿＿＿＿＿＿＿＿＿＿＿＿＿＿＿＿＿＿＿＿＿＿＿＿＿＿＿＿＿＿＿＿＿

＿＿＿＿＿＿＿＿＿＿＿＿＿＿＿＿＿＿＿＿＿＿＿＿＿＿＿＿＿＿＿＿＿＿＿

＿＿＿＿＿＿＿＿＿＿＿＿＿＿＿＿＿＿＿＿＿＿＿＿＿＿＿＿＿＿＿＿＿＿＿

＿＿＿＿＿＿＿＿＿＿＿＿＿＿＿＿＿＿＿＿＿＿＿＿＿＿＿＿＿＿＿＿＿＿＿

第二部分

填寫日期：＿＿＿＿＿＿＿

學校：＿＿＿＿＿＿　　班級：＿＿＿＿＿　　座號：＿＿＿＿　　性別：＿＿＿＿

一、你覺得我們使用歷史教科書的目的是什麼？

＿＿＿＿＿＿＿＿＿＿＿＿＿＿＿＿＿＿＿＿＿＿＿＿＿＿＿＿＿＿＿＿＿＿＿

＿＿＿＿＿＿＿＿＿＿＿＿＿＿＿＿＿＿＿＿＿＿＿＿＿＿＿＿＿＿＿＿＿＿＿

＿＿＿＿＿＿＿＿＿＿＿＿＿＿＿＿＿＿＿＿＿＿＿＿＿＿＿＿＿＿＿＿＿＿＿

＿＿＿＿＿＿＿＿＿＿＿＿＿＿＿＿＿＿＿＿＿＿＿＿＿＿＿＿＿＿＿＿＿＿＿

＿＿＿＿＿＿＿＿＿＿＿＿＿＿＿＿＿＿＿＿＿＿＿＿＿＿＿＿＿＿＿＿＿＿＿

＿＿＿＿＿＿＿＿＿＿＿＿＿＿＿＿＿＿＿＿＿＿＿＿＿＿＿＿＿＿＿＿＿＿＿

＿＿＿＿＿＿＿＿＿＿＿＿＿＿＿＿＿＿＿＿＿＿＿＿＿＿＿＿＿＿＿＿＿＿＿

二、有人曾說「如果只有用標準版教科書，學生對過去就會有相同的詮釋」，你同不同意這種說法？為什麼？

＿＿＿＿＿＿＿＿＿＿＿＿＿＿＿＿＿＿＿＿＿＿＿＿＿＿＿＿＿＿＿＿＿＿＿

＿＿＿＿＿＿＿＿＿＿＿＿＿＿＿＿＿＿＿＿＿＿＿＿＿＿＿＿＿＿＿＿＿＿＿

＿＿＿＿＿＿＿＿＿＿＿＿＿＿＿＿＿＿＿＿＿＿＿＿＿＿＿＿＿＿＿＿＿＿＿

＿＿＿＿＿＿＿＿＿＿＿＿＿＿＿＿＿＿＿＿＿＿＿＿＿＿＿＿＿＿＿＿＿＿＿

＿＿＿＿＿＿＿＿＿＿＿＿＿＿＿＿＿＿＿＿＿＿＿＿＿＿＿＿＿＿＿＿＿＿＿

＿＿＿＿＿＿＿＿＿＿＿＿＿＿＿＿＿＿＿＿＿＿＿＿＿＿＿＿＿＿＿＿＿＿＿

Abstract

"How Can You Learn History Without Textbooks? "
—Secondary Students' Perception of History Textbooks

Yi-Mei Hsiao

This paper reports results of the pilot study on how high school students perceive history textbooks in Taiwan. Textbooks are the most commonly used tool in history instruction in most countries including Taiwan. Although there has been a rich vein of research into textbooks, very few studies examined the students' interaction with textbooks. Understanding that it is an important and yet little explored field, the study examined Taiwanese students' ideas about textbook accounts and the role of textbooks

In this paper, the written responses of 42 students age 15-17 in 2 different schools in the northern Taiwan were analysed. Students were presented with one excerpt of textbook account and one extract of non-textbook account of the opium war in China (1842). Students were asked to choose a more credible account and explain their reasons. The results showed that about half of the students were unable to make the judgment because they did not know the criteria or reasons to do so. The other half of the students who were able to choose between accounts and their choices were based on emotional factors, familiarity and objectivity of the particular account.

The results also show students' ideas about the purpose of using history textbooks: basic material of historical knowledge, learning lessons from the past, preparing for exams, and propaganda. The findings suggest that historical accounts in textbooks have impact on students' ideas, but it is not necessarily related to the authority of textbooks. It is more related to students' preconceptions about the nature of history and the educational environment in Taiwan.

Abstract

How Can You Learn History Without Textbooks? —Secondary Students' Perception of History Textbooks

This paper reports results of the pilot study on how high school students perceive the role of textbooks. To them, Textbooks are the most commonsense tool in learning historical knowledge. Besides textbooks, Person Although the

How Can Pupils Profit from Historical Learner-centred Software?

Bettina Alavi[*]

Introduction

How do young learners work with historical software? What strategies are used by them? What historical competencies are stimulated and which not? What difficulties exist in this context?

These and other questions arise while producing interactive and multimedia-based learning arrangements which we did in Heidelberg in the face of the historical feature film "Gladiator" and the historical topic "The Straightening of the River Rhein in the Nineteenth Century". In doing so, trial and error with learners offers first impressions. However, valid results can only be achieved on an empirical basis. Therefore, it seems to be reasonable to analyse on a methodological basis how learners work with "historical" software. My studies are in early stages at the moment and can thus be seen as a preliminary survey for a bigger project. Today I will present to you some first results.

---

[*] Institut für Gesellschaftswissenschaften, Pädagogische Hochschule Heidelberg

State of research in Germany

In German-speaking didactics of the subject history there are no empirical studies yet in terms of learning strategies with historical software.[1] I could imagine this is different in countries you come from and I do ask you to play your part in this discussion. In foreign language didactics[2] in Germany - as well as in Anglophone countries - there are already existing surveys concerning this matter as well as research on interactive learning tasks[3]. This seems to be logical since the "market" (or field) for interactive learner-centred material is very well-developed in the domain of the acquisition of languages whereas the domain of historical learning is – by all means in German-speaking countries – comparatively decent.

In the field of media didactics[4] there is a lot to discover although the main focus is on the acquirement of general media competencies and not on didactic issues as such.

---

1 Eine erste Annäherung bieten aber Michele Barricelli, Ruth Benrath: „Ciberhistory". Studierende, Schüler und Neue Medien im Blick empirischer Forschung. In: Geschichte in Wissenschaft und Unterricht 54 (2003), S. 337-353, die die Nutzung einer „Infotain-ment-CD-ROM" zur Industrialisierung bei älteren Schüler/innen untersuchen.

2 Nicola Würffel: Strategiengebrauch bei Aufgabenbearbeitungen in internetgestütztem Selbstlernmaterial. Tübingen 2006. Dort finden sich viele weitere Literaturangaben.

3 Z.B. Johannes Eckerth: Fremdsprachenerwerb in aufgabenbasierten Interaktionen. Tübingen 2003, Ellis Rod: Task-based Language Learning and Teaching. Oxford 2003.

4 Manuela Paechter: Von der didaktischen Vision zum messbaren Indikator: Beispiele eines Qualitätssystems für medienbasierte Lehre. In: A. Sindler, C. Bremer, U. Dittler u.a. (Hrsg.): Qualitätsentwicklung in e-learning. Münster: Waxmann 2006. S. 55-71.

Analysis of the Learning Task

From my point of view the learning task is a teacher's model that challenges learners -respectively learning groups - to come up with a mostly problem-oriented communicative and/ or cognitive activity. The main focus of a learning task concentrates on communicative processes in order to arrive at a conclusion[5].

Even finding such a historically software-based learning task seemed to be very difficult. I checked pretty new learning software (published 2005) of an established historical schoolbook of a Secondary School. According to the publisher, the software completes and deepens topics of the historical schoolbook; the learners are supposed to be able to work on the software's content individually without any support of the teacher. Unfortunately, most sequences consist of a virtual tour with a final Multiple Choice Test or extracts of computer games. By definition, there were only **two types of learning tasks** on the software:

1. The learners are supposed to translate historical a visual resource into a chart or diagram (professional and methodological competence)
2. The learners are supposed to learn to know the components of a visual resource and are then able to reproduce it (methodological competence).

---

5 Vgl. Wolfgang Börner: Lernprozesse in grammatischen Lernaufgaben. In: Wolfgang Börner, Klaus Vogel (Hrsg.): Grammatik und Fremdsprachenerwerb. Tübingen: Narr 2002. S. 231-259.

The learners tested the two learning tasks. The second learning task seemed to ask too much of the learners. With the help of this task the learner's methodological competencies were actually meant to be enhanced, but unfortunately, they did not understand the content of the visual resource and were therefore unable to solve the problem. In the following this part of the research will thus be no longer taken into consideration.

However, it is remarkable that historical learning software, which actually claims to highlight learning, hardly provides any learning tasks at all. Obviously, the little range of learning tasks asks way too much of the target group: the learner's oral skills are assessed inappropriately. Hereby, they are unable to comprehend contents. This means that methodological competence cannot be conveyed irrespective of the content.

Furthermore, the **learning task** has to be analysed **critically**: What is the **content** all about? The learning task works up afterlife associations mediaeval Christian people had. These people were looking forward to the Judgement Day when all dead become judged by Christ: good people are directly sent to heaven whereas semi-good and bad people have to be answerable to Christ. He decides to send some people to heaven and some others forever to hell, together with Satan.

At this stage, a **problem in respect of content** becomes clear: actually, it is a matter of religious content and has only little to do with historical content. This religious content is indeed of central importance for the comprehension of mediaeval people and mediaeval governance although the learning software does not make a contribution to the classification of the historical impact. This has to be done in the history class. Thus, more complex historical processes of thinking are not encouraged explicitly.

The structure of the learning task

The learning task is constructed in a **linear** way:

        Firstly:Introduction to the content and assignment of tasks

        Secondly:Analysis of a visual resource

        Thirdly:Abstraction of the visual resource in a diagram

        Fourthly:Feedback with correct answers (animated diagram)

There is a wide range of **media**:

Visual media:The "Giebelfeld" (as an explanation: a Giebelfeld is usually a big illustration made of stone above the main door of mediaeval churches. In the following I will translate the term as "gable field").

Text:Explanatory texts for the visual resource and the assignment of tasks.

Films, music or recorded texts are missing. Therefore, multimedia components have to be cut back (the learners missed recorded texts a lot since they had a lot of text to read. It seems to be a general problem that most learning software provides way too much text.)

Interactivity of the learning task

The **visual resource** is divided in several segments. The learners can enlarge these segments and can thus, observe them in more detail. In a second step the learners are free to select various written information for each segment.

The **diagram** is in a basic set-up on hand. It needs to be labelled and provided with symbols. Connections are highlighted via lanes between the columns. They can only point to certain directions.

During the analysis of the historical visual resource the **interactivity** is just a pure exploration of given segments of the visual resource. There is only a learner's choice concerning the retention period, intensity and completeness when he or she is gathering information.

The diagram offers a much higher interactivity because of its numerous opportunities to complete it and thus, the chance to find out the answer for the learning task. Some segments can even be displaced several times.

What Historical Sphere of Competence Does the Learning Task Respond to?

In the field of methodological competencies there has to be an analysis of a visual resource. In the context of professional competencies the structuring of religious contents is demanded.

It's about a transfer task that requires both substantial reading skills and the ability to abstract. However, the transfer task ends with the saving of certain know-how.

There is neither a task regarding the **function** of afterlife associations on the gable window of churches nor a task concerning the **diffusion rate** or the **consequences** of peoples every day life and the status of the church. Thus, the level of meaning and historical contexts won't be achieved, but the learning task remains on a level of amazement in terms of altering religious ideas of mediaeval Christian people. Consequently, the religious content is not incorporated into the historical context.

Certain difficulties of the software cause several didactic problems:

Feedback

There is no feedback while working on the learning task and only the complete solution can be compared with a master answer provided. This encourages working meticulously but prevents the learners from being organised and well-structured. On the other hand, it was possible to observe strategies the learners applied to in various situations as long as the problem solving was planned to be very complex.

Programming errors in the face of the diagram

It was very difficult to place the lanes, which guarantee the correct connection of the contents between the segments, in a proper way. Sometimes even lanes that were connected correctly did not match their predetermined position. As a result, the learners started complaining and accused the programmer badly. However, on the other hand it was possible to see several learners following their original plan consequently without losing control by technical problems.

Arrangement on the screen

The visual resource and the diagram do not appear simultaneously on the screen. Every time the learners needed further information they had to go forth and back in the programme and they finally had to restart the diagram again and again to type in their newly gathered information. This wasn't very motivating for the learners at all, but surprisingly they gradually developed strategies to avoid these difficulties while completing the diagram. Thus, they additionally experienced several point of views and designed the diagram on a higher level than it was actually planned.

Cultural pre-knowledge

The learning task takes an adequate cultural knowledge concerning knowledge of Christianity for granted. This applies to the decoding of symbols (such as nimbus and wings) as well as to biblical indirectnesses (such as "who is Christ? Petrus? Angels?"). Consequently, the learning task can only be done by learners who are equipped with this kind of knowledge.

Level of abstraction

The diagram is a very abstract transfer of the gable window. Lots of elements of the gable window were cleared (e.g. Petrus and the angels). The learners have read several segments so far. Nevertheless, they still don't know to what kind of segment information the page goes back to. The body of the gable window is not equivalent to the model. In the original gable window the earth is located at the very bottom and the hell is not pictured at all whereas the model provides earth and hell on the same level. Thus, only learners who notice that the gable window has two sides (right side for the badies, left side for the goodies) are able to start labelling the columns automatically. I guess that the programme engineer was influenced by his cultural knowledge and thought "the hell must obviously be at the bottom".

Consequently, the question arises:

How could one choose this learning task, especially in the face of these enormous restrictions?

Initially, because of the learning **task's transferability** (historical analysis of a visual resource that is abstracted into a diagram) to other historical contents. Thus, the observable strategies to solve problems and the demanded historical competencies become more and more exemplary.

Secondly, because of the good (even though linear) structure of the learning task and the "**big steps**" provided. That made the learners work individually and on their own for quite a long time. This kind of learner-centred learning with a lot of self-control makes it possible to observe the learners thinking intensively (anyway, it's definitely more successful than working without learner's self-control).

Furthermore, the learning task serves as a preliminary task to deepen the history **lesson in school**. The contents of the schoolbook (The role of religion in people's mediaeval life) are illustrated by the learning results. In the subject history this can be carried on to the level of meaning and relevance. Plus, the learners are already familiarised with the topic since the medium is in line with the epoch – the European Middle Ages - dealt with in school. On the one hand, knowledge and strategies the learners acquired in the history lesson do influence their work on the software, but on the other hand, the teacher is not present and the learners work individually and on their own.

The learners

It's about 6th grade learners (**12 years old**) of a Secondary School who are taught the subject history for the very first year. In the context of the

German divided school system the Secondary School is a mid-level institution. Schooldays normally end with successful exams after class 10. Most learners then start learning a profession. The school is located in a small village in the direct environment of Heidelberg. It's a rural area with only a few migrant families. The learners have done a special programme for advanced reading competencies. Hence, they are all very fast readers with a brilliant reading technique and are all able to comprehend the message of texts almost immediately. The learners religious education is well-trained by the religious instruction class in school. In larger cities learners probably would have had more problems with the religious content of the learning task. I meet and see the learners every week while observing students doing their practical training there. The learners like the subject history a lot. That's because the teacher prefers teaching problem-oriented. It means the teacher always uses a problem as a starting point. Then, in a second step the learners are supposed to come up with different theses. Thereby imaginations arise and the learners establish a relationship to their every day life. They are used to speculate, to offer suggestions to solve a problem and to ask questions. They were introduced to the analysis of historical visual resources, but not in every single detail (6th graders!). Most learners wanted to participate in the study, but finally, there were 8 of them taking part (4 boys, 4 girls) in groups of two. For this reason, it is a small study which offers only insights and needs a lot more differentiation. Most learners are used to work with computers although they predominantly use it during leisure time to surf the internet or to play games. They write word-documents and do vocabulary training with the help of the computer. Up to now, computers weren't used in the history lesson at all.[6]

The method

The learners were filmed while they were working on the learning task in groups of two. With the help of this video screening both the learners activities in front of the screen and their verbal - as well as their non-verbal - statements are documented. I was always present while the learners were working, but actually mainly because of the almost non-working recorder. Nonetheless, the relationship between researcher and learners is a problem which needs to be taken into consideration since the learners had the possibility to ask me questions as soon as they had lost the right track. Honestly, they did ask questions, but only at very difficult stages.

The method I used is called "Verbal Reports on Thinking". Actually, this method is originally used in psychology, but it gradually influences the research on learning and teaching, too.[7] The learners were asked to talk as much as possible about what they were doing while they were working on the learning task, especially in respect of: what they were doing or what they were going to plan as well as their impressions and feelings. There is no need to conceal that the expressiveness of this method's results are discussed controversially. However, the method seems to be reasonably approved in terms of the exploration of how learners react when solving problems by means of well-structured tasks. Moreover, the method contains the advantage

---

6 The learners were asked several questions concerning their private use of computers before the actual work on the learning task started.

7 Nicola Würffel: Protokolle Lauten Denkens als Grundlage für die Erforschung von hypertextgeleiteten Lernprozessen im Fremdsprachenunterricht. In: Andreas Müller-Hartmann u.a. (Hrsg.): Qualitative Forschung im Bereich Fremdsprachen lehren und lernen. Tübingen 2001. S. 163-186.

that the results can be analysed both qualitatively and quantitatively.

The method was slightly modified by having two learners in front of one screen in order to have them solving problems communicatively. Hereby, the learner's process becomes transparent and simultaneously, the learner's cooperation while concentrating on the task becomes observable. It was very fruitful to divide the learners in groups of two because they were talking to each other permanently. Some of them are probably used to it since they play computer games together in front of one screen. Furthermore, most groups came up with totally different strategies to solve problems which were discussed and tested immediately. After the video screening the data were transcribed into verbal data and were placed in a scale next to the data of the screen activities. These data were – especially because of the little number of learners – analysed mainly qualitatively. That means, it was tried to reconstruct cognitive processes. At some points also quantitative data were analysed (e.g. the retention period for the analysis of the visual resource and the number of "go back clicks" to the visual resource.)

Before and after the work on the learning task as well as one week later the learners had to fill in a standardised questionnaire. The first questionnaire focused on the computer use, the second one demanded first evaluations of the learning task whereas the third one concentrated on the acquired knowledge and its relevance for the learners.

Some first results of the research:

Cognitive strategies of problem solving

The encouragement of historical competencies

Difficulties in historical learning

Cognitive Strategies of Problem Solving

Two basic models of problem solving strategies

The four learning groups followed two basic models of problem solving strategies which were unequally successful:

Model 1: „Now, our theory is the following ...“ Or: to systematise and to transfer!

The learners observed the visual resource thoroughly and started to **systematise** the image format immediately (they said: "That's the devil's side and that is the, sort of, good side"). They tried to consolidate their newly gained basic systematics (they came up with: "The angel there separates good from bad.") and tried to advance it (they said: "Heaven is above"). Thereby, they correct wrong classifications (<u>slaves</u> bend down) on the basis of further information (<u>humans</u> bend down). They transferred these systematics of the image format to the diagram; as soon as anything is unclear they argue for the systematics they worked out already (e.g. they said: "I mean in terms of the order of different levels. Thus, heaven is above...") and insist on realising it (learner 1: "Come on, we just said the goodies are left side, the badies right side!" Learner 2: "Oh yes, you're right!"). The learner's solution was predicated on the basis of the same systematics of image and diagram. Plus, they articulated it like this ("Now, our theory is the following..."). Thereby, they were very successful by being able to label the columns immediately and could relate the symbols and connections – via the correct lanes - to its corresponding places.

Model 2: *"We just read through it and check out what we are supposed to do next!"* Or: To adjust oneself to individual information. That actually means to surrender from the very beginning.

The second group is completely different: These learners observe the visual resource thoroughly, too. They recognised lots of details but weren't able to transfer them to the systematics of the image format. The components of the image stay unconnected side by side. The work on the diagram makes the learners insecure because of a lack of "theory" (there's no system noticeable): the columns get all sorts of labelling and everything seems to be possible and thus, gets tested. Even after 25 minutes these learners stated ideas like: "That's definitely were the heaven has to be…" They needed a lot more time to solve the problems and mainly got to the correct answer via the process of elimination. Consequently, the connection to the visual resource as a reference to the correct answer gradually got lost. While the learners of model 1 always focused on the visual resource and its systematics to have a basis for every single argument – although unconsciously –, the learners of model 2 gradually lost the coherence and thus, the right track. These learners gravitated only into the diagram's task and tried to solve the learning task immanently. Finally, this led to trial and error and they weren't able to solve the task in time. Those who nevertheless completed the task had lots of mistakes.

The comparison of both models illustrates that it seems to be inevitably necessary to offer the learners systematic support or at least the hint that systematisation is the key to successful work.

Cooperation strategies

The cooperation of the partners was of great importance for the successful work on the learning task. This was basically done by verbal as well as by non-verbal communication. In doing so, it is to highlight that all groups operated as teams. That means, the main focus was always on the answer and not on rivalry (e.g. "That's what I said already!"). Nonetheless, there were cooperation strategies that were very fruitful whereas others, unfortunately, did not aid one another.

Successful cooperation strategies were:

Supportive strategies

The learners made sure whether their partner was already as fast in reading and in reading comprehension as they had read and comprehended the text themselves. Partly, they read the text out aloud to each other. They searched for interactive areas collectively and supported each other even when the corresponding partner had the mouse ("Look, do you see these two bits? Click on them, they are both highlighted!"). These successful groups of two did not cut their own path and did not left their partner alone. It worked because they always asked for the okay to do the next step.

The communicating of solutions

Those learners who helped each other via nearly perfect communication were eminently successful ("I just want to show you how I would suggest to do it!"). Plus, they had the hardheadedness to achieve their common purpose.

They did not cancel the solution but managed to happily resolve it. Every time the initial idea was wrong they surprisingly profited from this solution and eliminated the wrong bits and pieces during their following work consequently.

Balancing between partners

In successful working groups one partner balanced his colleague's part as soon as he or she wasn't as concentrated as before. The lack of concentration was signalled in a mimic way (by stifling a yawn, rubbing one's eyes) as well as in a verbal way ("Sorry, I lost the track!"). The still concentrated learner kept working and tried to encourage his partner to come back.

Less successful strategies were:

Interruption of the partners thread

It happened a lot that one learner was thinking about an alternative to transfer his idea interactively while his partner suddenly interrupted him verbally with a completely different command ("Stop! Go back once more please!"). Thus, the train of thoughts couldn't be completed. Especially such a complex learning task demands feedback in between, otherwise it is very hard for the learners to realise what they have in mind.

To discourage the partner hastily

In some cases one learner could easily be discouraged by his partner encouraging him to stop his current activity immediately ("Leave it! It seems as if there is a reason for it!"). This happened with special emphasis as soon as the software was founded guilty. Anyhow, the software should be programmed correctly. The learner shifts the responsibility on to the software whereas the operating partner is unable to contradict.

Furthermore, some learners always suggested restarting the software immediately as soon as any little problem occurred. This discouraged the correspondent partner a lot, too. The partner becomes desperate as the already existing work is challenged permanently.

Transfers from history lessons

While the learners were solving problems they applied to three successful strategies that were obviously taught during the previous school year. Thereby, it wasn't about general or professional knowledge but about learning strategies.

On the one hand, all learning groups observed the visual resource very thoroughly before they started collecting additional information. They speculated a lot about what they had observed, discussed several details and tried to establish relationships. Not until quite a long time they started getting interested in additional information. The learners are used to this kind of approach since they learned it in the history lesson.

Secondly, the learners were already familiarised with the fact that a visual resource's structure can become transparent by decoding its symbols. The following statements illustrate that the learners have already experienced a lot about symbolism of images: learner 1: "Maybe they are kings!", after that learner 2: "But they haven't any crowns!", hereon learner 1: "But he has a nimbus?!".

Thirdly, the learners all knew from previous history classes how to label a diagram properly since all learning groups stuck to the same order: labelling of the columns, fitting the columns with components and creating connections between the columns.

I liked it a lot to see that learners do learn something in the history lesson which helps them to solve problems personally and individually.

Difficulties

Strangeness by difference (That's what we call "Alterität")

What was difficult for the learners?

The imagination of the Court at Judgement Day was difficult to comprehend for the pupils. For them the angels appeared to be in hell. However, on earth angels separate the good from the bad and half bad people and send them directly to heaven or to court. Even in Christian areas this perception is no longer up to date. Thus, this "Strangeness by Delay" is very difficult to explain. It means that some things are completely different today than they were in past time: In this case "strange" does not imply something exotic. This phenomenon has to be paid special attention to in today's historical learning processes. Actually, that's a platitude which nevertheless becomes fairly obvious in this case.

Language

The learners usually skip difficult items (such as "mandorla") assuming that it is of no further importance for solving the problem anyway. Reading as such seems to be very unpopular as the learners try to avoid as much reading as possible. However, most explanations concerning the image's components are normally not appropriate for the learner's age. Again, that leads to discouragement. Nevertheless, the learners usually accept these discouragements. They do not search for a glossary or try finding it out by asking me questions. This **avoidance strategy** becomes reinforced by the programming of the learning task: "If you have read all...." does not describe the task (6 relevant explanations regarding the components) in detail and admits to proceed without knowing exactly whether the learners checked the task properly or not. Obviously, the learners are used to these avoidance strategies since they probably do it the same way when working with textbooks.

The lack of reference to the learner's imaginativeness

The learners top the information of the learning task off in a different way. On the one hand, they use knowledge they experienced in class. On the other hand they come up with knowledge according to their leisure time experience: thus, the devil is compared to the monster in "Harry Potter" whereas the symbol of the Libra, which represents the court, is well-known from all kind of films. One learner recognised the gable field as: "that's what I've seen in holiday when I visited a church together with my parents at Lake Constance". He was probably right since these images are very widespread in Germany. Nonetheless, the learning task does not go back to the learner's imaginativeness at all. Thus, the learners are not encouraged when they start constructing imagination.

Feedback

The importance of feedback becomes obvious if one observes a learning group that works on a task for quite a long time in an unoriented way and finally gets corresponding but wrong answer. The feedback can also be immanent as long as it is transparent for the learners: the learners realised pretty soon that the diagram's lanes matched only one single place and couldn't be removed afterwards. Every time the learners restarted the software and thus, had to fill in the diagram again, they always began placing the lanes since they had got an immanent feedback regarding this little trick.

Learning effects

What sort of learning competencies was actually enhanced by the learning task?

After one week the learners were able to reproduce at least parts of the learning task and/ or could remember the results of the task even though on different language levels. While some learners drew the diagram (although partly incomplete) some others came up with little narrative anecdotes in order to produce new relations. There was only one learner who integrated what he had learned one week before: "People were very devout these days." This result illustrates that the religious content was at least partly understood and kept in mind. Nevertheless, there was only one learner being able to establish a relationship to current moral concepts. Only a few learners were able to acquire the facts in a narrative way whereas most learners counted on their visual memory.

The learners did very well in organising issue-related learning processes in teams in order to solve problems. In this case the learners were at least partially supported by the software.

The analysis of a visual resource as a method was preconditioned in the learning task and wasn't enhanced partially. It had to be introduced in the history lesson; otherwise the learners wouldn't have managed to complete the task successfully. The creation of the historical context is also planned and provided by the teacher. Unfortunately, this wouldn't have been necessary since the learners came up with their own approaches individually. One learner said: "They planned to make the people believe that every time they thought they had done something wrong they had to avoid going to hell. Therefore, they did everything the king said to them. Because they did not want to go to hell."

This learner has captured the function of the visual resource and is able to express it in his own words. Unfortunately, the software does not support this learning process. Thereby, the learners fall far short of what they normally do in the history lesson.

To draw a conclusion, even though a little one, I wish to have more didactic-methodological elaborated and sophisticated learning tasks. They are not supposed to stand out because of brilliant medial finesse, but because of the advancement of expert competencies in order to make learners being interested in learner-centred software.

中文節譯

學生如何從「學習者為本」的 歷史學習軟體中得益？

Bettina Alavi　著

徐兆安[*]　節譯

　　在德國以至英語國家中，相對於外語學習的軟體的可觀發展，歷史學習軟體無疑較為落後。亦由是故，至今尚未有有關歷史學習軟體中學習策略及方法的實證研究。本文將針對歷史學習軟體中的「學習任務」與學生的反應作分析。所謂「學習任務」，是教師設計予學生的架構，讓他們在其中進行以問題為中心的溝通或認知活動。一個「學習任務」的主要目的在於達至結論的溝通過程。要找到有這種「學習任務」的軟體，實在十分困難，最後，筆者以一套在 2005 年出版，附於某本有信譽的中學歷史教科書的軟體作為研究樣本。

　　這套軟體的內容有不少問題。本文集中考察的，是其中一個「學習任務」：要求學生將圖像資料（石畫）轉成圖或表。對圖像資料的分析，可視為方法能力的訓練；該「任務」要求學生勾勒出其宗教內容的結構，則是專門知識能力的訓練。可惜的是，它以中世紀基督徒的宗教觀為主題，但卻並沒有提供其歷史的背景與脈絡，不能啟發更複雜的歷史思考。這轉載資料的「任務」雖要求閱讀及摘要的能力，但它最後並沒有交代其內容的脈絡：既沒有涉及石畫描繪死後世界的作用，也無討論這種死後觀如何

---

[*] 清華大學歷史研究所碩士班

影響人們的日常生活，及教會在其中的位置。因此，學生不能藉此思考其中的意義，及其歷史脈絡，只能片面地驚嘆中世紀基督徒的宗教思想。結果，宗教內容並沒有被置於歷史脈絡當中。

此外，軟體的設計上也為教學造成若干問題。軟體只有在學生完成整個任務後，才會給予標準答案。在進行學習任務的途中，軟體並不會提出反應。這鼓勵他們精準地答題，但同時也使他們不能有組織而結構分明地解決問題。又如，圖像資料與圖表並不同時顯示在屏幕上，若學生需要更多資料，便要來回於圖像與圖表之間，最後更要重新啟動圖表來輸入新找到的資料。這本應使學生不耐煩，但令人驚喜的是，學生卻能在學習的過程中，摸索出避免這些技術問題的方法。此外，因為圖像的主體與圖表的架構不同，學生在看過幾個部分的畫像後，還不能把它跟圖表對起來。在原本的石畫中，人間是在最底部，而地獄則不在圖中，但在圖表中，人間與地獄卻被並列。只有察覺到石畫有兩面（右面是惡，左面是善）的學生，才能對照石畫與圖表的各部分。至於軟體的文字內容，則有影片的旁述及「任務」的解說等，但學生常常跟不上這些文字內容，因為文字資料實在太多了，這也是大多數學習軟體的通病。

既然這個軟體有如此多的限制，為何仍選擇它呢？首先，由於此「任務」的性質是轉載的，所以可清楚觀察學生解決問題的策略，以及所需的歷史能力。其次，此「任務」有較好的結構（雖然是線性的），已提供學生各主要步驟，所以他們可以在一段較長的時間內，各自獨立工作。這種「學習者為本」的學習大都讓學生自主自控，便於集中觀察他們的思考。再者，此「任務」是與學生們所上的歷史課是相對應的，由此，我們一方面可以觀察到歷史課如何影響他們應用這套軟體，另一方面，也可知道他們在老師不在時，是如何進行學習的。

本研究將運用「口述思考進程」(Verbal Report on Thinking) 的方法，以八位十二歲，第一年修讀歷史課並從未用過電腦來上該堂課的中學生

（按：約等於台灣的國中一年級）為研究對象。這種方法要求研究對象盡量把他們手上所做的、計畫要做的及心中的印象與感覺都說出來。我們不難理解，「口述思考進程」的可靠度頗具爭議性，但若將它應用在研究學生如何回應結構完整的「學習任務」上，則應是無大問題的。

研究的初步結果有三方面，首先是解決問題的認知策略方面。結果顯示能立刻想到要把「任務」內容系統化，並提出自己的一套理論的學生，比沒有理論思考的學生更成功地解決問題。成功地解決問題的學生，都有較好的合作策略：例如充分照顧同學的進度；交換對問題的不同意見，而非取消問題；互相補足對方的集中力等。較差的策略，則有打斷同學的思路，及轉移問題的焦點（如歸咎於軟體設計），降低同學解決問題的決心等。

其次，研究的結果也顯示歷史課訓練對學生的影響。學生全都先把軟體提供的圖像資料詳細地觀察完，然後再找尋額外的資料。他們從歷史課上已習慣了這種學習方式。此外，歷史課令他們習慣從符號中解讀出資訊，也授予應用圖表的技巧。這都令他們能獨立解決問題，實在令人欣慰。

最後是軟體所反應歷史學習的困難。其中特別值得注意的，是「時代的陌生感」：看來是同一事物，但過去與現在卻完全不同。這是很難向學生解釋的。此外，學生並不需要完全理解其中所有概念與名詞，就可完成軟體所設的任務，這種「逃避」完整理解的態度，在他們面對教科書時，也同樣是常見的。

學生在學習過程中展現出把課堂知識與日常知識聯繫的聯想力，卻由於軟體未能回應而沒有發揮的機會。軟體缺乏回應的設計，則往往使學生耗費長時間，最後卻得到錯誤的答案。總結軟體的學習成果，一星期以後，只有一個學生能把軟體上的資訊與其本身的認識綜合，而亦只有少部分學生才能以敘事的方式獲得軟體上的資訊，大部分學生則是靠圖像式的

記憶來把它們硬記住的。軟體也沒有顧及學生會如何以自己的語言表現他們所得到的資訊，亦由是故，學生們在運用軟體學習時的表現比他們在歷史課上來得差。總的來說，筆者希望未來能有在教學方法上更先進的「學習任務」。這並不能靠悅目的媒體來達成，而是要在歷史專業能力上有所進步，才能使學生對「學習者為本」的軟體更有興趣。

Hunting and Gathering the Past: Whose History and How Do We Teach It?

Stanley Hallman-Chong[*]

Canada, being a land of immigrants has a long heritage of multiculturalism even though this national reality was not always encouraged by official policy. In fact Canada has an equally long tradition of suppressing minority rights and expression. Indeed we have had about 200 pieces of legislation banning religious and cultural practices amongst our Aboriginal peoples and restricting the influx of people having Asian or African heritage. Furthermore, we have had about 250 years of slavery, and instances of mass incarceration of ethnic groups during periods of hysteria towards "foreigners in our midst". After WW II however, in light of world attention on the horrors of racism, Canada steadily repealed its discriminatory policies one after another. Today, no government can hope to win an election without appealing to the "ethnic vote". As well, a new generation of teachers and scholars have gained an appetite for not only exotic cuisine, but also for ethnic and minority stories that lay tantalizing in our past. Yet in our efforts to develop an inclusive history curriculum, we recognize that it is impossible to include every single story of every single community. It would likewise be unfeasible

[*] Toronto District School Board

to equalize the amount of content that is taught about each community as a way of ensuring equity.   If the amount of content is not the issue, by what principle then can we broaden our history curriculum to reflect our multicultural past? As we are settling the question of whose story should we tell, we have to also deal with the question, how should these stories be told?

Perhaps contrasting the depiction of minority groups with the representation of the majority Canadian groups i.e. the British and French, may provide a clearer picture of omissions and next steps in Canadian history. When one looks at our historical portrayal of British and French Canadians, we find a collection of stories that describe a continuity of communities.   The past actions within these communities are also recognized as integral to their own survival and to the origin of Canada itself. For example, in popular culture the battles of Vimy Ridge and Dieppe are told again and again as the moments that defined Canadian identity. Needless to say the actors in these dramas are White men.   Confirming this trend,   a recent survey of adolescent historical understanding, found that agency is exclusively attributed to men of European background. By contrast,   when other groups are mentioned in the student accounts, they are seen as reacting to events rather than acting from clear intentions. This may be explained by how Aboriginal and minority pasts are included in our history textbooks and curriculums.   They are   usually snippets of isolated episodes.   We find little continuity between these episodes and our present society.

What is the effect of neglecting to portray the continuity and historical agency of minority groups in our national narrative?   First let us look at popular treatments of our Aboriginal past in school textbooks.   Canadian students no longer begin their study of history as we once did by first surveying the exploits of European explorers. Instead, we teach children that Aboriginal peoples inhabited the land thousands of years prior to the arrival of Europeans. Here, students learn about cultural universals including beliefs, lifestyle, dress, food, types of shelter, and work. Social organization is also taught, such as hierarchical structures, gender roles, and the process of community decision making. Essentially, this is Social Studies and not History. Compare this to what students learn when studying early European Communities such as the Viking.

Working with 11 and 12 year olds on this topic and asking them to compare what they learned about Aboriginal peoples and Europeans, the following observations were made. "We learn about names [of the Viking people] and dates about what the Vikings did. We also learned that they traveled around to discover things." On the other hand, students admitted that they learned nothing like this when they studied Aboriginal peoples. When asked why they thought they had not learned similar information, students responded saying, "because the Aboriginal people didn't do anything... They just moved around when they needed food." When asked what they suppose happened to the Aboriginal communities that they had studied, students said, "they probably all died out."

Most of our historical accounts in Canada include details about Aboriginal people in the early chapters preceding the accounts of our confederation as a (nation) state. Then suddenly, there is little mention of them again except in scraps where they fought on behalf of Europeans and when they lost their territories through treaties. This gap in our teaching about the continuity of minority communities cannot be addressed by including snippets of information in side bars. Historians such Timothy Stanley have suggested that Canadian history should include the study of systemic racism in our common past. In fact, our recent forms of the national narrative inspired by our desire to expunge our ghosts do inform the public of various acts of official discrimination. However, these stories explore minorities, more often than not as passive victims of discrimination rather than in terms of their resistance against exclusion.

The importance of developing an understanding of historical agency is many fold. Research has found that too many stories depicting minorities as victims, actually creates negative stereotypes in students. The result is that students come to resent the very people for whom they were meant to feel sympathy. (Samuda, 1986) Secondly, research also indicates that when students have not developed a concept of historical agency, they withdraw from social responsibilities and express the idea that the world is out of control. (Seixas, 1994) Moreover, it has been pointed out that when students see a particular group as exclusively possessing agency, students who do not belong to that group develop a further sense of powerlessness and marginalization. (Stanley, 2002) Lastly, it seems that without understanding minority communities in terms of their agency, notions of continuity are also compromised. That is, not understanding how communities acted to preserve themselves, these communities are not understood as enduring over time.

Exploring the dynamism and plurality within minority communities continues to be a shortcoming in our history curriculums, despite its good intentions to be inclusive. In Ontario for example, we ask our students to find out why Aboriginal nations such as the Iroquois sided with the British in conflicts with the Americans. Looking at Iroquois society as a whole, there is in fact much evidence to suggest that the majority of the Iroquois nation was steadfastly against alliance with British/Canadian interests. (Benn, 1998) This example of assimilating minority past into the agenda of majority concerns ignores divergent interests that deeply influenced the course of events in minority communities.   The curriculum's failure to explore the dynamism of Iroquois society and its heated debates over community policies creates a concept of Aboriginal peoples as a stagnant monolith.   Aboriginal peoples have a rich past of intentional acts from plotting to forge independent confederacies to negotiating united fronts protesting government policies. These actions shaped the various communities throughout time and into the present.   Today, as Aboriginal peoples litigate for treaty rights, they do it from an understanding of their ancestors' negotiations with past governments. Mainstream Canadians on the other hand have little understanding of this past while identifying Aboriginal peoples through the cultural artifacts of hunting and gathering societies.   Many Canadians think that it is impractical to revisit treaty rights because they associate these rights with anachronistic communities.

Another example of ignoring continuity and agency can be seen in the limited portrayal of early Chinese Canadians as simple exploited labourers. The fact that the Chinese community was able to maintain an uninterrupted and continuous presence in British Columbia within a decade of European occupation goes unnoticed in most textbooks and courses.   The establishment of Chinese rural settlements, as well as prosperous Chinese owned mines, and a variety of urban businesses are also ignored.   Furthermore, our history programs fail to note how the Chinese resisted countless race riots and laws designed to extirpate their community. (Wickberg, E. 1982) This resistance included enlisting government officials from China to mediate between the Canadian government and the Chinese Canadian community.   Since these developments are not mentioned, the endurance of the Chinese community is not understood. The same can be said of other minority communities. Surveys of teachers inevitably identify early Black Canadians as linked to their escape from American slavery, but few are able to describe how any of the early Black settlements took specific actions to remain in Canada. The course of these actions would enlighten us on how different communities changed while affecting change in the larger community.

Generally, Canadians believe that multiculturalism is a product of government policies conceived in the 1960's rather than as an integral part of our origin. Most likely this is because our earlier difficulties in dealing with diversity is seen as a repudiation of multiculturalism, rather than as part of its development. Corroborating many studies on similar topics in the U.S., it is common for students to see present acceptance of diversity as arising from a "sudden realization that we should recognize the equality of all people."

The point of infusing minority history with concepts like agency and continuity is to go beyond purely the study of racism. Indeed our Canadian past is filled with incidents of discrimination, but it is also filled with other things. Identifying minority past with racism serves only to isolate that past from other aspects of our common past. We want to teach students that when they look at the past through certain concepts, they can find events that are significant to us today. Furthermore, this significance is not determined solely by group identity. Minority pasts then is not significant because many people are minorities. Instead, significance must be seen as something that is meaningful between groups. We can shout the political slogan that when one is victimized, we are all victimized. However, research suggests that such slogans have few positive effects on student understanding.

To quote Peter Seixas, we want students to "Demonstrate how an event, person or development is significant either by showing how it is embedded in a larger, meaningful narrative OR by showing how it sheds light on an enduring or emerging issue." I would suggest that one enduring issue, is understanding how to live with diversity. The past sheds light on this, not by simply showing us that bad things use to happen, nor to show us that if we do this, it would be like those bad things back then. Instead, we can use the past to construct an understanding of an emerging multicultural society. Through understanding how human intentions and conflicts change societies we get a better understanding of what we have become. Looking at past mistakes does not necessarily show us how to do things right, but plainly to see that actions do have consequences. We see that minor players and even those who were purposely suppressed in the past do impact the course of social development. Will this keep minority students engaged in schools and embroil them in the social fabric? Perhaps not, but if history is to include minority stories, they must bear some significance to where we are today. If not, we may as well repeat those famous words from Pumba in the Disney movie Lion King, "it doesn't matter, its in the past."

中文全譯

狩獵與採集過去：
誰的歷史以及我們怎麼教它？

Stanley Hallman-Chong　著

葉毅均　譯

　　加拿大作為移民樂土，早有多元文化主義 (multiculturalism) 的遺產，儘管官方政策並不總是樂見此一發展。事實上，加拿大有同樣悠久的、壓迫少數族群權利的歷史。我們曾有兩百個左右的法條禁止原住民的宗教及文化活動，乃至於限制亞洲和非洲移民的湧入。更有甚者，我們曾經有將近兩百五十年的奴隸制度存在，以及當所謂「外人在我們之中」(foreigners in our midst) 的歇斯底里時期，對於特定族群的大規模監禁案例發生。然而，在二次大戰之後，有鑑於種族主義所帶來的恐慌受到舉世矚目，加拿大開始逐步廢除其歧視政策。時至今日，沒有一個政府可以不顧族群票源而寄望勝選。同時，教師與學者中新的一代，也開始不僅僅滿足於異國料理，更冀圖了解過去深受壓抑的少數族群的故事。但是在我們發展一種包羅萬有的歷史課程的努力當中，我們發現不可能囊括所有群體的每一個故事。如果針對每個群體的授課內容在數量上加以平衡，以確保每個群體的平等地位，這也同樣是不切實際的。假若授課內容的量不是重點，那麼依照什麼原則，可以使我們擴展我們的歷史課程以反映我們多元文化的過去？當我們在討論應該講述誰的歷史時，我們也同樣應該探討該如何說這些故事。

　　或許對照一下對少數族群的描繪與佔加拿大多數的族群，亦即英裔和法裔的呈現，可以對加拿大歷史中的缺漏與為下一步該怎麼走，提供一個較為清晰的圖像。檢視對於英裔和法裔加拿大人的歷史描述，我們可以找到成堆的故事來說明其群體的延續性。這兩個族群的集體事蹟，無論對其自身生存來說，或對加拿大的由來而言都是不可或缺的。舉例來說，維米嶺 (Vimy Ridge) 與第厄普 (Dieppe) 等戰役在通俗文化中被一再地述說，並成為定義加拿大認同的關鍵。在這些戲劇化事件裡的主角不消說當然是白人。與此相應，最近一項針對青少年歷史認知的研究也發現，他們認為加拿大歷史上的能動性 (agency) 率皆由這些歐洲移民所掌握。相對地，當這些學生的敘述中提及其他族群的時候，往往將之視為針對事件而被動地做出反應，而非出自明確的主動意圖而行動。這點可以在原住民與少數族群的歷史如何被我們的歷史教科書和課程所納入來求得解釋，此二者通常被當作孤立的插曲片段，缺少與我們當前社會的延續性。

　　在我們的國族敘事中忽視少數族群的延續性與歷史能動性會有何後果？首先讓我們看一看學校教科書裡一般對原住民歷史的處理。加拿大學生學習歷史已不再像我們從前那樣，從歐洲探險家的事蹟開始講起。取而代之的是，我們教導孩子原住民幾千年來就已在此地居住，遠早於歐洲人的到來。學生們在此學習到的是，包括他們的信仰、服飾、食物、居所型態與工作等等的文化世界。此外，社會組織也包含在內，諸如階層結構、性別角色、以及群體決策的過程。從基本上來說，這是社會研究 (Social Studies) 而非歷史 (History)。試以此為基礎比較學生對於早期歐洲社群如維京人的學習內容。

　　請十一歲和十二歲的學童比較他們對於原住民和歐洲移民所學習內容的差異，得到的結果如下：「我們學到維京人所作所為的相關人名與日期。我們也知曉他們四處遊歷以發現事物。」另一方面，學生們坦承他們並未在學習原住民的時候得到類似的知識。當被問及何以如此之時，學生

們回應說：「因為原住民什麼事都沒幹……他們僅僅會為了食物而遷徙。」問他們認為原住民群體最後怎麼了，學生們回答：「他們大概全都絕種了。」

　　加拿大大部分的歷史敘述在談到我們成為一個國家的聯邦體制之前，都包含了細數原住民的章節。但在此之後，除非當原住民為了歐洲人而出征，或者因為簽約而喪失土地，才會被零星提及，否則近乎湮沒而不彰。這個少數族群歷史延續性的空白，並不能在我們的教學上透過補充片段的資訊來獲得解決。歷史學家如 Timothy Stanley 已經建議，加拿大的歷史應該納入對於我們過去裡的系統性種族主義的研究。事實上，我們最近的國族敘事形式，已經受到我們致力驅鬼的渴望所激勵，也確實使得大眾開始了解官方各式各樣的歧視。然而，這些探討少數族群的故事，常常將少數族群當作是不公平待遇的消極受害者，而非著重於少數族群對抗排外時所做的努力。

　　開發對歷史能動性之理解的重要性是多方面的。研究顯示，太多將少數族群描繪成受害者的故事，實際上在學生們的心目中創造了負面形象。結果是學生們開始憎恨他們原本應該加以同情的對象 (Samuda, 1986)。其次，亦有研究顯示，當學生缺少歷史能動性的概念，他們就會喪失社會責任的觀念，並得出一種世界已然失控的想法 (Seixas, 1994)。更有甚者，學者指出，當學生們將特定群體看成獨掌能動性的團體，那些不屬於此一群體的學生就容易產生更深一層的無力感與被邊緣化的感覺 (Stanley, 2002)。最後，如果不能理解少數族群的能動性，其延續性也同樣會遭受損害。也就是說，不了解群體如何主動作為以求自保，也就不能了解這些群體何以歷久而不墜。

　　探索少數族群內部的動力與多元性有所不足，仍舊是我們歷史課程中的一項缺失，儘管其用意是為了無所不包而加以論及。舉例而言，在安大略省 (Ontario)，我們要求學生找出為何原住民部落如易洛魁人 (Iroquois)

會在英美衝突中協助英方。事實上，就易洛魁社群整體而論，有許多證據顯示大多數的易洛魁人始終堅持反對與英國／加拿大的利益結盟 (Benn, 1998)。這種同化少數族群的過去，以求將之收編納入多數族群的關懷的做法，忽視了深刻影響少數族群的歷史事件發展過程中，少數族群本身的不同利益所在。歷史課程欠缺探討易洛魁社群的動力及其內部有關路線之爭的熱烈辯論，使得原住民部落看似冥頑不靈的龐然大物。原住民的過去其實充斥著有意識的行動，從籌畫各自獨立的聯盟，到協商成立聯合陣線以對抗政府政策。這些行動在過去形塑了各個不同的群體，直至今日也還是如此。正如今日的原住民部落在爭取他們法律上的權利時，是從其先祖過去與歷屆政府洽談的經驗出發的。然而，多數加拿大人並不了解這些歷史，僅僅透過狩獵和採集社會的文化製成品來認識原住民部落。許多加拿大人認為重新審視原住民的法律權利是不切實際的，因為他們聯想到的原住民部落都是早已不合時宜的。

忽視延續性與能動性的另一個例子，可以在少數將早期華裔加拿大人簡單描繪為被剝削的勞工中看到。卑詩省 (British Columbia) 的華人社群有能力在歐洲裔佔領的那十年裡維繫自身的生存，此一事實在大多數的教科書與課程中從未得到注意。華人鄉村開墾地的建立，以及繁榮的華人自有採礦地，和各種城市商販也同樣被忽略了。況且，我們的歷史教育從未提及華人如何抵抗無數次的種族暴動，以及專門設計用來根除華人社群的法律 (Wickberg, E. 1982)。這些華人的抗拒包括尋求中國官員的幫助，以調解加拿大政府和加拿大華人社群兩方。由於這些發展未曾得到引述，華人社群的韌性也就不被了解。同樣的情況也適用於其他少數族群。教師們大多無可避免地將早期加拿大黑人的來歷歸諸自美國奴隸制中脫逃，但幾乎沒有人能說明，這些早期黑人聚居地如何採取了特定作為以居留加拿大。這些作為可以啟發我們，不同群體中的改變如何可以影響及於更大群體的變化。

　　一般來說，加拿大人相信多元文化主義是政府在 1960 年代構想出來的政策產物，而非我們自身起源的真實成分。這極有可能是由於我們在早期處理多樣歧異性 (diversity) 所帶來的諸多困難，被視為對於多元文化主義的一種拒斥，而不知這正是多元文化主義發展過程中的一部分。這呼應了許多美國對於類似課題的相關研究，學生們通常會將現下對於多樣性的坦然接受，視為來自於「突然頓悟我們應該承認所有人的平等。」

　　在少數族群歷史中注入能動性和延續性的概念，重點是為了超越純粹對於種族主義的研究。我們加拿大的歷史的確充滿了歧視事件，但也還有其他事物。將少數族群的過往等同於種族主義，只會使之疏離出我們共同的過去。我們希望教導學生的是，當他們透過某些概念來認識過去，能夠發現對今天的我們來說仍有意義的事件。更進一步而言，這個意義不是單靠群體認同而生的。各個少數族群的過去之所以有意義，不是因為許多人本身就是少數族群。相反地，意義必須來自於跨越族群的定義。我們固然可以高喊政治口號，說道每當有一個人受害，我們就全部成為受害者。然而研究顯示，這樣的口號對於學生的理解來說，並沒有太多正面的效應。

　　用 Peter Seixas 的話來說，我們希望學生們「說明一個事件、人物或一項發展何以有意義，要麼是展現它嵌入一個更大的、意味深長的敘事，要麼就是展示它如何闡明一個持續已久或即將浮現的議題。」我所建議的是，其中一個持久的議題是了解如何與多樣性共存。歷史在此所闡明的，不是簡單地告訴我們壞事曾經發生過，也不是說如果我們也這麼做，將再度重蹈覆轍。相反地，我們可以利用過去來建立一種對形成中的多元文化社會的理解。透過了解人類的意圖與衝突如何改變社會，我們將對我們自身何以至於今日有更好的理解。鑑往事之非不必然能使我們知道如何可以做得更好，但卻能直接使我們知道任何作為確實會帶來某些後果。我們看到那些弱勢者，乃至於在過去受到存心迫害的人，的確影響了社會發展的進程。這是否將促使少數族群的學生就此專心致志於學校生活，並使他們

從而融入社會結構？或許不然，但如果歷史要納入少數族群的故事，這些故事就必須為今天的我們帶來某些意義。否則的話，我們或許就會重複迪士尼電影《獅子王》中龐巴 (Pumba) 的名言：「這不重要，這已經是過去的事了。」

學生應該學習怎樣的中國歷史

張 元*

一、前言：不一樣的中國歷史

這學期我學了很多，以前極討厭歷史的我，現在甚至感興趣起來，也稍微感受到中國文學中，文字中的張力美在那裡。上課聽了許多故事，從來不曾想打瞌睡；但又不僅是聽故事，還學了怎樣去培養感受歷史人物的方法，怎麼在字裡行間讀出作者的意味。讀到許多道德、人品、學識上古人遙不可及的成就，有時心裡也暗自勉勵自己。我的感覺是這不僅僅是堂歷史課，還是學思考、學人生哲學的課。[1]

　　這是一位學生在期末考卷上寫的一段話，這位學生選修了筆者在2004 年所擔任，屬於通識教育歷史領域的一門課：「中國典籍中的歷史世界」。筆者看到考卷上這一段文字時，首先想到這位學生這學期所學的「歷史」與以前她所學的，很不一樣，差別很大；同屬「歷史」的課程，有著很大的不同，此一現象，值得探討。許多學生也提及這門歷史課與他們過去所上的歷史課很不一樣，差別很大；過去的歷史課只不過是在記一些年代、人名、地名等等，不知道為什麼要學這些，只是記、只是背，覺

---

* 清華大學歷史研究所
1 張元，〈歷史課堂教學的新程式──故事、閱讀與書寫〉，《臺大歷史學報》第 37 期，2006 年 6 月，頁 346。

得十分痛苦，回想起來，都是不愉快的學習經驗。他們可能什麼都沒學到，也可能留下了一些十分模糊，卻相當負面的印象；這不是獨特的個人經驗，而是很普遍的情形。例如：一位知名的經濟學者，說到中國歷史，心中的印象是：「從古到今，史書斑斑記載的那些聖君明王的豐功偉業，要人民以君為天，寄一切希望於聖明君主的那一套思想；其實都是統治者為了鞏固其權位，甚至萬世一系的家族事業而編造出來的迷幻藥。」[2]這是《歷史月刊》上一篇文章中的一小段文字。這段文字表示他對中國歷史的知識，就是如此簡單，如此負面。而這些知識，就是他在中學與大學的歷史課程中所得到的，留在他心中的，主要的也就是這些而已。

這樣學習歷史的學生為數很多，因為大多數的學生是在同一個教學程式中學習這門科目。同樣的教科書，或者同樣形式的教科書，儼然占據教學過程中的主要地位，教師與其說是在教「歷史」，不如說是在教「歷史教科書」；教學的目標也很清楚，就是要學生在重要的考試中，如各級的升學考試，取得高分，順利進入理想的學校。在這樣的大環境下，教師為考試而教，學生為考試而學，其方法只有一項，就是死記硬背教科書中的文字，因此，在學生的心目中，歷史只是一門「背誦的科目」，簡稱「背科」。當然，我們也可以看到許多優秀的歷史老師，一直努力把歷史教得既讓學生喜愛，又讓學生感到真有收穫，只是這樣的老師有多少呢？為數似乎不多。優秀老師的精彩教學，其他老師知道嗎？似乎知道的也不多。在這樣的以升學為導向的教學環境中，舉目所見，無非升學參考書，考試測驗卷等，便於學生死記硬背的工具；相對而言，提供教師正常教學的各種教學理論，以及課堂教學中實用的資料、教案，也就十分有限。所以，一位歷史老師要成為深受學生喜愛與懷念的老師，需要克服的困難很多，需要抵抗的壓力也很大。我們看到，一些優秀的歷史老師在艱困的環境中

---

2 馬凱，〈為什麼愈大的官愈不顧人民死活〉，《歷史月刊》第 223 期，2006 年 8 月，頁 74。

堅持理想，努力不懈，可以說是臺灣教育界最寶貴的資產。

　　中國大陸的情形，筆者所知有限，就一點親身的經驗看來，情況甚為類似。三年前的一個晚上，八點多鐘，我們幾個人走進了著名的江蘇省揚州中學，見到教室大樓燈火通明，但卻鴉雀無聲，趨前一看，每一個學生的桌上擺滿了各科的教科書，這幅景象，對我而言，只能用「觸目驚心」來形容。大概也在同一年，東吳大學舉辦一場關於文獻學的研討會，來了幾位大陸這方面的專家。其中有一場的研討主題是歷史教學，主持人請大陸的學者談談對歷史教學的看法，其中有一位學者說，我們對進到系裡的學生所做的第一件事，就是要他們把中學所學的歷史都忘掉，不然很不好教。許多人聽了，都覺得十分新奇，甚至感到不可思議。最近讀到大陸歷史教學的著名學者寫的一篇文章，也提到了相似的看法。這位學者寫道：「前些年，就有些教師反應，剛進大學的高分學生『左』得可愛，要幫他『洗腦子』。還有學生大罵中學歷史教育是騙人的。這樣的情況現在是少了呢？還是更多？這些學生是幸運的，他們進了大學，還有機會『洗腦子』，那麼大量的沒有進大學的學生又如何了呢？只要我們負責任的『靈魂工程師』，就應當把它當一件非常嚴重的事情，看一看，想一想。」[3]

　　大家都知道，中國大陸的歷史教育長期以來受到馬克思唯物史觀的影響，所以有「左得可愛」之說。今天，隨著馬克思思想唯物史觀的退潮，歷史教育的指導思想也有了一些明顯的變化。今年（2006 年）9 月 3 日，臺灣的《中國時報》上有一篇有關上海歷史科新教材的報導，其中有一段是這樣寫的：「新版歷史教材的一位作者指出，新教材借鑑法國歷史家布勞岱爾的觀念：應當用一種包容文化、宗教、習俗、經濟和思想的『總體性歷史』的新方法來解析歷史，新教材目的是強調領導人和戰爭的傳統中解救歷史教學，讓人民和社會成為新的重點課題。」我讀了這段報導，感

---

[3] 轟幼犁，〈獒奶、狼奶、狗奶和人奶〉，《中學歷史教學參考》2006 年 1-2 期，頁 7。

到馬克思唯物史觀退位了，布勞岱的年鑑學派史觀取而代之；蘇聯的影響退去了，歐美的影響立即補了進來。我想要問的只是：中國的歷史教育一定要有一個西方的理論來作為指導思想嗎？

臺灣的情形如何？臺灣繼承民國初年以降的歷史教育，難道就未曾受到西方思想的影響嗎？值得我們好好地反思一下。

二、強調講述歷史事實，有其背景

中華民族是一個重視歷史的民族，各個時代都有傑出的歷史家以及精彩的歷史著作，這些豐厚的史學著述一直是中國傳統文化的特色所在。但這一史學傳統到了近代無可避免地受到西方史學的挑戰，也無可避免地發生了明顯的轉變，出現了所謂的「現代史學」。現代史學怎樣從傳統史學中演繹、變化、發展出來，至今仍與傳統史學之間有著怎樣的關係，這是近代學術思想史中，「傳統」學術「現代化」的一個部分，也是至今仍然需要學者仔細研究的一項課題，不是我的這篇小文所能討論，也不是我的能力所能處理。我們不妨略述學界的一般觀點，作為討論的背景。

如果我們說，中國大陸以外，臺灣的中國史研究是繼承著民國以來，「科學史學」為主的這股潮流繼續前進，大概不會遭到太多的反對。「科學史學」指何而言？最早可以追溯到「新史學」的呼喚者梁啟超，在這場史學革命中，梁啟超無疑是首揭批判傳統史學大纛的旗手，而他就是以「歷史科學」或「科學的歷史」為主要觀念，致使「新史學」的主流始終環繞著「科學化」的觀念。接著有重大影響者，應推胡適，胡適一再強調「實驗主義」，同時提倡「科學方法」。他的一些話，直到今天，人們仍能琅琅上口。如：「有幾分證據，才說幾分話。」以及「科學精神在於尋求事實，尋求真理；科學態度在於撇開成見，擱起感情，只認得事實，不跟著感情走。」至於「大膽的假設，小心的求證。」這句名言，更是無人不

知。但對於臺灣史學影響來說,大概沒有人超過傅斯年。而傅斯年的史學理念明白見於所撰〈歷史語言研究所工作之旨趣〉一文,在這篇重要的文獻中,傅斯年明白表示,「史料中可以得到最大量的客觀知識,堅實的事實只能得之於最下層的史料之中。」以及「只要把材料整理好,則事實自然明顯。」而「史學本是史料學」、「上窮碧落下黃泉,動手動腳找材料」同樣也是傅氏的名言。傅斯年儘管未再強調「科學」二字,但其精神仍然是偏重於這一方面的。[4]

二十世紀五十年代,臺灣在經濟上接受美國援助的挹注,思想文化上向美國學習也成了時代的潮流與趨勢,史學自不例外。於是,向社會科學學習,成了研究歷史的重要取向;社會科學提供了理論與方法,傳統典籍只不過是供人驅使的一堆材料而已。這樣的觀念,似乎仍然瀰漫在臺灣的歷史學界,只不過「社會科學」的具體內容有了一點改變而已。[5]

歷史研究的觀念與態度,必然對歷史教學產生重大影響,然而,這種觀念與態度不可能直接反映在歷史課堂教學上,而是經過一個「簡化」的過程。例如,昔日強調的科學與方法,不可能用於課堂教學,於是科學與方法的結論就成了它的化身,老師教、學生學這些結論,就好像學到了科學與方法。昔日重視的史料與證據,同樣不可能用於課堂教學,於是藉由史料與證據得出來的事實就成了它的化身,老師教、學生學這些事實,就好像可以取代了史料與證據。所以,我們看到長期以來,歷史課堂所呈現的,就是對於「事實」的講述與記憶。在這樣的背景下,歷史老師自然認為,教好歷史就是講很多的「事實」,補充許多教科書上所沒有的「事實」;歷史老師犯的最大過失,就是把「事實」講「錯」了。其結果,歷

---

4 請參閱:許冠三,《新史學九十年 1900 –》(香港:中文大學出版社,1986)自序;第一章,梁啟超:存真史、現活態、為生人;第五章,胡適:注重事實服從證據;第七章,傅斯年:史學本是史料學。

5 請參閱:許冠三,〈三十五年(1950-1985)來的臺灣史界變遷〉,《新史學九十年 1900 –》(下冊,1988),頁 241-273。

史課就成了一門「背科」，一門學生學習之時不覺絲毫樂趣，學完之後回想起來十分厭煩的課程。

歷史研究的方法，無法完全用於課堂教學，這一點無人置疑。但歷史教學只是老師講述事實嗎？等而上之，把學者的研究成果傳達給學生，也都只教「現成的知識」，這樣就可以了嗎？學生學習「歷史」這門課程，連一點歷史知識的性質、結構和方法都不涉及，就能夠達到「強化學生思考與分析能力」的教學目標嗎？[6]教歷史要教歷史知識的性質、結構和方法，這個觀念並不複雜，何以長期以來未能落實於課堂教學？歷史學的研究態度與觀念，特別是對於「事實」的強調，是否造成一定的影響，致使歷史老師認為只講事實，就符合歷史學的研究，就等於教了歷史知識的性質、結構與方法？更進一步，強調歷史知識就是「事實」的知識，是否成了歷史老師探究歷史知識的性質、結構和方法時難以超越的障礙？是否如此，值得探討。

我們常聽到一種說法，學生學習必須循序漸進，小學、中學的歷史課只須講述「歷史事實」，學生只須記得重大的事件，傑出的人物，主要的制度和大概的學說；至於對歷史知識性質的了解，結構的掌握和方法的練習，那是大學歷史系，甚至是歷史研究所學生的學習對象。這種說法十分普遍，我不知道是否受到上述「科學」的歷史學，追求「事實」的影響，但它確實是老師講歷史不談知識結構、方法的重要理由。這個理由可以成立嗎？

筆者不認為中學階段不適宜講述歷史知識的結構與方法。西方學者研究得知，歷史知識的最基本工作，如利用原始材料，作為證據，討論問題，在小學階段即可實施，而且可以取得一定成果。[7]筆者自己雖然沒有

---

6 《高級中學課程標準》，教育部編印，1995 年發布，1996 年出版。

7 請參閱：Keith C. Barton and Linda S. Levstik, *Teaching History for the Common Good* (Lawrence Erlbaum Associate, Inc.2004), pp.185-205.

在中、小學擔任歷史課程的機會，但在大學的一些通識課程中，可以了解學生在前一階段的學習情況。筆者可以清楚感到，學生對於著重歷史知識結構與方法的教學，十分陌生，卻甚感興趣，同時也覺得很有收穫。2006年，筆者在清華大學開了一門講述近代史學大師錢穆的課：「錢穆與中國傳統史學」，原先當作人文社會學系歷史學程的進階課程，但全校各系、各年級學生都來選修，其性質已從一門「歷史系」的專業課程，轉變成為「歷史領域」的通識的課程。一位化工系一年級的學生，在期中考的試卷上寫道：「讀錢先生的作品，那種嚴謹的思辨過程，循序漸進，鋪陳事件的歷程有條不紊，思緒清晰，對於歷史資料的蒐集的精細，熟讀牢記，更進一步可揣想當時情境、對話、心態。在我的看法中（不知是否恰當），傳統史學就像一本理性中不失感性的厚書，既是邏輯嚴密，卻又自然而然於字裡行間透露著感情。中國數千年來，先人的智慧、思想，如同大浪侵襲而來（過去對於歷史的理解似乎停留在老師所說的『歷史資料』層面，總是在了解過去的教訓與事實，徒有什麼鑑往開來的空洞思想）。」[8]這段話中，我們可以看到，這位學生把一年級下學期所上的歷史課與過去的歷史課作了對比，過去的只是一些資料、一些事實，卻要從中得到什麼教訓，自然感到相當空洞。但這一門歷史課，所看到的是歷史家的工作，包括精細的蒐集資料、嚴謹的思辨過程、有條不紊的鋪陳事件、揣想當時情境心態，這樣的歷史，既有嚴密邏輯的理性，又有字裡行間的感情，於是，古人的智慧、思想就如同大浪襲來。筆者認為「如同大浪襲來」不失為一個很漂亮的形容，相信也是一種很真切的感受；學生上歷史課，老師能夠引導的極致，不也就是如此嗎？值得一提的是，與這位學生相同的看法，一樣的感受，佔了班上的大多數。所以，筆者在檢討這門課的教學時，第一個想到的，就是：「講述歷史知識的組成結構、研究方法，不但

8　張元，〈教歷史，要教歷史知識的結構與方法——談清華大學的一門歷史課〉，《歷史月刊》第 223 期，2006 年 8 月，頁 117。按：文中括號為該生所寫。

不會過於艱深枯燥，反而會引起學生的學習興趣。比起只教歷史上的表面現象，或只講述一些歷史學者的論點，也就是一些『現成』的知識，講結構與方法，更會受到學生的歡迎。我相信，不只是清華大學的學生喜歡，所有的大學生都喜歡；不只是大學生喜歡，中學生也會喜歡。」[9]

三、試擬傳統史學的理論結構

如果，我們要問，人類的歷史知識中，有沒有「放諸四海而皆準」的結構和方法？我們應該首先要問，所謂的「結構和方法」指何而言？如果只是在最基本的層次，就是談及「歷史知識」，必須想到：問題、資料、分析、論證，以及最後回答問題、加以表述等，如同 Mary Fulbrook 在 *Historical Theory* 一書中所說歷史的「典範」(paradigm) 中的第一層次 (A. theoretical, internal or implicit paradigms[10])，我想，這應該是古、今、中、外，無有不同的。舉例來說，宋代大學者朱熹 (1130-1200)，認為關於井田被廢的既有解釋，無論從資料的解讀、史事的理解、意義的闡釋等方面，都不能令人滿意；於是撰有〈開阡陌辨〉一文，對於井田之廢，詳加述論。我們可以清楚看到，舉凡今天史學家無不重視、強調的治史要項，諸如：提出有意義的問題、選取重要資料、進行嚴謹論證、結合歷史情景、運用歷史想像等，朱熹此文無不具備，而且十分細膩精審，至於說明事物情理以及闡述歷史意義，雖然不為今天歷史學者所贊同，卻也突顯了中國傳統史學的特色。[11]我們可以說，八百年前的中國學者，探討歷史問題，

---

9 同上，頁 119。

10 Mary Fulbrook, *Historical Theory* (London, Routedge,2002), pp.34,35. 宋家復先生指出，本文的解讀欠妥。筆者只是藉以說明中國傳統史學敘述亦有其結構而已。感謝宋先生指正。

11 請參閱：張元，〈朱子講歷史之六：廢井田與開阡陌〉，《歷史月刊》第 218 期，2006 年 3 月，頁 114-118。

其嚴謹、細密、深刻，較諸受到西方影響下的中國現代史學，可以說是毫不遜色，完全符合歷史知識結構和方法的基本要求。

基本上結構和方法上的相同，並不表示中國傳統史學的「結構」和「方法」和今天所見深受西方學術影響的現代史學完全一樣。如果，我們再問：中國傳統史學的結構與方法，有何特點？我們固然可以在一些專精傳統學術的近代學者的著作中，見到一些十分精闢的見解，[12]但總覺得欠缺較為完整、便於現代人們閱讀或認識的論述。闡述傳統史學的理論結構，這項工作原非筆者所能勝任，由於不把傳統史學的結構和方法大致描繪出來，作為歷史教學上選取資料、解讀文本，以及理解過去的依據，則此一議題難以為續，故而只有拋磚引玉，略作嘗試。錯誤不妥之處在所難免，惟有敬請方家多予指正。

傳統上，對過去的理解來自典籍。如何讀懂典籍呢？最初步的工作就是認識其中的字與詞，這是最初步的工作，也是真確地認識過去的第一步。於是，我們看到重要的歷史典籍都有相當詳盡的「注釋」，其中大部分就是對於字和詞的解釋。當然，史書的注釋，其形式多來自經書的注釋，但不要忘了，所謂「經書」，在大多數古人觀念裡也是一種「歷史典籍」。例如：在朱熹觀念裡，《易經》與《詩經》都是「歷史典籍」，都是我們認識過去的重要依據，《尚書》、《春秋》、《周禮》更是如此。所以，《史記》有三家注，《漢書》有顏師古注，《後漢書》有李賢注，《三國志》有裴松之注。這是大家所熟知的，其中《三國志》注較特殊，字、詞的解釋不多，而其他三史的注釋，字、詞的解說儼然成為主要部分。不過，我們應該注意到，史書的注釋不只是一個字或詞的解說，不是前人做過後人就不再做的工作；這是一種前後相繼的傳統，後人對前賢的解釋有

---

12 例如：柳詒徵，《國史要義》（臺北：中華書局，1971）；錢穆，《中國史學發微》（臺北：東大圖書公司，1989），《中國歷史研究法》（臺北：聯經公司，錢賓四先生全集版）等論著。

所不滿，就提出新解，新的解釋不但更有理據，而且更為深入。這裡可以舉一個例子略作說明。

漢武帝天漢二年，西元前 99 年，李陵孤軍進擊匈奴，匈奴單于調動八萬騎兵對付李陵，雙方激戰。《資治通鑑》卷 21，記有其中一個片段，曰：「陵軍步鬥樹木間，復殺數千人，因發連弩射單于，」胡三省的注釋，重點在「連弩」一詞，是這樣寫的：「服虔曰：三十弩共一弦也。張晏曰：三十絭共一臂也。貢父曰：皆無此理。蓋如今之合蟬，或併兩弩共一弦之類。余據《魏氏春秋》，諸葛亮損益連弩，以鐵為矢，矢長八寸，一弩十矢俱發。今之划車弩，梯弩亦損益連弩而為之，雖不能三十臂共一弦，亦十數臂共一弦。」[13]

我們看到，顏師古引用了服虔和張晏的注，[14]劉攽（貢父）不同意，提出新的解說；但胡三省也不同意劉攽的意見，再提出一個解說。劉攽是北宋時人，也是《資治通鑑》的主要作者之一，他本人專精史學，[15]與其兄劉敞、姪劉奉世，有漢史「三劉」之稱。劉攽不贊同前人解釋的理由是「無此理」，因為他想不通一弦如何可以射出三十支矢，他認為射出兩支是可以理解的。那麼，胡三省又怎麼看呢？胡三省從資料之中，以及實際事物中，找出證據，認為三十支矢共一弦確實不大可能，但十支矢共一弦，應有其可能。我們可以看到，史書上一個「詞」的解說，愈到後代愈為精細，而且理由更為充足，既是史學注釋上的明顯發展，也是歷史知識的思考更加細緻深入。

我們讀懂了資料中的文字和詞彙，就可以相信這些資料了嗎？也就是說，古代留下的資料，可以不加甄別地採信、利用嗎？我們可以看到，就

13　《資治通鑑》，（新校標點本）頁 714。

14　《漢書》卷 54，〈李陵傳〉，（新校標點本）頁 2454。師古曰：「張說是也。」

15　《宋史》卷 319，〈劉攽傳〉：「攽所著書百卷，尤邃史學。作《東漢刊誤》，為人所稱。預司馬光修《資治通鑑》，專職漢史。」新校標點本，頁 10388。

是號稱「聖人」的著作，其真實性如何，到了宋代也不免遭到質疑，皮錫瑞在其所著《經學歷史》一書中，稱宋代為「經學變古時代」，[16]特加說明。其實，對於資料的考信，最晚可以追溯到司馬遷所說：「夫學者載籍極博，猶考信於六藝。《詩》、《書》雖缺，然虞夏之文可知也。」[17]這裡特別提到宋代，主要鑑於宋代在史籍資料考信方面，取得很高的成就，出現了《通鑑考異》這樣一部精細辨別資料可信與否，如何解釋的專著，徐炳昶稱之為「全世界最早批評史料的一部大書」，指出其特點，說明其意義。[18]到了清代，乾嘉學者對於典籍校刊、版本整理、史事考證、名物訓詁等用力甚勤，成就可觀。王鳴盛說他的著作是：「考其事蹟之實，俾年經事緯，部居州次，記載之異同，見聞之離合，一一條析無疑。」[19]雖為王氏自述之言，庶幾可以反映學者的努力與其取得之成果。這是傳統史學另一著重之處。

若問：傳統中國史學家選取資料，加以組織、安排、表述的重點是什麼？我們可以說，那是以「人」為主的敘事方式，「人」的表現最受重視，相比之下，人所做的「事」，則是第二義了。我們可以從傳統史學著作的體裁中明確看到，主要的史書屬於「紀傳」與「編年」二體，但編年體的史書，其內容與重點基本上與紀傳體無異。也就是說，按時間序列編寫的史書，其中所陳述者，仍是一個個人物的所作所為、所言所行，與紀傳體無大差別。此外，就是像《通典》、《文獻通考》，屬於的「政書」類史書，其中許許多多的人們意見，仍是構成此類著作的重要成分，「人」依舊扮演重要角色。於是，我們在史書中讀到的，幾乎都是一個人的出

---

16 皮錫瑞，《經學歷史》（臺北：藝文印書館，1966），頁 202-255。

17 《史記》卷 61，〈伯夷列傳〉（北京：中華書局，1959），頁 2121。

18 徐炳昶，《中國古史的傳說時代》（桂林：廣西師範大學，2003）頁 25。徐炳昶接著說：「但此後進展得很慢，并沒有在歷史界中成為一個大運動。西歐直到 19 世紀中葉以後，批評史料的風氣才大為展開，而且進步很快，在歷史界中成為一種壓倒一瓦的形勢。」

19 王鳴盛，《十七史商榷·自序》（臺北：廣文書局，1971），頁 1。

身，幼年時的獨特表現，進入官場或社會後的所作所為，對時政或時代的批評和意見，以及，當時人們對他的評論與觀感等等。就像錢穆所說：「歷史記載人事，人不同，斯事不同。人為主，事為副，未有不得其人而能得於其事者。」[20]今天看來，這樣的史學觀點顯然偏頗，有欠全面，但這也說明了傳統中國史學的特色所在。也許，此一頗具特色的「觀點」，似可符合 Mary Fulbrook 所說的「典範」中的第二層次 (B. contextual or perspectival paradigms[21])。

由於傳統史書的記載以人為主，而其表述方式則以摘錄這位人物的資料，加以編排、組織而成，其目的無非是要將這位人物最直接、最具體的呈現出來。除了「曰」、「論」、「贊」、「議」、「評」和「按」等明確表示是著者意見看法，其他皆從資料中選錄、擷取、安排，鋪陳一篇完整的敘事。這種讓資料說話，撰者在敘事過程中，盡量以資料為主，只是扮演輔助的角色。這種表述方式，沿襲已久，直到今天，我們心目中的史學大師，如王國維、陳寅恪、陳垣和錢穆，其史學論著，無不保有此一形式與精神。[22]

最後，我們要問一個最重要的問題：學生為什麼要學歷史？培養學生理性地理解過去的能力，也就是歷史的思維能力，或許是今天我們最容易想到的答案。這樣的答案當然不錯，甚至很好，然而如果我們進一步問：學生有了歷史思維「能力」，又是為了什麼？如果只是增強學生對「過

---

20 錢穆，〈略論中國史學〉，《現代中國學術論衡》（臺北：東大圖書公司，1984），頁104。

21 Mary Fulbrook, *Historical Theory,* pp.34,37.

22 當代史學名著之中，不少仍是承襲傳統史學，採用選錄資料的方式撰成，例如：范文瀾，《中國通史簡編》（北京：人民出版社，1955）；郭廷以，《近代中國史綱》，（香港：中文大學，1980）。不過這樣的表述方式似乎日見式微，例如：陳永發的《共產革命七十年》（臺北：聯經出版社）；許倬雲，《萬古江河》（臺北：英文漢聲出版社，2006），皆已不採傳統的敘事方式，而是完全由著者敘述，屬於西方史學的敘事方式。

去」的「認知」，只是強調「知識」的「能力」，而不能用於實際的生活，不能有助於實際事務的處理，不能有益於人的一生，這種為求知而求知的知識態度，或許可以得到今天學者的稱讚，但與主張「經世致用」的傳統史學顯然大相逕庭。

關於歷史有其致用的目的，王夫之在《讀通鑑論》中，有一句話，講得很清楚。他說：「所貴乎史者，述往以為來者師也。為史者，記載徒繁，而經世之大略不著，後人欲得其得失之樞機以效法之無由也，則惡用史為？」[23]王夫之的意思是史的目的或功用，在於作為今人的典範或誡鑑；而能否有此功效，則端看史書是否具備「經世之大略」，也就是歷史中人們如何面對問題，如何處理事情的情況。如果史書中具備了這樣的內容，讀者得以掌握「得失之樞機」，也就是懂得了成敗的道理，這樣的歷史才是有其效用的。不然，寫得再多，也屬徒然。

我們作進一步的探討，可以知道，「得失之樞機」只是道理而不是技巧，有其深義在焉。朱熹對學生講歷史，十分強調從歷史中只能學到人世間的「道理」，學不到任何做事的「技巧」或「計謀」。從歷史中學習前人的謀略、技巧，依樣畫葫蘆，是做不成事的，是不對的。因為人世間的道理，是歷史知識中的「人文價值」，也是學習者應該認真理解的「基本觀念」。這些人世事務中的道理，甚至可以與自然界相呼應，應是我們立身行事的依據。[24]再舉王夫之的話，作為此一理念的例證。王夫之談到三國人物時，非常推崇管寧，他說：「漢末三國之天下，非劉、孫、曹氏之所能持，亦非荀悅、諸葛孔明之所能持，而（管）寧持之也。」理由呢？管寧在遼東講授詩書，提倡禮儀，就是為天下存道統，為君子續學統，不因動亂而文明無以為繼。王夫之說：「見之功業者，雖廣而短，存之人心風

23　王夫之，《讀通鑑論》（北京：中華書局，1975），頁 156。

24　請參閱：張元，〈朱子講歷史之五：歷史中的道理與技巧〉，《歷史月刊》第 215期，2005 年 12 月號，頁 95。

俗者，雖狹而長。一日行之、習之，而天地之心，昭垂於一日；一人聞之、信之，而人禽之辨，立達於一人。」[25]就是進一步探究人世的道理，把人的作為，與人的心意，以及自然萬物的理據（天地之心），綜而論之，得出的一個十分深刻的看法，以褒揚管寧。

現代學者如何談論此一觀念？深於傳統史學者，仍然堅持此一理念與目標，並依之撰述。例如，王國維轟動一時的大文章〈殷周制度論〉[26]，主要立論在於：「殷周間之大變革，自其表言之，不過一姓一家之興亡與都邑之移轉；自其裡言之，則舊制度廢而新制度興，舊文化廢而新文化興。又自其表言之，則古聖人之所以取天下，及所以守之者，若無以異於後世之帝王；而自其裡言之，則其制度文物與立制之本，乃出於萬世治安之大計，其心術與規模，迥非後世帝王所能夢想也。」又說：「周之所以綱紀天下，其旨則在納上下於道德，而合天子、諸侯、卿大夫、士、庶民，以成一道德之團體。周公制作之本意，實在於此。」[27]其立論之依據仍在聖人之心術，此今人久已不彈之舊調。柳詒徵在其闡明傳統史學大義的名著《國史要義》中，也多有論述。例如，他說：「吾國聖哲深於史學，故以立德為一切基本。必明於此，然後知吾國歷代史家所以重視心術端正之故。若社會上下道德蕩然，且無先哲垂訓，詔以特立獨行，絕不能產生心術端正之史家。」又說：「謂史之義出於天，讀者亦且茫昧而不解。是又可以董子之言解之。《春秋繁露・玉杯》篇曰：『人受命於天，有善善惡惡之性，可養而不可改，可豫而不可去，若形體之可肥癯而不可得革也。』是故史之為書，所以善善惡惡也。善善惡惡者，人之性受命於天者也。吾國之為史者，其淺深高下固亦不齊，而由經典相傳，以善善惡惡

---

25 王夫之，《讀通鑑論》，頁 247。

26 郭沫若說：「（〈殷周制度論〉）是一篇轟動了全學術界的大論文，新舊史家至今都一樣地奉為圭臬。」見〈古代研究的自我批判〉，《十批判書》第一節（重慶：群益出版社，1945）。

27 王國維，〈殷周制度論〉，《觀堂集林》（北京：中華書局，1959）卷十，頁 2。

之性從事於史，則一也。」全書最後，柳詒徵是這樣寫道：「近世承之宋明，宋明承之漢唐，漢唐承之周秦。其由簡而繁，由繁而簡，固少數聖哲所創垂，亦經多數人民所選擇。此史遷所以必極之於究天人之際也。《大學》曰：『物有本末，事有終始，知所先後則近道矣。』又曰：『其本亂而末治者，否矣。』吾之人本主義，即王氏所謂合全國為一道德之團體者。過去之化若斯，未來之望無既。通萬方之略，弘盡性之功。所願與吾明理之民族共勉之。」[28]在這三段話中，我們可以看到像是「吾國聖哲」、「先哲垂訓」、「心術端正」、「受命於天」、「道德之團體」等現代史學非但不談，甚且避之唯恐不及的詞彙與觀念，既可以說明傳統史學與今天我們史學觀念相去之遙遠，也可以作為傳統史學有其獨特個性的明證。至於柳氏最後所言，「通萬方之略，弘盡性之功」，終究不失為一極崇高之理想與極偉大之抱負，即使不能使人心嚮往之，也應足以讓人讚嘆不已。

　　人之本性秉於天，乃傳統史學最為基本之觀念，因之可以說學術大原出於天，學術發展之目的，無非促使人人發揮本性。此一理念之下，期勉人人的所作所為、一言一行，皆合於義理，使社會成為一道德之團體。而史學之目的也不外將人之所以為人的尊貴意義，加以呈現；人世間的理想社會，加以實現。這固然是一個十分「主觀」的觀點，我們今天非但不能接受，甚至不易理解，但是，這卻是回答了一個最根本的問題，也提出了一個最高遠的理想，展現了一個最獨特的理論。我們不辭傅會之嫌，是否也可以看作是 Mary Fulbrook 所說 paradigm 中的第三層次 (C. metatheoretical) 或 paradigm proper？[29]也許，傳統史學之理念與 Mary Fulbrook 的理論不能完全符合，但至少說明，傳統史學不是很簡單的事實敘述，隨意褒貶，而是有其結構，且是十分謹嚴的結構。

28　柳詒徵，《國史要義》，頁 88，137，239。
29　Mary Fulbrook, *Historical Theory*, pp.35,41.

四、傳統史學運用於歷史教育的例證

我們今天所說「傳統史學」的理念與觀點，在過去漫長的歲月裡，曾經發揮過「歷史教育」的功效嗎？當然是有的，而且為數可觀。這裡只舉出幾個著名的例子，略作分析。

蘇軾是宋代著名學者、文學家，也在政壇上有所表現，更是中國人家喻戶曉的歷史人物，他在幼年時的「歷史教育」，同樣也是中國讀書人幾乎無不知曉的著名故事。《宋史‧蘇軾傳》開頭寫道：「蘇軾字子瞻，眉州眉山人。生十年，父洵游學四方，母程氏親授以書，聞古今成敗，輒能語其要。程氏讀東漢〈范滂傳〉，慨然太息，軾請曰：『軾若為滂，母許之否乎？』程氏曰：『汝能為滂，吾不能為滂母邪？』」[30]這段記載的重點有二，一是「聞古今成敗，能語其要」，意思是學習的對象是事情的發展演變，以及其中的道理，而不只是事情的經過；二是事情之中，人物為天下蒼生，為正義公理，最後犧牲生命的志節表現，最為感人，講述者只要真情流露，聽講者年紀雖小，亦能觸動。

謝道韞可以說是中國歷史上最為聰慧的女子，《世說新語‧賢媛篇》與《晉書‧列女傳》中關於她的記載，讀來讓人懷想讚嘆不已。《晉書‧列女傳》開頭幾句是：「王凝之妻謝氏，字道韞，安西將軍奕之女也。聰識有才辯。叔父安嘗問：『《毛詩》何句最佳？』道韞稱：『吉甫作誦，穆如清風；尹吉甫詠懷，以慰其心。』安謂有雅人深致。」謝道韞唸的這四句，出於《詩經‧大雅》的〈烝民〉，是周宣王時尹吉甫歌誦大臣仲山甫所作的詩。仲山甫是一位「不侮鰥寡，不畏強禦」，深得人們尊敬喜愛的大臣。謝道韞唸出了這四句，明顯期望負有重責大任的叔父，要做到像尹

30　《宋史》卷 338，（新校標點本）頁 10801。

吉甫詩中的仲山甫。謝安是一位何等敏銳的人物，立即聽出了姪女的心意，所以說了一句漂亮的話「雅人深致」讚美她。問題是，謝道韞何以立即想到這四句？一定是仲山甫的形像，尹吉甫的稱頌，長久在其心中，是她十分重視的歷史知識。這樣的歷史知識，既強調經世致用的功能，也是依據人們的心意與感情，來認識、評論古代的人與事。

　　諸葛亮可以說是中國人最喜歡的歷史人物，文學、戲劇中的諸葛孔明固然深受百姓大眾所喜歡，就是史書記載的諸葛武侯，也同樣得到讀書人的敬重與感佩。《三國志・諸葛亮傳》記他的出場曰：「亮躬耕隴畝，好為〈梁父吟〉，身長八尺，每自比於管仲、樂毅，時人莫之許也。」《三國志》的裴松之注，引《魏略》的話：「亮在荊州，以建安初與潁川石廣元、徐元直、汝南孟公威等俱游學，三人務於精熟，而亮獨觀其大略。」[31]這兩段記載可以反映青年諸葛亮對於認識「過去」的態度，以及他在讀書方面的表現。諸葛亮不願「務於精熟」，不下沒有用處的死工夫，而是「觀其大略」，只是摘取重點，細加玩味。而學習的目的，在於經世致用，以管仲與樂毅為典範。諸葛亮治蜀極有成效，陳壽在〈論贊〉中說道：「邦域之內，咸畏而愛之，刑政雖峻而無怨者，以其用心平而勸戒明也。」[32]陳壽解釋諸葛亮治蜀，績效優異，其因有二，一是「用心平」，即其為人民不為一己的心意，人們無不感動；另一是「勸戒明」，就是律令刑罰的各項規定十分清楚，使人人有所遵循。王夫之特別強調前者，不以後者為然。他說：「諸葛公曰：『惟淡泊可以明志。』君與大臣之志明，則天下之臣民之志定。豈恃綜核裁抑以立綱紀哉！」[33]我們應該特別注意王夫之的觀點，想一想他所說「君與大臣之志明，則天下臣民之志定」這句話的理據是什麼？這已經不是一個今天大家談論的「歷史」問題，而是一個屬於

31　《三國志》卷 35，（新校標點本）頁 911。
32　同前，頁 934。
33　王夫之，《讀通鑑論》，頁 388。

人生人性的「理念」問題。但此一「理念」從何而來，有無依據？有無價值？有無意義？看來都不是能夠輕易否定的。

我雖然只舉了三個例子，但它絕不是很獨特的人物事例，像蘇軾、謝道韞和諸葛亮的對「過去」的認識和所受的影響，在傳統典籍中隨處可見。我們只要稍加閱讀，就會清楚感受。如同一位 2004 年修習「中國典籍中的歷史世界」的學生，在上完一學期課程之後，很有所感，自動自發地寫了這樣一段文字：「我覺得閱讀古人經典，可以發現書中非常講究道德修養，志為天下的理念。『獨善其身，兼善天下』這大概是古時候讀書人的基本原則與最高理想吧！可是我們現在身處的環境，一個講求現實利益的世界，檯面上有多少人是想為人民做事？從小就是被教導要把書讀好，以後才有出路。汲汲營營為讀書，國小念好書，為了能擠進一個升學率高的國中；國中讀好書，為了能考到一個明星高中；高中讀好書，為了考上一個有名氣的國立大學外加一個有『錢』途的科系。當然古人也有很多人是為了功名而讀書，但是在最開始讀書的用意，不就是成為一個有德的人，並使自己有能力為天下做事？不知道是不是我想太多，總覺得讀了古代的一些經典文字，心中總有些許惆悵空虛。」[34]這位學生比較了典籍記載中古人與現代人「開始讀書時的用意」，引發了很深的感慨。筆者只是想問：古人「開始讀書時的用意」在古代典籍隨處可見，為什麼要等到選讀了這門課，才有所了解，才把古人的作為與自己的環境作一對比？大學的學生們不是已經讀了很多中國歷史，為什麼與學習者最有關聯的事，如古人「開始讀書的用意」，他們幾乎全無知悉？答案很簡單，典籍中的歷史，或傳統中的歷史與我們今天國、高中，甚至大學課堂上的歷史，中間隔著一堵很厚的牆。學生一旦從牆上打了一個洞，看見了牆外的天地，比較一下與自己所處的世界，崇高的理想不再遙不可及，人性的光輝不再

---

34 張元，〈歷史課堂教學的新程式：故事、閱讀與書寫〉，頁 348。

是教條八股，一時之間，頓感惆悵空虛，幾乎無法適應。但我相信，這樣一番試煉，對於學生的成長，以及成為一個可以為未來的「歷史」負責的人，必定有其助益。

典籍之中所體現之傳統史學要旨，殊少出現於當代各種歷史教科書中；歷史教科書中所見，則多為現代史學之研究成果，其間差異十分明顯。從歷史教育方面著眼，我們應該如何思考此一問題呢？我認為，應從兩個方面考慮：一、典籍中的記載與現代史學的研究，何者最接近那真實的過去？二、學生學習認識、理解過去之時，採取與今日生活十分隔閡的古代傳統史學，還是與今日生活十分接近的現代史學研究成果，容易達到學習的目標？

典籍中的資料，一般來說性質同於「第一手資料」，現代的研究成果，則較同於「第二手資料」。我們當然知道，「第一手資料」不見得必然較「第二手資料」更接近「過去的真實」。但是，如果現代的研究，在資料解讀上為了配合某種「理論」，而有所忽略或扭曲，其研究成果，必然遠離過去的真實，殆可斷言。遠離過去真實的研究成果，不能通過時間的考驗，必遭淘汰，亦可斷言。清末康有為撰《新學偽經考》，扭曲《漢書》文句原意，以配合公羊春秋今文家之改制理論，此書一出，震驚學界，轟動士林。但錢穆撰〈劉向歆父子年譜〉一文刊布，按諸史書文句，一一闡述其原意，康有為扭曲、穿鑿、傅會之手法，完全顯露，無所遁形。[35]此後，視《左傳》、《周禮》等古文經書，係劉歆助王莽篡位而偽造之說，已不復為人們所相信，《新學偽經考》不再被視為一本有價值的歷史著作，就是一個著名的例子。相反地，如果現代研究能真切地掌握典籍資料的原意，其成果應較資料本身更能接近那真實的過去。

然而，什麼叫作「真切掌握資料原意」？又頓成問題。我們了解資料

---

35 請參讀：錢穆，〈劉向歆父子年譜·自序〉，《西漢經學今古文平議》（臺北：東大圖書公司，1971），頁 2-7。

中一字一句的確解，讀懂了全文的意思，就是真切的理解了嗎？恐怕未必。古人所言，有其深意，或意在言外，我們能否領悟、體會？古書所記，有其體例，布局結構皆有其義，我們是否了然於心？皆需考慮。柳詒徵說：「初學不第不可遽謂前人不逮吾儕，且不得謂吾人於前人所撰著悉已了解。深造自得不易言，姑先儲前哲研究撰著之識，得其通涂，再求創闢異境。此雖不敢以律上智，然世之中材最多，循此或可無弊耳。」[36]他的意見，今天看來不無迂腐之嫌，但他說前人著作，了解不易，需要下一番工夫，仍不失為值得重視的經驗之談。相反地，這些工夫全然欠缺，心態上只把古書所載視為「材料」，僅供吾人編排驅使，必然不能「真切地掌握資料原意」，也是可以斷言的。

至於第二個問題，學生在學習理解、認識過去之時，傳統典籍還是現代著作，較易取得成效。答案是明顯的，典籍資料不但文字古奧，而且觀念獨特，皆與學生的生活經驗相去甚遠。所以，以古典資料作為歷史教學的「主要」依據，從學生學習的角度來看，並不妥當。作為輔助資料使用之時，非但需要精細挑選，清楚解說，而且應該針對學生閱讀能力，改寫成他們易於了解的文字。

五、安排中國歷史課程的三項建議

學生「應該」學習怎樣的中國歷史？筆者試著結合一些理論觀點與實際情況，提出幾點粗淺的看法，供大家參考。

首先，利用現代研究成果，勾勒出歷史發展演變的圖像。傳統史學名家輩出，名著如林；現代史學論著極豐，汗牛充棟。若用於歷史教學，必須經過一番選擇，從教學角度來看，學生首先需要的歷史圖像（big

---

36 柳詒徵，《國史要義》，頁 126。

picture），仍以取自現代史學的研究成果為宜。司馬遷的《史記》成書於二千年前，儘管其中精彩敘事至今令人欣賞、讚嘆，但二千年來的史學發展，特別是近百年來，新方法的引入，提出了新見解，足以取代舊學說。講到黃帝、蚩尤，徐炳昶的〈我國古代部族三集團考〉[37]完全可以取《史記‧五帝本紀》而代之。講到戰國時代的合縱、連橫，徐中舒《先秦史論稿》[38]、楊寬《戰國史》[39]中的論述即與司馬光《資治通鑑》中的記載出入甚大，亦可完全取而代之。

從另一方面看，近代史家對於時代圖像的精彩論述，為我們理解提供了簡明但十分深刻的架構，最宜用於教學。例如：中國中古時代，門第士族成了歷史舞台的主角，胡漢之間對立與融合的戲碼不斷，構成了時代樂章的主旋律。陳寅恪的有關研究，特別是他提出的「開隴文化本位政策」，對於此一時期的歷史理解，最有幫助。再舉一例，日本學者內藤虎次郎首先提出，宮崎市定予以增補改進的關於「唐宋變革」的學說，無疑仍是講述從中古時代轉向近世中國最為清楚有力的說明，在教學上仍有其無可取代的價值。如果講到中國近代歷史，三千年未曾有之變局，西洋人之入中國實為主要原因，美國學者如費正清（J. K. Fairbank）提出的「刺激與反應」之說，也不失為可以介紹的解釋之一；相對來說，范文瀾依據馬克思理論所撰寫的《中國近代史》，其中若干觀點，則不妨視為另一種解釋。

歷史教學必然受制於歷史研究，兩者固然不應該視為生產者與推銷者之間的關係，因為歷史教學與歷史研究的實施程序並無基本不同，都是問

37　徐炳昶，〈我國古代民族三集團考〉，《中國古史的傳說時代》，頁 42-147。
38　徐中舒，〈魏齊爭霸與合縱連橫〉，《先秦史論稿》（成都：巴蜀書社，1992），頁 224-266。
39　楊寬，〈合縱連橫和兼併戰爭的變化〉，《戰國史》（臺北：臺灣商務印書館，1997），頁 341-422。

一個有意義的問題、蒐取資料、提出論證、回答問題、加以表述等等，[40]只是繁簡有別而已，這是歷史教師必須清楚認識的觀念。但是，歷史老師不能無視歷史研究的新成果，歷史研究的主要觀點應該出現在各級的歷史課堂上，老師備課之時，面對汗牛充棟的現代歷史論著，「選擇」就十分重要。選擇最為重要，最多共識的「觀點」，建構起最為重要的「歷史圖像」，應該是最能取得教學成果的做法。

其次，從傳統史學的素材中，挑選精彩的故事。歷史教學除了主要「架構」之外，「細節」也很重要。今天我們看到，許多歷史老師在課堂上補充了許多事實經過、制度規定、學說要點等等「細節」，學生清楚知道，這些內容，主要是為了考試，結果非但考過即忘，而且留下了「極討厭」的印象。我們又看到，目前歷史課時不斷縮減，高中階段一個學期的歷史課，要講完整部中國歷史，細節補充幾乎成了不可能的空想。但是，教授歷史，課堂講述之外，提供閱讀資料也是不可或缺的重要方法。八十年前，何炳松撰寫〈歷史教授法〉，強調補充材料的重要，認為「應該看作同教科書一樣」，[41]就明白指出，歷史教學不能只是教歷史教科書，也不能只是依靠老師的講述，「補充教材」不可缺少。今天看來，此一主張仍然正確。因之，若在課堂講述上可以補充一些細節，或在課堂教學之外，提供學生閱讀材料，我們應該選取怎樣的內容呢？以筆者自己的授課經驗，可以清楚看到，從典籍資料中，選取教學內容，可以得到很好的效果。

中國史籍以「人」為主，史籍中的人物敘述，主要方式是藉由許多故事，勾勒出其人特有的氣質與精神。紀傳體固然如此，編年體亦復如此。

---

40 Michael Gorman, "The 'structured enquiry' is not a contradiction in terms: focused teaching for independent learning" *Teaching History* 92(1998,London) 20-25. 亦見：張元，讀 *Teaching History92*,20-25.《清華歷史教學》第十五期，2004，頁 145-148。

41 何炳松，〈歷史教授法〉（原載《教育雜志》，第十七卷，第二、三號，1925年）《何炳松論文集》（北京：商務印書館，1990），頁 376。

舉例來說，鄭國的子產是春秋時代人物，事蹟見於編年體的《左傳》，「鄭子產」也是張蔭麟所撰《中國史綱上古篇》中第一位以整節描述的「人物」，他的敘述，就是一連串十分精彩、有趣而且具有意義的「故事」。[42]這些故事中所呈現的精彩、趣味與意義，是今天的教科書中幾乎沒有的；卻也是學生聽了，或讀了之後，不只是喜歡，而且可以受到感動的。諸葛亮則是另一個例子，我們講歷史中的諸葛亮，不應只講教科書中有限的幾句話，也不應利用《三國演義》中的過於神奇的故事，而是應該利用史書中的記載，特別是古代史家的卓見。撰寫《三國志》的陳壽之外，注《三國志》的裴松之，以及著有《讀通鑑論》的王夫之，都有極其精卓的論述。裴松之與王夫之對於諸葛亮的施政與心志，認識深刻，闡釋精闢，我們在教課講述之時，略加援引，學生也能受到感動。[43]再說，明君聖主，史上固然少見；但賢臣良吏，何代無之？閱讀這些載於史冊，垂為典範的人物，動人之處乃其心意與志節的卓絕表現，讓後人懷想、追慕不已，而不是他有過人的智慧與傑出的才能。這樣的歷史記載，對於資質一般的學習者尤有啟發的功效；這種藉由歷史陳述人世間的道理，也是中國數千年的傳統文化之中，饒有特色之處。今天的歷史教育，是否應該予以繼承？我們必須要想一想。我們是不是為了「與世界接軌」，捨棄以「人」為主的傳統史學觀點，強調「文化、宗教、習俗、經濟和思想的『總體性歷史』」這種年鑑學派的取材觀點？如果中國歷史課所講的，都是飲食、住房、服裝、貨幣、城市、資本、市場、技術之類的內容，這種「總體性歷史」，學生會覺得有趣嗎？會受到感動嗎？會因此而喜歡歷史嗎？我們也要好好想一想。我不知道正面答案的理由為何，我是看不出有任何的可能

42　張蔭麟，《中國史綱上古篇》（臺北：正中書局，1951），頁75-80。

43　有一位學生說：「老師上課講的那些故事我也認為頗能幫了解時代的背景與想法，至今講諸葛亮的那節課我仍深印腦海，我那時深受感動。」請參見：張元，〈歷史課堂教學的新程式：故事、閱讀與書寫〉，頁327。

性。

　　如果問一般受過教育的社會大眾，我們如何知道過去？可能的答案有二，一是歷史教科書，但那是要「背誦」的，所以是令人「討厭」的；二是稗官野史中的故事與小說，雖然讓人覺得有趣、喜歡，但是不是「歷史」，終究不能無疑。如果，我們利用典籍中的故事，選出精彩者，講得生動有趣，而又把時代的特色和人們的心態，作了恰當的描繪；或者選取了同樣性質的資料，學生讀來興趣盎然，實際上就是提供了一條真正進入過去，了解歷史的道路。[44]

　　第三，引導學生學習，必須講求方法。我們既依據現代史學的研究成果勾勒歷史的骨架，又從傳統典籍中挑出精彩的故事，作為血肉，展現精神，即可構成十分理想的中國歷史課程嗎？筆者並不這麼認為，主要理由是，今天課堂教學的主體不應再是老師，教學過程不應該是老師準備好、組織好教材，綱舉目張，有條不紊地講給學生聽。今天，任何教學理論都強調教學應「以學生學習為中心」，老師只是處於引導的地位。所以，教材的選取、安排固然重要，教學方法的設計、實施同樣重要。

　　筆者不認為坊間各種各樣的「課程教學方法」、「課程教學手冊」之類書籍，對於教授歷史有很大的幫助，是歷史老師應該熟讀的。筆者覺得有兩類論著特別重要，作為歷史教學的工作者，必須熟悉。一是關於學生學習的理論著作，二是關於歷史教學的理論著作；前者是對學生的學習能力所作的探討，後者基本上是對學生所學習的歷史知識所作的分析。關於這兩類著作，中國學者貢獻甚為有限，從中國傳統學術中發展出來的論述，幾乎未曾聽聞。由於不論是學生的學習心理與認知能力，還是歷史知識的

44　敏隆講堂的一位學員王怡然說：「我改變了對歷史的感受，以前討厭要『背』的歷史教科書，很愛故事、小說。上課後，發現這兩種觀點都無法幫助我進入那個時代，要去對話、去想像、去像胡三省（通鑑的注釋者）一樣，找到一絲絲的道理。」〈上張元老師通鑑有感〉，《敏隆講堂季刊》第 21 期 (2006)，頁 23。

性質、結構與方法，都可以做出比較屬於「客觀」的論述，我們應該潛心學習，力求全面理解與切實掌握，不能因為未見於傳統史學，而有所排斥抵制，或掉以輕心，不加聞問。

就以最為重要的歷史知識的概念來說，英國學者提出「實質概念」與「第二層次概念」的說法，又對第二層次概念之中的時序、變遷、因果、證據、解釋和神入等，清楚界定，詳予說明，[45]就是一項巨大的貢獻。這些「概念」，非但對於學生了解「歷史知識」極為重要，對於老師的教學同樣也是極為重要。學生理解了這些概念，知道歷史學習不是只記住一些「事實」，而是一個論證的過程；老師熟悉這些概念，在教學中加以運用，一定可以產生很有效率的引導功能。從另一方面看，這些「概念」與前文所述傳統史學的結構方法、主要論點，並無矛盾不合，不能並存之處。我們反而可以看到，兩者的有機結合，相輔相成，更能把歷史課程教得深刻動人，學生真正獲得學習的益處。

傳統史學的理念與今天歷史教學的概念，並不互相排斥，而是相輔相成，我們可以從昔日歷史教學的事例中得到印證。上文提及朱熹的〈開阡陌辨〉，說明八百年前的中國大學者思考歷史問題的步驟、程序及其表現出來的嚴謹、深細，與今日史學界的要求，可以說是一般無二。我們相信，朱熹在講述歷史時運用的方法應該也是如此，朱熹的講述經由弟子記載下來，見於《朱子語類》，提供了更為清楚的例證。我們從《朱子語類》卷 79 與卷 81，有關三監之亂與周公東征的記載中，可以看到朱熹如何講述歷史。他一開始就說，商紂暴虐，人們想把他趕走，商亡之後，人們想到主人被殺，宗廟被毀，想法就有了改變，醞釀出後來反周的舉動。這裡，朱熹注意到，時間不同，人們對同一對象的想法有了差異，再進一

---

45 請參讀：Peter Lee, "Putting Principle into Practice: Understanding History" *How Students Learn History in the Classroom* (Washington, D. C.: The National Academies Press, 2005), pp.41-72.

步說明變化的原因。朱熹又說，管叔、蔡叔被武庚用酒灌醉，聽從武庚，起事作亂。後來周公作〈酒誥〉，一再叮嚀不可喝酒，必定是由此事引起。不過，朱熹這樣講述，並無足夠的資料依據，然而朱熹有所說明：「其中想煞有話說，而今書、傳只載得大事，其中更有機權曲折在。」意思是今天所見典籍，只能記載大概，有許多關鍵的變化與曲折的過程都沒能記下來。這裡朱熹談到了資料的性質、局限，以及運用的原則。朱熹講周公東征以他自己所寫的《詩集傳》中〈破斧〉一詩的解釋作為閱讀資料，要學生從這段資料中找出最為關鍵的詞句（好話頭），並對學生久久不能掌握緊要之處，只在邊緣的地方計較，很不以為然，幾乎生了氣。朱熹認為最關鍵的詞句，就是能否體會東征將士的心意，能否有一番「神入」的功夫，領悟到高遠的理想。[46]從朱熹的這一堂歷史課，我們可以看到今天所說的「第二層次概念」，八百年前的大學者幾乎都已注意到了。

從人心之正大，體悟到天地之情，這是八百年前大學者的期盼，當然不宜成為今天歷史課的目標。但是，筆者認為，一個學生，如果在理解過去的學習過程中，對於古代的偉大心靈與崇高理念能夠有所感悟，其識見眼光、人生態度多少受其影響；其立身行事、言行舉止也應該會有所反映。這樣的歷史課程內容，不也成了為社會培養好公民，而建立的一個管道嗎？再說，今天的學生讀到這樣的內容，必定覺得只是說教，只是可笑嗎？應該不是如此。相反地，志節之士的卓絕表現，自有其動人的力量，課堂中只要有所呈現，學生就能感受。北京大學歷史系三年級的徐碩，作為交換學生，到新竹清華大學一個學期，上了我開的一門課，就深深感到

---

46 請參閱：張元，〈朱子講歷史之四：三監之亂與周公東征〉，《歷史月刊》第 209 期，2005 年 6 月號，頁 103-105。又：朱熹所說的「好話頭」，即《詩集傳·破斧》中他所說的：「雖披堅執銳之人，亦皆能以周公之心為心，而不自為一身一家之計，蓋亦莫非聖人之徒也。學者於此熟玩而有得焉，則其心正大，而天地之情真可見矣！」

傳統史學的動人力量，不妨視為一個小小的見證。[47]

　　簡言之，歷史老師要知道，學生走進教室時，心中不是一張白紙，而是有著千奇百怪的想法，需要老師去調整與引導；也要知道，歷史課不是把現成的知識，整理好了交給學生，而是帶領學生進入過去，去思考、想像與體會；更要知道，最能直接反映過去的典籍資料，有其精義，完全不需藉西方理論加以說明。有了這樣的認識，進而時時想到學生的學習心理、歷史教學的概念與傳統史學的理念，並在課堂教學之時，安排教材，設計教法，不斷實驗、改進，這樣才能教好學生應該學習的中國歷史。

　　總之，學生的學習心理與認知能力，有其結構與層次；歷史課程中的歷史知識，有其概念與類別；傳統史學亦是結構謹嚴，層次分明；三者之間，如何作有機的結合，創造出最為精彩的中國歷史課程，將中國歷史與文化的精義發揮出來，為現代社會培養可以理性理解過去，明白人世道理的好公民，正是今天講授中國歷史的老師們應該肩負起來的責任。

六、小結：教學依據應該取自傳統

　　近年來，國民中學與高級中學的「中國歷史」課程時數大幅減少，這是「中國歷史」課程面臨的外在危機；但是，以往很長的一段時間，課程時數不能算少， 這門課程的教學成效並不佳良，這樣看來，影響中國歷史教學的最基本因素，應與課時多少無關。長久以來，學生上課讀書，老

47　徐碩說：「以前，由於接觸得很少，所以對於傳統史學難免有些誤解，認為不過是考據而已。但上課時，才有了望洋興嘆之感。傳統史學也重考據，如錢穆先生之《先秦諸子繫年》就是一部考據極為精闢之作，但傳統史學絕非限於考據。讀《國史大綱》、《秦漢史》一些偏重史論的著作，其洋洋灑灑、縱橫馳騁的氣魄，使我讀之慨然。《中國學術思想論叢》、《中國近三百年學術史》之中所描述的時代處境中人物對人生、對理想的持守，更令我體會到錢先生那深切的人文關懷。此時，我才真正體會到傳統史學的無窮魅力。」〈錢穆與中國傳統史學的上課感想〉，《歷史月刊》第 223 期，2006 年 8 月號，頁 120。

師講課教書，似乎都是為了考試，而且考試的方式十分刻板，不死記硬背不能得到高分，這是十分普遍的情形，或謂此一情況未能改觀，一切皆屬空談。但是，考試方式與命題技術的改進與革新，不可能與教材、教法的具體內容無關；不可能依據目前的教材教法，只是在考試的「技術」上作若干改變，就可以取得改進歷史教學的成效。筆者認為，面對目前中國歷史教學的窘境，想要有所獻替，發揮這門課程應有的功效，應該從最根本的地方，也就是歷史教育的理論依據，加以思考。

中國歷史教學的理論依據，應該是傳統的中國史學，而不應該是馬克思、布勞岱的史觀或理論，也不應該是蘭克、韋伯，或者社會科學者的觀念或理論。我們都同意，不論是馬克思、布勞岱，或者蘭克、韋伯，以及柯靈烏、克羅齊，都有極宏大，極精深的歷史理論，都能予吾人很多的啟發，但是這些理論是否能與中國典籍中的資料融會貫通？能否對中國歷史作出精彩動人的解釋或說明？在在讓人懷疑。以中國史料之足，適西方理論之履，扞格扭曲，在所難免。往日情事，歷歷在目，奚可不引以為戒？

中國傳統史學，著重之處為何？是帝王將相的履歷生平？是事情經過的表面敘述？是無需證據的任意褒貶？是道德訓誨的史事例證？應該都不是的。傳統史書，呈現出怎樣的特色？是檔案資料不加剪裁的堆積？是舞文弄墨炫耀才華的園地？是阿諛諂媚巴結討好的工具？還是心懷不滿伺機報復的手段？應該也都不是的。從中國傳統史書中呈現出來的傳統史學，內容豐富、敘事優美之外，層次分明、結構嚴謹、思慮細密、理想高遠，早已形成完整深刻的理論，足以作為今天教授中國歷史時的重要依據。如何將此理論依據與實際教學結合起來，取得成果，應是吾人今天努力的目標。

Abstract

What Kind of Chinese History Should Student Learn?

Chang Yuan

What I would like to say here is related to the two different modules I taught separately in 2004 and 2006. One was called *the Historical World in Chinese Classical Historiography*; the other was *Qian Mu and Traditional Historiography*. It was interesting to observe the reaction of my students in class. They always had something to complain about in other modules they had, but they announced that the two modules I taught were very different; they actually enjoyed them! I have been wondering: what exactly made such a difference? Which part of the course exactly delighted my students? I intend to explore more on this topic:

I understand that students found the materials I included in the modules interesting, but it was not just that. I did not simply choose whatever I believed may interest my students. There were all sorts of choices to be made in terms of selecting materials and presenting them to the students. That is to say, I needed to get a tight grasp of where these materials stood in the original books, and to hold a true understanding about the intention of the author. Only then would I be able to bring out the meanings of the materials, and leave a powerful impression upon the students.

In other words, there are serious issues involved concerning the materials themselves. If a teacher does not consider these issues, he or she cannot make a history class approachable to students, in spite of interesting materials. So what kind of issues am I referring to here? I believe they are about the basic ideas and principles of Chinese Traditional Historiography, as well as its overall structure.

The history class today at school is dominated by a homogenous way of teaching, largely controlled by the way our textbooks are arranged and the prioritisation of exams. However I believe there is a third reason contributing to this fact: history is widely seen as a scientific knowledge. The New History Movement in China in 1920s had such slogans as 'Make History scientific'. As a consequence, the idea that one should pursue evidential grounds of historical knowledge and leave subjective feelings and judgment behind has left a long-term impact among the intellectuals. Especially prominent are Hu

Shi and Fu Sinian. With limited hours of history lessons each week, it is impossible to demonstrate the detailed process of critical methods at work. As a result, in class the teacher can only present the conclusions as so called 'historical facts'.

I believe even today a majority of our teachers still believe that what they tell students is 'facts' of the past, which are worth memorising, because that helps for exams. And the biggest mistake a history teacher can make is to mix up these historical 'facts'. However, could it be exactly this kind of belief that results in the fact that students tend to have negative feelings about history lessons? One of my students told me, 'I felt painful when I studied history, as I was forced to memorise all the facts without being given a reason.' In my opinion, it is not the teacher's fault. Teachers are willing to do their job properly and do not like to see their students suffer. So what is to blame? Could it be the confusion about the nature, structure, and critical methods of history?

To make Chinese History an interesting subject to students, one may find it beneficial to review the perspectives and principles of Chinese Traditional Historiography. To base one's teaching on Chinese Traditional Historiography it is necessary to have some understanding about it. There are books about Chinese Traditional Historiography by Liu Yizheng and Qian Mu, but it is not easy for modern readers to understand. Also, the principles they discussed are difficult to be put into practice nowadays. Perhaps what we can do is to re-examine Chinese Classical Historiography, and to recognise the main concerns, structure, and purpose of the content. In other words, we should unfold a clear structure of it, and we can look into the outcome, which may also be called the 'theory'.

I just started to work on the project here. You can see that I have provided explanations for difficult words and phrases. I also discussed the credibility of the data, and the main purpose of the historical records. I tried to highlight the qualities of some certain way of expression. And I have talked about the ultimate goal of studying history. For all of these I have made brief statements and given some examples. What I have been trying to do is to demonstrate that Chinese Traditional Historiography is not entirely useless, as Liang Chichao claimed during the New History Movement. There is always something extraordinary in Chinese Classical Historiography. As long as we take a closer look, we can discover interesting parts and integrate them into the lecture in class or as a supplementary reference to look into after class. When we read along the historical narratives in the Chinese Classical Historiography carefully, we can see that the history illustrated there is more than a record of a series of events. History can be inspiring. All aspects of Chinese Classical

Historiography can be useful in teaching, from the basic understanding of the texts, to the ultimate ideals of humanity. It is not only interesting for students, but also helps them to consider important issues in life. I have provided some examples as to how our ancestors studied history as an illustration.

I cannot overemphasize the importance of Chinese Traditional Historiography. However I do not mean to revive the old way of history teaching. Neither do I believe that studying Chinese Traditional Historiography is the only available path. My point is that we should remember it is no simple work to understand Chinese Traditional Historiography, among which layers of meanings are intertwined. It is fascinating. Before we make use of it in teaching, it is essential to know in which place of the book does the material stand. It is the same with all other resources we can use in Chinese history teaching; we should know where they belongs and find a good way to put it into our teaching, in order to achieve the best results.

It is true that Chinese Classical Historiography, in spite of being magnificent works, are after all hundreds or thousands years old. While modern Chinese academic world is moving ahead fast and changing rapidly, especially under the constant influence from western culture, there is no reason to ignore latest innovative theories. We should try to make use of them instead. Some of the modern interpretations to Chinese history are fairly significant and help drawn a clear outline to our historical development. They can not only replace some of the conclusions we had drawn from Chinese Classical Historiography, but also benefit our teaching, and thus being useful when we design our history lesson. Besides, western scholars have done massive research on both theory and practice in history education, and we should also integrate the result into our teaching.

However, even so, the data in Chinese Classical Historiography can still serve as invaluable teaching material, such as the description of the character, his or her childhood behaviour, the things he or she has done, and how that reflects the Zeitgeist. It is of my humble opinion that this approach would motivate students more than a flat narration of historical facts, or a lecture about food, living conditions, fashion, capitalism, commerce and techniques. Students may thus decide that a history lesson can be amiable. I also would like to point out: one can observe from Chinese Classical Historiography that our ancestors did not simply record historical events and top up with a little moral teaching; it is a surprise to see that Zhu Zi from eight hundred years ago already deployed the teaching concepts as valued by western scholars.

There are two major problems we are facing today in Chinese History Education: there are too few teaching hours devoted to it, and teaching style is determined by exam preparation. But there seems to be another fundamental issue that should be addressed. That is, what kind of history should we teach in class? It is not just a matter of choice of topics. It is not a matter of 70 per cent of social history, or 30 per cent of women studies. It should be about the history theories which we base on to conduct the perspective of our history teaching.

If we pause for a moment and examine the history theories on our teaching today, we will discover that its perspective is far away from what our ancestors believed in the old times. We select some of the materials from the gigantic collection of Classical Historiography in teaching, but hardly pay attention to their original purpose. My intention today is to bring this phenomenon to your attention, and see if we can improve this situation. I have further made clarification about the content of Chinese Classical Historiography, and I would like to prove that after my own demonstration, this kind of material can be useful and popular in history teaching.

What kind of Chinese history should our students learn? If we think from students' position, we should ask instead: why should students study history, especially Chinese history? This is too big a topic, and I only would like to discuss one aspect of it: how to make a Chinese History lesson interesting to students, so that they feel motivated and actually learn something in class? Students always claim that they enjoy listening to stories, especially those about the historical characters. It is exactly something we can easily find in the Chinese Classical Historiography, which can serve as abundant teaching resources for teachers. One question is, could these 'stories' actually help us to reach the teaching goals illustrated within our history education? I have little doubt about that. Let me say that again: I believe we can gain lots of understanding about history from these 'stories', including understanding about an era, how to interpret data and how to interpret a text which carries multiple meanings. Based on the stories, teachers can create questions for discussion in the classroom. What we emphasis on history education today is the ability to understand the past, and that, I believe can be achieved through this. If we work on this really hard and carefully, students may be able to understand the meanings behind the behaviours of the historical characters and the purposes of the authors. What is more, students may even be inspired in relation to their ideals and main issues in life, and be further directed on the path to the ultimate goal of our traditional culture, 'Reach the ultimate goodness' （止於至善）.

By the way, in my article I mentioned a book, *Historical Theory* by Mary Fullbrook, as it served a great inspiration to me.

國家圖書館出版品預行編目資料

學生如何學歷史？
——歷史的理解與學習國際學術研討會論文集

張元‧蕭憶梅主編. – 初版. – 臺北市：臺灣學生，2012.05
面；公分

ISBN 978-957-15-1550-2 (平裝)

1. 歷史教育 2. 文集

603.3   100021662

學生如何學歷史？
——歷史的理解與學習國際學術研討會論文集

主　　　編：張　　元　　●　　蕭　　憶　　梅
文 字 編 輯：貢　　　　舒　　　　瑜
美 術 編 輯：周　　　　湘　　　　雲
出　版　者：臺 灣 學 生 書 局 有 限 公 司
發　行　人：楊　　　　雲　　　　龍
發　行　所：臺 灣 學 生 書 局 有 限 公 司
　　　　　　臺北市和平東路一段七十五巷十一號
　　　　　　郵 政 劃 撥 帳 號：00024668
　　　　　　電　話　：（02）23928185
　　　　　　傳　眞　：（02）23928105
　　　　　　E-mail：student.book@msa.hinet.net
　　　　　　http://www.studentbook.com.tw
本 書 局 登
記 證 字 號：行政院新聞局局版北市業字第玖捌壹號
印　刷　所：長 欣 印 刷 企 業 社
　　　　　　新北市中和區永和路三六三巷四二號
　　　　　　電　話　：（02）22268853

定價：新臺幣六五〇元

西 元 二 〇 一 二 年 五 月 初 版